# 30 DAYS TO THE GMAT CAT

# 30 DAYS TO THE GMAT CAT

**Mark Alan Stewart, J.D.**
**and**
**Frederick J. O'Toole, Ph.D.**

Macmillan • USA

30 Days to the GMAT CAT

Macmillan General Reference USA
A Simon & Schuster Macmillan Company
1633 Broadway
New York, NY 10019-6785

Macmillan Publishing books may be purchased for business or sales promotional use. For information please write: Special Markets Department, Macmillan Publishing USA, 1633 Broadway, New York, NY 10019.

Graduate Management Admission Test, GMAT, Graduate Management Admission Council, and GMAC are registered trademarks of the Graduate Management Admission Council.

An ARCO book

Macmillan is a registered trademark of Macmillan, Inc.
ARCO is a registered trademark of Prentice-Hall, Inc.

ISBN: 0-02-861834-3
Library of Congress Number: 97-070078

Manufactured in the United States of America

10 9 8 7 6 5 4 3 2 1

# About The Authors

**Mark Alan Stewart** is an attorney (J.D., University of California at Los Angeles) and private test preparation consultant based in Southern California. He is one of today's leading authorities in the field of standardized exam preparation, bringing to this publication more than a decade of experience in coaching college students as they prepare for the GMAT. His other Macmillan (ARCO) publications for graduate-level admissions include:

- *GMAT CAT: Answers to the Real Essay Questions*
- *30 Days to the LSAT*
- *GRE-LSAT Logic Workbook*
- *GRE-LSAT-GMAT-MCAT Reading Comprehension Workbook*
- *Perfect Personal Statements—Law, Business, Medical, Graduate School*
- *Words for Smart Test-Takers*
- *Math for Smart Test-Takers*

**Frederick J. O'Toole** (Ph.D. Philosophy, University of California) is a Professor of Philosophy at California State Polytechnic University, San Luis Obispo. His areas of specialization include Critical Thinking, Symbolic Logic, and History and Philosophy of Science. He brings to this publication over two decades of experience teaching students critical thinking concepts and skills. His other publications include:

- *GMAT CAT: Answers to the Real Essay Questions*
- *30 Days to the LSAT (Macmillan Publishing Company, 1997)*
- *Critical Thinking Interactive Exercises, (Philosophical Documentation Center, 1993)*
- *The Fundamentals of Modern Logic (Blake Publishing, 1977)*

# THE 30-DAY PROGRAM

**DAY 1**

Get to Know the GMAT

1

**DAY 2**

The Computer-Adaptive GMAT and General Test-Taking Strategies

8

**DAY 3**

Critical Reasoning Lesson 1: Basic Skills and Strategies

16

**DAY 7**

Quantitative Ability Lesson 2: Arithmetic

63

**DAY 8**

Quantitative Ability Lesson 3: Mini-Test and Review (Arithmetic)

74

**DAY 9**

Sentence Correction Lesson 1: Format, Strategies, Grammer

82

**DAY 13**

Analytical Writing Assessment Lesson 2: Analysis of an Issue

117

**DAY 14**

Analytical Writing Assessment Lesson 3: Analysis of an Argument

121

**DAY 15**

Quantitative Ability Lesson 4: Algebra—Basic Concepts

125

**DAY 19**

Reading Comprehension Lesson 2: Question Types

160

**DAY 20**

Reading Comprehension Lesson 3: Mini-Test and Review

170

**DAY 21**

Quantitative Ability Lesson 7: Geometry, Part 1

177

**DAY 25**

Practice Test, Review of Section 1: Analytical Writing Assessment

210

**DAY 26**

Practice Test Section 3: Quantitative Ability

213

**DAY 27**

Practice Test Review of Section 3: Quantitative Ability

222

# Authors' Acknowledgements

The authors wish to thank Linda Bernbach at ARCO for her editorial assistance. Mark Stewart also wishes to thank: Eva Anda and Patrick Cunningham for their contributions; Christine Poe and Diane Wagster for their clerical assistance; and Annette Davis for her support and encouragement. Fred O'Toole would like to thank his beautiful ladies, Joyce Connelly and Oona O'Toole, for their patience and support.

## CREDITS

The directions for the GMAT sections and the AWA scoring guide that appear in this publication are reprinted with the permission of Graduate Management Admission Council, the copyright holder.

"The Artful Encounter," by Richard Wendorf, *Humanities,* Vol. 14, No. 4 (July/August 1993), pp. 9–12. Published by The National Endowment for the Humanities.

"Images of Dorothea Lange," by Therese Thau Heyman, *Humanities,* Vol. 14, No. 5 (September/October 1993), pp. 6, 8–10. Published by The National Endowment for the Humanities.

"Large Format Expands Little Buddha," by Bob Fisher, *American Cinematographer,* Vol. 75, No. 5 (May 1994), p. 41.

"Health Care and the Constitution: Public Health and the Role of the State in the Framing Era," by Wendy E. Parmet, *Hastings Constitutional Law Quarterly,* Vol. 20, No. 2, pp. 279–281, 285–286; reprinted by permission of University of California, Hastings College of Law and Wendy E. Parmet. © 1993 by University of California, Hastings College of Law.

"The American Renaissance," by James S. Turner, *Humanities,* Vol. 13, No. 2 (March/April 1992). Published by The National Endowment for the Humanities.

## Day 1

# Get to Know the GMAT

### Today's Topics:

1. Purpose of the GMAT
2. Who designs and administers the GMAT?
3. Is the GMAT required for admission to graduate business schools?
4. The computer-adaptive GMAT at a glance
5. Scoring, evaluation, and reporting
6. Registering to take the GMAT

Today you will familiarize yourself with the format and content of the GMAT, learn how the exam is scored and evaluated, and become acquainted with the registration process. Tomorrow (Day 2) you will examine the computer-adaptive GMAT environment, along with basic test-taking strategies.

## PURPOSE OF THE GMAT

The Graduate Management Admission Test (GMAT) is designed to provide admission officers, counselors, and prospective applicants with predictors of academic performance in the advanced (graduate-level) study of business and management. GMAT scores are only one of several factors considered in an admission decision. Other factors include undergraduate grade point average (GPA), work and other experience, recommendation letters, and application essays (personal statements).

## WHO DESIGNS AND ADMINISTERS THE GMAT?

The Educational Testing Service (ETS) developed and administers the GMAT in consultation with the Graduate Management Admission Council (GMAC). ETS also conducts ongoing research projects aimed at improving the test. The GMAC develops guidelines, policies, and procedures for the graduate business school admission process and provides information about the admission process to the graduate business schools and to prospective applicants. The GMAC consists of representatives from more than 100 graduate business schools. Both ETS and the GMAC are nonprofit organizations.

1

## IS THE GMAT REQUIRED FOR ADMISSION TO GRADUATE BUSINESS SCHOOL?

Approximately 850 graduate business schools worldwide *require* GMAT scores for admission. Approximately 450 additional graduate business schools use (but don't require) GMAT scores to access applicants' qualifications. Schools that do not require GMAT scores usually have relatively lenient admission standards or are located outside of the United States.

## THE COMPUTER-ADAPTIVE GMAT AT A GLANCE

The total testing time for the computer-adaptive GMAT is three and a half hours. The format for the exam is as follows:

| Section | Time | Questions |
| --- | --- | --- |
| **Tutorial** | **untimed** | |
| **Analytical writing assessment (AWA)** | **60 minutes** | **2 topics** |
| Analysis of an issue | 30 minutes | 1 topic |
| Analysis of an argument | 30 minutes | 1 topic |
| Break | 5 minutes | |
| **Quantitative section** | **75 minutes** | **37 (27 scored, 10 unscored)** |
| Problem solving | | 23–24 |
| Data sufficiency | | 13–14 |
| Break | 5 minutes | |
| **Verbal section** | **75 minutes** | **41 (30 scored, 11 unscored)** |
| Critical Reasoning | | 14–15 |
| Sentence Correction | | 14–15 |
| Reading Comprehension | | 12–14 |

The two AWA sections are always administered first (before the Quantitative and Verbal sections). The Quantitative and Verbal sections can be administered in either order.

The use of calculators is prohibited, but you can use the following materials during the exam:

- Scratch paper (provided for all sections)

- Pencils (provided for all sections)

- Silent timing devices (the GMAT CAT interface indicates *elapsed* time)

### The CAT System: Tutorial, Practice, and Demonstration of Competence

The GMAT is now administered entirely by computer. To ensure that you are comfortable with the CAT (Computer-Adaptive Test) system before the test begins, you can choose to have the CAT system lead you through a tutorial. You can also choose to practice using the system by responding to sample questions. The tutorial teaches you how to do the following:

- Use the mouse

- Scroll the screen display up and down

- Select and change a response

- Confirm a response and move to the next question

- Access the online help

- Access the directions for the current test section

- Access the onscreen timing clock

- Use the AWA word processing features

To further ensure that you are sufficiently capable of handling the computerized aspect of the GMAT CAT, before beginning the actual timed exam, you must demonstrate adequate competence in performing these tasks. Although the tutorial and practice questions are optional, demonstration of competence with the CAT system is *required* before testing begins. You will examine the computer-adaptive GMAT environment in detail tomorrow (Day 2).

## The Two 30-Minute AWA Sections

Each of the two Analytical Writing Assessment (AWA) sections involves a 30-minute writing task. One section is entitled "Analysis of an Issue," and the other section is entitled "Analysis of an Argument." The AWA sections are always administered *first*, before all other sections of the GMAT. However, the two AWA sections can be administered in either order.

**Selection of topics.** The CAT randomly selects two topics (one of each type) from 180 different topics (90 of each type). The GMAC prereleases all 180 topics by publishing them at the official GMAT website (http://www.gmat.org). However, please note that the topics are not included in the printed version of the *GMAT Information Bulletin.*

**Mechanical aspects of preparing and recording your response.** Scratch paper is provided for taking notes and constructing outlines. You must record your actual essay responses electronically, using the word processor built into the GMAT CAT. Unless the GMAC decides otherwise, handwritten responses are not permitted.

**Evaluation of essay responses.** Within one week after the test, two different ETS graders at ETS regional sites independently read and rate your AWA responses. Evaluation is on a 0–6 scale, and your final score is the average of the four separate ratings assigned, rounded to the nearest one-half point. In the event of a large discrepancy in ratings between the two graders, a third evaluator might rate your essays as well. In evaluating your responses, the graders focus on your thought process (reasoning) as well as on how effectively you write. For more detailed information about AWA scoring and evaluation, see Day 12.

## Unscored or Pretest Questions

The Quantitative and Verbal sections each include several unscored or pretest questions that are interspersed or "embedded" among the scored questions. You will not be able to distinguish between scored and pretest questions. ETS includes pretest questions to assess the integrity, fairness, and difficulty of new questions that might appear as scored questions on future exams.

## The 75-Minute Quantitative Section

The Quantitative section measures your basic mathematical skills, your understanding of basic concepts, and your ability to reason quantitatively, solve quantitative problems, and interpret graphic data. A typical Quantitative section covers the more elementary aspects of the following:

- Arithmetical operations
- Integers, factors, and multiples
- The number line and ordering
- Decimals, percentages, and ratios
- Exponents and square roots
- Arithmetic mean
- Operations with variables
- Algebraic equations and inequalities
- Geometry, including coordinate geometry

Algebraic concepts on the GMAT are those normally covered in a first-year high school algebra course. The GMAT does not cover advanced mathematical concepts such as trigonometry and calculus, geometry theorems, and formal proofs.

The Quantitative section uses two different question types:

- Problem solving (23–24 questions)
- Data sufficiency (13–14 questions)

*Problem Solving* questions require you to solve a mathematical problem and then select the correct answer from among five answer choices. Each *Data Sufficiency* question consists of a question followed by two statements (labeled 1 and 2). You must analyze each of the two statements to determine whether it provides sufficient data to answer the question. Although their formats differ, these two question types include similar content.

The exam intersperses the *Data Sufficiency* questions among Problem Solving questions. Here is a typical sequence of questions (keep in mind that the exact sequence and number of questions per type might differ somewhat on your exam):

| Questions 1–2 | Problem solving |
|---|---|
| Questions 3–7 | Data sufficiency |
| Questions 8–13 | Problem solving |
| Question 14 | Data sufficiency |
| Question 15 | Problem solving |
| Question 16 | Data sufficiency |
| Questions 17–21 | Problem solving |
| Questions 22–27 | Data sufficiency |
| Questions 28–34 | Problem solving |
| Question 35 | Data sufficiency |
| Questions 36–37 | Problem solving |

Remember that 10 of the 37 Quantitative questions are pretest (unscored) questions. These pretest questions are interspersed among scored questions. You will not be able to tell pretest questions from scored questions.

## The 75-Minute Verbal Section

The Verbal section includes three different question types:

- Critical Reasoning (14–15 questions)
- Sentence Correction (14–15 questions)
- Reading Comprehension (12–13 questions)

*Critical Reasoning* questions are designed to evaluate your ability to understand, criticize, and draw reasonable conclusions from arguments. The exam presents each argument in a brief one-paragraph passage. *Sentence Correction* questions are designed to evaluate your command of the English language and of the conventions of formal standard written English. Areas tested include grammar, diction, and syntax. *Reading Comprehension* questions are designed to measure your ability to read carefully and accurately, to determine the relationships among the various parts of the passage, and to draw reasonable inferences from the material in the passage. The exam presents the questions as a series of four distinct sets, each set including three (brief) questions. All questions in one set pertain to one particular passage. The passages are drawn from for a variety of subjects, including the humanities, the social sciences, the physical sciences, ethics, philosophy, and law.

Each Verbal section contains all three question types. Here is a typical sequence of questions (keep in mind that the exact sequence and number of questions per type might differ slightly on your exam):

| Questions 1–3 | Sentence Correction |
|---|---|
| Questions 4–5 | Critical Reasoning |
| Questions 6–8 | Reading Comprehension |
| Question 9 | Sentence Correction |
| Questions 10–11 | Critical Reasoning |
| Questions 12–14 | Sentence Correction |
| Questions 15–17 | Reading Comprehension |
| Questions 18–21 | Critical Reasoning |
| Questions 22–24 | Sentence Correction |
| Questions 25–26 | Critical Reasoning |
| Question 27 | Sentence Correction |
| Questions 28–30 | Reading Comprehension |
| Questions 31–33 | Critical Reasoning |
| Questions 34–35 | Sentence Correction |
| Questions 36 | Critical Reasoning |
| Questions 37–39 | Reading Comprehension |
| Question 40 | Critical Reasoning |
| Question 41 | Sentence Correction |

Remember that 11 of the 41 Verbal questions will be pretest (unscored) questions. As in the Quantitative section, the unscored questions are interspersed among the scored questions, and you will not be able to tell pretest questions from scored questions.

## The Two Optional Five-Minute Breaks

You can pause for a brief break (up to five minutes) immediately after the two 30-minute AWA sections *and* after the first of the two multiple-choice sections. A word of warning: These optional breaks must not exceed five minutes each, for if you pause too long between sections, the exam session automatically terminates and no responses or scores are tabulated or reported.

## Post-Test Procedures

After completing the $3\frac{1}{2}$ hour GMAT CAT, you are not quite finished. Immediately after the exam, the CAT system asks you the following:

- Whether you want an unofficial score report (for all but the AWA sections) at this time (Remember that if you request a score report at this time, you waive your right to cancel your scores.)

- To which schools you want to send your score reports (the system provides a complete list of graduate business schools)

- Several questions about your test-taking experience (to provide feedback to ETS so that it can continue to refine and improve the test)

Finally, test-center procedures require that you turn in all scratch paper and pencils provided to you at the test center.

---

## SCORING, EVALUATION, AND REPORTING

---

### How the GMAT CAT Is Scored

Because of the GMAT CAT's interactive nature, the scoring system for the Quantitative and Verbal sections is a bit tricky. Your score for each of these two sections is based on both the *correctness* of your responses and the *difficulty level* of the questions. For example, if you fail to complete a section, you can nevertheless achieve a relatively high score by continuing to respond correctly to more difficult (and usually more time-consuming) questions.

Test takers receive four scores for the GMAT:

- A scaled *Quantitative* score, on a 0–60 scale, based on the correctness of responses to and difficulty level of the scored *Quantitative* questions

- A scaled *Verbal* score, on a 0–60 scale, based on the correctness of responses to and difficulty level of the scored *Verbal* questions

- A *total* score, on a 200–800 scale, based on both the *Quantitative* and *Verbal* scores

- An *AWA* score, on a 0–6 scale, which averages (to the nearest one-half point) the four ratings of the test taker's responses to the two AWA topics

### Interpreting Your GMAT Scores

For each of your four GMAT scores, you receive a percentile rank (0–99%). A percentile rank of 60%, for example, indicates that you scored higher than 60% of all test takers (and lower than 39% of all test takers). Percentile ranks for Quantitative, Verbal, and total scores indicate how a test taker performed relative to the entire GMAT test-taking population during the most recent three-year period. The percentile rank for AWA, however, is based only on more current administrations. (For more about interpreting scores, see Day 30.)

### Reporting Scores to Test Takers and to the Schools

Unofficial Quantitative, Verbal, and total scores are available to you at the testing center *immediately* after you complete the exam. Within 10 days after testing, ETS mails to you an official score report for all four sections (however, the test itself is not disclosed). Concurrently, ETS mails a score report to each school that you have designated to receive your score report (you can send reports to as many as five schools without incurring an additional fee). ETS is currently considering, but has not yet implemented at press time, methods for electronic transmission of scores to the schools. Also, at this time score reports do *not* include test takers' AWA responses; however, the GMAC is examining possible methods of disclosing AWA responses to the schools.

### How the Schools Evaluate GMAT Scores

Each business school develops and implements its own policies for evaluating GMAT scores. Some schools place equal weight on GMAT scores and GPA, others weigh GMAT scores more heavily, whereas others weigh GPA more heavily. ETS reports your three most recent GMAT scores to each business school receiving your scores and transcripts. Most schools *average* reported scores; a minority of schools consider only your *highest* reported score. A few schools have adopted a *hybrid* approach by which they average reported scores unless there is a sufficiently large discrepancy between scores, in which case the school considers only your highest score.

## REGISTERING TO TAKE THE GMAT

The following information provides an *overview* of the GMAT registration process. Always consult the current printed *GMAT Bulletin* or the GMAT Website (http://www.gmat.org) for the latest information on testing, registration, and fees.

### When Should You Take the GMAT?

Most graduate business schools admit new students for the fall term only. Although application deadlines vary among the schools, if you plan to take the GMAT no later than the December prior to matriculation, you will be sure to meet application deadlines at *all* schools. Ideally, you should take the GMAT early enough so that you can take the exam a second time if necessary and still meet application deadlines. In any event, take the GMAT at a time when you are sure that you have adequate time to prepare for the exam.

You can take the GMAT at any time, even during your freshman or sophomore year of college. However, because the intellectual abilities that the GMAT evaluates are largely developed during your four years of college, postponing the test might allow for further intellectual development and higher GMAT scores. Most candidates who take the GMAT while still in college wait until late in their junior year or early in their senior year to do so. If you are still in college, consider postponing the GMAT until after you have taken the following types of courses:

- Critical thinking and logic (for GMAT Critical Reasoning questions as well as for the AWA section)

- English composition (for GMAT Sentence Correction questions and the AWA sections)

- Courses in the humanities and social sciences (for GMAT Reading Comprehension questions and for the "Analysis of an Issue" portion of the AWA section)

- Basic algebra and basic geometry (for GMAT Quantitative questions)

### Where and When Is the GMAT Offered

The GMAT CAT is administered at approximately 400 different testing centers throughout North America and at selected sites outside North America. These testing centers are located at various colleges, universities, secondary schools, ETS field offices, and Sylvan Technology Centers. The pencil-and-paper GMAT may still be offered at selected international sites (outside of North America) where the computer network is not yet complete.

Unlike the pencil-and-paper GMAT, which is offered only four times a year, the CAT is offered almost continuously. Currently, most test centers administer the CAT during three weeks each month. Testing hours and days may vary among test centers. The GMAC's goal is for all test centers to be open 10 hours a day, six days a week, all year long. Although you might be able to take the test within as little as two days after scheduling an appointment, busier testing centers may experience backlogs up to several weeks.

### How to Register for the GMAT

Registration for the computer-adaptive GMAT is by appointment at one of the computer-based testing centers. Candidates can register for the GMAT by any of the following methods:

- Candidates can call the test center of their choice directly.

- Online registration is available (with a Visa, MasterCard, or American Express card) at the following URL: http://www.gmat.org.

- ETS is establishing a National Registration Center and a central toll-free telephone number for registration (this toll-free registration service might be available by the time you register).

## How to Retake the GMAT

You can retake the GMAT as often as you want; however, to take the exam a second time, you must wait until the next month following your initial exam. For example, if you take the GMAT initially any time in November, you can retake the test any time in December. An additional waiting period is imposed after retests as well. At press time, the GMAC had not yet settled on the length of these subsequent waiting periods. (Contact ETS for current information.)

## How to Cancel Your GMAT Scores

You can cancel your GMAT scores at any time *during* the test or *immediately after* completing the test. Also, as noted earlier, if you take too long a break between exam sections, the exam session automatically terminates and your responses and scores (if any) are canceled. If you request an unofficial score report (immediately after the test), you cannot cancel your scores. If you do not request an unofficial score report, you can cancel your scores at any time *within one week after the test*. Score reports sent to the business schools note score cancellations (although the reports do not note the scores themselves). A record of score cancellation will not hurt your chances of admission.

## How to Register for the GMASS

The Graduate Management Admission Search Service (GMASS), offered by the GMAC, is designed to help candidates become aware of full-time and part-time graduate programs, admission procedures, and financial aid opportunities. If you sign up for the GMASS, you are included on a mailing list that the GMAC provides to the schools, and you automatically receive information from those schools that are looking for applicants that match your background characteristics (as you indicate when you register for the GMAT). Participation in GMASS is voluntary, free, and currently available on a one-time-only basis. (The GMAC is considering offering the GMASS on a monthly, bimonthly, or quarterly basis in the future; contact the GMAC for current information.)

## How to Find Further Information About Registration Policies and Procedures

For detailed information about GMAT registration procedures, consult the official GMAT Website (http://www.gmat.org) or refer to the printed *GMAT Bulletin*, published annually by the GMAC. This free bulletin is available directly from the GMAC as well as through career-planning offices at most four-year colleges and universities. The *GMAT Bulletin* provides detailed and current information about the following:

- Test center locations, telephone numbers, and hours of operation

- Accommodations for disabled test takers

- Requirements for admission to the GMAT

- Registration and reporting fees

To obtain a GMAT Bulletin or other information about the GMAT, you can contact ETS as follows:

- By mail:

  GMAT
  Educational Testing Service
  P.O. Box 6103
  Princeton, NJ 08541-6103

- By courier or express delivery:

  Distribution and Receiving Center
  225 Phillips Boulevard
  Ewing, NJ 08628-7435

- By telephone:

  (609) 771-7330
  (a toll-free number may also be available)

- By e-mail:

  gmat@ets.org

- On the World Wide Web:

  http://www.gmat.org

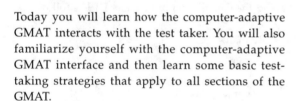

# Day 2

## The Computer-Adaptive GMAT and General Test-Taking Strategies

### Today's Topics:

1. How the computer-adaptive GMAT works
2. The GMAT CAT interface
3. Scoring your best on the GMAT

Today you will learn how the computer-adaptive GMAT interacts with the test taker. You will also familiarize yourself with the computer-adaptive GMAT interface and then learn some basic test-taking strategies that apply to all sections of the GMAT.

## HOW THE COMPUTER-ADAPTIVE GMAT WORKS

### How the CAT "Builds" a Customized Test for Each Test Taker

The Quantitative and Verbal sections of the GMAT CAT *interact* with you by continually tailoring the test's difficulty level to your abilities. How does the CAT accomplish this? The initial questions presented to you are moderately difficult. If you respond incorrectly to these questions, the CAT presents questions that are somewhat easier (although not necessarily similar in content). If you respond correctly to the initial questions, the CAT poses questions that are more difficult (although not necessarily similar in content). As a result, questions presented later in a

section are more likely than earlier questions to match your ability—that is, they will be neither too easy nor too difficult. The CAT does *not* adjust difficulty level by increasing or decreasing the total *number* of questions presented.

The CAT selects appropriate questions from a large bank of questions, categorized by content and difficulty. Thus, although the overall content (the topics covered) and the total number of questions is the same for all test takers, the CAT presents each test taker with a *distinct* set of 37 questions for the Quantitative section and 41 questions for the Verbal section.

### Skipping Questions, Returning to Questions, and Finishing a Section

**The CAT does *not* let you skip questions.** Given the interactive design of the test, this makes sense. The computer-adaptive algorithm cannot determine the appropriate difficulty level for the next question without a response (correct or incorrect) to each question presented in sequence.

**The CAT does *not* let you return to any question already presented (and answered).** Why? The computer-adaptive algorithm that determines the difficulty of subsequent questions depends on the correctness of prior responses. For example, suppose that you answer question 5 incorrectly. The CAT responds by posing slightly easier questions. Were the CAT to let you return to question 5 and change your response to the correct one, the questions following question 5 would be easier than they should have been, given your amended response. In other words, the process by which the CAT builds your score would be undermined.

**The CAT does *not* require you to finish each section.** The CAT gives you the *opportunity* to respond to a total of 78 questions (37 Quantitative and 41 Verbal). However, the CAT does *not* require you to finish each section. If you fail to respond to all 37 (or 41) questions, the CAT nevertheless calculates a score based on those questions you did answer. (ETS will establish a minimum number of responses required for a score report, but has not yet determined that number at press time.)

### Are Scores for the GMAT CAT Comparable to Scores for the Pencil-and-Paper GMAT?

In October 1996, ETS conducted a research study that established the relationship between the scores of the GMAT CAT and the pencil-and-paper version. Although the results of this study are not yet available to the general public, they have been provided to the schools to allow them to compare GMAT CAT scores with pencil-and-paper scores.

### Do Computer-Literate Test Takers Have an Advantage on the CAT?

In developing the CAT, ETS has taken every measure to eliminate any advantage a computer-literate test taker might have on the test. Test takers use only the mouse (not the keyboard) during the Quantitative and Verbal sections, so no keyboard commands are involved. The word processor used for the AWA section is very basic, incorporating only a few simple editing features that all users can quickly and easily master. The tutorial, practice, and required demonstration of competence prior to the test are designed to ensure further a level playing field for all test takers. Despite all efforts to eliminate any advantage that a computer-literate test taker might have, a test

taker who is experienced with a mouse or who is a fast and accurate typist might in fact be at a slight advantage.

### Advantages of the CAT over the Pencil-and-Paper GMAT

The GMAT CAT offers several advantages over the pencil-and-paper version:

- The CAT offers greater flexibility and convenience for test takers. The CAT is available at any time during the year, and candidates can schedule an appointment by telephone.

- Unofficial scores are available *immediately* on competition of the test.

- Official scores are available within two weeks after the test.

- The CAT eliminates the chance of putting the right answer in the wrong place on the answer sheet.

- The CAT reduces the possibility of cheating. It is impossible to return to previous sections, work ahead to other sections, work beyond the expiration of an allotted time period, or glance at a neighbor's responses.

- The interactive feature of the CAT allows for accurate assessment with fewer questions, thus eliminating endurance as a significant factor.

- The CAT offers more opportunities for possible future refinements (see the section "What Changes Are in Store for the GMAT in the Future?" later in this chapter).

### Disadvantages of the GMAT CAT Compared to the Pencil-and-Paper Version

With the foregoing advantages come some disadvantages compared to the pencil-and-paper version:

- You have no chance to return to previous questions and reconsider responses or to "cross-check" different responses for consistency (cross-checking is especially helpful in the Reading Comprehension questions).

- The CAT favors those test takers who are more comfortable with and adept at using computers.

- The possibility of technical problems (hardware, software, network, or power failures) cannot be entirely eliminated.

- You have no opportunity later to review your customized test in order to assess your strengths and weaknesses. (Eventually, the CAT system will provide for exam disclosure; however, ETS and GMAC admit that implementation is years away.)

## What Changes Are in Store for the GMAT in the Future?

GMAC and ETS are currently exploring further refinements in the GMAT CAT and in the scoring and reporting process. Possible future refinements include the following:

- Customizing CAT scores for each school. For example, if a particular school determines that Reading Comprehension should be weighted more heavily than Critical Reasoning, scores could be automatically adjusted accordingly. (Currently, separate scores are not reported for the different components within the Quantitative, Verbal, and AWA sections.)

- Incorporating questions that measure other cognitive abilities as well as innovative questions that assess leadership skills and listening skills.

- Refining the computer-adaptive algorithm to enable test takers to review previous questions and change responses to questions.

## THE GMAT CAT INTERFACE

The figure on page 11 shows the GMAT CAT interface including a hypothetical AWA topic.

### The CAT Title Bar

A dark title bar appears across the top of the computer screen at all times, during all test sections (you cannot hide the title bar). The title bar displays three items:

- The time elapsed for the section (left corner)

- The name of the test section (middle)

- The current question number and total number of questions on the current section (right corner) (Quantitative and Verbal screens only)

### The CAT Toolbar

A series of six buttons appears in a toolbar across the bottom of the computer screen at all times. Here is what each button does.

**The "Quit Test" button.** Click this button to stop the test and cancel your scores for the entire test. If you click the Quit Test button, a dialog box appears on the screen and asks you to confirm this operation.

**The "Exit Section" button.** Click this button if you finish the section before the allotted time expires and want to proceed immediately to the next section. A dialog box appears on the screen and asks you to confirm this operation.

**The "Time" button.** Click this button to display the time remaining for the current section. The screen displays the time until you close it (by clicking on the button again). The time is displayed in minutes and seconds. You should refrain from clicking the Time button to check the time remaining, because the screen displays the time elapsed at all times. (If you have trouble computing the time remaining from the time elapsed, don't expect a high Quantitative score!)

**The "Help" button.** Click this button to display the directions at the top of the screen. Because you will already be familiar with the directions for all sections, you probably will have no need to check the directions by clicking this button.

**The "Confirm Answer" button.** When you click the Next button to proceed to the next question, a Confirm Answer dialog box appears asking you to confirm your response. After you confirm your response, the interface presents the next question, and you cannot go back and change your response to the prior question. If the Confirm button is dark, the Confirm Answer function is enabled (that is, you've selected a response to the current question);

Time elapsed

CAT Title bar

Name and Number
of Text Section

Help/Directions

AWA Topic

The AWA
Editing screen

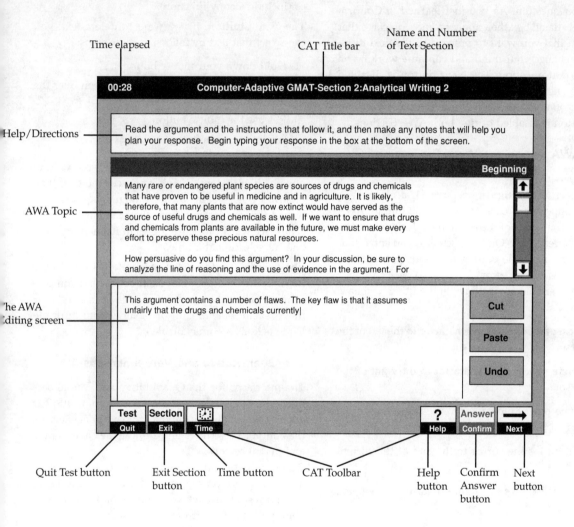

**00:28    Computer-Adaptive GMAT-Section 2:Analytical Writing 2**

Read the argument and the instructions that follow it, and then make any notes that will help you
plan your response.  Begin typing your response in the box at the bottom of the screen.

**Beginning**

Many rare or endangered plant species are sources of drugs and chemicals
that have proven to be useful in medicine and in agriculture.  It is likely,
therefore, that many plants that are now extinct would have served as the
source of useful drugs and chemicals as well.  If we want to ensure that drugs
and chemicals from plants are available in the future, we must make every
effort to preserve these precious natural resources.

How persuasive do you find this argument?  In your discussion, be sure to
analyze the line of reasoning and the use of evidence in the argument.  For

This argument contains a number of flaws.  The key flaw is that it assumes
unfairly that the drugs and chemicals currently|

Cut

Paste

Undo

Test | Section | [clock]
Quit | Exit | Time

? | Answer | →
Help | Confirm | Next

Quit Test button

Exit Section
button

Time button

CAT Toolbar

Help
button

Confirm
Answer
button

Next
button

if the button appears light, the function is disabled (you have not yet selected a response to the current question). (The Confirm Answer function is automatically disabled during the AWA section.)

**The "Next" button.** Click this button to proceed to the next question. As you just learned, a Confirm Answer dialog box then appears, and you can either confirm that you want to proceed to the next question or change your mind and continue working on the current question. The Next button is disabled (appears light) until you select a response to the current question (by clicking one of the five ovals), and the button is disabled during both AWA Sections.

## The AWA Screen and Word Processing Features

As shown in the figure on page 11, a clear AWA screen appears for each of the two 30-minute AWA topics. (The screen of the figure includes the first few lines of a response.) On these screens, you enter your responses using the editing functions provided by the CAT word processor.

Here are the navigational and editing keyboard keys available:

- **Backspace** removes the character to the left of the cursor.

- **Delete** removes the character to the right of the cursor.

- **Home** moves the cursor to the beginning of the current line.

- **End** moves the cursor to the end of the current line.

- **The arrow keys** move the cursor up, down, left, or right.

- **Enter** moves the cursor to the next line.

- **Page Up** moves the cursor up one page (or screen).

- **Page Down** moves the cursor down one page (or screen).

- **Tab** is disabled (that is, it does not function).

Because the Tab key is disabled, skip a line (by pressing Enter twice) to indicate paragraph breaks.

In addition to editing keys, the CAT word processor includes mouse-driven Cut, Paste, and Undo functions (note that the CAT word processor does *not* include a copy function).

**The "Cut" button.** If you want to delete text, you can select that text by following these steps:

1. Hold down your mouse button.
2. Sweep the I-beam cursor on the screen over the text that you want to delete.
3. Release the mouse button.
4. Click the Cut button.

**The "Paste" button.** If you want to move text from one position to another, select and cut the text, then position the I-beam on the screen wherever you want to move the text, then click the Paste button. (The CAT word processor stores in its memory only one cut selection at a time.)

**The "Undo" button.** Click this button to undo the most recent Delete, Cut, or Paste action that you performed. (The CAT word processor stores only your most recent Delete, Cut, or Paste action; multiple Undo actions are unavailable.)

## The Quantitative and Verbal Screens

The interfaces for the Quantitative and Verbal sections are similar. As in the AWA section, a title bar appears across the top, and a toolbar appears across the bottom. These next figures show the Quantitative and Verbal screens.

**Responses.** As you will notice, only one question at a time appears on the screen for these sections. To select a response, click your mouse on the circles or "bubbles" to the left of the response. (You cannot select the responses with the keyboard.) Note that the answer choices are *not* lettered A, B, C, D, and E.

**The vertical scrollbar.** For many GMAT questions, the screen is split vertically. The left side displays the problem or passage, and the right side displays the answer choices. All Reading Comprehension passages, and possibly some Critical Reasoning passages, will be too long to view on the screen in their entirety. To scroll up and down these passages,

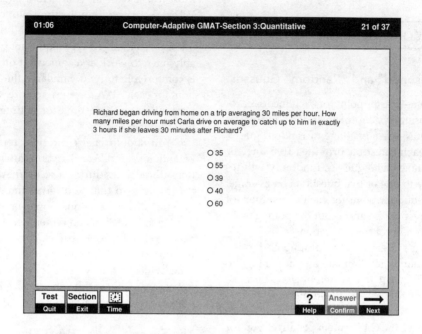

Richard began driving from home on a trip averaging 30 miles per hour. How many miles per hour must Carla drive on average to catch up to him in exactly 3 hours if she leaves 30 minutes after Richard?

- ○ 35
- ○ 55
- ○ 39
- ○ 40
- ○ 60

Test   Section     ?   Answer   →
Quit   Exit   Time     Help   Confirm   Next

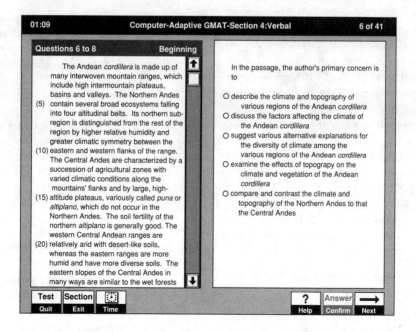

**Questions 6 to 8**     **Beginning**

The Andean *cordillera* is made up of many interwoven mountain ranges, which include high intermountain plateaus, basins and valleys. The Northern Andes
(5) contain several broad ecosystems falling into four altitudinal belts. Its northern sub-region is distinguished from the rest of the region by higher relative humidity and greater climatic symmetry between the
(10) eastern and western flanks of the range. The Central Andes are characterized by a succession of agricultural zones with varied climatic conditions along the mountains' flanks and by large, high-
(15) altitude plateaus, variously called *puna* or *altiplano*, which do not occur in the Northern Andes. The soil fertility of the northern *altiplano* is generally good. The western Central Andean ranges are
(20) relatively arid with desert-like soils, whereas the eastern ranges are more humid and have more diverse soils. The eastern slopes of the Central Andes in many ways are similar to the wet forests

In the passage, the author's primary concern is to

- ○ describe the climate and topography of various regions of the Andean *cordillera*
- ○ discuss the factors affecting the climate of the Andean *cordillera*
- ○ suggest various alternative explanations for the diversity of climate among the various regions of the Andean *cordillera*
- ○ examine the effects of topography on the climate and vegetation of the Andean *cordillera*
- ○ compare and contrast the climate and topography of the Northern Andes to that the Central Andes

Test   Section     ?   Answer   →
Quit   Exit   Time     Help   Confirm   Next

use the vertical scrollbar just to the right of the passage.

## SCORING YOUR BEST ON THE GMAT

### Making "Reasoned" and "Random" Guesses

By deducting one-quarter point for each incorrect response, the scoring system for the pencil-and-paper GMAT eliminates any advantage of random guessing. Because each question provides five answer choices, a test taker who guesses randomly will respond correctly to one of five questions on average. Deducting one-quarter point for each of the four (of five) incorrect responses cancels out the point gained for the one (out of five) correct response.

The scoring system for the computer-adaptive GMAT also attempts to eliminate any advantage to random guessing, but in a different way. Because correct responses to easier questions receive less weight in your score than correct responses to difficult questions, the CAT system penalizes you for incorrect responses by posing easier subsequent questions. You can then redeem yourself by responding correctly to these subsequent questions and increasing the level of difficulty. Conversely, if you guess randomly on a question that is too difficult for you and happen to select the correct response, the CAT system will catch on to your luck by posing even more difficult questions, which you will also have trouble with and will probably answer incorrectly.

Because the CAT system requires that you respond to every question presented to you before you can move on to another question, the test actually forces you to guess if you don't have a reasoned response among the five choices. What does this suggest in terms of a strategy? What it boils down to is the following:

- It is neither to your advantage nor disadvantage to make random guesses.

- If you must guess, try to make a reasoned or educated guess. Eliminate obvious wrong-answer choices, and go with your hunch.

### Managing Your Time

Most test takers can complete the Quantitative and Verbal sections within the time allotted. However, to read, consider, and respond to all 37 Quantitative questions and all 41 Verbal questions, you will probably have to work at a somewhat quicker pace than is comfortable for you. Similarly, the 30-minute time limit for each AWA response requires a lively writing pace, allowing little time for editing, revising, and fine-tuning.

You should check the time remaining on the Quantitative and Verbal sections after every 10 questions (three times during a section). Adjust your pace accordingly so that you have time to consider all questions in the section. However, don't be a constant clock watcher, and remember that you have no need to click that onscreen clock button (you can determine the time remaining based on the elapsed time, which is always visible in the screen's upper-left corner). Concentrate on the question at hand, not on the time remaining.

### The Seven Deadly GMAT Sins

1. **Perfectionism.** On an exam as important as the GMAT, you can easily adopt a stubborn, perfectionist frame of mind—one in which you insist on responding correctly to each question before moving on to the next one. The design of the CAT itself contributes to this mind set, because your reward for correct responses to difficult questions is greater than your reward for easier questions. Nevertheless, a stubborn, perfectionist attitude might be self-defeating, because it restricts the number of questions that you attempt, which in turn can hold down your score. As you take the mini-tests and the full-length practice test in this book, get comfortable with a quick pace by adhering strictly to the time limits imposed. Set aside your perfectionist tendencies, and remember: You can miss quite a few questions and still get a high GMAT score. Develop a sense of your optimal pace—one that results in the greatest number of correct responses.

2. **Overconfidence.** Perhaps you think you are a math "wiz" and that the Quantitative GMAT

questions won't pose any real challenge; or perhaps you think you have good command of English and believe that the Sentence Correction questions will be a breeze. If so, you're already on your way to disappointing GMAT scores. The single most common mistake GMAT takers make is to hurry through what they consider to be "easy" questions. Many incorrect responses are the result of careless errors and oversights, not lack of intellectual ability or knowledge.

3. **Over-analysis.** GMAT questions are not designed to trick you. In fact, the testing service goes to great lengths to ensure that all questions are clear and unambiguous and that each question has one best response. As long as you believe your thinking is fairly clear as you read and consider a question, do not second-guess your own judgment as to which response is correct. You'll probably be wasting valuable time.

4. **The passive mind set.** While taking the GMAT, it is remarkably easy to fall into a passive mode—one in which you let your eyes simply pass over the words while you hope that the correct response jumps out at you as you scan the answer choices. Fight this tendency by interacting with the test as you read it. Keep in mind that each question on the GMAT is designed to measure a specific ability or skill. Thus, when presented with each new question, try to adopt an active, investigative approach to the question. Ask yourself the following:

- What skill is the question measuring?

- What is the most direct thought process for determining the correct response?

- How might a careless test taker be tripped up on this type of question?

Use your pencil to help keep you in an active mode. Make brief notes on your scratch paper. Draw diagrams and flow charts as needed to keep your thought process clear and straight.

5. **Obsession with scores.** Perhaps you have a particular business school in mind as your first choice, and you think that you need a particular GMAT score to gain admission to that school. Setting a goal for your GMAT scores is understandable. However, try not to concern yourself as much with your scores as with what you can constructively do between now and exam day to improve your performance.

6. **Cramming and burnout.** Preparing for the GMAT is a bit like training for an athletic event. You need to familiarize yourself with the event, learn to be comfortable with it, and build up your endurance. At some point—around exam day, you hope—your motivation, interest, and performance will peak. Cramming for the GMAT makes little sense; it takes several weeks to get comfortable with the exam, to correct poor test-taking habits, to develop an instinct for recognizing wrong-answer choices and to find your optimal pace.

On the flip side, there is a point beyond which additional study and practice confer little or no additional benefit. Devoting one month of your attention, energy, and concern to the GMAT is plenty of time. Don't drag out the process by starting several months in advance or by postponing the exam to give yourself more time than you really need for preparation.

7. **Unrealistic expectations.** Every test taker wants a "perfect" score on the GMAT, and in theory, any test taker is capable of attaining it. In reality, however, each individual is constrained by his or her innate abilities and talents. Accept your limitations. With regular study and practice, you will perform as well as you can reasonably expect to perform. Also be realistic about the benefits you expect from this or any other GMAT preparation book. There is only so much that you can do in 30 days—or even 300 days—to boost your GMAT score.

# Critical Reasoning Lesson 1: Basic Skills and Strategies

## Today's Topics:

1. Critical Reasoning at a glance
2. Anatomy of a Critical Reasoning problem
3. Strategies for dealing with Critical Reasoning problems
4. Managing your time
5. Identifying the main point or conclusion of an argument
6. Identifying the unstated conclusion of a passage
7. Making inferences from given premises
8. Detecting assumptions involved in an argument
9. Assessing the effect of additional information

Today you will familiarize yourself with the format of the Critical Reasoning problems, learn strategies for handling the questions, and learn five of the eight basic Critical Reasoning skills tested on the GMAT.

## CRITICAL REASONING AT A GLANCE

**Number of questions:** 14–15 (interspersed with Reading Comprehension and Sentence Correction)
**Average time per question:** 1 ³/₄ minutes
**Basic format:**

- Brief passage containing an argument followed by a question and five answer choices.

**Ground rules:**

- Scratch paper is permitted and provided.
- Each question is considered independently.

- No penalty (deduction) is assessed for incorrect responses.

- **Terminology of formal logic presupposed:** none

- **Logical concepts presupposed:**

  - Argument
  - Issue
  - Premise
  - Conclusion
  - Assumption

**Primary Critical Reasoning skills tested:**

- Identifying the main point or conclusion of an argument

- Making inferences or drawing conclusions from given premises

- Identifying assumptions of an argument

- Assessing the effect of additional information on an argument

- Identifying the unstated conclusion of an argument

- Identifying the method of reasoning employed in an argument

- Detecting reasoning errors

- Recognizing arguments that have similar structure or employ a similar method

## ANATOMY OF A CRITICAL REASONING PROBLEM

Critical Reasoning problems have three elements:

1. A brief passage that contains an argument or a set of facts. The writing style and format of the passages vary considerably from problem to problem. In addition, the content of the passages covers a broad spectrum of topics.

2. A question dealing with the argument or the information stated in the passage. There are only eight basic question types, but the phrasing of each type varies extensively.

3. Five answer choices, from which you are to choose the *best*.

Here is a typical example:

An auto mechanic who is too thorough in checking a car is likely to subject the customer to unnecessary expense. On the other hand, one who is not thorough enough is likely to miss some problem that could cause a serious accident. Therefore, it's a good idea not to have your car checked until a recognizable problem develops.

Which one of the following, if true, casts the most doubt on the argument?

(A) A mechanic can easily detect mechanical problems that can cause serious accidents even before they become recognizable to the customer.

(B) Due to the high cost of skilled labor, some auto garages limit the amount of time spent on auto checkups.

(C) Drivers who are not trained mechanics usually have difficulty recognizing that their car has a problem.

(D) Many mechanics spend neither too little nor too much time when checking a car for problems.

(E) Most people cannot afford to have their cars checked for problems regularly.

## STRATEGIES FOR DEALING WITH CRITICAL REASONING PROBLEMS

It's important to have a plan in mind before you begin any complex task. This is especially true when dealing with the Critical Reasoning questions on the GMAT. Knowing in advance how you will approach each problem is just as important as having the requisite knowledge to solve the problem. The following three-step approach will help you work through the test methodically and answer the questions with the greatest possible speed and accuracy.

### Step One: Read the Question Stem Carefully

**Identify the problem type.** When reading the question *stem* (the question itself, apart from the passage and answer choices), try to determine which Critical Reasoning skill the question is testing, then decide which task you need to perform to reach the answer.

**Follow directions carefully.** Pay close attention to any special directions mentioned in the question. For example, if the question directs you to assume that the information stated in the passage is true, do so even if some or all of it seems to be false. Or, if the question directs you to assume that each of the answers is true, do so even if they state something that you believe is false.

### Step Two: Read the Passage Carefully

**Identify the premise (or premises) and the conclusion.** With the task firmly in mind, read the passage very carefully. What you look for when reading the passage depends entirely on the task that you are performing. In most cases, however, it is important to begin by determining which statements in the passage are *premises* of the argument and which statement is the *conclusion*. After you do so, you should underline the key words in the premises and conclusion, leaving out as much of the unnecessary verbiage as possible.

**Pay attention to key words.** You must pay careful attention to detail when reading the passage, and you must confine your understanding of the topic under discussion to the information stated in the passage unless specifically directed otherwise. In other words, pay very close attention to facts, numbers, percentages, and the stated relationships among them, and do not make superfluous assumptions or draw unwarranted conclusions. Pay particular attention to words and phrases that have logical meanings. Such words as *all, some, none,* and *most,* and such phrases as *only if* and *given that,* signify logical relationships that are crucial to understanding an argument's reasoning.

**Put your knowledge of the topic aside.** Treat each topic as though you knew nothing whatsoever about it other than what is stated in the passage. It is extremely important that you focus on the argument's *logic* rather than on the argument's *content*. Never choose an answer simply because you happen to believe that it is true or because you agree with it, and conversely, never reject an answer simply because you believe that it is false or because you disagree with it. Keep this in mind: Critical Reasoning questions test your ability to recognize correct and incorrect reasoning; they do *not* test your knowledge of the topic under discussion. Keep this in mind as well: An argument can employ correct reasoning even if all statements in the argument are *false,* and conversely, an argument can employ incorrect reasoning even if all the statements in the argument are *true.*

### Step Three: Read the Answers Carefully

If you don't know the answer or none appears to you to be the best, narrow down the alternatives by eliminating those that appear to be the *worst* answers, then make a guess.

## MANAGING YOUR TIME

The advice in the preceding strategies can be summed up in two simple maxims:

- Know what you're looking for before you go looking.

- If you're unsure of how to find what you're looking for, don't waste too much time looking.

This is important advice in light of the fact that you have only an average of 1 3/4 minutes to come up with the correct answer for a problem. Of course, this does not mean that you can or should spend only 1 3/4 minutes on each problem, but does serve to highlight the importance of wise time management.

The first maxim points out the importance of being methodical in your approach to each problem. One obvious reason for this is that being methodical saves time. The second maxim points out the importance of making the best use of your time in handling a problem—more specifically, the importance of not letting yourself get bogged down. Some questions on the test are much harder than others. Therefore, you might have to guess on a few questions to finish on time. Also, you have to develop a strict time schedule and keep close track of time.

## IDENTIFYING THE MAIN POINT OR CONCLUSION OF AN ARGUMENT

The ability to identify premises and conclusions of arguments correctly is essential to answering almost all the Critical Reasoning questions on the GMAT. Therefore, this skill warrants close attention and complete mastery.

Conclusion questions are typically worded as follows:

- Which of the following best expresses the main point of the passage?

- The conclusion of the argument is best expressed by which of the following?

An argument's final conclusion typically expresses the argument's main point. In arguments that contain more than one conclusion, the final conclusion is the statement that is supported by other statements but does not itself support any other statement; intermediate conclusions are statements that are supported by other statements and that, in turn, support further statements.

## Look for Indicator Words and Phrases

In most cases, you can quickly identify an argument's conclusion simply by paying close attention to key words and phrases in the passage. Here are some words and phrases commonly used to indicate that the sentence that follows is a conclusion:

| | | |
|---|---|---|
| therefore | entails that | allows us to infer that |
| shows that | as a result | hence |
| consequently | it follows that | proves that |
| implies that | so | it is likely that |
| thus | suggests that | demonstrates that |

In cases where such words and phrases are absent, you can identify the conclusion by first identifying the premises and then looking for the sentence that they are intended to support. Here are some words and phrases commonly used to indicate that the sentence that follows is a premise:

| | | |
|---|---|---|
| since | for | because |
| inasmuch as | follows from | given that |
| is suggested by | is proved by | for the reason that |
| is entailed by | assuming that | is substantiated by |
| is shown by | as a result | on the supposition that |

Now look at a few examples to see how these words and phrases can help you identify the conclusion of an argument.

### Example 3-1

Einstein is as great a cult figure as Madonna, *so* T-shirts with Einstein's picture on them will sell as well as shirts with Madonna's picture.

### Example 3-2

*Since* Einstein is as great a cult figure as Madonna, T-shirts with Einstein's picture on them will sell as well as shirts with Madonna's picture.

In Example 3-1, the word *so* indicates the conclusion; in Example 3-2, the word *since* indicates the premise. The argument in each of these examples is identical and can be rewritten as follows:

> **Premise:** Einstein is as great a cult figure as Madonna.
>
> **Conclusion:** T-shirts with Einstein's picture on them will sell as well as shirts with Madonna's picture.

Here's a more complicated example:

### Example 3-3

*Inasmuch as* Einstein is as great a cult figure as Madonna, *it is likely that* T-shirts with Einstein's picture on them will sell as well as shirts with Madonna's picture, *so* we should add them to our inventory.

Each of the three italicized expressions in Example 3-3 is an indicator. The first indicates a premise, the other two indicate conclusions. The word *so* indicates the final conclusion. The phrase *it is likely that* indicates the intermediate conclusion. You can rewrite this argument as follows to reveal its structure:

> **Premise:** Einstein is as great a cult figure as Madonna.
>
> **Intermediate conclusion:** T-shirts with Einstein's picture on them will sell as well as shirts with Madonna's picture.
>
> **Final conclusion:** We should add to our inventory T-shirts with Einstein's picture on them.

## Look for Rhetorical Questions

In addition to the use of these indicator expressions, another common way to signal an argument's conclusion is to express it as a rhetorical question or as an answer to a rhetorical question. The purpose of such questions is not to solicit information, but rather to emphasize a particular point or to raise a particular issue. Rhetorical questions typically (but not always) appear at the beginning of the passage. The remaining sentences in the passage are typically premises that support a position on the issue that the rhetorical question encompasses. Consider the following example:

**Example 3-4**

Can anyone really deny that abortion is morally wrong? After all, killing humans is wrong, and abortion is just another way of killing a human.

The rhetorical question in Example 3-4 leaves little doubt about the author's position on this issue. The way in which the question is posed clearly indicates that, at least for the author, this is not an open question. Generally, the more sarcastic the tone of the question, the more obvious the author's position on the issue that the question encompasses. The converse of this is generally the case as well. The conclusion of the argument in Example 3-4 is simply a restatement of the rhetorical question expressed in the first sentence—specifically, that abortion is morally wrong. The remaining sentences in Example 3-4 are premises that support this conclusion. You can rewrite the argument in Example 3-4 as follows:

**Premise:** Killing humans is wrong.

**Premise:** Abortion is just another way of killing a human.

**Conclusion:** Abortion is morally wrong.

Here's another example:

**Example 3-5**

Is abortion morally wrong or not? I would answer "no!" because while killing humans is morally wrong, abortion kills a fetus, and a fetus is not a human being.

The first sentence in Example 3-5 is a rhetorical question that raises the issue that the author wants to address. Next, the author indicates which side of this issue he or she is arguing—specifically, that abortion is not morally wrong. This is the argument's conclusion. The remaining statements in Example 3-5 are intended as reasons in support of this claim. In this example, the question itself does not make it obvious which side of the issue the author is arguing. The way in which the question is

posed indicates that this is, at least initially, an open question. In such cases, you must read on to find out which side of the issue the author arguing. You can rewrite the argument in Example 3-5 as follows:

**Premise:** Killing humans is morally wrong.

**Premise:** A fetus is not a human being.

**Premise:** Abortion kills a fetus.

**Conclusion:** Abortion is not morally wrong.

## A Procedure for Identifying the Main Point or Conclusion

Here's a brief summary of the procedure for identifying the main point or conclusion of an argument:

1. Scan the passage looking for conclusion and premise indicator words or phrases. These words and phrases provide important clues to the author's organizational scheme. Typically, you are looking for the argument's final conclusion, so in arguments with more than one conclusion, determine which sentences lead to or support other sentences in the passage. The final conclusion is the one that others support but does not itself support any others.

2. Alternatively, look for a rhetorical question in the passage; typically, this question appears at the beginning. The main point is either a restatement of this question or a direct answer to this question. If the author's position on the issue addressed in the question is not obvious from the way in which the question is asked, a quick scan of the passage usually tells you which side of the issue the author supports.

3. If the passage has no indicator expressions or rhetorical questions, the best way to proceed is to ask yourself what the author is trying to establish in the passage.

## IDENTIFYING THE UNSTATED CONCLUSION OF A PASSAGE

Unstated conclusion questions test your ability to follow a line of reasoning and reach the conclusion that most logically completes that line of reasoning.

In such questions, a blank replaces the last few words or the last sentence of the passage, and you must choose the answer that best fits in the blank. The best answer is the one that most logically completes the passage's reasoning process. When dealing with passages that leave the conclusion unstated, the best way to begin is to identify the passage's main ideas. Look for links between these ideas in the passage. Then look for an answer that ties together two of the main ideas that the passage does not link together. A more holistic approach is simply to ask yourself what the author is working toward or trying to establish in the passage.

## A Procedure for Identifying Unstated Conclusions

Here's the procedure for identifying an unstated conclusion:

1. Identify the passage's main ideas.
2. Look for links between the main ideas expressed.
3. Look for an answer choice that links together two of the main ideas that the passage does not link together.
4. As an alternative to steps 1–3, ask yourself what the author is trying to establish.

To illustrate this procedure, examine the following example:

**Example 3-6**

When we regard people to be morally responsible for their actions, we regard them as being the object of praise or blame with respect to those actions. But it seems evident that people cannot be the object of praise or blame for their actions unless they performed them of their own free will. Therefore, _____.

Which of the following best completes the preceding argument?

(A) People are morally responsible only for actions that they perform of their own free will.

(B) People are not morally responsible for actions that they did not perform.

(C) People can be blamed or praised only for actions that they perform of their own free will.

(D) People are morally responsible only for actions for which they can be blamed or praised.

(E) People who are not morally responsible for their actions cannot be blamed or praised for their actions.

The main ideas in Example 3-6's passage are (1) actions for which one is morally responsible, (2) praiseworthy and blameworthy actions, and (3) actions performed of one's own free will. Notice that the passage's first sentence ties together ideas 1 and 2, and the second sentence of the passage ties together 2 and 3. In this example, the conclusion that the author invites is one that ties together ideas 1 and 3. Looking at the answer choices with this in mind, the best response is A.

## Making Inferences from Given Premises

Inference questions test your ability to draw conclusions from the information stated in the passage—that is, your ability to determine what else *must* be true or *is likely* to be true, given that the statements in the passage are true. In problems of this type, the information in the passage functions as the premises of the argument and the candidate conclusions are among the answer choices.

### Inference Questions

Inference questions are typically worded as follows:

• If all the statements in the passage are true, which one of the following must also be true?

• Which one of the following conclusions is most strongly supported by the statements in the passage?

• Which of the following statements can be properly inferred from the passage?

Notice that there are three basic types of questions:

1. Questions that ask for the conclusion that *must be true* given the information in the passage

2. Questions that ask for the conclusion that is *most strongly supported* given the information in the passage

3. Questions that ask for the conclusion that can be *properly drawn or inferred* from the passage

The difference between the first two types of questions is significant. The conclusion that must be true given the information stated in the passage is the one that cannot conceivably be false, given this information. The conclusion that is most strongly supported by the information stated in the passage is the one that is most unlikely to be false (that is, most likely to be true), given this information.

Questions that ask for what can be "properly inferred" or "properly drawn" from the passage are somewhat tricky. For an inference to be "proper," it must be made in accordance with acceptable inference rules or meet certain standards of acceptable inference. In the case of *deductive* reasoning, these rules and standards are designed to ensure that the truth of the premises *guarantees* the truth of the conclusion, whereas in the case of *inductive* reasoning, the rules and standards are designed to ensure that the truth of the premises makes it *highly likely* that the conclusion is true. Basically, questions that ask what conclusion you can "properly" infer or draw from the statements in a passage can be understood in two ways: as asking either for the conclusion that must be true, or for the conclusion that the passage most strongly supports.

Without training in formal logic, you pretty much have to "fly by the seat of your pants" when dealing with these problems. However, you shouldn't just guess the answers for these problems. There are some definite guidelines or procedures that you want to follow.

## A Procedure for Dealing with "Must Be True" Inference Questions

Here's the procedure for dealing with questions that ask you to find the statement that *must be true* given the information stated in the passage:

1. Read the passage very carefully. If necessary, underline the premises (or list them on separate lines), leaving out any unnecessary verbiage.

2. Read each of the answers, and ask yourself whether it can conceivably be false given that the sentences in the passage are true.

3. The correct answer is the one that cannot conceivably be false given the information stated in the passage.

To see how this procedure works, examine a simple example:

**Example 3-7**

Cheating on your taxes is lying, and lying, as we all know, is morally wrong.

If the statements in the passage are true, which one of the following must also be true?

(A) Cheating on your taxes is illegal.

(B) Cheating is morally wrong.

(C) Cheating on your taxes is morally wrong.

(D) Lying is cheating.

(E) Cheating is immoral.

First, read the passage very carefully. Underline the premises, leaving out the unnecessary verbiage, as follows:

Cheating on your taxes is lying, and lying, as we all know, is morally wrong.

Second, read each answer in turn and determine whether it can conceivably be false, given the information stated in the premises. The correct answer is the one that cannot conceivably be false, given this information.

Can A conceivably be false given the stated information? The answer is yes, because the given information does not explicitly mention anything about what is legal or illegal. Remember, don't make *any* assumptions beyond what the passage states explicitly.

Can B conceivably be false given the stated information? Again, the answer is yes, because the given information does not state that *all kinds* of cheating are lying. It states only that a particular kind of cheating (cheating on your taxes) is lying.

Can C conceivably be false given the stated information? In this case, the answer is no, because if all tax cheating is lying, and all lying is morally wrong, then all tax cheating *must* be morally wrong. Response C is the correct answer.

After finding an answer that must be true given the information, you need not continue considering the other answers. You have found the correct answer, so simply record it and move on to the next problem.

Here's a slightly more complicated example:

**Example 3-8**

All professors are outgoing, and all outgoing people are popular, but even so, some introverts are professors.

If the preceding statements are true, which one of the following must also be true?

(A) All popular people are outgoing.

(B) All outgoing people are professors.

(C) Some introverts are popular.

(D) No introverts are professors.

(E) No introverts are popular.

First, read the passage very carefully. Underline the premises, leaving out the unnecessary verbiage, as follows:

All professors are outgoing, and all outgoing people are popular, but even so, some introverts are professors.

Next, read each of the answers, and ask yourself whether it can conceivably be false, given that the underlined sentences are true.

Can A conceivably be false, given the information stated in the premises? The answer is yes, because the passage states that all outgoing people are popular, and this premise is consistent with the conclusion that not all popular people are outgoing.

Can B conceivably be false, given the information stated in the premises? The answer is yes, because the passage states that all professors are outgoing people, and this premise is consistent with the conclusion that not all outgoing people are professors.

Can C conceivably be false, given the information stated in the premises? The answer is no, because if all professors are outgoing and all outgoing people are popular, then all professors must be popular. However, if all professors are popular and some introverts are professors, then some introverts must be popular. Response C is the correct answer.

A variation of this type of question asks not for the single statement that must be true, but rather for the answer that is the exception (that is, the statement that need not be true given the stated information). In this case, the question is worded as follows:

If the preceding statements are true, all the following statements must also be true except the following:

In this version of the question, four of the five answer choices must be true and only one need not be true. Your job is to find the one that need not be true given the information in the passage. The procedure for dealing with this type of question is the same as previously described. The only difference is that the correct answer is the one that could conceivably be false given the stated information.

## A Procedure for Dealing with "Most Strongly Supported" Inference Questions

Here's the procedure for dealing with questions that ask you to find the statement that is *most strongly supported* given the information stated in the passage:

1. Read the passage very carefully. If necessary, underline the premises (or list them on separate lines), leaving out any unnecessary verbiage.

2. Read each of the answers, and determine how likely it is to be true given the information stated in the passage.

3. Use a simple four-point scale to score each of the answers (for example, 1 for very unlikely, 2 for not very likely, 3 for somewhat likely, 4 for very likely). The correct answer is the one that gets the highest score.

To see how this procedure works, consider the following example:

**Example 3-9**

Dogs taken to humane shelters are routinely checked for rabies. The dog that bit the little boy was obtained from the humane shelter just a day before it bit the boy.

If the statements in the passage are true, which of the following is most strongly supported?

(A) The humane shelter technicians never make mistakes when testing dogs for rabies.

(B) The dog contracted rabies after it was released from the shelter but before it bit the boy.

(C) The dog does not have rabies.

(D) The little boy has rabies.

(E) The humane shelter technicians are incompetent.

With the information stated in the passage in mind, rank each of the answers using the four-point scale.

The score for A is 2. Response A is not very likely, because the information in the passage really doesn't address itself to the issue of whether the testing procedures are reliable.

The score for B is 2. Although it is possible that the dog contracted rabies during this brief period, without additional information regarding the dog's whereabouts and so on, it is difficult to assess the likelihood that this is the case.

The score for C is 4. The fact that the dog was tested for rabies just a short time before the incident makes it very likely that the dog was not rabid at the time of the incident.

The score for D is 1. The likelihood that D is true is a function of the likelihood that C is true, so if it is very likely that the dog does not have rabies, the little boy is very unlikely to have rabies.

The score for E is 2. Although it is possible that the technicians are incompetent, the stated information does not support that claim.

Reviewing the scores, you determine that response C is most strongly supported, and thus is the correct answer.

## A Procedure for Dealing with "Properly Inferred" Inference Questions

You can also use the preceding procedure to deal with questions that ask you to find the statement that is *properly inferred* from the information in the passage. You simply expand the four-point scale to a five-point scale, assigning 5 to answers that must be true.

## DETECTING ASSUMPTIONS INVOLVED IN AN ARGUMENT

An *assumption of an argument* is a statement that the argument does not express but that must be true if the conclusion is to be true. Put simply, an assumption is a missing piece of information required to support the conclusion.

In looking for the assumptions in an argument, you can use the author's stated information as a guide to the author's hidden assumptions. Typically, hidden assumptions in arguments serve to connect key ideas in the author's reasoning. Authors fail to state these connections explicitly because they believe that their audience already accepts them or that they are too obvious to state.

Assumption questions are typically worded as follows:

- The conclusion of the argument is properly drawn if which one of the following is assumed?

- For the argument to be logically correct, it must make which of the following assumptions?

- Which one of the following is an assumption on which the argument in the passage depends?

- Which of the following is a presupposition in the argument?

The exact conditions that must be satisfied for an argument to be "logically correct," or for the conclusion to be "properly drawn," differ depending on the argument type. As a general rule, however, the more unlikely it is for the conclusion to be false given that the premises are true, the more "logically correct" the argument. Therefore, to find an assumption that will make the argument logically correct, you look for a statement that, when taken with the stated premises, significantly increases the likelihood that the conclusion is true. Moreover, among a selection of possible assumptions, the one that increases this likelihood the most will be the best candidate.

Consider the following brief argument:

**Example 3-10**

All humans have inherent worth; this is why they have an inalienable right to privacy.

This argument can be rewritten as follows:

**Premise:** All people have inherent worth.

**Conclusion:** All people have an inalienable right to privacy.

As it stands, the preceding argument is not compelling; that is, the stated premise does not, by itself, ensure that the conclusion is true or even that it is highly likely to be true. The assumption required to make this argument logically correct must fill this logical gap. Moreover, to fill the logical gap, the assumption must connect the key ideas in the argument in such a way that it is either impossible or highly unlikely for the conclusion to be false given the stated premise. In Example 3-10, you can fill the argument's logical gap with the following statement:

Anything that has inherent worth has an inalienable right to privacy.

Adding this statement to the argument ensures that the conclusion is true, given that the premises are true—as the following reconstruction of the argument clearly demonstrates.

**Assumption:** Anything that has inherent worth has an inalienable right to privacy.

**Premise:** All people have inherent worth.

**Conclusion:** All people have an inalienable right to privacy.

## A Procedure for Finding Assumptions

To find an assumption that makes the argument logically correct, follow this procedure:

1. Identify the premises and the conclusion of the argument.
2. Locate the logical gap in the argument. Typically, the stated premises and the conclusion link together key ideas in the passage. In most cases (but not all), the logical gap is an unstated link between two of these key ideas.

    Alternatively, ask the following question: What additional information is required to ensure the truth of the conclusion?
3. Look for an answer choice that either (1) connects key ideas in the argument in such a way that when you add this statement to the argument's

stated premises, the argument's conclusion either cannot be false or the likelihood of its being false is greatly diminished, or (2) provides information that, when taken with the given premises, prevents the conclusion from being false or makes it highly unlikely that the conclusion is false.

To see how this procedure works, take a look at an example written in the style of a GMAT problem:

### Example 3-11

Captive animals exhibit a wider range of physical and behavioral traits than animals in the wild, and this is why researchers who study them are able to study a wider range of genetic possibilities than researchers who study wild animals.

For the preceding argument to be logically correct, it must make which one of the following assumptions?

(A) Animals that are captive exhibit a wider range of physical and behavioral traits than animals that are wild.

(B) Animals that permit researchers to study a wide range of genetic possibilities are better research subjects than animals that do not.

(C) The wider the range of the physical and behavioral traits in a population of animals, the greater the range of their genetic possibilities.

(D) Captive animals are studied more than wild animals.

(E) Animals in the wild exhibit a narrow range of physical and behavioral traits.

You can rewrite the passage's argument as follows:

**Premise:** Captive animals exhibit a wider range of physical and behavioral traits than animals in the wild.

**Conclusion:** Researchers who study captive animals are able to study a wider range of genetic possibilities than researchers who study wild animals.

This argument has an obvious logical gap between the premise and the conclusion. You can determine the assumption required to fill this gap simply by asking what information, in addition to the stated premise, is required to ensure that the conclusion is true. In this instance, a little thought reveals that the required information must link the range of physical and behavioral traits with the range of genetic possibilities. Moreover, they must be linked in such a way that the wider the range of physical and behavioral traits, the wider the range of genetic possibilities. Turning to the answer choices with this in mind, C is obviously the best choice.

## ASSESSING THE EFFECT OF ADDITIONAL INFORMATION

Questions of this type begin with a passage that contains an argument. Your task is to assess the effect additional information has on the argument. There are basically just two types of problems:

1. Those that ask you to select the answer that *strengthens* the argument.

2. Those that ask you to select the answer that *weakens* the argument.

Additional-information-assessment (AIA) questions are worded in a variety of ways. To avoid confusion, it is important to remember that there are just two types of problems: strengthen problems and weaken problems. The following questions indicate some of the various ways in which the exam might express these question types.

AIA questions that ask you to select the choice that *weakens* the argument are worded variously, as follows:

- Which of the following, if true, would refute the argument in the passage?

- Which one of the following, if true, casts the most doubt on the argument?

- Which one of the following, if accepted by the authors, would require them to reconsider their conclusion?

- Which of the following, if true, most seriously calls the preceding conclusion into question?

- The argument is most vulnerable to which of the following criticisms?

- Which of the following, if true, most seriously undermines the author's contention?

- Which of the following, if true, most substantially weakens the argument?

AIA questions that ask you to select the choice that *strengthens* the argument are worded variously, as follows:

- Which of the following, if true, most strengthens the argument?

- Which of the following would provide the most support for the preceding conclusion?

- Which of the following supports the conclusion in the preceding passage?

- The conclusion in the preceding argument would be more reasonable if which one of the following were true?

- Which of the following, if true, would confirm the author's conclusion?

- Which one of the following, if true, provides the most support for the argument?

### Weakening an Argument

There are basically three ways to weaken an argument: undermine a major assumption of the argument, attack one of the premises of the argument, or suggest an alternative conclusion that you can infer from the given premises. In problems that ask you to choose a statement that weakens an argument, the correct answer does one of these three things. For this reason, it is important at the outset when working these problems to identify the premises, the conclusion, and the major assumption of the passage's argument.

### A Procedure for Finding the Statement That Weakens an Argument

Here's the procedure to find the statement that *weakens* an argument:

1. Identify the argument's premises and conclusion.

2. Identify the argument's major assumption.

3. Look for an answer choice that does one of the following:

a. Undermines the major assumption

b. Attacks a stated premise

c. Suggests an alternative conclusion that you can infer from the stated premises

4. The correct answer is one that does any one of the preceding.

To see how this procedure works, take a look at the following example:

### Example 3-12

Mountain lion sightings in outlying areas of Los Brisas have increased dramatically over the past two years. Hence, the population of mountain lions must be increasing.

Which of the following, if true, most effectively weakens the preceding argument?

(A) People have become more active in outdoor activities during the past two years.

(B) The mountain lion habitat has dramatically diminished over the past two years.

(C) The human population in the outlying areas of Los Brisas has dramatically increased over the past two years.

(D) The number of television programs about mountain lions has increased dramatically during the past two years.

(E) Reports of people and animals being killed by mountain lions have increased dramatically over the past two years.

The premise and conclusion of Example 3-12 are easy to identify: The premise is the first statement, and the conclusion is the statement that follows the word *hence*. The major assumption in Example 3-12 is that the population of humans in the outlying areas of Los Brisas has remained relatively constant over the two-year period. Given this assumption, an increase in sightings strongly indicates an increase in the population of mountain lions. Without this assumption, however, the argument is weakened considerably. The answer choice that most directly challenges this assumption is C, so C is the correct answer.

### Strengthening an Argument

There are two ways to strengthen an argument: offer support for the argument's major assumption, or provide additional evidence for the conclusion (that is, evidence beyond what the given premises state). In a problem that asks you to choose a statement that strengthens an argument, the correct response does one of these two things.

### A Procedure for Finding the Statement That Strengthens an Argument

Here's the procedure to find the statement that *strengthens* an argument:

1. Identify the argument's premises and conclusion.

2. Identify the argument's major assumption.

3. Look for an answer choice that does either of the following:

a. Offers support for the major assumption

b. Provides additional evidence for the conclusion

4. The correct answer is one that does either of the preceding.

To see how this procedure works, take a look at the following example:

### Example 3-13

The portrayal of violence on television and in movies has increased dramatically over the past 10 years. It is primarily for this reason that we have seen a dramatic increase in the rate of violent crime during the last decade.

Which one of the following, if true, provides the most support for the argument?

(A) Liberal sentencing policies over the past 10 years have resulted in reduced sentences for perpetrators of violent acts.

(B) Persons who commit violent acts are less prone to being influenced by portrayals of violence.

(C) Recent studies have shown that repeated exposure to portrayals of violence significantly increases the tendency to commit violent acts.

(D) The number of homeless people has increased dramatically during the last decade.

(E) Due to severe overcrowding during the past decade, prisons have been forced to release violent criminals before they have served their full sentences.

The premise and conclusion in Example 3-13 are relatively easy to identify. The phrase *It is primarily for this reason that* indicates that the first sentence in the passage is the premise; the conclusion follows this phrase. The argument's major assumption is that exposure to portrayals of violence results in violent acts. Answer choices A, D, and E state plausible alternative reasons for the increase in violence and, as such, might be considered as providing additional support for the conclusion. However, neither A, D, nor E directly support the argument's main contention that increased portrayals of violence are the "primary" reason for the increase in violent acts. Answer choice B weakens the argument because it undermines the argument's major assumption, so you can eliminate it. Answer choice C supports the argument's major assumption and thus is the best answer.

# Critical Reasoning Lesson 2

## Today's Topics:

1. Recognizing reasoning errors
2. Identifying the method of arguments
3. Recognizing similarities between arguments

Today you will learn how to recognize reasoning errors, identify the method of arguments, and recognize similarities between arguments.

## RECOGNIZING REASONING ERRORS

In GMAT problems involving reasoning errors, the passage contains an argument that employs a questionable argumentative technique or fallacy. Your task is to identify the flaw or error in the reasoning. Such problems do not require you to identify the fallacy by its traditional name; instead, you must select the best description of the reasoning error from the answer choices.

Reasoning error questions are typically worded as follows:

- Which of the following is the best statement of the flaw in the argument?

- Which one of the following indicates an error in the reasoning leading to the conclusion in the argument?

- Which one of the following questionable argumentative techniques does this passage employ?

The best way to prepare for this type of question is to become familiar with the various types of reasoning errors catalogued below.

## Statistical Fallacies

The two most common statistical reasoning fallacies are the *fallacy of the biased sample* and the *fallacy of the small or insufficient sample*. Both involve sampling errors. The fallacy of the biased sample is committed whenever the data for a statistical inference is drawn from a sample that is not representative of the population under consideration. The fallacy of the small or insufficient sample is committed whenever too small a sample is used to warrant confidence in the conclusion or whenever greater reliability is attributed to the conclusion than the sample size warrants. These two fallacies are commonly referred to as fallacies of "hasty generalization."

Here's an example of an argument that commits the fallacy of the biased sample:

**Example 4-1**

In a recent survey conducted on the Internet, 80 percent of the respondents indicated their strong disapproval of government regulation of the content and access of Web-based information. This survey clearly shows that legislation designed to restrict the access or to control the content of Internet information will meet with strong opposition from the electorate.

The preceding argument draws the data for its inference from a sample that is not representative of the entire electorate. Because the survey was conducted on the Internet, not all members of the electorate have an equal chance of being included in the sample. Moreover, people who use the Internet are more likely to have an opinion on the topic than people who do not. For these reasons, the sample is obviously biased.

Here's an example of an argument that commits the fallacy of the insufficient sample:

**Example 4-2**

I met my new boss at work today and she was very unpleasant. Twice when I tried to talk with her, she said that she was busy and told me not to interrupt her again. Later, when I needed her advice on a customer's problem, she ignored me and walked away. It's obvious that she has a bad attitude and is not going to be easy to work with.

The data for this argument's inference is insufficient to support the conclusion. Three observations of a person's behavior are not sufficient to support a conclusion about that person's behavior in general. Obviously, the boss could just have been having a bad day or been engrossed in other things.

## Causal Reasoning Fallacies

**The "after this, therefore because of this" fallacy.** This fallacy is by far the most common causal fallacy, and the one most likely to appear on the GMAT. This is the fallacy of concluding on insufficient grounds that because event X occurred *after* some other event Y, Y must have *caused* X. Many common superstitions are examples of this fallacy (for example, having a black cat cross your path or walking under ladders). The error in arguments that commit this fallacy is that their conclusions are causal claims that the evidence insufficiently substantiates. In most instances of this fallacy, the only evidence that is offered to support the causal claim is a positive correlation between two conditions or events; the one that occurs first is identified as the cause, the one that follows is identified as the effect. Typically, the causal connection between the two events is implausible given our general understanding of the world.

Here are two typical examples of the "after this, therefore because of this" fallacy:

**Example 4-3**

Ten minutes after walking into the auditorium, I began to feel sick to my stomach. There must have been something in the air in that building that caused my nausea.

**Example 4-4**

The stock market declined shortly after the president's election, thus indicating the lack of confidence that the business community has in the new administration.

Example 4-3 posits a causal connection between two events simply on the basis of one occurring before the other. Without further evidence to support it, the causal claim based on the correlation is premature. Example 4-4 is typical of modern news reporting. The only evidence that this argument offers to support the implicit causal claim that the president's election caused the decline in the stock market is the fact that the election preceded the decline. Although the election might have been a causal factor in the stock market's decline, to argue that it is the cause without additional information and auxiliary hypotheses that make the causal connection plausible is to commit the "after this, therefore because of this" fallacy.

**The slippery slope fallacy.** On a slippery slope, you cannot gain a foothold, so after you start to slide, you continue to slide until you crash to the bottom. Similarly, in this fallacy, it is assumed without justification or proof that after one event occurs, a series of events will occur that will end with some undesirable consequence. Because the undesirable consequence is to be avoided, it is reasoned that the initiating event is also to be avoided. Typically, arguments of this type provide no evidence that the causal sequence that they foretell is the only possible scenario of events. In most cases, a little reflection reveals that the scenario is not even very likely. Without the assumption that each step in the sequence of events is inevitable, the argument is not convincing. This fallacy is also commonly referred to as the domino fallacy.

Here's an example of the slippery slope fallacy:

**Example 4-5**

If pornography is not outlawed once and for all, the spread of pornographic literature will lead to an increase in sex-related crimes such as rape and incest. This in turn will lead to a general moral decay in the society that will cause an increase in crimes of all sorts. Eventually, a complete breakdown of law and order will occur, leading ultimately to the total collapse of civilization as we know it. We certainly don't want this to happen, so we had better outlaw pornography before it's too late to do anything about it.

## Unwarranted Assumption Fallacies

Unwarranted assumptions are assumptions that have no merit or independent justification.

**The fallacy of composition.** The fallacy of composition is committed when a characteristic of individual members of a group is assumed, without warrant, to apply to the members of the group collectively. This fallacy is commonly referred to as the "part-whole" fallacy. Although in some cases a property of an individual is transferable to the group of which the individual is a member, this certainly isn't always the case. The fallacy of composition mistakenly assumes that this transference always holds.

Here is an example of the fallacy of composition:

**Example 4-6**

All physical objects are made of atoms. Atoms have no color. This book is a physical object, so it has no color.

This example mistakenly assumes that a property that the parts lack is a property that the whole lacks as well. A little reflection shows that this assumption is false in this case.

**The division fallacy.** The division fallacy is the converse of the composition fallacy. In this case, the fallacy is committed when a property of a group is mistakenly assumed to hold to the individuals that make up the group. This fallacy is commonly referred to as the "whole-part" fallacy. Although in some cases a property of a group is transferable to the individuals in the group, this certainly isn't always the case. The division fallacy mistakenly assumes that this transference always holds.

Here is an example of the division fallacy:

**Example 4-7**

The GMAT is a challenging exam. Therefore, every problem on the GMAT is a challenging problem.

This example assumes that a property of the whole exam applies to each part of the exam. Clearly, the exam could be challenging even if some of the problems were not challenging.

**The false dichotomy fallacy.** A common unwarranted-assumption fallacy, the false dichotomy fallacy is committed when one assumes, without warrant, that there are only two alternatives, then reasons that because one of the alternatives is false or unacceptable, the other must be true or accepted. Of course, in cases where there are in fact only two alternatives, and this fact is obvious or justifiable, this pattern of reasoning is highly effective and acceptable. Typically, arguments afflicted with this fallacy offer no evidence to support the claim that only two alternatives are available, and a little reflection reveals that this claim is not self-evident. This fallacy is commonly referred to as the "black-and-white" fallacy.

Here is an example of the false dichotomy fallacy:

**Example 4-8**

Either we put convicted child molesters in jail for life or we risk having our children become their next victims. We certainly can't risk this, so we had better lock up these criminals for the rest of their lives.

The argument in Example 4-8 assumes that only two alternatives are possible. The statement offers no evidence to support this claim, and a little reflection reveals that the claim obviously has no validity. Although child molestation is a difficult problem to deal with, it is unlikely that the only solution to the problem is the one that the argument mentions. It is also unlikely that the advocated solution is the only way that we can protect children from becoming the victims of convicted offenders.

## Irrelevant Appeals Fallacies

**Irrelevant appeals** attempt to persuade others to accept a conclusion by appealing to matters that are not relevant to the truth or correctness of the conclusion.

They are considered reasoning errors because they violate the requirement that the reasons offered in support of a claim provide evidence that the claim is true or correct. In other words, such appeals mistakenly view the goal of argumentation to be simply persuasion rather than the attainment of the truth.

**Appeal to ignorance.** The *appeal to ignorance* is one of the most commonly used ploys to gain acceptance of a claim. The basic form of this fallacy is to argue that a claim is true (or false) solely on the grounds that no one has demonstrated or can demonstrate that the claim is false (or true).

Here's an example of an argument that employs an appeal to ignorance.

**Example 4-9**

Scientists have not established any causal link between smoking and lung cancer, hence we must simply accept the fact that smoking does not cause lung cancer.

Inability to prove that something is true (or false) cannot, by itself, be taken as evidence that it is false (or true). If this were accepted as a principle of logic, it would follow, for example, that our inability to prove the existence of God would lead immediately to the conclusion that God does not exist, and that our inability to prove that UFOs don't exist would lead immediately to the conclusion that UFOs exist.

**Appeal to public opinion.** Another commonly used ploy to gain acceptance of a claim is to appeal to public opinion or to what most persons believe. Instead of using evidence or reasons to support the truth of the claim, the argument's author resorts to consensus prejudices, beliefs, traditions, or customs to gain acceptance of the conclusion. The author relies on peer pressure and peer acceptance to persuade the unwary, uncritical listener or reader. Typically, the argument doesn't offer any evidence that is relevant to the truth of the argument's claim. This fallacy is a favorite of politicians and advertisers.

Here's an example of an argument that employs an appeal to public opinion.

**Example 4-10**

Rick O'Flanagan's newest novel, *Seldom More Often Than Frequently,* has been on the best-seller list for 25 weeks in a row. It must be a good book; after all, 30 million readers can't be wrong.

In this example, the only reason given for the claim that the novel is a good book is that 30 million people have read it. A little reflection tells you that this, by itself, is not a good reason for this claim. After all, it is also true that 30 million people regularly read tabloids, but this is surely not evidence that the tabloids are in any sense good.

**Appeal to authority.** Another common appeal used to gain acceptance of a claim is the appeal to authority. In place of evidence that supports the claim, authors often resort to the testimony or expertise of others to support the claim. This practice is not always suspect. As a matter of fact, people often rely on other people or sources when accepting claims. We do this, for example, when appealing to scientists, textbooks, doctors, and other experts to support our beliefs. This practice becomes suspect when there is a question about the competence, reliability, qualifications, motives, prejudices, and so on, of the persons or sources on whom we are relying.

Here's an example of an argument that employs an appeal to authority:

**Example 4-11**

Geena Goodlooks is one of this country's most respected and honored actresses. You can be certain that when she says welfare reform is needed, it has to be true.

In this argument, you have to wonder about the relevance of Geena's testimony to the truth of the claim that it supports. The argument offers no evidence that justifies its reliance on her testimony on this topic. The fact that she is a "respected and honored" actress hardly qualifies her as an expert on the need for welfare reform.

## Fallacies of Refutation

*Fallacies of refutation* are committed in criticizing the arguments of others. Refutation fallacies occur whenever the critic focuses on aspects of the argument that are irrelevant to the reasoning employed in the argument or the truth of the claims that make up the argument. The basic tactic in criticisms that commit fallacies of this type is to scrupulously avoid attacking the argument, and instead attack the author, a side issue, or a deliberately weakened version of the argument.

**Attacking the author.** Attacks on the argument's author take three forms. The attack focuses either on the character, the motives, or the behavior of the person presenting the argument. The aim of the attack in all three cases is to discredit the conclusion of the person's argument. Assaults of this type are rarely, if ever, relevant to the reasoning employed in the argument or the truth or correctness of the conclusion. They are irrelevant for the simple reason that an arguer's personal character, motives, or behavior are rarely relevant to the correctness of his or her reasoning or the truth of the statements employed in the reasoning. Criticisms that employ attacks of these types are commonly known as *ad hominem* arguments—arguments against the person. On the GMAT they occur in one of three forms:

*Attacking the author's character.* Here's an example of a counterargument that employs an attack on the *character* of the person advancing the argument:

**Example 4-12**
   When you realize that the man who is trying to convince you that he would be the best president this country has ever seen is in fact a womanizer and an illegal drug user, it's not difficult to draw the conclusion that his arguments are completely unacceptable.

   This example attacks the presidential candidate's arguments by pointing out repugnant characteristics of the candidate. No attempt is made to consider or attack the candidate's arguments.

*Attacking the author's motives.* Here's an example of a counterargument that employs an attack on the *motives* of the persons advancing the argument:

**Example 4-13**
   The radio and television industry has been lobbying against proposed changes in the laws governing the use of publicly owned transmission frequencies. But just keep this in mind: No matter how good the industry's arguments might be, broadcasters stand to lose a great deal if the proposed changes become law.

Example 4-13 dismisses the radio and television industry's arguments out of hand on the grounds that broadcasters have a vested interest in the outcome. The tactic exhibited in Example 4-13 is commonly called "poisoning the well" because it condemns the argument's source to discredit the argument.

*Attacking the author's behavior.* Here's an example of a counterargument that employs an attack on the behavior of the person advancing the argument:

**Example 4-14**
   My esteemed colleague accuses me of misappropriating taxpayers' funds for my own personal use. Well, it might interest you to know that he has the unenviable distinction of having spent more on so-called fact-finding trips to exotic locations all around the world than anyone else in Congress.

   The fallacy exhibited in Example 4-14 is commonly called the "you too!" or "two wrongs don't make a right" fallacy. In this example, the politician makes no attempt to attack the colleague's argument; rather, the focus of the attack is to accuse the person of similar questionable behavior or wrongdoing.

**Attacking a side issue.** Another fallacious refutation tactic commonly employed is to divert attention away from the argument under consideration and focus instead on a side issue. The popular name for this refutation tactic is "red herring," which comes from the fox hunting practice of dragging a cooked herring across the fox's trail to divert the hounds from the scent. The aim of this tactic is simply to obfuscate and avoid the argument instead of offering apt reasons to reject an argument.

   Here's an example of a counterargument that employs the "red herring" fallacy:

**Example 4-15**
   Mandatory life sentences for three-time felons is a bad idea. People who think such sentences are a good idea argue that they will stop violent crime. But if we really want to stop violent crime, instead of locking people up, we should stop portraying violence in movies and on television.

In Example 4-15, the critic shifts attention away from the issue of whether mandatory life sentences should be used to combat violent crime to a related but different issue. Instead of attacking the arguments of the proponents of mandatory life sentences, the critic proposes an alternative solution to the problem. Obviously, however, merely proposing a different solution to a problem cannot, by itself, be taken as evidence that competing solutions and the arguments that support them are necessarily mistaken or incorrect.

**Attacking a weakened version of an argument.** A critic commits the "straw man" fallacy by misrepresenting an opponent's argument deliberately to make it easier to criticize, or so obviously implausible that no criticism is required. Although the misrepresented version is usually only a caricature of the opponent's argument, the author treats the "straw man" version as equivalent to the original. Because the new version is a significantly weakened version of the original argument, the critic seldom has difficulty defeating it.

Here's an example of a counterargument that employs the "straw man" fallacy:

**Example 4-16**
The "right-to-die" bill currently being considered by Congress implies that it's acceptable to take the lives of weak and frail old people who cannot defend themselves. However, anyone who has an ounce of decency knows that this is just plain wrong, so we must make every effort to defeat this legislation.

In Example 4-16, the critic distorts the argument in favor of the legislation by drawing a highly questionable inference from it. The attack then focuses on the purported implication that is quite easy to defeat.

## Reasoning Errors Involving the Use of Language

**The fallacy of equivocation.** This fallacy occurs when a key word or phrase that has more than one meaning is employed in different meanings throughout the argument. Because the truth of the premises

and the conclusion is in part a function of the meanings of the words in the sentences that express them, a shift in meaning of key terms in the argument leads the audience to draw conclusions from premises that do not in fact support them.

Here's an example of an argument that commits the fallacy of equivocation:

**Example 4-17**
Logic is the study of arguments, and because arguments are disagreements, it follows that logic is the study of disagreements.

Example 4-17 employs the word *argument* in two different meanings. In the first premise, *argument* means a discourse in which reasons are offered in support of a claim; the second premise defines *argument* as "a disagreement." If you adopt the second meaning, the first premise is false; if you adopt the first meaning, the second premise is false. Either way, the premises simply fail to support the conclusion.

**The fallacy of circular reasoning.** There are two basic forms of the fallacy of circular reasoning or "arguing in a circle." The first type occurs when a critic employs a restatement of the premise as the conclusion of the argument. The second type occurs when the premises presuppose the truth of the conclusion. Sound reasoning requires that the premises provide independent support for the conclusion. Obviously, merely restating the premises in the conclusion can hardly be regarded as independent evidence that the conclusion is true. Nor can the use of premises that presuppose the truth of the conclusion be regarded as independent evidence that the conclusion is true. In both of these cases, the critic is merely arguing in a circle. The circular reasoning fallacy is commonly referred to as the fallacy of "begging the question."

Here's an example of an argument that commits the first form of the fallacy of circular reasoning:

**Example 4-18**
Honesty is the best policy for the simple reason that it's best to adopt a practice that ensures that people are treated in a fair, truthful, and trustworthy manner.

In Example 4-18, the conclusion is a just restatement of the premise, because honesty just means being fair, truthful, and trustworthy.

Here's an example of an argument that commits the second form of the fallacy of circular reasoning:

**Example 4-19**

My boss told me that I was her favorite employee. It must be true, because there's no way she would lie to her favorite employee.

In Example 4-19, the arguer is trying to prove that he is the boss's favorite employee, but to support the premise that the boss would not lie to her favorite employee, he would have to accept the claim that he was the boss's favorite employee. To do this, however, is to assume the very thing that he is trying to prove.

---

## IDENTIFYING THE METHOD OF ARGUMENTS

In problems that ask you to identify the method of an argument, the passage states an argument and your task is to identify the reasoning technique that the argument employs. You are *not* required to identify the technique by name, but only to select from the answer choices the best description of the argument's general reasoning strategy.

The method of an argument is simply the way in which the author goes about establishing the conclusion, or in the case of a critical response to an argument, the way in which the author attempts to defeat the conclusion. An author might use many argumentative techniques when attempting to establish or defeat conclusions–too many to list here. However, familiarity with some of the basic strategies and techniques will prove to be helpful in dealing with these problems.

Note that not all the following methods of establishing or defeating conclusions are necessarily effective or logically correct. The issue in the problems under discussion is merely to identify the method that the author has used, not to determine whether the method is effective or logically correct. Determining the latter is an entirely different matter.

The exam typically words method questions as follows:

Which of the following most accurately characterizes the argumentative strategy used in the passage?

The argument proceeds by:

Which one of the following argumentative techniques is used in the passage?

The method of the argument is to:

The argument employs which one of the following reasoning techniques?

### Reasoning by Analogy

A common method employed in arguing for a conclusion is to use an *analogy.* Starting with a claim or situation that is familiar and unproblematic, the author argues that the issue in question is very much like the familiar case, and hence that what is true of it is probably true of the case in question. The following simple example demonstrates this method:

**Example 4-20**

The mushrooms that we saw in the forest yesterday are the same color, size, and shape as those that we saw in the grocery store today. Obviously, the mushrooms sold in the grocery store aren't poisonous, hence it is likely that the ones we saw in the forest aren't poisonous either.

### Citing an Authority

Another technique often employed when attempting to establish some claim is to cite an *authority* as the grounds or reason for accepting it. In these cases, the authority's or expert's testimony functions as the argument's premise, and the author's reasoning is that the audience ought to accept the conclusion simply because some expert or authority claims that it's true. Here's an example:

**Example 4-21**

Professor Lipscomb, my physics professor, warned us about the dangers of water and air pollution. That's why I'm supporting the Clean Air and Water initiative.

## Using Statistical Reasoning

Many arguments use statistics to establish claims. These arguments usually begin with the recitation of a statistical claim to the effect that some percentage of a certain group has a certain characteristic. Such an argument then indicates that because a given individual is in the group, the individual is likely (or unlikely) to have the aforementioned characteristic. Here are some examples:

### Example 4-22

Two percent of all vegetarians contract colon cancer. Because Sally is a vegetarian, it is unlikely that she'll get colon cancer.

### Example 4-23

Eighty percent of all logic students scored high on the GMAT. Henry is a logic major, so he probably scored high on the GMAT.

## Reasoning from Experience

People often accept past experience as a reason for believing that something *is* the case or *will be* the case. Authors who use this type of reasoning typically begin with a statement that delineates some experience that they or someone else has had. This stated experience then functions as a premise from which the authors argue that some, as yet unexperienced, event or situation will occur. Here's a well-worn example:

### Example 4-24

We have observed the sun rising countless times in the past, hence we can be assured that the sun will rise tomorrow.

A variation of the preceding method is to argue that some general claim is true on the basis of the observation of several instances of the claim. Arguments that employ this kind of reasoning typically begin with premises that document the observed instances; the conclusion typically asserts that what is true of the observed instances is true of all or most instances. Here is an example:

### Example 4-25

Don't worry! All the lettuce that we checked in the shipment was in excellent condition, so you can be assured that all the lettuce is okay.

## Causal Reasoning

Authors typically establish *causal conclusions* (conclusions that assert a causal relation between two events) either by *eliminative reasoning* or by noting a *significant correlation* between events.

**Eliminative reasoning.** Arguments that employ eliminative reasoning usually proceed by isolating a common feature of the events by a process of elimination. The arguer then deems the common feature to be the cause. The premises of such arguments usually describe testing procedures aimed at determining which, if any, of a set of properties are causally related to the event in question. Through experiment or observation, the arguer tries to eliminate each of these features as a causal candidate. The feature that resists these attempts is concluded to be the cause of the event under consideration. Here is an example:

### Example 4-26

Six customers of a fast-food restaurant developed food poisoning shortly after eating lunch there. An investigation revealed that they had all drunk different beverages but not all had eaten salads, soups, or french fries. However, they had all eaten chicken sandwiches prepared with different breads. The health department concluded that the cause of the food poisoning was poorly cooked chicken.

**Causal reasoning based on a significant correlation.** Arguments that assert a causal relation on the basis of a significant correlation between two circumstances typically begin with premises that document the correlation. The correlation is deemed significant if it is such that the suspected cause is not only present whenever the event occurs, but also absent whenever the event fails to occur. After establishing this, the argument concludes that the relation between the two events is a causal relation. Here is an example:

### Example 4-27

Every time that my car hits a pothole in the road, the engine misfires, but it never misfires when the road is smooth. Hence, hitting potholes is the cause of the misfiring.

## Disjunctive Reasoning

Another common method used to establish a conclusion is to show that it is the only acceptable alternative by ruling out all other possibilities. Here is an example:

### Example 4-28

If Sean went to the beach, he either drove his own car or went with a friend. But Sean's car is in the garage, so he must have gone with a friend, because he was seen at the beach early this morning.

## Conditional Reasoning

Conditional arguments usually proceed by first stating a conditional statement, then asserting or denying the antecedent (the "if" clause) or the consequent (the "then" clause) of the conditional statement. Here are some examples:

### Example 4-29

Pigs can't fly. If they could, they would, but they don't, so they can't.

### Example 4-30

If it looks like a duck, walks like a duck, and quacks like a duck, then it's a duck. It looks, walks, and quacks like a duck, so obviously it's a duck.

### Example 4-31

Sam is a basketball player if he's over 6' tall. But Sam is only 5' 9", so he's not a basketball player.

## Common Rebuttal Techniques

**Discredit the arguer.** Among the most common methods employed to defeat or rebut an argument is to challenge the motives or the integrity of the person who is presenting the argument. The basic ploy

here is to attempt to discredit the argument by discrediting the arguer. Here are some examples:

### Example 4-32

The medical industry has argued vigorously that health-care reform is unnecessary, but we have to keep in mind that the medical industry stands to lose the most if new health-care legislation is passed.

### Example 4-33

Professor Martini has presented some strong arguments in favor of the theory of evolution, but none of them are acceptable because it is a well-known fact that Martini is an atheist.

**Redirect the argument.** Another common method used to defeat an argument is to direct attention away from the argument's main point to a different, though perhaps related, point, then attack or defend the other point rather than the main issue. Here is an example:

### Example 4-34

Mandatory life sentences for three-time felons are a bad idea. People who think that such sentences are a good idea argue that they will stop violent crime. But if we really want to stop violent crime, instead of locking people up we should stop portraying violent crimes on television and in movies, because that's where these criminals get their ideas in the first place.

**Reduce a premise to absurdity.** Authors often attempt to defeat an argument by showing that one of its major premises is false or absurd. A common way to do so is first to assume that the premise is in fact true, then show that this assumption leads to an obviously false or absurd claim. By showing that the premise leads to this result, the authors thereby show the premise itself to be false or absurd and thus defeat the argument that employs it as a major premise. Here's an example of this technique:

### Example 4-35

The evidence that condom use is an effective means to stop the spread of AIDS is hardly conclusive. But assume for the sake of argument that it is. By promoting condom use, we encourage young people to think that it's okay to be promiscuous, to have sex with prostitutes, to engage in homo-sexual activities—in short, to engage in the very activities that spread AIDS. So, rather than limiting the activities that spread this disease, we promote them by promoting condom use.

# RECOGNIZING SIMILARITIES BETWEEN ARGUMENTS

Parallel reasoning problems all begin with the same basic setup. The passage and each of the answer choices presents an argument. The task, however, can differ from problem to problem. In some cases, the problem asks you to find the argument that parallels the same *structure* as the argument in the passage; in other cases, the problem asks you to find the argument that employs the same *method of reasoning*; and other problems ask you to find the argument that contains the same *reasoning error* as the argument in the passage.

## Parallel Reasoning Question Types

Questions that ask you to find the argument that has the same structure or pattern of reasoning as the argument in the passage are typically worded as follows:

- The argumentative structure of which one of the following most closely parallels that of the argument in the passage?

- The pattern of reasoning displayed in the argument in the passage is most closely paralleled in which of the following arguments?

- Which of the following arguments contains a flawed pattern of reasoning parallel to that contained in the preceding argument?

- Which of the following, in its logical features, most closely parallels the reasoning in the passage?

Questions that ask you to find the argument that employs the same method of reasoning as the argument in the passage are typically worded as follows:

- Which of the following most closely parallels the reasoning in the argument presented in the passage?

- In which of the following is the method of reasoning most parallel to that in the preceding argument?

Questions that ask you to find the argument that contains the same reasoning error as the argument in the passage are typically worded as follows:

- Which one of the following arguments contains a flaw that is most similar to the one in the preceding argument?

- The faulty reasoning in which one of the following is most parallel to that in the preceding argument?

Each of these question types requires a slightly different approach, as the following sections discuss.

## Parallel Structure Problems

**Recognizing argument structure.** To get a basic idea of what is meant by logical "structure" or "pattern," consider the following pair of arguments:

**Example 4-36**
> All men are mortal. Socrates is a man. Hence, Socrates is mortal.

**Example 4-37**
> Every dog has a master. Fido is a dog. Therefore, Fido has a master.

Although the arguments in these examples are obviously about different topics, and hence quite dissimilar in content, they are alike in the way in which they present information about their topics. Each begins with a general statement claiming that all individuals in a certain class have a certain characteristic, followed by a particular statement that claims that a certain individual belongs to the class mentioned previously, and concluding that the individual has the characteristic mentioned previously. Because of these similarities, the "pattern" or "structure" of these two arguments is the same.

You can represent the basic pattern of Examples 4-36 and 4-37 as follows:

**Premise:** All A are B.

**Premise:** C is an A.

**Conclusion:** C is a B.

Note that the argument's content (that is, what the argument is about) is irrelevant when trying to determine the argument's structure; it is not *what* the argument says that is important, but rather *the way* in which the argument says it. The *order* of the premises and conclusion (for example, which is stated first or second) is also irrelevant when trying to determine the similarity of the structure of arguments. For example, consider the following pair of arguments that have the same structure but which present their premises and conclusions in different orders:

**Example 4-38**

People who are happy are content; hence, since Mary is happy, she must be content.

**Example 4-39**

John must be tall because he is a basketball player and all basketball players are tall.

The similarity in structure of these two arguments becomes readily apparent when you restate them and reorganize them as follows.

Here's the structure of Example 4-38:

**Premise:** All people who are happy are content.

**Premise:** Mary is happy.

**Conclusion:** Mary is content.

Here's the structure of Example 4-39:

**Premise:** All basketball players are tall.

**Premise:** John is a basketball player.

**Conclusion:** John is tall.

Determining an argument's pattern or structure is relatively easy so long as you focus on the way in which the argument is expressed rather than on what the argument expresses. In other words, focus on the syntax of the sentences that comprise the argument rather than on what the sentences mean.

## Parallel Structure Problems

Here's an example of a parallel structure problem as it would appear on the GMAT:

**Example 4-40**

Either the safe wasn't locked or it was opened by the burglar. But it wasn't opened by the burglar unless he knew the combination. So either it was unlocked or the burglar knew the combination.

The pattern of reasoning displayed in the argument in the passage is most closely paralleled in which of the following arguments?

(A) Either the Slugs or the Snails will win the Fruit Bowl. The Snails won't win unless they beat the Slugs. Hence, if the Slugs win the Fruit Bowl, the Snails didn't beat them.

(B) God is either unwilling or unable to prevent evil. But He is not unable unless He is not omnipotent. Hence, He is either unwilling or He is not omnipotent.

(C) Either gun control laws are passed or the number of crimes involving hand guns will continue to rise. But gun control laws won't be passed unless the National Rifle Association (NRA) supports them. Hence, if the NRA supports them, gun control laws will be passed.

(D) Professor Lascola is either a realist or an empiricist. But he is not an empiricist if he believes that some concepts are innate. So, if he believes that some ideas are innate, he is not a realist.

(E) Either smoking is harmful or the surgeon general's warnings about smoking cigarettes are incorrect. But studies have shown conclusively that smoking is harmful, hence the surgeon general's warnings are correct.

### How to Handle Parallel Structure Problems.

Here's the procedure for dealing with parallel reasoning problems that ask you to find an argument that has the *same structure or pattern of reasoning* as the argument in the passage.

First, make sure that you understand the structure of the argument in the passage. To do so, underline words such as *all, some,* and *no* (and their synonyms), and words and phrases such as *and, or, if, then,* and *if and only if* (and their synonyms). If you apply this advice to the passage in Example 4-40, the result is as follows:

> Either the safe wasn't locked or it was opened by the burglar. But it wasn't opened by the burglar unless he knew the combination. So either it wasn't locked or the burglar knew the combination.

So far, the structure looks like this:

**Premise:** Either _____ or _____.

**Premise:** _____ unless_____.

**Conclusion:** Either _____ or_____.

Next, think about the sentences that fill the blanks. Notice that the same sentence fills the first blank of the first premise as fills the first blank of the conclusion. Notice also that the same sentence fills the second blank of the second premise as fills the second blank of the conclusion. Notice further that you do not fill the second blank of the first premise and the first blank of the second premise with exactly the same sentence. You fill the first blank of the second premise with the negation of the sentence that fills the second blank of the first premise. After you fill in the blanks, the structure looks like this:

**Premise:** Either A or B.

**Premise:** Not B unless C.

**Conclusion:** Either A or C.

With this structure in mind, look at each of the answer choices to find the one with exactly the same pattern.

Answer choice A doesn't have the same structure as the argument in the passage. The structure of A is follows:

**Premise:** Either A or B.

**Premise:** Not B unless C.

**Conclusion:** If A, then not C.

Answer choice B has the same structure as the passage's argument. You can convince yourself that this is the case simply by replacing the letters in the schema for the passage's argument by the independent clauses of B.

Answer choice C does not have the same structure as the passage's argument. The structure of C is as follows:

**Premise:** Either A or B.

**Premise:** Not A unless C.

**Conclusion:** If C, then A.

Answer choice D does not have the same structure as the passage's argument. The structure of D is as follows:

**Premise:** Either A or B.

**Premise:** If C, then not B.

**Conclusion:** If C, then not A.

Answer choice E also does not have the same structure as the passage's argument. The following is the structure of E:

**Premise:** Either A or not B.

**Premise:** A.

**Conclusion:** B.

## Parallel Method of Reasoning Problems

Questions that ask you to find the argument that employs the *same method of reasoning* as the argument in the passage should be approached differently than those that ask for the argument that has the same structure or pattern of reasoning. Here's an example of this type of question as it would appear on the GMAT:

**Example 4-41**

> The economy is like a garden in that it experiences periods of growth and periods of latency. To thrive, gardens require human intervention by way of cultivation and fertilization. Hence, for the economy to thrive, human intervention—by way of government regulation and monetary stimulus—is required.

In which of the following is the method of reasoning most parallel to that in the preceding argument?

(A) It's true that domestic dogs are similar in many ways to wild wolves, but if dogs were immediately related to wolves, they could not be domesticated, because, to date, no one has ever successfully domesticated a wild wolf.

(B) Provided that the teeth of the dinosaur stegosaurus are like the teeth of the modern herbivores such as the horse and the cow, they are probably ancient ancestors of these animals. However, no evidence can be found that clearly supports this hypothesis. Hence, it is unlikely that modern herbivores descended from stegosauruses.

(C) Measurements taken from fossil remains of tyrannosaurus rex are indicative of the entire species only if we can be assured that they are representative. But since we cannot be certain of this, we cannot conclude that all these animals stood over 20 feet tall.

(D) Computers and machines are extremely complex artifacts just as plants and animals are extremely complex organisms. Machines and computers are made by intelligent beings; hence, plants and animals probably have an intelligent maker as well.

(E) It's a well-known law that any two objects that are similar to a third object are similar to one another. Hence, since George's and Cosmo's cars are similar to Elaine's, they must be similar to one another.

## How to Handle Parallel Method of Reasoning Problems.

Here's the procedure for dealing with parallel reasoning problems that ask you to find an argument that employs the same method of reasoning as the argument in the passage.

First, make sure that you understand the method employed in the passage's argument. In Example 4-41, the method employed is analogical reasoning. This argument likens the economy to a garden and posits that because gardens require human intervention to thrive, it follows that the economy also requires human intervention to thrive.

Next, look for an answer choice that employs analogical reasoning to reach the conclusion. In Example 4-41, the best response is D. Answer D likens complex artifacts to complex organisms and argues that because complex artifacts have an intelligent maker, it follows that complex organisms also have an intelligent maker.

## Parallel Reasoning Error Problems

Questions that ask you to find the argument that contains the *same reasoning error or flaw* as the argument in the passage should be approached in the same way as those that ask for the argument that employs the same method of reasoning. Here's an example of this type of question as it would appear on the GMAT:

**Example 4-42**

If abortion on demand were to become legal, there would be a great increase in abortions. And once abortion became commonplace, there would be a weakening of respect for human life in general. Once the respect for human life is weakened, we would see an increase in euthanasia of all kinds— the elderly, the mentally handicapped, and the physically disabled. Before long, we would get rid of anyone who is unpopular or unproductive. In short, it would threaten our civilization. Therefore, we should oppose any move to broaden the grounds of legal abortion.

The faulty reasoning in which one of the following is most parallel to that in the preceding argument?

(A) The portrayal of violence on television and in the movies is the main cause of violence in our nation. Hence, to get rid of violence in our nation, we must censor television shows and movies.

(B) Mandatory life sentences for three-time felons is a bad idea. People who think that such sentences are a good idea think that they will stop violent crime. But if we really want to stop violent crime, instead of locking people up we should eliminate the root cause of violent crime by ceasing to glamorize violence in movies and on television.

(C) It has been well established that smoking marijuana leads to heroin use, and that heroin use leads to drug addiction. Drug addiction, in turn, leads to crime to support the drug habit. The epidemic of drug-related crime is threatening the very core of our existence as a nation. Hence, to stop this threat, we must not legalize marijuana use.

(D) Parents are wrong to criticize their children for coming home late, smoking, watching too much television, and getting poor grades. After all, they do all these things and they're not all that smart themselves.

(E) Failure to comply with the directions contained in this chain letter will result in bad consequences. Jane Dugal received this letter and passed it on in the required 72-hour period. A week later, she won $6 million in the lottery. Sam Dorff received it but did not comply with the directions. Within a week after receiving it, he was trampled to death by a renegade elephant at the circus.

## How to Handle Parallel Reasoning Error Problems.

First, identify the reasoning error in the passage's argument. The argument in Example 4-42 commits the "slippery slope" fallacy. This argument purports that various events will occur as a result of legalizing abortion. The terminus of this sequence of events is a catastrophic event that we must avoid, and thus, states the argument, we should also avoid the initiating event.

Next, look for an answer choice that commits the "slippery slope" fallacy. In Example 4-42, the best response is C. Answer C links marijuana use to heroin use, links heroin use to drug addiction, links drug addiction to crime, and finally links crime to the nation's downfall. Because the downfall of the nation is to be avoided, the argument posits that marijuana use should be legally curtailed.

## RECAP OF DAY 4

Today three important topics were covered: reasoning errors, methods of argument, and parallel argument questions. Here is a brief checklist of the items covered under each topic:

- **Reasoning errors**

  Statistical fallacies

  Causal reasoning fallacies

  Unwarranted assumption fallacies

  Irrelevant appeals fallacies

  Fallacies of refutation

  Reasoning errors involving the use of language

- **Methods of argument**

  Reasoning by analogy

  Citing an authority

  Statistical reasoning

  Reasoning from experience

  Causal reasoning

  Disjunctive reasoning

  Conditional reasoning

- **Parallel argument questions**

  Parallel structure problems

  Parallel method of reasoning problems

  Parallel reasoning error problems

# Critical Reasoning Lesson 3: Mini-Test and Review

### Today's Topic:

Today you apply what you learned on Days 3 and 4 to a series of Critical Reasoning passages. After taking this mini-test under timed conditions, review the explanations that follow.

## MINI-TEST (CRITICAL REASONING)

**Number of questions:** 14
**Suggested time:** 24 minutes

**Directions:** For each question in this section, select the best of the answer choices given.

1. Sexual preference is not something over which persons have control. To hold a person accountable for something over which he or she has no control is irrational. Therefore, _____.

Which of the following best completes the preceding argument?

(A) It is rational to hold people accountable for things over which they have control.

(B) Sexual preference is a matter of personal choice and should not be answerable to any laws or customs of society.

(C) It is irrational to hold a person accountable for his or her sexual preference.

(D) Persons are often held accountable for things over which they have no control.

(E) Persons should not be held accountable for their sexual preference.

2. Is it wrong for doctors to lie about their patients' illnesses? Aren't doctors just like any other people that we hire to do a job for us? Surely, we would not tolerate not being told the truth about the condition of our automobile from the mechanic that we hired to fix it, or the condition of our roof from the carpenter that we employed to repair it. Just as these workers would be guilty of violating their good faith contracts with us if they were to do this, doctors who lie to their patients about their illnesses violate these contracts as well, and this is clearly wrong.

The conclusion of the argument is best expressed by which of the following?

(A) Doctors who lie to their patients about their illnesses violate their good faith contracts with their patients.

(B) Doctors often lie to their patients about their illnesses.

(C) Doctors are just hired workers like mechanics and carpenters.

(D) It is wrong for doctors to lie about their patients' illnesses.

(E) Doctors, like mechanics and carpenters, enter into good faith contracts with us when we hire them.

3. Testifying before the Senate committee investigating charges that cigarette manufacturers had manipulated nicotine levels in cigarettes to addict consumers to their products, tobacco executives argued that cigarette smoking is not addictive. The primary reason they gave in support of this claim was that cigarette smoking was not regulated by the Food and Drug Administration (FDA).

For the tobacco executives' argument to be logically correct, which of the following must be assumed?

(A) The FDA does not regulate substances that are not addictive.

(B) Substances that are not regulated by the FDA are not addictive.

(C) The FDA does not regulate some addictive substances.

(D) There is no scientific proof that cigarette smoking is addictive.

(E) The tobacco executives lied when they claimed that cigarette smoking was not addictive.

4. Sean: I think the university orchestra's performance of Beethoven's symphony was terrible.

Kelly: Why do you say that?

Sean: Because the way that the orchestra played it was not the way Beethoven intended it to be played.

What must be assumed for Sean's argument to be logically correct?

(A) Beethoven intended the symphony to be performed in a way different from the way that the university orchestra performed it.

(B) Only the composer of a musical work knows how it should be performed.

(C) In general, university orchestras cannot perform Beethoven's symphony in the way that it was intended to be performed.

(D) No performance of a composer's work that is not in keeping with the composer's original intention is a good performance.

(E) University orchestras lack the musical sophistication to do justice to Beethoven's symphony.

5. Tax laws are fair only if people don't earn different amounts of money or don't pay the same amount in taxes. The reasons for this are clear. If people earn different amounts of money but everyone pays the same amount in taxes, then those who earn more wind up keeping more, and those who earn less keep less. But if this is the case, tax laws are clearly unfair.

Which of the following, in its logical features, most closely parallels the reasoning used in the passage?

(A) If a person has talent but doesn't develop it, it is a waste. On the other hand, if one has talent and does develop it, it is a wonderful gift. Hence, talent is a wonderful gift only if it is not a waste.

(B) If Oona doesn't go to preschool, she will either stay at home or remain in day care. But, if she doesn't go to preschool, she will not learn to get along with other children. So, if she stays at home or remains in day care, she won't learn to get along with other children.

(C) Combustion will not occur if oxygen is not present. But if combustion doesn't occur, oxygen might nevertheless be present. Hence, the presence of oxygen is necessary but not sufficient for combustion to occur.

(D) If a person is depressed, he or she often loses the will to live, but if one loses the will to live, then life isn't worth living. Hence, life is worth living only if one is not depressed.

(E) If the energy industry is deregulated but energy-related businesses do not profit from the deregulation, Congress will reinstate regulations. But this will occur only if it can be demonstrated that energy-related businesses are likely to fail in the near future. Hence, either the energy industry is deregulated or it can be demonstrated that energy-related businesses are likely to fail in the near future.

6. A study of native born residents in Oonaland found that two-thirds of the children developed considerable levels of nearsightedness after starting school, while their illiterate parents and grandparents, who had no opportunity for formal schooling, showed no signs of this disability.

If the preceding statements are true, which of the following conclusions is most strongly supported by them?

(A) The visual stress imposed by reading and other class work caused the children's nearsightedness.

(B) People who are illiterate do not suffer from nearsightedness.

(C) Only people who have the opportunity for formal schooling develop nearsightedness.

(D) Only literate people are nearsighted.

(E) One-third of the children are illiterate.

7. Emily: The best reason I can think of for not using drugs is that drug use is illegal, and one ought to obey the law.

David: How can you, of all people, think that's a good reason when you rarely drive within the legal speed limit!

Which of the following questionable argumentative techniques does David employ in his response to Emily?

(A) Rejecting the conclusion of an argument on the basis of a claim about the motives of the person advancing the argument.

(B) Attacking the person's character rather than the argument.

(C) Criticizing an argument by pointing out an inconsistency between what a person says and the way in which he or she behaves.

(D) Misrepresenting an argument for the purpose of making it easier to attack.

(E) Drawing attention away from the real issue of the argument to a side issue, then attacking the side issue.

8. The budget deficit will continue to grow unless taxes are raised soon. However, that's not going to happen in the foreseeable future. The upshot is that if the budget deficit continues to grow, an almost unbearable debt will burden the next generation of taxpayers.

If the preceding statements are true, which of the following must be true?

(A) Taxes will be raised soon.

(B) The budget deficit will not continue to grow.

(C) The political climate will not change in the foreseeable future.

(D) The budget deficit will continue to grow, but an almost unbearable debt will not burden the next generation of taxpayers.

(E) An almost unbearable debt will burden the next generation of taxpayers.

9. To allow the press to keep its sources confidential is very advantageous to our country, because it is highly conducive to the interests of our nation that private individuals should have the privilege of providing information to the press without being identified.

The faulty reasoning in which one of the following is most parallel to that in the preceding argument?

(A) Freedom of the press is a fundamental feature of all democratic societies. Therefore, if a society has a free press, it is democratic.

(B) The primary reason for widespread unemployment in this nation is that large numbers of people across this great country of ours are out of work.

(C) In democratic societies, the press has an inviolable obligation to publish any news that is in the public interest to have published. Thus, in democratic societies, the press has a duty to publish news on any topic that the public shows interest in.

(D) Free tuition for out-of-state students would be advantageous to students who otherwise cannot attend this university. That's why free tuition ought to be implemented for these students.

(E) Free speech is very advantageous to this country because allowing people to speak their minds without restraint provides a nonviolent means to dissipate the pent up anger and frustration that results from governmental policies and decisions with which people do not agree.

10. There is clear evidence that the mandated use of safety seats by children under age four has resulted in fewer child fatalities over the past five years. Compared to the five-year period prior to the passage of laws requiring the use of safety seats, fatalities of children under age four have decreased by 30%.

Which one of the following, if true, most substantially strengthens the preceding argument?

(A) The number of serious automobile accidents involving children under age four has remained steady over the past five years.

(B) Automobile accidents involving children have decreased sharply over the past five years.

(C) The use of air bags in automobiles has increased by 30% over the past five years.

(D) Most fatal automobile accidents involving children under age four occur in the driveway of their home.

(E) The number of teenage drivers has increased by 30% over the past five years.

11. The divorce rate of couples who live together before they get married is twice as high as that of couples who do not live together before marriage. Thus it is evident that living together before getting married damages a couple's chance for a successful marriage.

The argument proceeds by:

(A) Reaching a causal conclusion on the basis of a correlation between two circumstances.

(B) Generalizing about all couples on the basis of evidence about only those who later divorce.

(C) Neglecting evidence about couples who are happily married.

(D) Isolating a common feature through a process of elimination and concluding that this feature is causally related to the event under investigation.

(E) Reaching a general conclusion on the basis of an unrepresentative sample.

12. Ten years ago, the death rate from Neural Synapse Deficiency (NSD) related causes was 5% of all persons infected with the dreaded anti-synapse virus (ASV) that causes it. Today, the corresponding figure has risen to over 15%. This is clear evidence that over the past 10 years, the rate of propagation and the malignancy of the virus have increased substantially.

Which of the following, if true, most substantially strengthens the argument in the preceding passage?

(A) ASV screening and detection methods have dramatically improved over the past decade.

(B) The number of ASV-infected persons has increased tenfold over the past 10 years.

(C) The number of persons who are willing to submit to ASV screening has increased significantly over the past 10 years.

(D) The number of recognized NSD-related causes of death has remained relatively constant over the past 10 years.

(E) New drugs have been developed over the past 10 years that significantly abate the debilitating effects of the NSD virus.

13. Lycopene, glutathione, and glutamine are powerful antioxidants that neutralize the free radicals that the body produces as a result of routine bodily processes. An excess of these free radicals in your system causes rapid aging because they accelerate the rate of cellular damage. Aging is simply the result of this damage. Thus, to slow down aging, it is necessary to supplement your diet with these antioxidants on a daily basis.

Which of the following, if true, most seriously undermines the author's contention?

(A) Most persons aren't concerned with the effects of aging until it is too late to do anything about it.

(B) Exercise associated with normal daily activities effectively neutralizes and dissipates the free radicals that are produced as a result of routine bodily processes.

(C) The cost of antioxidants is exorbitantly high and well beyond the budget of most consumers.

(D) Only overweight people who do not exercise on a daily basis are likely to have an excess of free radicals in their systems.

(E) Smoking cigarettes is one of the main causes of cellular damage in humans.

14. Does having a large amount of money guarantee happiness? Results of a recent survey overwhelmingly confirm that having a sizable quantity of money is the key to happiness. In the survey, 78% of those who responded who also claimed that they possessed a large amount of money said that they were happy.

    Which of the following, if true, most seriously calls the survey finding into doubt?

    (A) No clear quantitative definition of "large amount of money" was provided to the respondents.

    (B) No clear qualitative definition of "happiness" was provided to the respondents.

    (C) Most of the respondents who claimed to have a large amount of money in fact did not.

    (D) Many people are happy even though they do not possess a great deal of money.

    (E) Many people who have a great deal of money are not happy.

# Quick Answer Guide

## Mini-Test: Critical Reasoning

1. C
2. D
3. B
4. D
5. D
6. A
7. C

8. E
9. B
10. A
11. A
12. D
13. B
14. C

## EXPLANATIONS

### 1. Unstated conclusion (moderate). Answer: C.

You can rewrite the passage's argument as follows:

**Premise:** Sexual preference is not something over which persons have control.

**Premise:** Holding a person accountable for something over which he or she has no control is irrational.

The main ideas in the argument are (1) sexual preference, (2) things over which persons have control, (3) things for which persons ought to be held accountable, and (4) things that are irrational. The first premise links 1 and 2, the second premise links 2, 3, and 4. The unstated conclusion will have to link 1, 3, and 4.

Response C links 1, 3, and 4.

A is an incorrect response. Response A links 2, 3, and the opposite of 4.

B brings in information not mentioned in the passage.

D is an incorrect response. Response D links 2 and 3.

E is an incorrect response. Response E links 1 and the opposite of 3.

### 2. Conclusion (moderate). Answer: D.

The rhetorical question at the beginning of the passage introduces the issue that D discusses, which is whether it is wrong for doctors to lie about their patients' illnesses. The final sentence concludes that this practice is wrong because it is a violation of the good faith contract that we enter into when we hire the doctor.

A is a premise of the argument.

The passage does not support B. The passage does not state that doctors often lie to their patients about their illnesses, nor is this the passage's main focus. The main focus of the passage is to determine not whether doctors *do* but whether they *should* engage in this practice.

C is a premise of the argument.

The passage implies E.

### 3. Assumption (moderate). Answer: B.

You can represent the tobacco executives' argument as follows:

**Premise:** The FDA does not regulate cigarette smoking.

**Conclusion:** Cigarette smoking is not addictive.

The argument's logical gap that you need to fill is the link between substances that are regulated by the

FDA and substances that are addictive. Moreover, to make the argument logically correct, the link between them must be such that the fact that something is not regulated entails that it is not addictive. Response B is equivalent in meaning to the claim that all substances that the FDA does not regulate are not additive. This is exactly the assumption required to fill the gap in the tobacco executives' argument.

Response A does not fill the logical gap in the tobacco executives' argument. Response A is equivalent in meaning to the claim that all substances that are not addictive are not regulated by the FDA. The assumption required to fill the gap in the tobacco executives' argument is that all substances that the FDA does not regulate are addictive.

C does not fill the logical gap in the tobacco executives' argument. The fact that some of the substances that the FDA regulates are not addictive is irrelevant to the tobacco executives' argument. Their conclusion is based on the premise that cigarette smoking is *not* regulated, not that it *is* regulated.

D brings in information not mentioned in the passage. The claim asserted in response D, if true, could serve as an additional premise in support of the conclusion.

E brings in information not mentioned in the passage. The issue of whether the tobacco executives lied when they claimed that cigarette smoking is not addictive is irrelevant to the logic of their argument.

## 4. Assumption (moderate). Answer: D.

You can restate Sean's argument as follows:

**Premise:** The university orchestra's performance of Beethoven's symphony was not in accordance with the way that Beethoven intended it to be performed.

**Conclusion:** The university orchestra's performance of Beethoven's symphony was not a good performance.

The logical gap in Sean's argument that needs to be filled is the link between good performances and performances that are in accordance with the way in which the composer intended the music to be performed. Moreover, to make the argument logically correct, this link must be such that the fact that

a performance is not in accordance with the composer's intentions regarding the way that the music should be played implies that the performance is not good. Response D is equivalent in meaning to the claim that any performance that is not in keeping with the composer's intentions regarding how the music be played is not a good performance. This is exactly the assumption required to fill the gap in Sean's argument.

Response A is not an assumption of Sean's argument. Response A simply restates the major premise of Sean's argument.

B does not fill the logical gap in Sean's argument. Response B is equivalent in meaning to the claim that all performances that are performed in the way that the composer intended are good performances. This, in turn, is equivalent to the claim that all performances that are not good are not performed in a way in which the composer intended. This latter claim, however, does not entail that performances that are not in accordance with the composer's intentions are not good performances.

C and D provide plausible explanations of why the university orchestra's performance of Beethoven's symphony was not in accordance with Beethoven's intentions. As such, C and D provide support for the major premise, but do not state assumptions of Sean's argument.

## 5. Parallel reasoning (challenging). Answer: D.

You can represent the passage's argument as follows:

**Premise:** If people earn different amounts of money but everyone pays the same amount in taxes, then those who earn more wind up keeping more, and those who earn less keep less.

**Premise:** If those who earn more wind up keeping more and those who earn less keep less, tax laws are clearly unjust.

**Conclusion:** Tax laws are just only if people don't earn different amounts of money or don't pay the same amount in taxes.

You can outline this argument's logical pattern as follows:

**Premise:** If P, then Q.

**Premise:** If Q, then not R.

**Conclusion:** R only if P.

You can represent the argument in response D as follows:

**Premise:** If a person is depressed, he or she often loses the will to live.

**Premise:** If one loses the will to live, then life isn't worth living.

**Conclusion:** Life is worth living only if one is not depressed.

A comparison of this argument with the preceding argument reveals that they share exactly the same logical pattern.

Response A is incorrect. You can represent the argument in response A as follows:

**Premise:** If a person has talent but doesn't develop it, it is a waste.

**Premise:** If a person has talent and does develop it, it is a wonderful gift.

**Conclusion:** Talent is a wonderful gift only if it is not a waste.

Unlike the argument in the passage outlined previously, the "if" clause of this argument's second premise is not the same as the "then" clause of the first premise.

B is an incorrect response. You can represent the argument in response B as follows:

**Premise:** If Oona doesn't go to preschool, she will either stay at home or remain in day care.

**Premise:** If Oona doesn't go to preschool, she will not learn to get along with other children.

**Conclusion:** If Oona stays at home or remains in day care, she won't learn to get along with other children.

Unlike the argument in the passage outlined previously, the "if" clause of this argument's first premise is the same as the "if" clause of the second premise.

C is an incorrect response. You can represent the argument in response C as follows:

**Premise:** If oxygen is not present, combustion will not occur.

**Premise:** If combustion does not occur, oxygen might nevertheless be present.

**Conclusion:** The presence of oxygen is necessary but not sufficient for the occurrence of combustion.

The main difference between this argument and the argument in the passage outlined previously is in their conclusions.

E is an incorrect response. You can represent the argument in response E as follows:

**Premise:** If the energy industry is deregulated but energy-related businesses do not profit from it, Congress will reinstate regulations.

**Premise:** Congress will reinstate regulations only if it can be demonstrated that energy-related businesses are likely to fail in the near future.

**Conclusion:** Either the energy industry is deregulated or it can be demonstrated that energy-related businesses are likely to fail in the near future.

The main difference between this argument and the argument in the passage outlined previously is in their conclusions.

## 6. Inference (easier). Answer: A.

The task in this problem is to find the answer choice that is most strongly supported—that is, the one that is most likely to be true, given that the information stated in the passage is true. The only difference cited in the passage between the children who developed nearsightedness and the parents and grandparents who did not have this disability is the fact that the children went to school whereas the parents and grandparents did not. The inference to be drawn from this information is that school activities that require the use of vision, such as reading, are somehow causally related to the nearsightedness. Admittedly, the information stated in the passage does not, by itself, prove that these activities are the cause of the children's nearsightedness, but it would provide strong support for this claim.

The passage does not strongly support response B. From the information in the passage, you can infer that there are some people who are illiterate and who also do not suffer from nearsightedness: the parents and grandparents of the children. However, it does not follow from this inference that *all* people who are illiterate do not suffer from nearsightedness, nor does this inference strongly support this latter claim.

The passage does not support response C. This response is equivalent in meaning to the claim that all nearsighted people have had the opportunity for formal schooling. Admittedly, the passage implicates formal schooling with nearsightedness, but the implication is that formal schooling is, in some instances, a significant difference between persons who are nearsighted and persons who are not.

The passage also does not support response D. This response is equivalent in meaning to the claim that all nearsighted people are literate. Although the passage implies that *some* illiterate people—the parents and grandparents of the nearsighted children—are not nearsighted, it does not follow from this implication that *all* illiterate people are not nearsighted, nor does this response strongly support this claim.

The passage does not support response E. The passage states only that "two-thirds of the children developed considerable levels of nearsightedness after starting school." No inference regarding the remaining one-third of the students is warranted.

### 7. Reasoning error (moderate). Answer: C.

Emily's argument against using drugs is based on the premise that one ought to obey the law. David rejects this premise, not by challenging its truth, but by claiming that Emily often behaves in ways that are inconsistent with it. In so doing, David argues "against the person" rather than against Emily's argument.

A and B are not consistent with David's response. David does not question Emily's motives for advancing the argument nor her character.

D is inconsistent with the passage. David does not restate or misrepresent Emily's argument in the passage.

Response E is also inconsistent with David's remark. The point of David's remark is not to draw attention away from the issue of Emily's argument, but instead to draw attention to an apparent inconsistency between Emily's pronouncement regarding obeying the law and her actions.

### 8. Inference (moderate). Answer: E.

The task in this problem is to find the answer that must be true—that is, the one that cannot conceivably be false, given that the information stated in the passage is true. You can represent the passage's premises as follows:

**Premise 1:** Either the budget deficit will continue to grow or taxes will be raised soon.

**Premise 2:** Taxes will not be raised soon.

**Premise 3:** If the budget deficit continues to grow, an almost unbearable debt will burden the next generation of taxpayers.

From premise 1 and premise 2, the following conclusion follows:

**Conclusion 1:** The budget deficit will continue to grow.

From conclusion 1 and premise 3, a second conclusion necessarily follows:

**Conclusion 2:** An almost unbearable debt will burden the next generation of taxpayers.

Because conclusion 2 necessarily follows from the passage's stated information, that conclusion cannot conceivably be false if this information is true.

The passage contradicts response A. The passage states that "given the current political climate, that's not going to happen in the foreseeable future." In this sentence, the pronoun "that" refers to the phrase "taxes are raised soon" in the previous sentence.

The passage implicitly contradicts B. From premise 1 and premise 2, it necessarily follows that the statement "The budget deficit will continue to grow" is true.

The passage does not support C. No information in the passage supports a prediction about what the political climate will be in the foreseeable future.

The passage contradicts D. From premise 1 and premise 2, the following conclusion necessarily follows:

**Conclusion 1:** The budget deficit will continue to grow.

From conclusion 1 and premise 3, a second conclusion necessarily follows:

**Conclusion 2:** An almost unbearable debt will burden the next generation of taxpayers.

Because D states a conjunction of two sentences, one of which must be false, D must be false.

### 9. Parallel reasoning (moderate). Answer: B.

You can represent the passage's argument as follows:

**Premise:** It is highly conducive to the interests of society that private individuals should have the privilege of providing information to the press without being identified.

**Conclusion:** To allow the press to keep its sources confidential is very advantageous to the country.

An examination of the reasoning in the preceding argument reveals that it is circular—that is, the conclusion simply restates the premise. What this argument boils down to is simply that it is good for the country to allow the press to keep its sources confidential because this is good for the country.

You can represent this argument as follows:

**Premise:** Large numbers of people across this great country of ours are out of work.

**Conclusion:** There is widespread unemployment in America.

The reasoning in this argument is circular. An examination of the conclusion reveals that it simply restates the premise.

Response A is incorrect. You can represent this argument as follows:

**Premise:** Freedom of the press is a fundamental feature of all democratic societies.

**Conclusion:** If a society has a free press, it is democratic.

This argument's reasoning is not circular; its conclusion is not a restatement of the premise. The premise is equivalent in meaning to the claim that all democratic societies have a free press—that is, if a society is democratic, it has a free press. The conclusion does not state this.

C is an incorrect response. You can represent this argument as follows:

**Premise:** In democratic societies, the press has an inviolable obligation to publish any news that is in the public interest to have published.

**Conclusion:** In democratic societies, the press has a duty to publish news on any topic that the public shows interest in.

The reasoning in this argument is not circular, because the conclusion does not restate the premise. Although the premise and the conclusion might initially appear to have the same meaning, a closer examination reveals that in the premise the phrase "in the public interest" means "that which is relevant to the public's well being," whereas in the conclusion, what the "public shows interest in" means "that which the public finds fascinating."

D is an incorrect response. You can represent this argument as follows:

**Premise:** Free tuition for out-of-state students would be advantageous to students who otherwise cannot attend this university.

**Conclusion:** That's why free tuition ought to be implemented for these students.

The reasoning in the preceding argument is not circular, because the conclusion does not restate the premise.

E is an incorrect response. You can represent the argument as follows:

**Premise:** Allowing people to speak their minds without restraint provides a nonviolent means to dissipate their pent up anger and frustration that results from governmental policies and decisions with which they do not agree.

**Conclusion:** Free speech is very advantageous to this country.

The reasoning in the preceding argument is not circular, because the conclusion does not restate the premise.

### 10. Assessing the effect of additional information (easier). Answer: A.

The task in this problem is to find an answer that strengthens the argument—that is, one that offers support for the major assumption of the argument or that provides additional evidence for the conclusion. You can represent the passage's argument as follows:

**Premise:** Compared to the five-year period prior to the passage of laws requiring the use of safety seats by children, fatalities of children under age four have decreased by 30%.

**Conclusion:** The passage of laws requiring the use of safety seats by children under age four has resulted in fewer child fatalities over the past five years.

The argument's major assumption is that there are no significant differences between the five-year period preceding the passage of the laws and the five-year period since their passage that could account for the decrease in fatalities. Response A supports this assumption.

B weakens the argument. The argument's major assumption is that there are no significant differences between the five-year period preceding the passage of the laws and the five-year period since their passage that could account for the decrease in fatalities. Response B undermines this assumption.

C, D, and E do not offer support for the argument's major assumption, nor do they provide additional evidence for the argument's conclusion.

### 11. Method (moderate). Answer: A.

The method that the passage's argument employs is to reach a causal conclusion on the basis of a correlation between two events. In this case, living together before marriage is correlated with a higher divorce rate. The conclusion drawn from this correlation is that living together before marriage increases the likelihood that the marriage will not succeed.

B and C are off focus. The task in this problem is to identify the method of the passage's argument, not to find fault with the argument.

D misinterprets the passage. The passage does not compare features possessed by couples who live together before marriage with features possessed by couples who do not, nor is one identified as the common feature by a process of elimination.

E is off focus. The task in this problem is to identify the method of the passage's argument, not to find fault with the argument. In any case, you cannot determine how representative the sample is based on the information that the passage states.

### 12. Assessing the effect of additional information (moderate). Answer: D.

The task in this problem is to find an answer that strengthens the argument—that is, one that offers support for the argument's major assumption or that provides additional evidence for the conclusion. You can represent the passage's argument as follows:

**Premise:** Ten years ago, the death rate from Neural Synapse Deficiency (NSD) related causes was 5% of all persons infected with the antisynapse virus (ASV) that causes it.

**Premise:** Today, the death rate from NSD-related causes is 15% of all persons infected with the ASV that causes it.

**Conclusion:** The rate of propagation and the malignancy of the ASV has increased substantially over the past 10 years.

The argument's major assumption is that no additional NSD-related causes of death have been discovered in the interim that could account for the increase in the death rate. In other words, the number of recognized NSD-related causes of death has remained relatively constant over the past 10 years.

B is the second best response. Response B provides additional evidence for the claim that the rate of propagation of the ASV has increased over the past 10 years; however, it does not provide additional evidence for the claim that the malignancy of the virus has increased over this period. The argument's conclusion states that *both* the rate of propagation and the malignancy of the virus have increased.

A, C, and E do not offer support for the argument's major assumption, nor do they provide additional evidence for the argument's conclusion.

### 13. Assessing the effect of additional information (moderate). Answer: B.

The task in this problem is to find an answer that weakens the argument—that is, one that undermines the argument's major assumption, attacks a stated premise, or suggests an alternative conclusion that you can infer from the premises. You can represent the passage's argument as follows:

**Premise:** Lycopene, glutathione, and glutamine are powerful antioxidants that neutralize the free radicals that the body produces as a result of routine bodily processes.

**Premise:** An excess in your system of the free radicals that are produced in the body as a result of routine bodily processes causes rapid aging.

**Conclusion:** To slow down aging, it is necessary to supplement your diet with these antioxidants on a daily basis.

The argument's major assumption is that daily ingestion of the antioxidants mentioned in the passage is the only way to rid your system of the free radicals produced as a result of routine bodily processes. Response B undermines this assumption.

A brings in information not mentioned in the passage. The passage does not discuss whether persons are concerned with the problem of aging or when that concern is realized.

C brings in information not mentioned in the passage. Admittedly, the high cost might prevent some people from using these antioxidants daily, but the fact that they are beyond the budget of most consumers does not attack a premise of the argument, nor does it subvert the major assumption of the argument or suggest an alternative conclusion.

D does not undermine the argument's major assumption, attack a stated premise, or suggest an alternative conclusion that you can infer from the premises.

E brings in information that the passage does not mention. The passage does not discuss additional causes of cellular damage such as smoking.

## 14. Assessing the effect of additional information (easier). Answer: C.

The task in this problem is to find an answer that weakens the argument—that is, one that undermines the argument's major assumption, attacks a stated premise, or suggests an alternative conclusion that you can infer from the premises. You can represent the passage's argument as follows:

**Premise:** Seventy-eight percent of the respondents said that they were happy.

**Premise:** The same 78% of the respondents claimed that they possessed a large amount of money.

**Conclusion:** Having a sizable quantity of money is the key to happiness.

Response C directly attacks the second premise, thereby calling the survey's findings into serious doubt. If C is true, the second premise is false. Consequently, the argument falls apart because the connection between having money and being happy is completely severed.

A and B state possible problems that could have an adverse effect on the survey's reliability, but neither of these responses directly attacks the truth of a stated premise, nor do they undermine the major assumption or suggest an alternative conclusion that you can infer from the premises.

D is consistent with the argument's conclusion. The conclusion does not state that everyone who is happy has a large amount of money, it states that persons who have a large amount of money are happy. Response D does not suggest an alternative conclusion that you can infer from the premises, nor does it undermine the argument's major assumption or attack a stated premise.

E contradicts the argument's conclusion. The conclusion states that persons who have a large amount of money are happy; response E states the opposite of this claim. Response D does not weaken the argument because it does not undermine the argument's major assumption, attack a stated premise, or suggest an alternative conclusion that you can infer from the premises.

## Day 6

# Quantitative Ability Lesson 1: Overview and Strategies

### Today's Topics:

1. The Quantitative section at a glance
2. Specific topics covered and frequency of appearance
3. Terminology presupposed by the Quantitative section
4. Assumptions underlying all Quantitative questions
5. Problem Solving questions
6. Data Sufficiency questions
7. Handling word problems
8. Managing your time

Today you will familiarize yourself with the format of the Quantitative section, survey the topics covered, and learn some general strategies and tips that apply to all Quantitative questions.

## THE QUANTITATIVE SECTION AT A GLANCE

**Time allotted:** 75 minutes
**Number of questions:** 37 total
- 27 questions are scored, 10 are unscored pretest questions

**Average time per question:** 2 minutes

**Basic Format:**
- All 37 questions are in multiple-choice format
- The exam poses 23–24 questions in a problem solving format
- The exam poses 13–14 questions in a data sufficiency format
- Data Sufficiency questions are interspersed with Problem Solving questions
- Approximately 50% of the questions are word problems ("real-life" scenarios)

**Ground rules:**

- Calculators are prohibited

- Scratch paper for performing calculations, solving equations, and so forth, is allowed and provided

**Broad areas covered:**
- Properties of numbers

- Arithmetical operations

- Algebraic expressions, equations, and inequalities (limited to what a first-year high school algebra course usually covers)

- Geometry, including coordinate geometry, intuitive geometry, and spatial visualization

- Data interpretation (statistical charts, tables, and graphs)

**Areas not covered:**
- Advanced algebra concepts

- Geometry theorems and formal proofs

- Trigonometry

- Calculus

**Abilities (skills) tested:**
- Proficiency in arithmetical operations

- Proficiency at solving algebraic equations

- Ability to convert verbal information to mathematical terms

- Ability to visualize geometric shapes and numerical relationships

- Ability to devise intuitive and unconventional solutions to conventional mathematical problems

---

## SPECIFIC TOPICS COVERED AND FREQUENCY OF APPEARANCE

Here's a breakdown of the specific areas covered in the Quantitative section, along with an estimate of how many questions (out of 37 total) from each area most test takers can expect:

**Properties of Numbers and Arithmetical Operations (12–15 Questions)**
- Linear ordering (positive and negative numbers, and absolute value)

- Properties of integers (factors, multiples, and prime numbers)

- Arithmetical operations

- Laws of arithmetic

- Fractions, decimals, and percentages

- Ratio and proportion

- Powers and roots

- Mean (average), mode, and median

- Sets

**Algebraic Equations and Inequalities (12–15 Questions)**
- Simplifying linear and quadratic algebraic expressions

- Solving equations with one variable (unknown)

- Solving equations with two variables (unknowns)

- Solving factorable quadratic equations

- Inequalities

**Geometry, Including Coordinate Geometry (5–8 Questions)**
- Intersecting lines and angles

- Perpendicular and parallel lines

- Triangles

- Quadrilaterals (four-sided polygons)

- Circles

- Rectangular solids (three-dimensional figures)

- Cylinders

- Pyramids

- Coordinate geometry

Interpretation of Statistical Charts, Graphs and Tables (2–3 Questions)

- Pie charts

- Tables

- Bar graphs

- Line charts

## TERMINOLOGY PRESUPPOSED BY THE QUANTITATIVE SECTION

The Quantitative section presupposes knowledge of certain terminology used in basic arithmetic, algebra, and geometry, including such terms as the following:

- Integer, factor, multiple, prime number, absolute value

- Product, sum, ratio, quotient, fraction, percent

- Square root, exponent

- Equation, inequality

- Isosceles, equilateral, hypotenuse (triangle)

- Parallel, perpendicular, bisect (lines and angles)

- Parallelogram, rectangle, cylinder

- Perimeter, area, volume

- Radius, diameter, circumference, arc (of a circle)

- Coordinate plane, origin, x-axis, y-axis

The lessons in this book will define and clarify all but the most elementary terms.

## ASSUMPTIONS UNDERLYING ALL QUANTITATIVE QUESTIONS

The official test directions for the Quantitative section explicitly instruct you to make the following assumptions:

- All numbers used are real numbers.

- All figures lie on a plane unless otherwise indicated.

- All lines are straight lines unless otherwise indicated.

- All angle measures are greater than zero.

## PROBLEM SOLVING QUESTIONS

Problem Solving questions require you to solve a mathematical problem and then find that solution among the five answer choices. This conventional test format should be quite familiar to you. Problem Solving questions vary widely in difficulty and complexity. Example 6-1, a word problem, is easier than average. (Remember: Word problems account for about half of the 40 Quantitative questions.) Take a minute or two to solve this problem.

**Example 6-1**

Susan purchased a 16-ounce soda. If she drinks 10% of the soda immediately before lunch and 20% of the remaining amount with lunch, approximately how many ounces of soda are left to drink after lunch?

(A)  11.2

(B)  11.5

(C)  12.0

(D)  12.8

(E)  13.0

As simple as Example 6-1 might seem, there are actually three distinct yet interrelated skills involved in handling the question:

1. A *verbal* skill (interpreting the verbal statement and converting it into proper mathematical expressions and operations)

2. A *mathematical* skill (calculating percentages)

3. *Efficiency* (your ability to determine the correct response in the fewest possible steps and calculations; Example 6-1, for example, tests your ability and willingness to round off numbers appropriately)

To see how these three skills come into play in Example 6-1, break down the analysis into distinct steps:

1. Recognize that the verbal statement calls for you to first determine 90% (not 10%) of 16 ounces (skill 1).

2. Determine 90% of 16 in either one or two steps: $.9 \times 16 = 14.4$ (one step) or $16 - (.1 \times 16) = 14.4$ (two steps) (skills 2 and 3).

3. Recognize that the verbal statement calls for you to determine 80% (not 20%) of 14.4 (skill 1).

4. Determine 20% of 14.4. You determine 20% before determining 80% because $2 \times 144$ (the two numbers stripped of extraneous zeros and decimal places) is obviously 288 (no pencilwork required), whereas $8 \times 144$ is not as obvious (pencilwork might be required) (skills 2 and 3).

5. Insert a decimal point in the number 288. Ask yourself what sized number you are looking for. The answer is a number somewhere between 1 and 5. Thus, 20% of 14.4 must be 2.88, not 28.8 or .288 (skill 3).

6. Round off 2.88 to 2.9 before subtracting from 14.4 (skill 3).

7. Subtract 2.9 from 14.4 (11.5—no pencilwork required) (skill 2).

8. Scan the answer choices for the closest number to 11.4 (the correct response is B).

## Interpreting Figures in the Problem Solving Format

Some Problem Solving questions are accompanied by figures (diagrams and pictures). Such figures are intended to provide information useful in solving the problems. They are drawn as accurately as possible *except* when a specific problem states that a figure is not drawn to scale. Rest assured: Figures are drawn in such a way that their visual appearance will not mislead or trick you.

## Tips for Handling Problem Solving Questions

**Tip 1: Size up the question first.** Try to assess which specific mathematical area the question is testing (for example, which mathematical rules and formulas come into play). Each question falls into one (or, in the case of "crossover" questions, two) of the specific

areas listed earlier in this lesson. By determining right up front what you are up against, you are already well on your way to dealing with the question.

**Tip 2: Determine how much time you're willing to spend on the problem, if any.** As noted earlier, questions vary widely in difficulty level, from simple arithmetic calculations to complex word problems. As you attempt the mini-tests and practice tests in this book, try to get a feel for your limitations in handling complex questions. Learn to recognize a tough question when you see it, so that you don't waste valuable time on it; take an educated guess (see tip 3) and move on.

**Tip 3: Size up the answer choices.** Before you attempt to solve a problem, examine the answer choices. These choices often provide helpful clues about how to proceed in solving the problem and about what sort of solution you should be looking for. Pay particular attention to the following:

- *Form.* Are the answer choices expressed as percentages, fractions, or decimals? Ounces or pounds? Minutes or hours? If the answer choices are expressed as equations, are all variables together on one side of the equation? As you work through the problem, convert numbers and expressions to the same form as the answer choices.

- *Size.* Are the answer choices extremely small numbers? Numbers between 1 and 10? Larger numbers? Negative or positive numbers? Do the answer choices vary widely in value, or are their values clustered closely around an average? If all answer choices are tightly clustered in value, you can probably disregard decimal points and extraneous zeros in performing calculations, but you should be very careful about rounding off. If the choices vary widely in value, you should be able to eliminate several choices that don't correspond to the general size of number that the question suggests. Notice that answer choices for Problem Solving questions are usually arranged in size order, from the smallest value to the largest.

- *Other distinctive properties and characteristics.* Are the answer choices integers? Do they all include a variable? Do one or more include radicals (roots)? Exponents? Is there a particular term, expression, or number that they have in common?

**Tip 4: Don't do too much work in your head.** Carelessness, *not* lack of knowledge or ability, is the leading cause of incorrect responses in GMAT Problem Solving questions. In manipulating expressions and performing calculations, use your pencil and scratch paper for all but the simplest mathematical steps.

**Tip 5: Look for wrong-answer choices that result from common errors.** The GMAT intentionally baits you with wrong-answer choices that result from making specific common errors in setting up problems and in calculation. Don't assume that your response is correct just because your solution appears among the five answer choices. Rely instead on your sense for whether you understood what the question calls for and performed the calculations and other steps carefully and accurately. In Example 6-1, if you erroneously added together 10% and 20% and subtracted the number 3 (based on that sum) from 16, you would have selected answer E. If you erroneously subtracted 20% from the original 16 ounces (instead of from 14.4 ounces), you would have selected C.

**Tip 6: Verify the appropriateness of your response before moving on.** After solving the problem and selecting a response, check the question again to verify that your response corresponds to what the question calls for (in terms of size, expression, units of measure, and so forth). If it does, and you are confident that your work was careful and accurate, don't spend any more time checking your work. Confirm your response and move on to the next question.

**Tip 7: Don't do more work than is necessary to determine the correct answer.** If the question asks for an approximation, the test maker is hinting that exact calculations might be time-consuming and that you can rely on rounded-off numbers as you work. Even if the question does not explicitly call for approximation (and the overwhelming majority of the questions do not), don't calculate exact figures when approximations will suffice.

# DATA SUFFICIENCY QUESTIONS

Each Data Sufficiency question includes a question followed by two statements (labeled 1 and 2). Your task is to analyze each numbered statement to determine whether it provides sufficient data to answer the question. The correct response to each Data Sufficiency question is one of the following:

- **A (the first oval)** if statement 1 *alone* suffices, but statement 2 alone does *not* suffice, to answer the question.

- **B (the second oval)** if statement 2 *alone* suffices, but statement 1 alone does *not* suffice, to answer the question.

- **C (the third oval)** if *both* statements 1 and 2 *together* suffice to answer the question, but *neither* statement *alone* suffices.

- **D (the fourth oval)** if each statement *alone* suffices to answer the question.

- **E (the fifth oval)** if statements 1 and 2 *together* do *not* suffice to answer the question.

## Interpreting Figures in the Data Sufficiency Format

Figures accompanying Data Sufficiency questions conform to the information given in the questions but do not necessarily conform to the additional information given in statements 1 and 2. Do *not* rely on a figure's visual scale when analyzing the question. For example, do not rely on figures alone to determine whether any of the following are true:

- Two line segments are equal in length

- Two angles are equal in measure

- Two lines are parallel or perpendicular

- Two triangles are similar

- Two segments of a pie chart are equal in size

The figure below illustrates this point. Take a minute or two to attempt the question, which is average in difficulty level. Remember not to let the apparent size of the two angles in question mislead you. Rely instead on the information in the question itself and in statements 1 and 2.

**Example 6-2**

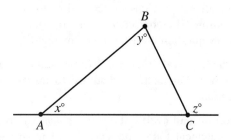

In the above figure, is $AB$ equal in length to $AC$?

(1) $x + y = z$

(2) $y = 180 - z$

This question involves angle measures of triangles. In all likelihood, then, the following rule is key in responding to the question:

> The sum of the three interior angles of a triangle equals 180.

You can state the rule algebraically using the variables $x$ and $y$ (as in the problem) along with the variable $a$ to represent the third interior angle:

$$x + y + a = 180$$

Notice that statements 1 and 2 both resemble the foregoing equation, at least to some extent. This is a good indication that you are on the right track in your approach to the problem. Next, express the foregoing equation in terms of $x$, $y$, and $z$. Because the line that includes $AC$ is a straight line, angles $z$ and $a$ are said to be *supplementary*—that is, the sum of their angle measures equals 180. Thus, you can express $a$ as $180 - x$, and can further refine the preceding equation using either of the following:

$$x + y + (180 - z) = 180$$

$$x + y - z = 0$$

Example 6-2 also involves relative lengths of triangle sides. Specifically, the question asks whether two particular sides are equal in length. If they *are* equal in length, the angles opposite those two sides

must be equal in measure (the triangle is isosceles). You can state this in terms of the preceding equation, using either of the following:

$$y = a$$

$$y = (180 - z)$$

Does statement 1 alone suffice to determine whether $y = 180 - z$? To answer this question, try substituting $180 - a$ for $z$ in statement 1:

$$x + y = z$$

$$x + y = (180 - a)$$

$$x + y + a = 180$$

Notice that the last equation is simply a statement of the rule that the sum of the angle measures of a triangle equals 180. Accordingly, statement 1 is true of any triangle and therefore is insufficient alone to determine whether AB=AC. Eliminate A as a viable answer choice. You can also eliminate D as a viable answer choice, because D also requires that 1 alone suffice to answer the question.

Now consider statement 2 by itself—that is, disregard statement 1. Notice that the equation provided in statement 2 indicates that $y$ is equal to the third interior angle (referred to as $a$ in this analysis). Statement 2 answers the question. Based on $y = 180 - z$, or $y = a$, the triangle is isosceles, and the sides opposite the equal angles are equal in length.

Because statement 1 alone is insufficient to answer the question while statement 2 alone is sufficient, the correct response is B. You need not consider the two statements together. (The answer to the question itself is yes, although it isn't necessary to go this far to respond to this or any other data sufficiency problem. Had neither statement 1 nor 2 alone sufficed to answer the question, you would have then considered both statements together to determine whether the correct response is C or E.)

## What Does "Sufficient" Mean?

In Data Sufficiency questions that ask for a particular value (for example, "What is the area of the circle?" or "What is the value of $x$?"), keep in mind that the question is answerable only if *one and only one value* results—not a range of numbers, not a positive or negative number, not an expression that includes a variable.

## What If Statements 1 and 2 Result in Conflicting Answers?

Conflicting answers won't result from the two statements. Rest assured that the information provided in statement 1 will *not* be inconsistent with the information provided in statement 2. Thus, if the correct response to a particular data sufficiency problem is D, the answer to the question posed will be the same, regardless of which statement is being considered. Although there is no inherent reason for this consistency (at least for questions whose correct response is D), the questions are designed this way to avoid confusion.

## Tips for Handling Data Sufficiency Questions

**Tip 1: Size up the question first, and don't get bogged down with "toughies."** As with Problem Solving questions, assess what specific mathematical area the question is testing. Determine right up front what you are up against and whether your time would be better spent on a question that involves a topic with which you are more proficient.

**Tip 2: Be sure to consider each statement alone.** After analyzing statement 1, you'll be surprised how difficult it can be to purge the information in statement 1 from your mind and start with a clean slate in considering statement 2. Be alert at all times to this potential problem.

**Tip 3: Don't do more work than necessary.** Keep in mind that the data sufficiency format does not require you to answer the question posed. You need only determine whether the information that the statements provide suffices.

**Tip 4: Use your pencil.** As with Problem Solving questions, don't try to do too much work in your head. Avoid careless errors by using your pencil and scratch paper for all but the simplest mathematical steps.

**Tip 5: Make educated guesses by eliminating answer choices.** Keep in mind that if statement 1 alone is insufficient to answer the question, you can eliminate both A and D. On the other hand, after determining that one of the statements alone suffices, you can eliminate C and E. Thus, if you are having trouble with one of the two statements but are confident about your analysis of the other statement, consider making a guess and moving on to the next question.

**Tip 6: Avoid C-itis and E-itis.** If you are relatively weak in handling Data Sufficiency questions, you might tend to choose responses C and E more frequently than the others. Why? If you are unable to perform a reasoned analysis of the problem regardless of how much information is provided, this inability will suggest to you that you can eliminate A, B, and D. Try to avoid this tendency.

## HANDLING WORD PROBLEMS

Word problems (problems expressed in "real-life" terms) account for approximately 50% of all Quantitative questions. (The remaining 50% are posed in a purely mathematical setting.) You can expect to see the following types of word problems on the GMAT:

- Discount and profit, tax, and commission

- Simple averages and weighted averages

- Motion (rate, speed, and flow)

- Measurement (units of time, weight, distance, volume, and so on)

- Work

- Mixture, proportion, and ratio

- Geometry

- Data interpretation

Word problems tend to be more difficult than average, because they require you to convert a verbal problem into mathematical terms, creating additional opportunity for mistakes on your part. GMAT word problems depend on reasonable, real-life assumptions that enable you to respond to the question posed. Do not second-guess the premise, split hairs in terms of the intended meaning of words or phrases, or read anything into the information provided that isn't there. The premise in Example 6-1 (page 61), for instance, fails to explicitly account for the possibility that someone other than Susan drank a portion of her soda during lunch. The question assumes (but doesn't explicitly state) that only Susan drank the soda. This is the sort of reasonable assumption that you are expected to accept in handling word problems. In fact, you *must* accept this assumption to respond to the question. Don't fight the test; you'll only defeat yourself.

## MANAGING YOUR TIME

Most test-takers find that they can finish the 75-minute Quantitative section within the time allotted without feeling rushed. Nevertheless, you must move at a steady pace. Your average time allotted per question is approximately two minutes. Keeping track of your elapsed time for each question is not only unnecessary but also distracting and time-consuming. You should, however, check the online clock every so often—perhaps every 10 minutes—to see whether you are on pace. If your pace is right, you will respond at the following rate:

- Ten questions within 20 minutes

- Twenty questions within 40 minutes

- Thirty questions within 60 minutes

- Thirty-seven questions within 75 minutes

## ABOUT THE OTHER QUANTITATIVE LESSONS IN THIS BOOK

The remaining eight Quantitative lessons in this book are divided into the three basic content areas of arithmetic, algebra, and geometry. These lessons are not intended to be comprehensive treatments of these mathematical subjects. Instead, they highlight those areas that are particularly confusing, are commonly misunderstood, or appear most frequently on the GMAT. If you need additional instruction in any particular area, obtain an appropriate mathematics text or workbook to supplement these lessons.

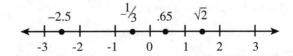

# Day 7

## Quantitative Ability Lesson 2: Arithmetic

### Today's Topics:

1. Real numbers
2. Absolute values
3. Integers
4. Laws of arithmetic
5. Fractions
6. Ratios and proportion
7. Decimals
8. Percent
9. Exponents (powers)
10. Roots
11. Arithmetic mean (simple average) and median
12. Combinations

Today you will review basic terminology, concepts, and rules of arithmetic, focusing on particular areas that bear most directly on GMAT Quantitative questions.

## ABOUT TODAY'S LESSON

The topics covered today are basic building blocks for more complex GMAT quantitative problems. Most of what you read here should be review. Nevertheless, pay close attention, because any misunderstanding or confusion about a basic concept might have an adverse effect on your Quantitative score. Moreover, some GMAT questions involving only the basic concepts examined here can be surprisingly difficult.

## REAL NUMBERS

A *real number* is any number on the real number line (see figure below). All real numbers except zero are either positive or negative.

A real number $x$ is less than another real number $y$ if $x$ appears to the left of $y$ on the real number line.

If $x < y < z$, then $x$ is to the left of both $y$ and $z$ on the number line, whereas $y$ is to the left of $z$ on the number line. In other words, $y$ is between $x$ and $z$.

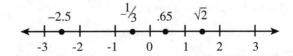

## ABSOLUTE VALUE

The *absolute value* of a real number refers to the number's distance from zero (the origin) on the number line. The absolute value of x is indicated as |x|. Although any negative number is less than any positive number, the absolute value of a negative number can either be less than (example 1), equal to (example 2), or greater than (example 3) a positive number:

1. $|-7| = 7 < |8|$
2. $|-7| = 7 = |7|$
3. $|-7| = 7 > |6|$

## INTEGERS

*Integers* include the set of all "counting" numbers on the number line: { . . . –3, –2, –1, 0, 1, 2, 3 . . . }. *Even* integers are divisible by 2 (an even integer divided by 2 yields an integer quotient), whereas *odd* integers are not divisible by 2 (the quotient is not an integer). Zero is an integer, but it is neither even nor odd.

### Operations on Integers

Here are some observations about the results of operations (addition, subtraction, multiplication, and division) on integers:

**Addition and subtraction**

- (integer) ± (integer) = integer

- (even) ± (even) = even (or zero, if the two integers are the same)

- (even) ± (odd) = odd

- (odd) ± (odd) = even (or zero, if the two integers are the same)

**Multiplication and division**

- (integer) × (integer) = integer

- (nonzero integer) ÷ (nonzero integer) = integer, but only if the numerator is divisible by the denominator

- (odd) × (odd) = odd

- (even) × (nonzero integer) = even

- $\frac{even}{2}$ = integer

- $\frac{odd}{2}$ = noninteger

### Properties of the integer 1

If *n* is a nonzero real number:

- $n \times 1 = n$

- $\frac{n}{1} = n$

- $\frac{n}{n} = 1$

### Properties of the integer 0 (zero)

If *n* is a real number:

- $n \pm 0 = n$

- $n \times 0 = 0$

- $\frac{0}{n} = 0$

- $\frac{n}{0}$ = undefined

- $\frac{0}{0}$ = indeterminate

You will not encounter undefined or indeterminate numbers on the GMAT; questions explicitly restrict denominators to nonzero values wherever necessary to avoid these numbers.

### Factors, Multiples, and Prime Numbers

**Factors and multiples.** Where the product of a nonzero integer x and another integer is an integer y, x is said to be a *divisor* or *factor* of y. In other words, if y is divisible by x, x is a factor of y (and, conversely, y is said to be a *multiple* of x). By definition, the absolute value of an integer is greater than or equal to that of any of its factors. Consider the integer 30:

- There are 16 factors (8 positive, 8 negative) of 30: {1, –1, 2, –2, 3, –3, 5, –5, 6, –6, 10, –10, 15, –15, 30, and –30}.

- The number 30 is a multiple of (divisible by) 16 different integers.

Remember these important points about factors:

- Any integer is a factor of itself.

- The number 1 is a factor of all integers.

- The integer zero has no factors and is not a factor of any integer.

- A positive integer's largest factor (other than itself) is never greater than half the integer's value.

**Prime numbers.** A *prime number* is a positive integer having only two factors: 1 and the number itself. In other words, a prime number is not divisible by any integer other than itself and 1. The set of prime numbers up to and including 31 includes 2, 3, 5, 7, 11, 13, 17, 19, 23, 29, and 31. One and zero are not prime numbers.

**Shortcuts to determining factors (divisibility).** Determining factors of large integers can be difficult. Keep in mind the following rules to help you determine quickly whether one integer is a multiple of (is divisible by) another integer:

- If the integer ends in 0, 2, 4, 6, or 8, the number is divisible by 2.

- If the sum of the digits is divisible by 3, the number is divisible by 3.

- If the number formed by the last two digits is divisible by 4, the number is divisible by 4.

- If the number ends in 5 or 0, the number is divisible by 5.

- If the number meets the tests for divisibility by 2 and 3, the number is divisible by 6.

- If the number formed by the last three digits is divisible by 8, the number is divisible by 8.

- If the sum of the digits is divisible by 9, the number is divisible by 9.

---

## LAWS OF ARITHMATIC

The laws of arithmetic are the fundamental tools to use in combining and simplifying mathematical expressions. Keep in mind the following basic laws of arithmetic, which you will put to use repeatedly in GMAT quantitative problems.

**Commutative laws**

- $a + b = b + a$

- But $a - b \neq b - a$ (unless $a = b$)

- $ab = ba$

- But $\frac{a}{b} \neq \frac{b}{a}$ (unless $a = b$)

**Associative laws**

- $a + (b + c) = (a + b) + c$

- But $a - (b + c) \neq (a - b) + c$

- $a(bc) = (ab)c$

- But $\frac{ab}{c} \neq \frac{ac}{b}$ or $\frac{a}{bc}$

**Distributive laws**

- $a(b + c) = ab + ac$

- $a - (b + c) = a - b - c$

- $\frac{a+b}{c} = \frac{a}{c} + \frac{b}{c}$

- But $\frac{a}{b+c} \neq \frac{a}{b} + \frac{a}{c}$

The second distributive law indicated above is a particular favorite of the testing service. It is surprisingly easy to overlook minus signs when simplifying expressions.

---

## FRACTIONS

A fraction is a number of the form $\frac{x}{y}$ ($y \neq 0$). $x$ is referred to as the *numerator,* and y is referred to as the *denominator.* A *mixed number* includes an integer and a proper fraction (for example, $7\frac{5}{6}$). To convert a mixed number to proper fraction, multiply the denominator by the integer, add the product to the numerator, then place the sum over the original denominator:

$$7\frac{5}{6} = \frac{(6)(7)+5}{6} = \frac{47}{6}$$

## Addition and Subtraction of Fractions

To add or subtract two fractions having the same denominator, add together the two numerators:

$$\frac{3}{7} + \frac{5}{7} = \frac{8}{7}$$

$$\frac{8}{5} - \frac{11}{5} = -\frac{3}{5}$$

To add or subtract two fractions having *different denominators*, determine a multiple common to both denominators. For each fraction, multiply the numerator and denominator by an integer that results in that common denominator. In the following example, 12 is the lowest common multiple of 4 and 3, and is referred to in the context of the fraction as the *lowest common denominator*:

$$-\frac{13}{4} + \frac{8}{3} =$$

$$-\frac{(13)(3)}{(4)(3)} + \frac{(8)(4)}{(3)(4)} =$$

$$-\frac{39}{12} + \frac{32}{12} = -\frac{7}{12}$$

## Multiplication of Fractions

To multiply one fraction by another, multiply the two numerators and multiply the two denominators (the denominators need not be the same):

$$\left(\frac{13}{2}\right)\left(-\frac{3}{7}\right) = -\frac{39}{14}$$

To simplify the multiplication, always look for the possibility of canceling factors common to either numerator and either denominator, as shown in the below figure.

$$\frac{18}{7} \cdot \frac{7}{12} = \frac{\cancel{18}^3}{\cancel{7}^1} \cdot \frac{\cancel{7}^1}{\cancel{12}^2} = \frac{3}{2}$$

## Division of Fractions

On the GMAT, problems involving operations with fractions typically involve *complex fractions*, which express either the numerator or denominator (or both) as a fraction and/or as a sum or difference of two terms. To simplify complex fractions, try the following four steps:

1. Combine fractions within the numerator as well as fractions within the denominator (canceling common factors wherever possible).

2. If the denominator is not already a fraction itself, express it as such by placing it in a numerator over the denominator 1.

3. Invert (switch) the terms of the fraction by which you are dividing. (The inverted fraction is called the *reciprocal* of the original fraction.)

4. Multiply the two resulting simple fractions, canceling common factors, if possible.

The figure below figure shows two examples that involve steps 2 through 4.

$$\frac{\frac{2}{3}}{\frac{11}{5}} = \frac{2}{3} \cdot \frac{5}{11} = \frac{10}{33}$$

$$\frac{\frac{5}{9}}{\frac{15}{1}} = \frac{\frac{5}{9}}{\frac{15}{1}} = \frac{5}{9} \cdot \frac{1}{15} = \frac{\cancel{8}^1}{9} \cdot \frac{1}{\cancel{15}^3} = \frac{1}{27}$$

## RATIOS AND PROPORTION

A *ratio* is an expression of proportion or comparative size. The size of a number $x$ relative to that of a number $y$ ($y \neq 0$)—that is, the ratio of $x$ to $y$—can be expressed as either $x{:}y$, $x$ to $y$, or $x/y$. Just as with fractions, you can reduce ratios to lowest terms by canceling common factors. Let's put all this in a verbal context. Given 12 males and 16 females, all the following are true:

- The male/female ratio is 12:16, 3:4, $\frac{12}{16}$, or $\frac{3}{4}$.

- The ratio of males to females is 12 to 16, or 3 to 4.

- The number of males is $\frac{12}{16}$ (or $\frac{3}{4}$) the number of females.

- The number of males multiplied by $\frac{16}{12}$ (or $\frac{4}{3}$) equals the number of females.

- The female/male ratio is 16:12, 4:3, $\frac{16}{12}$, or $\frac{4}{3}$.

- The ratio of females to males is 16 to 12, or 4 to 3.

- The number of females is $\frac{16}{12}$ (or $\frac{4}{3}$) the number of males.

- The number of females multiplied by $\frac{12}{16}$ (or $\frac{3}{4}$) equals the number of males.

Remember: The order of the terms of a ratio is very important. For instance, in the foregoing example, the ratio of males to females is 12 to 16 $\left(\frac{12}{16}\right)$, not 16 to 12.

## DECIMALS

You can express any real number in decimal form. The value of digits in a decimal number depends on their position (place) relative to the decimal point. For example, consider the number 938.421:

- The numeral 9 is the "hundreds" digit, and it has a place value of 100 (three places to the left of the decimal point).

- The numeral 3 is the "tens" digit, and it has a place value of 10 (two places to the left of the decimal point).

- The numeral 8 is the "ones" digit, and it has a place value of 1 (one place to the left of the decimal point).

- The numeral 4 is the "tenths" digit, and it has a place value of $\frac{1}{10}$ (one place to the left of the decimal point).

- The numeral 2 is the "hundredths" digit, and it has a place value of $\frac{1}{100}$ (two places to the left of the decimal point).

- The numeral 1 is the "thousandths" digit, and it has a place value of $\frac{1}{1,000}$ (three places to the left of the decimal point).

Accordingly:

938.421 =

$9(100) + 3(10) + 8(1) + 4(1/10) + 2(1/100) + 1(\frac{1}{1,000})$

$= 900 + 30 + 8 + \frac{4}{10} + \frac{2}{100} + \frac{1}{1,000}$

Without a calculator, multiplying and dividing numbers having two or more decimal points can be quite time-consuming. Consider the following examples:

$$(297.36)(14.98) \qquad \frac{1653.67}{76.74}$$

Calculators are not permitted on the GMAT. Fortunately, the GMAT does not require you to crunch numbers like these. Where large numbers or numbers with two or more decimal places appear on the GMAT, rest assured that you can determine the correct answer without making exact calculations, by rounding off or by approximating. GMAT questions that include decimals typically involve fractional or percentage equivalents and conversions (see the next section) rather than number crunching.

## PERCENT

*Percent* means *per hundred*. Percents are usually less than 100, but they can be 100 or greater as well. Any percent can also be expressed as a fraction or in decimal form. Here are some examples:

- 37% = 37 out of 100 = $\frac{37}{100}$ = .37

- 284% = $\frac{284}{100}$ = 2.84

- 5% = 5 out of 100 = $\frac{5}{100}$ = .05

- 3.4% = 3.4 out of 100 = $\frac{3.4}{100}$ = $\frac{34}{1000}$ = .034

- $x$% = $x$ out of 100 = $\frac{x}{100}$ = $\frac{1}{100}(x)$ = .01$x$

- $\frac{1}{4}$% = $\frac{1}{4}$ out of 100 = $\frac{\frac{1}{4}}{100}$ = $\left(\frac{1}{100}\right)$ (.25) = .0025

A percentage expressed as a negative number indicates decrease. Otherwise, the number system includes no such thing as a negative portion or percentage.

### Fractional and Decimal Equivalents of Percents

**Changing a percent to a decimal (and vice versa).** The preceding examples used multiple steps to express percentages in terms of decimal equivalents.

A quicker way to change a percent to a decimal is simply to move the decimal point two places to the left, and remove the percent sign. Conversely, to change a decimal to a percent, move the decimal point two places to the right and add the percent sign. Note the following examples:

- $9.5\% = .095$
- $.4\% = .004$
- $123\% = 1.23$
- $.003 = .3\%$
- $.704 = 70.4\%$
- $13.661 = 1,366.1\%$

**Changing a percent to a fraction (and vice versa).** To change a percent to a fraction, simply remove the percent sign and divide by 100 (simplify by canceling common factors). Reverse the process to change a fraction to a percent (simplify by canceling common factors). Note the following examples:

- $23\% = \frac{23}{100}$
- $2.891\% = \frac{2.891}{100} = \frac{2,891}{100,000}$
- $810\% = \frac{810}{100} = \frac{81}{10} = 8\frac{1}{10}$
- $\frac{4}{5} = \frac{4}{5}(100\%) = \frac{400}{5}\% = 80\%$
- $\frac{3}{8} = \frac{3}{8}(100\%) = \frac{300}{8}\% = \frac{75}{2}\% = 37\frac{1}{2}\%$

**Guarding against errors in converting one form to another.** To guard against conversion errors on the GMAT, keep in mind the general size of the number with which you are working. For example, a test taker in a hurry might carelessly (and incorrectly) express

- $.09\%$ as $.9$ or $\frac{9}{100}$
- $\frac{.4}{5}$ as $.8\%$
- $668\%$ as $66.8$ or $.668$

One good way to check your conversion is to verbalize the original expression, perhaps rounding off the original number to a more familiar one. In the first of the preceding examples, think of .09% as just under .1%, which is one-tenth of a percent, or a thousandth (a pretty small number). In the second example, think of $\frac{.4}{5}$ as just under $\frac{.5}{5}$, which is $\frac{1}{10}$, or 10%. Think of 668% as more than six times a complete 100% or between 6 and 7.

## Common (Testworthy) Fraction, Decimal, and Percent Equivalents

Certain fractional and decimal equivalents of common percents occur frequently enough on the GMAT that you should memorize them. These fractions, percentages, and decimals are favorites of the testing service because they reward test takers who recognize quicker ways to determine answers to questions. The equivalents in the table below should make your work with percent problems much easier.

| PERCENT | DECIMAL | FRACTION |
|---------|---------|----------|
| 50% | .5 | $\frac{1}{2}$ |
| 25% | .25 | $\frac{1}{4}$ |
| 75% | .75 | $\frac{3}{4}$ |
| 10% | .1 | $\frac{1}{10}$ |
| 30% | .3 | $\frac{3}{10}$ |
| 70% | .7 | $\frac{7}{10}$ |
| 90% | .9 | $\frac{9}{10}$ |
| $33\frac{1}{3}\%$ | $.33\frac{1}{3}$ | $\frac{1}{3}$ |
| $66\frac{2}{3}\%$ | $.66\frac{2}{3}$ | $\frac{2}{3}$ |
| $16\frac{2}{3}\%$ | $16\frac{2}{3}$ | $\frac{1}{6}$ |
| $83\frac{1}{3}\%$ | $.83\frac{1}{3}$ | $\frac{5}{6}$ |
| 20% | .2 | $\frac{1}{5}$ |
| 40% | .4 | $\frac{2}{5}$ |
| 60% | .6 | $\frac{3}{5}$ |
| 80% | .8 | $\frac{4}{5}$ |
| $12\frac{1}{2}\%$ | .125 | $\frac{1}{8}$ |
| $37\frac{1}{2}\%$ | .375 | $\frac{3}{8}$ |
| $62\frac{1}{2}\%$ | .625 | $\frac{5}{8}$ |
| $87\frac{1}{2}\%$ | .875 | $\frac{7}{8}$ |

## Finding a Percent of a Number

Consider the following question: *What is 35% of 65?* There are three methods of finding a percent of a given number:

    (1) Proportion,   (2) Decimal,   (3) Fractional

**Proportion method.** Equate $\frac{35}{100}$ with the unknown number divided by 65:

$$\frac{x}{65} = \frac{35}{100}$$

$$\frac{x}{65} = \frac{7}{20}$$

$$x = \frac{455}{20}$$

$$x = \frac{91}{4}$$

$$x = 22\frac{3}{4}$$

**Decimal method.** Change 35% to .35:

$$(.35)(65) = 22.75$$

**Fractional method.** Change 35% to $\frac{35}{100}$:

$$(\frac{35}{100})(65) = (\frac{7}{20})(65) = \frac{(7)(13)}{4} = \frac{91}{4} = 22\frac{3}{4}$$

Most test takers find the fractional method to be the easiest and quickest to use, but you might prefer one of the other methods.

## Finding a Number When a Problem Gives a Percent

Consider the following question: *7 is 5% of what number?* You can use the proportion method to find a number when a problem gives a percent. However, most test takers find it easier to set up a different equation—one that states algebraically exactly what the question asks verbally.

The proportion method is as follows:

$$\frac{5}{100} = \frac{7}{x}$$

$$5x = 700$$

$$x = 140$$

Compare the verbal equation method:

$$7 = .05x \quad (7 \text{ is } .05 \text{ of } x)$$

$$700 = 5x$$

$$x = 140$$

## Finding What Percent One Number Is of Another

Consider the following question: *12 is what percent of 72?* You can use the proportion method to solve this problem, but you will probably find the fractional method easier and more intuitive.

The proportion method is as follows:

$$\frac{x}{100} = \frac{12}{72}$$

$$x = \frac{1,200}{72}$$

$$x = \frac{50}{3}$$

$$x = 16\frac{2}{3}\%$$

You can solve the same problem using the fractional method:

$$\frac{12}{72} = \frac{1}{6} = 16\frac{2}{3}\%$$

## Finding the Percent of Increase or Decrease

On the GMAT, percent problems often involve percent change (increase or decrease). Consider the following question:

10 increased by what percent is 12?

In handling such questions, keep in mind that the percent change always relates to the value *before* the change. First, determine the amount of the increase—2 in this case. Next, compare that increase to the original number (before the change) by a fraction—$\frac{2}{10}$ in this case. Ten increased by $\frac{2}{10}$ (or 20%) is 12.

You can use the same procedure for percent decrease. Consider the following question:

12 decreased by what percent is 10?

As before, first determine the amount of the change (2), then compare the change with the original amount (before the decrease)—12 in this case. The fractional decrease is $\frac{2}{12}$. Twelve decreased by $\frac{2}{12}$ (or $\frac{1}{6}$ or $16\frac{2}{3}\%$) is 10. (Did you remember $16\frac{2}{3}\%$ from the conversion table on page 68?)

Notice that the percent increase from 10 to 12 (20%) differs from the percent decrease from 12 to 10 ($16\frac{2}{3}$%). The reason for this is that you determine the change based on the original number (before the change), and that number is different in the two questions.

---

## EXPONENTS (POWERS)

---

An *exponent* (or *power*) refers to the number of times that a number (called the *base* number) is multiplied by itself. For example, $n^3 = (n)(n)(n)$; $n$ is said to be (raised to the third power) or "cubed." An exponent can be an integer or a fraction, a positive number or a negative number. On the GMAT, however, exponents are usually limited to positive integers.

### Exponents and Ordering

Raising numbers to powers can have surprising effects on the *size* and *sign* (negative or positive) of the base number. This is a favorite area for GMAT test questions. Here are some useful observations about the impact of exponents on ordering (the position along the real number line):

- (positive base) raised to (any exponent) = (positive number)

- (negative base) raised to (even integer) = (positive number)

- (negative base) raised to (odd integer) = (negative number)

- (base number >1) raised to (exponent greater than 1) increases the number

- (base number between 0 and 1) raised to (exponent greater than 1) decreases the number toward 0

- (base number between −1 and 0) raised to (odd exponent greater than 1) increases the number toward 0

- (base number less than −1) raised to (odd exponent >1) decreases the number

### Combining (Simplifying) Terms That Include Exponents

The rules relating to combining base numbers and exponents can be quite confusing. Here are some observations about the results of operations (addition, subtraction, multiplication, and division) on terms (numbers and variables) that include exponents. Keep in mind that most forms of combining are prohibited.

**Addition and subtraction.** You can't combine base numbers or exponents when adding or subtracting two terms unless base numbers are the same and exponents are the same.

$$a^x + a^x = 2a^x \text{ (okay to combine)}$$

$$a^x + b^x \text{ (cannot be combined)}$$

$$a^x + a^y \text{ (cannot be combined)}$$

**Multiplication and division.** When multiplying or dividing you can combine different base numbers, but only if the exponents are the same:

$$a^x \cdot b^x = (ab)^x$$

$$\frac{a^x}{b^x} = \left(\frac{a}{b}\right)^x$$

You can combine exponents, but only if base numbers are the same. When multiplying terms, add the exponents. When dividing terms, subtract the denominator exponent from the numerator exponent.

$$a^x \cdot b^x = (ab)^x$$

$$\frac{a^x}{a^y} = a^{x-y}$$

### Additional Exponent Rules

The figure below shows a few more exponent rules that you should know.

$$\left(a^x\right)^y = a^{x \cdot y} \qquad \left[\left(a^2\right)^5 = a^{10}\right]$$

$$a^{x/y} = \sqrt[y]{a^x} \qquad \left[a^{2/3} = \sqrt[3]{a^2}\right]$$

$$a^{-x} = \frac{1}{a^x} \qquad \left[a^{-2} = \frac{1}{a^2}\right]$$

$$a^{-x/y} = \frac{1}{a^{x/y}} = \frac{1}{\sqrt[y]{a^x}} \qquad \left[a^{-1/2} = \frac{1}{a^{1/2}} = \frac{1}{\sqrt{a}}\right]$$

$$a^0 = 1 \quad (a \neq 0)$$

## Common (Testworthy) Exponential Values

The exponential values (numbers) indicated in the below table occur frequently on the GMAT, so you should memorize them.

| | POWER & CORRESPONDING VALUE | | | | | | |
|---|---|---|---|---|---|---|---|
| BASE | 2 | 3 | 4 | 5 | 6 | 7 | 8 |
| 2 | 4 | 8 | 16 | 32 | 64 | 128 | 256 |
| 3 | 9 | 27 | 81 | 243 | | | |
| 4 | 16 | 64 | 256 | | | | |
| 5 | 25 | 125 | 625 | | | | |
| 6 | 36 | 216 | | | | | |

## ROOTS

A *square root* of a number $n$ is a number that multiplied by itself equals $n$. (Roots are denoted by *radical* signs, as in $\sqrt{n}$ and $\sqrt[3]{n}$.) The GMAT does not require that you calculate exact roots (square or otherwise) of large numbers. The exam might, however, ask you to *approximate* or determine parameters of square roots (or other roots). For example, $\sqrt[3]{50}$ lies somewhere between 3 and 4 ($3^3 = 27$, $4^3 = 64$). This range will probably suffice to respond to a GMAT question. The rules for roots (examined below) are quite similar to those for exponents.

## Roots and Ordering

As with exponents, the root of a number can bear a surprising relationship on the *size* and *sign* (negative versus positive) of the number. This again is a favorite area for test questions. Here are some useful observations:

- If $n > 1$, then $1 < \sqrt[3]{n} < \sqrt{n} < n$.

- If $0 < n < 1$, then $0 < n < \sqrt{n} < \sqrt[3]{n} < 1$ (notice that the square root is larger than its square, and the cube root is even larger).

- The *square* root of any negative number is an *imaginary* number (not a real number). (You will not encounter imaginary numbers on the GMAT.)

- Every negative number has exactly one cube root, and that root is a negative number [(–)(–)(–) = (–)]. The same holds true for all other *odd*-numbered roots of negative numbers.

- Every positive number has two square roots: a negative number and a positive number (with the same absolute value). The same holds true for all other *even*-numbered roots.

- Every positive number has only one cube root (a positive number). The same holds true for all other *odd*-numbered roots.

## Combining and Simplifying Terms That Include Roots

The GMAT also covers the rules for combining terms that include roots. Terms under different radicals cannot be combined under a common radical if you are *adding* or *subtracting* them:

$$\sqrt{x}\sqrt{y} \neq \sqrt{x+y}$$
$$\sqrt{x} - \sqrt{y} \neq \sqrt{x-y}$$
$$\sqrt{x} + \sqrt{x} = 2\sqrt{x} \quad \left(\text{not}\sqrt{2x}\right)$$

However, terms under different radicals can be combined under a common radical if you are *multiplying* or *dividing* them (as long as the root is the same—for example, two square roots):

$$\sqrt{x}\sqrt{y} = \sqrt{xy}$$
$$\frac{\sqrt{x}}{\sqrt{y}} = \sqrt{\frac{x}{y}}$$
$$\sqrt{x}\sqrt{x} = x$$

On the GMAT, radicals and roots often occur in equations. To simplify such an equation, squaring both sides of the equation is often a good idea, as in the following example:

$$\sqrt{x+2y} = 7$$
$$x + 2y = 49$$

## Common (Testworthy) Exponents and Roots

Some square and cube roots occur frequently enough on the GMAT that you should memorize them. The numbers in the table below should make your work with roots much easier.

Common square roots >10:

$\sqrt{121} = 11$
$\sqrt{144} = 12$
$\sqrt{169} = 13$
$\sqrt{196} = 14$
$\sqrt{225} = 15$
$\sqrt{625} = 25$

Cube roots from 2 to 10:

$\sqrt[3]{8} = 2$
$\sqrt[3]{27} = 3$
$\sqrt[3]{64} = 4$
$\sqrt[3]{125} = 5$
$\sqrt[3]{216} = 6$
$\sqrt[3]{343} = 7$
$\sqrt[3]{512} = 8$
$\sqrt[3]{729} = 9$
$\sqrt[3]{1,000} = 10$

# ARITHMETIC MEAN (SIMPLE AVERAGE) AND MEDIAN

## Arithmetic Mean (Simple Average)

You determine the *arithmetic mean*, or *simple average*, of a set of numbers or other terms by adding the terms together and dividing the resulting sum by the number of terms in the set. For example, if $A$ equals the average of five terms—$v, w, x, y$ and $z$—you can express $A$ as follows:

$$A = \frac{v + w + x + y + z}{5}$$

## Median

In a set of numbers ordered from least to greatest, the *median* is the middle value (if the series includes an odd number of terms) or the average of the two middle values (if the series includes an even number of terms). Thus, the median of five terms—$a, b, c, d,$ and $e$ (in order of value)—is $c$, whereas the median of four terms—$a, b, c,$ and $d$ (in order of value)—is $\frac{b+c}{2}$.

For the same set of values, the mean (average) and the median can be, but are not necessarily, the same. Here's an example:

The set $\{3,4,5,6,7\}$ has both a mean and median of 5.

The set $\{-2,0,5,8,9\}$ has a mean of 4 but a median of 5.

## "Sum-of-the-Digits" Problems

Problems involving arithmetic mean (average) inherently involve the "sum of the digits" that are being averaged. On the GMAT, you might encounter either an arithmetic mean or a pure "sum-of-the-digits" problem that involves a string of numbers so long that determining their sum could involve time-consuming calculations. When approaching such a problem, keep in mind that there is probably a quicker way. (Remember: One of the skills that the GMAT measures is your ability to recognize quick ways to solve the problems.) Consider, for example, the following set of numbers:

$$\{-17, -15, -12, -6, -3, 0, 3, 6, 12, 15, 18, 21\}$$

Notice that all positive numbers, with the exception of 18 and 21, have a negative-number counterpart. All these numbers add up to 0 and can be ignored in computing the sum of the digits. You need to consider only the numbers 18 and 21, as well as the negative number –17. The numbers 18 and –17 average out to 1. Thus, the sum of all the digits is 21 + 1, or 22. Similarly, when comparing the sum of two *sets* of digits, instead of computing both sums, cancel out digits common to both sets.

# COMBINATIONS

A *set* involves a group of two or more numbers or other terms. A GMAT question might ask you to determine the number of *possible combinations* of terms within one set or among terms in two sets. For example, consider the following two sets:

Set 1: $\{a, b, c, d, e\}$

Set 2: $\{x, y, z\}$

How many distinct sets of five members are possible by combining three members from Set 1 with two members from Set 2? In formal mathematics (more specifically, the field of probability), such problems usually call for the use of *factorials*. On the GMAT, however, these problems are usually simple enough to analyze less formally and more intuitively.

There isn't anything conceptually difficult about the question in the preceding paragraph. You simply need to be methodical and careful as you tally up all possibilities. Here's a method that you should apply to any such problem: Combine terms as far to the left as possible before moving to the right. To answer the above question, in the example, first consider all possible combinations from Set 1 that include *a*:

{*a b c*}

{*a b d*}

{*a b e*}

{*a c d*}

{*a c e*}

{*a d e*}

Next, consider all combinations including *b*, aside from those already accounted for (in other words, move to the right only):

{*b c d*}

{*b c e*}

{*b d e*}

Next, consider all combinations including *c*, aside from those already accounted for (in other words, move to the right only):

{*c d e*}

All three-member combinations including *d* and *e* have already been accounted for. Thus, there are a total of 10 possible three-member combinations from Set 1. Similarly, from Set 2 there are a total of three possible two-member combinations:

{*x y*}

{*x z*}

{*y z*}

Therefore, the total number of combinations asked for by the question is 30 ($10 \times 3$).

## Quantitative Ability Lesson 3:
## Mini-Test and Review (Arithmetic)

Today you will apply what you learned from the previous two lessons (Days 6 and 7) to a 20-question mini-test, which includes both Problem Solving and Data Sufficiency questions.

### INSTRUCTIONS

Attempt the following 20 Quantitative questions under simulated exam conditions. After completing the mini-test, review the explanations that follow. Preceding the explanation for each question, the question type and difficulty level are indicated. Because the concepts covered here are relatively basic, this mini-test is a bit easier *overall* than the average difficulty level of a GMAT Quantitative section.

### MINI-TEST (QUANTITATIVE ABILITY)

**Number of questions:** 20
**Suggested Time:** 35 minutes

1. A clerk's salary is $320.00 after a 25% raise. Before the clerk's raise, the supervisor's salary was 50% greater than the clerk's salary. If the supervisor also receives a raise in the same dollar amount as the clerk's raise, what is the supervisor's salary after the raise?

   (A) $370
   (B) $424
   (C) $448
   (D) $480
   (E) $576

2. Which of the following has the largest numerical value?

   (A) $\frac{3}{5}$

   (B) $\frac{2}{3} \times \frac{3}{4}$

   (C) $\sqrt{.25}$

   (D) $.9^2$

   (E) $\frac{.2}{.3}$

3. If $abc \neq 0$, and if $0 < c < b < a < 1$, is $\frac{a^4 b^3 c^2}{b^2 c d^2} < 1$?

   1. $a = \sqrt{d}$

   2. $d > 0$

   (A) Statement 1 alone is sufficient to answer the question, but statement 2 alone is not sufficient

   (B) Statement 2 alone is sufficient to answer the question, but statement 1 alone is not sufficient

   (C) Both statements together are needed to answer the question, but neither statement alone is sufficient to answer the question

   (D) Either statement by itself is sufficient to answer the question

   (E) Not enough facts are given to answer the question

4. $\dfrac{1\frac{1}{8}}{4\frac{1}{8}-3\frac{2}{3}} =$

   (A) $\dfrac{4}{81}$

   (B) $\dfrac{2}{5}$

   (C) $\dfrac{3}{7}$

   (D) $\dfrac{15}{23}$

   (E) $\dfrac{27}{11}$

5. If * represents a digit in the five-digit number 62,*79, what is the value of *?

   1. 62,*79 is a multiple of 3.

   2. The sum of the digits of 62,*79 is divisible by 4.

   (A) Statement 1 alone is sufficient to answer the question, but statement 2 alone is not sufficient

   (B) Statement 2 alone is sufficient to answer the question, but statement 1 alone is not sufficient

   (C) Both statements together are needed to answer the question, but neither statement alone is sufficient to answer the question

   (D) Either statement by itself is sufficient to answer the question

   (E) Not enough facts are given to answer the question

6. If $x$ and $y$ are negative integers, and $x - y = 1$, what is the least possible value of $xy$?

   (A) 0

   (B) 1

   (C) 2

   (D) 3

   (E) 4

7. Diane receives a base weekly salary of $800 plus a 5% commission on sales. In a week in which her sales totaled $8,000, what was the ratio of her total weekly earnings to her commission?

   (A) 2:1

   (B) 3:1

(C) 3:2

(D) 5:2

(E) 8:5

8. Susan has selected exactly three crayons, each a different color, from a crayon box. How many crayon colors were represented in the box before her selection?

   1. Exactly four distinct three-crayon color combinations were represented in the box before Susan selected three crayons.

   2. Just before Susan's selections, the box contained exactly five crayons.

   (A) Statement 1 alone is sufficient to answer the question, but statement 2 alone is not sufficient

   (B) Statement 2 alone is sufficient to answer the question, but statement 1 alone is not sufficient

   (C) Both statements together are needed to answer the question, but neither statement alone is sufficient to answer the question

   (D) Either statement by itself is sufficient to answer the question

   (E) Not enough facts are given to answer the question

9. $\dfrac{\frac{3a^2c^4}{4b^2}}{6ac^2} =$

   (A) $\dfrac{ac^2}{8b^2}$

   (B) $\dfrac{ac^2}{4b^2}$

   (C) $\dfrac{4b^2}{ac^2}$

   (D) $\dfrac{8b^2}{ac^2}$

   (E) $\dfrac{ac^2}{6b^2}$

10. If the product of two integers $x$ and $y$ is negative, what is their difference?

    1. $x + y = 2$

    2. $-3 < x < y$

(A) Statement 1 alone is sufficient to answer the question, but statement 2 alone is not sufficient

(B) Statement 2 alone is sufficient to answer the question, but statement 1 alone is not sufficient

(C) Both statements together are needed to answer the question, but neither statement alone is sufficient to answer the question

(D) Either statement by itself is sufficient to answer the question

(E) Not enough facts are given to answer the question

11. Which of the following is nearest in value to $\sqrt{664} + \sqrt{414}$?

(A) 16

(B) 46

(C) 68

(D) 126

(E) 252

12. The average of six numbers is 19. When you take away one of those numbers, the average of the remaining five numbers is 21. What number did you take away?

(A) 2

(B) 9

(C) 10

(D) 12

(E) 31

13. If $xy \neq 0$, is $x > y$?

1.   $|x| > |y|$

2.   $x = 2y$

(A) Statement 1 alone is sufficient to answer the question, but statement 2 alone is not sufficient

(B) Statement 2 alone is sufficient to answer the question, but statement 1 alone is not sufficient

(C) Both statements together are needed to answer the question, but neither statement alone is sufficient to answer the question

(D) Either statement by itself is sufficient to answer the question

(E) Not enough facts are given to answer the question

14. What is the greatest value of a positive integer $n$ such that $3^n$ is a factor of $18^{15}$?

(A) 15

(B) 18

(C) 30

(D) 33

(E) 45

15. If $x$, $y$, and $z$ are consecutive negative integers, and if $x > y > z$, which of the following must be a positive odd integer?

(A) $xyz$

(B) $x + y + z$

(C) $x - yz$

(D) $x(y + z)$

(E) $(x - y)(y - z)$

16. Three salespeople—A, B, and C—sold a total of 500 products among them during a particular month. During the month, did A sell more products than B sold as well as more products than C sold?

1.   A sold 166 products during the month.

2.   C sold 249 products during the month.

(A) Statement 1 alone is sufficient to answer the question, but statement 2 alone is not sufficient

(B) Statement 2 alone is sufficient to answer the question, but statement 1 alone is not sufficient

(C) Both statements together are needed to answer the question, but neither statement alone is sufficient to answer the question

(D) Either statement by itself is sufficient to answer the question

(E) Not enough facts are given to answer the question

17. If $x < -1$, which of the following is smallest in value?

    (A) $-\dfrac{.9}{x^3}$

    (B) $-\sqrt[3]{x}$

    (C) $\left(\sqrt[3]{x}\right)^2$

    (D) $\dfrac{1}{\sqrt[3]{x}}$

    (E) $x^3$

18. Machine $X$, Machine $Y$, and Machine $Z$ each produce widgets. Machine $Y$'s rate of production is one-third that of Machine $X$, and Machine $Z$'s production rate is twice that of Machine $Y$. If Machine $Y$ can produce 35 widgets per day, how many widgets can the three machines produce per day working simultaneously?

    (A) 105

    (B) 164

    (C) 180

    (D) 210

    (E) 224

19. At a particular ice cream parlor, customers can choose among five different ice cream flavors and can choose either a sugar cone or a waffle cone. Considering both ice cream flavor and cone type, how many distinct triple-scoop cones with three different flavors are available?

    (A) 10

    (B) 15

    (C) 20

    (D) 30

    (E) 35

20. There is enough food at a picnic to feed either 20 adults or 32 children. All adults eat the same amount, and all children eat the same amount. If 15 adults are fed, how many children can still be fed?

    (A) 4

    (B) 6

    (C) 8

    (D) 9

    (E) 10

# Quick Answer Guide

## Mini-Test: Arithmetic

| | | | |
|---|---|---|---|
| 1. | C | 11. | B |
| 2. | D | 12. | B |
| 3. | A | 13. | E |
| 4. | E | 14. | C |
| 5. | C | 15. | E |
| 6. | C | 16. | A |
| 7. | B | 17. | E |
| 8. | C | 18. | D |
| 9. | A | 19. | C |
| 10. | E | 20. | C |

# EXPLANATIONS

### 1. Percent (moderate). Answer: C.

$320 is 125% of the clerk's former salary. Expressed algebraically:

$$320 = 1.25x$$
$$32,000 = 125x$$
$$\$256 = x \text{ (clerk's salary before the raise).}$$

Thus, the clerk received a raise of $64 ($320 − $256). The supervisor's salary before the raise was as follows:

$$\$256 + 50\% \text{ of } \$256 =$$
$$\$256 + \$128 =$$
$$\$384$$

The supervisor received a $64 raise. Thus, the supervisor's salary after the raise is $448 ($384 + $64).

### 2. Equivalent forms of numbers (easier). Answer: D.

Convert all expressions to decimal form:

(A) $\frac{3}{5} = .6$

(B) $\left(\frac{2}{3}\right)\left(\frac{3}{4}\right) = \frac{1}{2} = .5$

(C) $\sqrt{.25} = .5$

(D) $(.9)(.9) = .81$

(E) $\frac{.2}{.3} = \frac{2}{3} \approx .66$

### 3. Exponents (moderate). Answer: A.

Before analyzing the two statements, simplify the fractional expression by canceling $b^2$ and $c$ from both numerator and denominator. The simplified fraction is $\frac{a^4 bc}{d^2}$. Given statement 1, $a^2 = d$. Substituting $a^2$ for $d$ in the fraction: $\frac{a^4 bc}{a^4} = bc$. Given that $b$ and $c$ are both positive but less than 1, $bc < 1$, and the answer to the question is *yes*. Statement 1 alone suffices to answer the question. However, statement 2 alone is insufficient to answer the question. Even if $d$ is greater than zero, statement 2 fails to provide sufficient information to determine the relative values of the numerator and denominator. A sufficiently small $d$-value relative to the values of $a$, $b$, and $c$ results in a quotient greater than 1, whereas a sufficiently large relative $d$-value results in a quotient less than 1.

### 4. Complex fractions (easier). Answer: E.

First, convert all mixed numbers into proper fractions:

$$\frac{\frac{9}{8}}{\frac{33}{8} - \frac{11}{3}}$$

Next, combine the two fractions in the denominator over their lowest common multiple, which is 24:

$$\frac{\frac{9}{8}}{\frac{99}{24} - \frac{88}{24}}$$

$$\frac{\frac{9}{8}}{\frac{99-88}{24}}$$

$$\frac{\frac{9}{8}}{\frac{11}{24}}$$

Eliminate the fractional denominator by multiplying the numerator by the denominator's reciprocal. Then simplify by factoring:

$$\frac{9}{8} \times \frac{24}{11} = \frac{9}{1} \times \frac{3}{11} = \frac{27}{11}$$

### 5. Integers (moderate). Answer: C.

If the sum of the digits of a number is divisible by 3, the number is also divisible by 3. The sum of the digits in the number 62,*79, excluding *, is 24. Thus, if the number is a multiple of (divisible by) 3, * = 0, 3, 6, or 9. Thus, statement 1 alone is insufficient to answer the question. Given statement 2, * = 0, 4, or 8. Thus, statement 2 alone is insufficient to answer

the question. Statements 1 and 2 together establish that * = 0, and so both statements together suffice to answer the question.

### 6. Integers (easier). Answer: C.

The first step is to solve for $x$: $x = y + 1$. Using negative integers with the smallest absolute value yields the smallest product. $y = -2$, and $x = -1$. Accordingly, $xy = 2$.

### 7. Percent and ratio (moderate). Answer: B.

You can express Diane's commission as (.05)(8,000) = $400. You can add her commission to her base salary as follows: $800 + $400 = $1,200 (total earnings). The ratio of $1,200 to $400 is 3:1.

### 8. Sets (challenging). Answer: C.

Statement 1 alone is insufficient to answer the question. For example, letting letters represent colors, the box could include four crayons and four different colors—A, B, C, and D—offering four distinct three-crayon combinations: {ABC}, {ABD}, {ACD}, and {BCD}. As an alternative, the box could include five crayons but only three different colors—{A,A,A,B,C}—offering four distinct three-crayon combinations: {ABC}, {AAA}, {AAB}, and {AAC}. Statement 2 alone is also insufficient to answer the question. Prior to Susan's selection, the box could have represented anywhere from three to five colors. Again, using letters to represent colors, possible combinations include {AAABC}, {AABCD}, and {ABCDE}, to list just a few. Together, statements 1 and 2 suffice to answer the question. Exactly three colors must be represented in a box of five crayons offering exactly four three-crayon combinations. Again, using letters to represent colors, the configuration must be {AAABD}. All other five-crayon configurations of three or more colors offer too many three-crayon color combinations. The closest is {A,A,B,B,C}, which offers five combinations: {AAB}, {AAC}, {ABC}, {ABB}, and {BBC}.

### 9. Exponents (easier). Answer: A.

You can simplify by multiplying the numerator fraction by the reciprocal of the denominator:

$$\frac{3a^2c^4}{4b^2} \times \frac{1}{6ac^2}$$

Factor out 3, $a$, and $c^2$ from both numerator and denominator:

$$\frac{ac^2}{4b^2} \times \frac{1}{2} = \frac{ac^2}{8b^2}$$

### 10. Integers (moderate). Answer: E.

Given $xy < 0$, either $x$ or $y$ (but not both) must be negative. Despite this restriction, statement 1 alone is insufficient to answer the question because it specifies one equation in two variables. Statement 2 alone is also insufficient. Although $x$ must equal either $-2$ or $-1$ ($x$ must be a negative integer), $y$ could be any positive integer. Considering statements 1 and 2 together, because there are two possible values of $x$ ($-2$ and $-1$) in the equation $x + y = 2$, the difference between $x$ and $y$ could be either 4 or 6. Thus, statements 1 and 2 together are insufficient to answer the question.

### 11. Roots (easier). Answer: B.

You need not calculate either root because the question asks for an approximation. The number 664 is slightly greater than 625, which is $25^2$. The number 414 is slightly greater than 400, which is equal to $20^2$. Thus, the sum of the terms is just over 45 (approximately 46).

### 12. Arithmetic mean (moderate). Answer: B.

You can solve this problem quickly if you simply compare the sums. Before you take away the sixth number, the sum of the numbers is 114 ($6 \times 19$). After you take away the sixth number, the sum of the remaining numbers is 105 ($5 \times 21$). The difference between the two sums is 9, which is the value of the number that you took away.

### 13. Absolute value (moderate). Answer: E.

You must consider both positive and negative values for $x$ and $y$. Given $|x| > |y|$, an $x$-value of either 4 or $-4$ and a $y$-value of 2, for example, satisfies the inequality but results in two different answers to the question. Thus statement 1 alone is insufficient to answer the question. Similarly, given $x = 2y$, if you use negative values for both $x$ and $y$ (for example,

$x = -4$ and $y = -2$), the answer to the question is *no*; however, if you use positive values (for example, $x = 4$ and $y = 2$), the answer to the question is *yes*. Thus, statement 2 alone is insufficient. Statements 1 and 2 together are still insufficient. For example, if $x = -4$ and $y = -2$, both statements 1 and 2 are satisfied, $x < y$, and the answer to the question is *no*. However, if $x = 4$ and $y = 2$, both statements 1 and 2 are satisfied, but $x > y$, and the answer to the question is *yes*.

### 14. Exponents (challenging). Answer: C.

$$18^{15} = 3^{15} \times 3^{15} \times 2^{15} = 3^{30} \times 2^{15}$$

$3^{30}$ is clearly greater in value than $2^{15}$. Thus, the greatest value of $n$ is 30.

### 15. Integers (moderate). Answer: E.

Given that $x$, $y$, and $z$ are consecutive negative integers, either one integer is odd or two integers are odd. Also, a negative number multiplied by a negative number yields a positive number. With this in mind, consider each answer choice in turn:

   (A) $xyz$ must be negative and even.

   (B) $x + y + z$ must be negative; however, whether answer B is odd or even depends on whether one or two of the three integers are odd.

   (C) $x - yz$ must be negative (because $yz$, a positive number, is subtracted from the negative number $x$). However, whether answer C is odd or even depends on whether one or two of the three integers are odd. $yz$ must be even; however, $x$ could either be even or odd.

   (D) $(y + z)$ must be negative and odd. Thus, the product of $x$ and $(y + z)$ must be positive (either odd or even).

   (E) $(x - y)$ must be odd and positive. $(y - z)$ must be odd and positive, because $y > z$. The product of the terms must therefore be odd and positive.

### 16. Proportion (easier). Answer: A.

Given that a total of 500 products were sold, statement 1 alone suffices to answer the question. If A sold 166 products, A sold just less than one-third of the total number. Either B or C must sell more than one-third, and the answer to the question is *no*.

Statement 2 alone is insufficient to answer the question. If C sold 249 products, A could have sold anywhere from 0 to 251 products; if A sold either 250 or 251 products, A also sold more products than either B or C. However, if A sold 0–249 products, A did not sell more products than B or C.

## 17. Roots/Exponents (moderate). Answer: E.

From the largest to smallest (left to right on the number line), the order is: (B), (A), (D), (C), (E). (B) must be a positive number greater than 1. (A) must be a positive non-integer between zero and 1. (D) must be a negative non-integer between zero and –1. (C) must be greater than (to the right of) $x$, between $x$ and –1 on the number line. (E) must be smaller than $x$ (to the left of $x$ on the number line).

## 18. Ratio (moderate). Answer: D.

The ratio of $X$'s rate to $Y$'s rate is 3 to 1, and the ratio of $Y$'s rate to $Z$'s rate is 1 to 2. You can express the ratio among all three as 3:1:2 ($x$:$y$:$z$). Accordingly, $Y$'s production accounts for one-sixth of the total widgets that all three machines can produce per day. Given that $Y$ can produce 35 widgets per day, all three machines can produce $(35)(6) = 210$ widgets per day.

## 19. Sets (moderate). Answer: C.

{A, B, C, D, E} represents the set of ice cream flavors. Ten triple-scoop combinations are available: {ABC}, {ABD}, {ABE}, {ACD}, {ACE}, {ADE}, {BCD}, {BCE}, {BDE}, and {CDE}. Each of these combinations is available on either of the two cone types. Thus, the total number of distinct ice cream cones is 20.

## 20. Proportion (moderate). Answer: C.

If 15 adults are fed, three-fourths of the food is gone. One-fourth of the food will feed $\left(\frac{1}{4}\right)(32)$, or 8, children.

## Day 9

# Sentence Correction Lesson 1: Question Format and Strategies— Grammar Lesson (Part 1)

### Today's Topics:

1. Sentence Correction at a glance
2. Anatomy of a Sentence Correction problem
3. Ten tips for handling Sentence Correction problems
4. Testworthy Rules of Grammer
5. What's *not* covered in Sentence Correction problems
6. The sentence as a unit
7. Distinguishing adjectives and adverbs
8. Adjectives with linking verbs
9. Comparative and superlative adjectives
10. Personal pronouns and case
11. Relative pronouns

Today you will familiarize yourself with the format of Sentence Correction problems and learn some basic strategies for handling these problems. Then you will examine specific rules of English grammar and guidelines for effective sentences as tested by GMAT Sentence Correction problems.

## SENTENCE CORRECTION AT A GLANCE

**Number of questions:** 14–15 (11–12 scored questions, 3–4 pretest questions)
**Suggested time per question:** 1–1$\frac{1}{2}$ minutes

**Directions provided on the test:** "In each of the following sentences, some part of the sentence or the entire sentence is underlined. Beneath each sentence you will find five ways of phrasing the underlined part. The first of these repeats the original; the other four are different. If you think the original is the best of these responses, choose the first response; otherwise, choose one of the others. Select the best version.

"This is a test of correctness and effectiveness of expression. In choosing answers, follow the requirements of standard written English; that is, pay attention to grammar, choice of words, and sentence construction. Choose the answer that produces the most effective sentence; this answer should be clear and exact, without awkwardness, ambiguity, redundancy, or grammatical error."

**This section tests your ability to distinguish between:**

- Correct and incorrect English grammar, according to the requirements of standard written English

- Awkward and effective sentence construction

- Ambiguous and clear sentences, in terms of how effectively they convey their intended meaning

- Proper and improper use of English words and idiomatic phrases

**Primary areas tested:**
- The sentence as a unit

- Adjectives and adverbs

- Proper pronoun case

- Subject-verb agreement

- Pronoun-antecedent agreement

- Verb forms (tense, voice, and mood)

- Pronoun reference

- Misplaced parts and dangling modifiers

- Subordination and coordination

- Parallelism

- Diction (word usage and idioms)

**Specific areas not tested:**
- Punctuation (except comma placement)

- Jargon, slang, and colloquialisms

- Terminology of English grammar

- Vocabulary

- First- and second-person pronoun case (infrequently tested)

# ANATOMY OF A SENTENCE CORRECTION PROBLEM

Each Sentence Correction problem includes three distinct elements: the sentence, the first answer choice, and the remaining answer choices.

## The Sentence

Each Sentence Correction problem begins with a sentence. Part or all of this sentence is underlined. The sentences are formal in style (albeit not necessarily correct), not conversational. Most of the sentences involve topics from a variety of academic disciplines; some sentences, however, involve topics of more general or popular interest.

## The First Answer Choice

The first of the five answer choices merely restates exactly the underlined part of the original sentence; there is no need to read this first answer choice.

## The Remaining Answer Choices

Each of the remaining answer choices presents an alternative to the underlined part (the first answer choice).

## An Example of a Sentence Correction Problem

Example 9-1 shows how these elements come together in a Sentence Correction problem.

**Example 9-1**

Patrice, a virtuoso according to the classical musician community, plays in a unique style of which is all her own, and her playing also embodies a warmth prevalent during the golden age of violin playing.

(A) a virtuoso according to the classical musician community, plays in a unique style of which is all her own, and her playing also embodies

(B) considered a virtuoso by classical musicians, plays in a style all her own, which at the same time embodies

(C) who is regarded by the community of classical musicians as being a virtuoso, plays in a unique style all her own and embodies

(D) regarded by the community of classical musicians as a virtuoso, who plays in a style all her own while at the same time embodying

(E) whom the community of classical musicians would consider to be a virtuoso, plays in a unique style all her own while at the same time embodying

## Analysis of Example 9-1

The original sentence (answer choice A) suffers from the following three problems:

1. The phrase "classical musician community" is confusing. It is unclear whether the adjective "classical" refers to the noun "musician" or to the noun "community." The best answer choice *must* remedy this problem.

2. In the phrase "style of which is," the preposition "of" is superfluous and unnecessary. The idiomatic expression "of which" might be proper in some other context, but is improperly used here. The best answer choice *must* remedy this problem.

3. The sentence intends to convey that, although the warmth of Patrice's playing is reminiscent of a style prevalent during the European golden age, her style is nevertheless distinct and unique in other ways. The original sentence A does not convey this idea as effectively as it could.

B is the best response. It remedies all three problems with the original sentence. Notice that B is not necessarily an ideal or "perfect" sentence. The first clause employs the passive voice ("considered . . . by classical musicians") rather than the preferred active voice ("classical musicians consider"). Nevertheless, B is the best response among the five choices.

C is faulty in two respects. First, the phrase "as being" is an improper idiomatic expression. Second, the word "and" sets up two parallel objects, each of which refers to the subject "Patrice." However, the verb "embodies" should refer to Patrice's playing

style, not to Patrice herself. Using the terminology of English grammar, C is said to suffer from faulty parallelism in grammatical construction.

D is not a complete sentence. The subject "Patrice" is followed by two modifying clauses (the first begins with "regarded," and the second begins with "who"). Thus, although the three problems present in the original sentence are absent in D, answer choice D is clearly incorrect.

E suffers from two problems. First, the verb "would consider" is a subjunctive (hypothetical) form of the infinitive "to consider." The original sentence, however, expresses the community's view of Patrice as factual. Thus, E distorts the intended meaning of the original sentence. Second, the word "embodying" improperly refers to Patrice instead of her playing style.

---

# TEN TIPS FOR HANDLING SENTENCE CORRECTION PROBLEMS

---

### Tip 1: Pick Up the Pace

Most test takers need less time to answer the average Sentence Correction problem than they do to answer a Critical Reasoning or Reading Comprehension question. Thus, although you will have 75 minutes to attempt a total of 41 Verbal questions, plan on devoting an average of only 60 to 75 seconds to each Sentence Correction problem and more time to the other Verbal questions. (If you are particularly weak in the area of Sentence Correction, you may wish to spend as much as 90 seconds on each Sentence Correction problem.)

### Tip 2: Take Your Time in Reading Each Response

The qualitative distinction between the best response and another response can be quite subtle. If you hurry through a Sentence Correction problem, you can easily overlook the distinction. The key might lie, for example, in the inclusion or exclusion of one word. Take your time, and read with great precision and care.

## Tip 3: Read *All* the Answer Choices

More than one answer choice might be grammatically correct. Thus, don't hasten to select a response merely on this basis. Another response might be clearer or less awkward and therefore better. Read them all!

## Tip 4: Trust Your Ear

If a response doesn't sound right as you read it in the context of the sentence, eliminate it. There's no need to analyze it any further.

## Tip 5: Don't Let Nonsensical Responses Throw You

If a response seems confusing or unclear, don't assume that you are at fault for not understanding the sentence. Some answer choices will simply not make much sense. Don't waste your time analyzing the response to determine why it is grammatically incorrect. Eliminate it!

## Tip 6: Eliminate Responses That Introduce New Errors

At least one or two responses are likely to include one or more grammatical problems apart from the ones in the original sentence. You can eliminate these quickly, without bothering to try them out in the original sentence.

## Tip 7: Eliminate Responses That Change the Meaning of the Original Sentence

If a response alters, distorts, or confuses the original sentence's meaning, it is *not* the best response, even if it is grammatically correct (it probably won't be, anyway).

## Tip 8: Resolve Close Calls in Favor of Briefer Responses

If you are undecided between two responses, resolve in favor of the briefer (more concisely worded) response. However, don't misuse this approach. Don't assume that shorter responses are automatically better than longer ones. Apply this technique only when your choice comes down to a coin flip.

## Tip 9: Avoid Hyper-Correction

Probably the most common Sentence Correction mistake among GMAT test takers is the tendency to insist on finding fault with the original sentence. Keep in mind that in approximately one out of five Sentence Correction problems, the original sentence is the best among the five choices.

## Tip 10: Verify Your Response Before Moving On

Before confirming your response, check your selection by reading the entire sentence, filling in your chosen response. If it sounds right, confirm your response and move on.

---

## TESTWORTHY RULES OF GRAMMAR

For the remainder of today's lesson, you examine the most "testworthy" rules of English grammar and guidelines for effective sentences and proper diction. (This lesson continues tomorrow.) This review is not intended to be comprehensive. Some topics are treated in detail, others are discussed only briefly, and others are excluded entirely, all depending on the extent to which the topics are tested in GMAT Sentence Correction problems.

Most native English speakers should find these lessons sufficient for the GMAT. However, non-native English speakers and native English speakers who are particularly weak in this area should supplement these lessons with additional study. The following resources are highly recommended:

- *Prentice Hall Reference Guide to Grammar and Usage,* by Muriel Harris, published by Prentice Hall.

- *Harbrace College Handbook,* by John C. Hodges, Winifred Bryan Horner, and Suzanne Strobeck Webb, 12th Edition, published by Harcourt Brace Johanovich, College & School Division.

- *The Macmillan College Handbook,* by Gerald Henry Levin, 2nd Edition, published by Macmillan College Division.

## What's *Not* Covered in Sentence Correction Problems?

In Sentence Correction problems, some concepts get more emphasis than others, and some are not tested at all. Specifically, Sentence Correction items do not test the following:

- *Punctuation.* The GMAT does not test rules for using periods, colons, semicolons, dashes, hyphens, quotation marks, apostrophes, and so forth. The exam does test rules for using *commas,* but only indirectly. For example, a Sentence Correction answer choice might be incorrect because misplaced commas create confusion or ambiguity as to the sentence's meaning.

- *Jargon, slang, and colloquialisms.* Sentence Correction problems do not require you to distinguish between formal standard written English and less formal writing—including jargon, slang, and colloquialisms.

- *Vocabulary.* Sentence Correction problems focus on grammar and usage of ordinary words, not on vocabulary. You need not develop an erudite vocabulary or learn long lists of obscure words just for the GMAT.

- *First- and second-person pronouns.* First-person pronouns include *I, my, mine, me, we, our, ours,* and *us.* Second-person pronouns include such words as *you, your,* and *yours.* Sentence Correction problems infrequently test these pronouns mainly because the sentences included in these problems are academic in nature and do not include self-references or dialogue.

## The Sentence as a Unit

### Comma Splices and Fused (or Run-on) Sentences

A *main clause* is any clause that can stand alone as a complete sentence. Do not link two sentences (main clauses) without any punctuation (the result is a *fused sentence*) or with only a comma (the result is a *comma splice*). If you use a comma between two main clauses, always follow the comma with one of the following words: *and, or, not, but, yet, for,* or *so.* For example:

> **Fused sentence:** Dan ran out of luck Mike continued to win.
>
> **Comma splice:** Dan ran out of luck, Mike continued to win.
>
> **Proper:** Dan ran out of luck, but Mike continued to win.

### Sentence Fragments

A sentence must include both a subject and a predicate; otherwise, it is a *sentence fragment* and cannot stand alone. Sentence fragments are usually easy to recognize. An especially long sentence fragment, however, can escape detection if you are not reading carefully. For example:

> Although the wind died down, from one corner of the attic above the garage, nevertheless the distinctive whistling sound as well as a draft.

### Subordination Versus Coordination

An effective sentence places appropriate grammatical emphasis in its different parts. Main ideas should receive greater grammatical emphasis than dependent elements. You can achieve *subordination* of a dependent clause to the main clause by using the following:

- Words modifying relative pronouns: *which, who,* and *that*

- Words establishing *time* relationship: *before, after, as,* and *since*

- Words establishing a *causal* relationship: *because* and *since*

- Words of *admission* or *concession*: *although, though,* and *despite*

- Words indicating *place*: *where* and *wherever*

- Words of *condition*: *if* and *unless*

You can achieve *coordination* of two clauses that should receive equal grammatical emphasis by using such words as *and, but,* and *so.* Do not use two main clauses linked by coordinating words where subordination is called for to convey the intended meaning. For example:

**Confusing:** Jose and Victor were identical twins, *and* they had completely different ambitions.

**Better:** *Although* they were identical twins, Jose and Victor had completely different ambitions.

**Better:** *Although* Jose and Victor were identical twins, they had completely different ambitions.

Main clauses linked by coordinating words should be similar in length to suggest grammatical balance. If one main clause is much shorter than another, reconstruct the sentence by *subordinating* the shorter clause to the longer one. Here are a few examples:

**Unbalanced:** Julie and Sandy were the first two volunteers for the fund-raising drive, *and* they are twins.

**Better:** Julie and Sandy, *who* are twins, were the first two volunteers for the fund-raising drive.

**Unbalanced:** Julie and Sandy, *who* are twins, are volunteers.

**Balanced:** Julie and Sandy are twins, *and* they are volunteers.

Stringing together two or more subordinate clauses usually results in an awkward and confusing sentence. Reconstruct such sentences to either separate or assimilate the clauses. For example:

**Awkward:** Barbara's academic major is history, *which* is a very popular course of study among liberal arts students, *who* are also contributing to the popularity of political science as a major.

**Better:** Barbara's academic major is history, which along with political science is a very popular course of study among liberal arts students.

## DISTINGUISHING ADJECTIVES AND ADVERBS

*Adjectives* are used to modify (qualify or restrict the meaning of) nouns and pronouns. *Adverbs* are used to modify verbs, verbals, adjectives, and other adverbs. Here are a few examples:

- The pencil was *extremely* sharp. (The adverb "extremely" modifies the adjective "sharp," which in turn modifies the noun "pencil.")

- The movie ended *suddenly*. (The adverb "suddenly" modifies the verb "ended.")

- The Canadian figure skater can jump *particularly* high. (The adverb "particularly" modifies the adverb "high," which in turn modifies the verb "jump.")

Although adverbs usually end in *ly*, whereas adjectives do not, there are many exceptions. For example:

- *Likely* reason (adjective)

- Walked *fast* (adverb)

## ADJECTIVES WITH LINKING VERBS

Be sure to use the appropriate modifier after verbs such as *look, feel, sound, smells,* and *tastes,* which you can use either as *action* verbs or as *linking* verbs. Here are two related examples:

- He looks *awful*. (The verb "looks" links the subject "he" to its complement, the adjective "awful.")

- He looks *awfully* good. (The adverb "awfully" modifies the adjective "good," which is the complement of the subject "he.")

## ADJECTIVES: COMPARITIVES AND SUPERLATIVES

Comparatives and superlatives are usually created either by adding an *er* (or *ier*) or *est* (or *iest*) to the end of an adjective or by preceding the adjective with such words as *more, less, most,* or *least.* Do not use both methods together. Here's an example:

**Proper:** Francis is *more healthy* than Greg.

**Proper:** Francis is *healthier* than Greg.

**Improper:** Francis is *more healthier* than Greg.

Use the *comparative* form of an adjective or adverb to compare *only two* members of a class. Use the *superlative* form to compare *three or more members* of a class. For most adjectives and adverbs, the comparative form simply adds *er* to the end of the word, whereas the superlative forms add *est*. The following table lists comparative and superlative forms of various adjectives and adverbs.

| Comparative Form | Superlative Form |
| --- | --- |
| brighter | brightest |
| greater | greatest |
| fewer | fewest |
| lesser | least |
| more | most |
| better | best |

## PERSONAL PRONOUNS AND CASE

*Case* refers to the inflectional form of a pronoun or possessive noun. There are three cases: *subjective* (or *nominative*) case, *possessive* (or *genitive*) case, and *objective* case. *Reflexive* pronouns (or *self* pronouns) are used as objects in referring to the sentence's subject. The following table indicates the proper personal pronouns for each case.

| | Subjective Case | Possessive Case | Objective Case | Objective Case (Reflexive) |
| --- | --- | --- | --- | --- |
| First-person singular | I | my, mine | me | myself |
| First-person plural | we | our, ours | us | ourselves |
| Second-person singular | you | your, yours | you | yourself |
| Second-person plural | you | your, yours | you | yourselves |
| Third-person singular | he, she, it | his, her, hers, its | him, her, it | himself, herself, itself |
| Third-person plural | they | their, theirs | them | themselves |

## Subjective Case

You should use a pronoun's subjective case as the subject of a verb, as the subject complement (following a linking verb), and when comparing subjects of understood (unstated) verbs. Here are three examples (one of each):

- *She* flew in from the east coast. ("She" is the subject of "flew.")

- It was *she* who flew in from the east coast. (The verb "was" links the subject "It" and its complement, "she.")

- *She* flew further than *he* [flew]. ("He" is the subject of the understood verb, "flew.")

## Possessive Case

The possessive case is most frequently used to indicate *possession,* although the case is also used to indicate *origin* or *source.* Here are three examples (one of each):

- The baseball players took *their* respective turns at bat. (Each player *possesses* a turn at bat.)

- Baseball's continuing popularity as a sport lies in *its* tradition. (Tradition is the *origin* of baseball's popularity.)

- *His* hitting a single resulted in more runs than his hitting a home run. (The single was the *source* of more runs.)

Use the possessive case immediately before a *gerund* (a verb ending in *ing* and used as a noun). Here are a few examples:

- I admire *their* (not *them*) *cooperating* with one another.

- *Its showing* its teeth indicates that the dog is afraid.

## Objective Case

You should use the objective case for objects of verbs, prepositions, and infinitives, as well as when comparing objects of understood (unstated) verbs. Here are some examples:

- Because he did not *see her*, he walked right *by her.* ("Her" is the object of the verb "see" and the object of the preposition "by.")

- He hoped *to see her* as he walked by the restaurant. ("Her" is the object of the infinitive "to see.")

- In looking for his mother and father, he noticed her before [*noticing*] *him.* ("Him" is the object of the understood verb "noticing.")

Use the objective case for either the subject object of an infinitive (a verb preceded by *to*):

- The boss expects *him to write* the proposal. ("Him" is the subject of the infinitive "to write.")

- All employees expect the boss *to promote* either *him* or Carla. ("Him" is the object of "to promote.")

## Reflexive Pronouns

As noted earlier, reflexive pronouns are used as objects (in the objective case) in referring to a sentence's subject (that is, to *self*). Be careful not to use these pronouns in any other context. Here's an example of a reflexive pronoun used properly:

In striving to understand others, we also learn more about *ourselves* (not *us*).

Be sure to use only proper (standard) versions of these reflexive pronouns:

- *Ourselves,* not *ourself* or *our own selves*

- *Themselves,* not *theirselves, theirself, themself, their own self,* or *their own selves*

Here are a few sentences that illustrate this point:

- We have only *ourselves* (not *ourself*) to blame for the plight of the endangered black thrush bird.

- Musicians cannot please their audiences and themselves (not *theirselves*) all the time.

## RELATIVE PRONOUNS

A *relative pronoun* introduces a subordinate clause and should relate to a noun in the preceding clause. (You examine subordinate clauses in detail on day 10.) Words that can function as relative pronouns include *which, who, that, whose,* and *whom.*

### Which, Who, and That

Use *which* to refer to things; use *who, whose,* and *whom* to refer to particular persons; and use *that* to refer to either things or to people in general. The following sentences use these relative pronouns properly:

- The third page, *which* had been earmarked, contained several typographical errors.

- The third performer, *whose* name was Amanda, was the best of the group.

- The first department *that* fails to meet its production deadline will be eliminated.

- Employees *that* (or *who*) fail to meet their sales quotas will be fired.

### That and Which

The relative pronouns *that* and *which* are often confused. The choice can greatly affect a sentence's meaning. Consider the first example sentence in the preceding section, along with a variation of that sentence:

- The third page, *which* had been earmarked, contained several typographical errors.

- The third page *that* had been earmarked contained several typographical errors.

The first sentence merely describes the third page as earmarked, whereas the second sentence says that the page containing the errors was the third earmarked page.

### Who and Whom (or Whoever and Whomever)

The relative pronouns *who* and *whom* are often confused. Use *who* and *whoever* in referring to a noun (or pronoun) in the *subject case.* Use *whom* in referring to a noun (or pronoun) in the *object case.* To make sure that you are using these words correctly, isolate the clause containing the relative pronoun, transform the clause into a question, and answer the question using an appropriate pronoun. If you answer the question using a subject-case pronoun, then *who* (or *whoever*) is proper. For example:

- It was the Northerners *who* initiated the battle. (Who initiated the battle? *They* did [subject case].)

- *Whoever* the victor might be deserves the spoils of battle. (Who is the victor? *She* is [subject case].)

- First aid will be available to *whoever* requires it. (Who requires first aid? *He* does [subject case].)

If you answer the question using an object-case pronoun, then *whom* (or *whomever*) is proper. For example:

- The battle was initiated by Sherman, with *whom* the President sided. (With whom did the President side? With *him* [object case].)

- The bloodiest battle was initiated on behalf of those for *whom* life was most precious. (For whom was life most precious? For *them* [object case].)

# Sentence Correction Lesson 2: Grammar Lesson (Part 2)

### Today's Topics:

1. Subject-verb agreement
2. Pronoun-antecedent agreement
3. Verb forms
4. Pronoun reference
5. Misplaced parts and dangling modifiers
6. Parallelism
7. Shifts in mood, voice, tense, and perspective
8. Word usage—the GMAT "hit" list
9. Idioms—the GMAT "hit" list

Today you will examine more specific rules of English grammar and guidelines for effective sentences for GMAT sentence correction problems. You will also review some particularly common (and testworthy) word-usage and idiom problems.

## SUBJECT-VERB AGREEMENT

A verb should agree in number (singular or plural) with its subject. Do not let intervening words and clauses between the subject and its verb mislead you. In all the following sentences, "parade" is the subject of the singular verb "was":

- The parade of cars *was* spectacular.

- The parade as well as the fireworks *was* spectacular.

- The parade, along with the fireworks, *was* spectacular.

- The parade of cars and horses *was* spectacular.

Subjects joined by *and* are usually plural. For example:

- The chorus *and* the introduction *need* improvement.

Subjects joined by *or, either . . . or,* or *neither . . . nor* are usually singular. For example:

- *Either* the chorus or the introduction *needs* improvement.

- *Neither* the chorus *nor* the introduction *needs* improvement.

However, if one subject is singular and one is plural, the verb should agree with the nearer subject. Compare these two sentences, for example:

- Either the rhythm or the *lyrics need* improvement.

- Either the lyrics or the *rhythm needs* improvement.

**91**

Subjects preceded by *every* or *each* call for singular verbs. Here are two examples of each:

- Every possible cause *has* been investigated.

- Every possible *cause* and *suspect was* investigated.

- Each adult and child here *speaks* fluent French.

- Each one of the children here *speaks* fluent French.

A *collective* noun or a noun of *quantity* can call for either a singular verb or a plural verb, depending on whether the noun is used in a singular or plural sense. Here are two examples of each:

- Four years *is* too long to wait. (This sentence uses "four years" in a singular sense.)

- Four years can *pass* by quickly. (This sentence uses "four years" in a plural sense.)

- The majority *favors* the Republican candidate. (This sentence uses "majority" in a singular sense.)

- The majority of the voters here *favor* the Republican candidate. (This sentence uses "majority" in a plural sense.)

A linking verb usually agrees with its subject rather than its complement:

- Unexpected delays *are* the reason for the higher cost.

- The reason for the higher cost *is* unexpected delays.

## PRONOUN-ANTECEDENT AGREEMENT

An *antecedent* is the word (or words) to which a pronoun refers. A pronoun should agree in number with its antecedent. Use singular pronouns in referring to singular antecedents. Use plural pronouns in referring to plural antecedents.

**Singular:** Studying other artists actually helps a young *painter* develop *his* or *her* own style.

**Plural:** Studying other *artists* actually helps young painters develop *their* own style.

Singular pronouns are usually used in referring to such antecedents as *anyone, each, either, neither, one, everyone,* and *everybody.* For example:

- *Neither* of the two countries imposes an income tax on *its* citizens.

- *One* cannot be too kind to *oneself.*

Use either singular or plural pronouns to refer to *collective nouns,* depending on whether the collective noun is used in a singular or plural sense. For example:

- The legislature hesitates to punish *its* (not *their*) own members for ethics violations.

- The planning committee recessed, but Jack continued to work without *them* (not *it*).

## VERB FORMS

### Tense

*Tense* refers to how a verb's form indicates time. The following indicates the six tenses and their corresponding verb forms, using the singular form of the confusing verb *to have* as an example:

- **Simple present:** He *has* enough money to buy a new car.

- **Simple past:** He *had* enough money after he was paid to by a new car.

- **Simple future:** He *will have* enough money after he is paid to buy a new car.

- **Present perfect:** He *has had* enough food but *has* continued to eat anyway.

- **Past perfect:** He *had had* enough food but *had* kept eating anyway.

- **Future perfect:** He *will have had* enough food once he *has* finished eating the dessert.

Use single-word verbs for the simple tenses. Precede a verb with *has* (or *have*) in the present-perfect tense, *had* in the past-perfect tense, and phrases such as *will have* in the future-perfect tense. Be careful not to mix or shift tenses within a sentence. Here are a few examples of *improper* shifting of tense:

- He *will have* enough money after he *was* paid.

- He *had had* enough food but *continued* to eat anyway.

- He *had* enough food but *will continue* to eat anyway.

With many verbs, you use the same form for all tenses except that you add *ed* for the past tenses, as in *walk, walked*. However, other verbs use distinctive forms for different tenses, such as *see, saw,* and *seen*. It is impossible to list here all the various distinctive forms for commonly used verbs. Use your ear to determine whether the form sounds correct. Non-native English speakers should review verb forms by consulting a comprehensive English grammar text.

## Active and Passive Voices

*Transitive* verbs are verbs with direct objects. *Intransitive* verbs do not take objects. For example:

**Transitive:** The student read the book. ("Book" is the object of the transitive verb "read.")

**Intransitive:** The student was tired of reading the book. ("Tired" is the subject complement of the subject "student," not the object of the intransitive linking verb "was.")

You can usually convert the object of a transitive *active* verb to the subject of a transitive passive verb. For example:

**Active voice:** Computers *perform* repetitive tasks tirelessly.

**Passive voice:** Repetitive tasks *are performed* tirelessly by computers.

While grammatically correct, the passive voice is somewhat awkward; accordingly, the active voice is usually preferred. In some instances, however, the passive voice might be appropriate for impact or effect; for example:

Sunrise over the Tetons *is surpassed* in beauty only *by* the sun itself.

## Progressive Verb Forms

You use *progressive* verb forms to suggest an action in progress by adding an *ing* to the verb and preceding it with a participle such as *am, is,* or *be*. Here are a few examples:

- I must *be going*.

- She *is preparing* a feast.

- They *have been planning* the party for some time.

You can use progressive verb forms in any of the six tenses:

**Present:** She is preparing a feast.

**Past:** She was preparing a feast.

**Future:** She will be preparing a feast.

**Present perfect:** She has been preparing a feast.

**Past perfect:** She had been preparing a feast.

**Future perfect:** She will have been preparing a feast.

Infinitives and verbals (clauses with gerunds) can also take the progressive form as well as more than one tense (but not all tenses). As with ordinary verbs, be careful not to mix tenses or shift from one tense to another. Here are four sentences that use progressive verb forms properly:

**Present:** *To go* to war is to travel to hell.

**Present perfect:** *To have gone* to war is *to have traveled* to hell.

**Present:** *Seeing* the obstacle *allows* him to alter his course.

**Present perfect:** *Having seen* the obstacle *would have allowed* him to alter his course.

## The Subjunctive Mood

*Mood* (or *mode*) refers to the manner in which the action or state in a sentence is conceived, as indicated by verb form. The English language includes three moods: indicative, imperative, and subjunctive.

The *indicative* mood is used to make factual statements and ask factual questions. This is the most commonly used mood.

The *imperative* mood is used to issue commands, give directions, or make requests, as in the following examples:

- Hurry up.

- Please hold your applause.

GMAT sentence correction problems do not usually use the imperative mood.

The *subjunctive* mood is used to express a wish or a contrary-to-fact condition. Subjunctive verb forms can be tricky because they are distinctive and idiomatic. (As a result, this is one of the GMAT's favorite areas of grammar.) Here are a few examples of the use of the subjunctive:

- I wish it *were* earlier.

- Suppose he *were* to speed up suddenly.

- If the college had not increased its tuition, I *would* have enrolled.

You can also properly use *should* and *had* in the subjunctive mood to express a contrary-to-fact condition, as in the following examples:

- *Should* he drive too fast, he would surely have an accident.

- *Had* he driven slower, he would have avoided an accident.

The subjunctive mood is also properly used in clauses of recommendation, request, suggestion, or demand using the word *that*:

- Ann suggested *that we go* to the Chinese restaurant.

- I insist *that you be* quiet.

## PRONOUN REFERENCE

A pronoun should refer clearly to its intended antecedent (the noun or noun clause to which the pronoun refers). One way to avoid confusion as to a pronoun's antecedent is to place the pronoun as near as possible to its antecedent (as in the second sentence that follows). Another way to avoid confusion is to replace the pronoun with its antecedent (as in the third sentence that follows):

**Unclear:** Minutes before Kevin's meeting with Paul, *his* wife called with the bad news. (It is unclear whose wife called.)

**Clear:** *Kevin's* wife called with the bad news minutes before his meeting with Paul.

**Clear:** Minutes before Kevin's meeting with Paul, *Kevin's* wife called with the bad news.

Be particularly careful with pronoun references to antecedents in the possessive case. For example:

**Unclear:** Although *Frank's intentions* were honorable, *he* was misunderstood.

**Clear:** Although Frank had honorable intentions, he was misunderstood.

Pronouns such as *it, you, that,* and *one* are often used in a vague or obscure manner, without clear reference to an antecedent. Here are some examples:

**Vague:** When one dives in without looking ahead, *you* never know what will happen. (It is unclear whether "you" refers to the diver or to the broader *one*.)

**Clear:** *One* never knows what will happen when *one* dives in without looking ahead.

**Clear:** When *you* dive in without looking ahead, *you* never know what will happen.

**Vague:** When the planets are out of alignment, *it* can be disastrous. ("It" has no antecedent.)

**Clear:** Disaster can occur when the planets are out of alignment.

## MISPLACED PARTS AND DANGLING MODIFIERS

### Misplaced Modifiers

A *modifier* is a word or group of words that restricts, describes, or qualifies another word or group of words. Modifiers include prepositional phrases, adjectives, and adverbs, as well as adjective, adverbial, and subordinate clauses. You should usually place modifiers as near as possible to the word or words that they modify, as long as the resulting sentence is idiomatically correct. Otherwise, it might be unclear as to whom or what the modifier refers. Here are two examples:

**Misplaced:** *Nearly dead*, the police finally found the victim.

**Better:** The police finally found *the victim, who was nearly dead*.

**Unclear:** Bill punched Carl while wearing a mouth protector.

**Clear:** While wearing a mouth protector, Bill punched Carl.

Merely joining related parts, however, does not necessarily ensure that you are clearly conveying the intended meaning. Look at these two sets of examples:

**Unclear:** *Nathan* can read the newspaper and can shave *without his glasses*. (It's unclear as to whether "without his glasses" refers only to "shave" or to both "shave" and "read the newspaper.")

**Unclear:** *Without his glasses*, Nathan can read the newspaper and can shave. (This version implies that these are the only two tasks that Nathan can perform without his glasses.)

**Clear:** *Even without his glasses*, Nathan can read the newspaper and shave.

**Unclear:** Exercising *frequently* contributes to a sense of well being.

**Clear:** *Frequent* exercise contributes to a sense of well being.

**Clear:** Exercising contributes *frequently* to a sense of well being.

Modifiers such as *almost, nearly, hardly, just*, and *only* should immediately precede the words that they modify, even if the sentence sounds correct with the parts separated. For example:

**Misplaced:** Their one-year old child *almost* weighs *40 pounds*.

**Better:** Their one-year old child weighs *almost 40 pounds*.

Note the position of *only* in the following sentences:

**Clear:** *Only the assistant* was able to detect obvious errors.

**Unclear:** The assistant was *only* able to detect obvious errors.

**Unclear:** The assistant was able to *only* detect *obvious errors*.

**Clear:** The assistant was able to detect *only obvious errors*.

## Split Infinitives

An *infinitive* is the plural form of a transitive (action) verb, preceded by *to*. Do not separate *to* from its corresponding verb. Here are two improper examples (the second is a bit more subtle):

- The executive was compelled *to*, by greed and ambition, *work* more and more hours each day.

- Meteorologists have been known *to* inaccurately *predict* snowstorms.

## Split Clauses or Sentence Bases

Do not split a sentence base or core (the sentence stripped of its modifying phrases). Also, do not split any clause that you should treat as a single grammatical unit. Here are some examples:

**Split:** The value of the dollar *is not*, relative to other currencies, *rising* universally.

**Better:** The value of the dollar *is not rising* universally relative to other currencies.

**Split:** The government's goal this year *is to provide* for its poorest residents *an economic safety net*.

**Split:** *The government's goal* is to provide an economic safety net *this year* for its poorest residents.

**Better:** The government's goal this year is to provide an economic safety net for its poorest residents.

## Dangling Modifiers

A *dangling modifier* is one that fails to relate clearly to any particular word or group of words in the sentence. Correct dangling-modifier problems by reconstructing the sentence. For example:

**Dangling:** *By imposing* artificial price restrictions on oil suppliers, these suppliers will be forced to lower production costs. (This sentence makes no reference to the person or entity imposing the restrictions.)

**Better:** Imposition of artificial price restrictions on oil suppliers will force these suppliers to lower production costs.

**Dangling:** *Set by an arsonist,* firefighters were unable to save the burning building. (This sentence makes no reference to whatever was set by an arsonist.)

**Better:** Firefighters were unable to save the burning building from *the fire set by an arsonist.*

## PARALLELISM

Use the same (or *parallel*) construction for all sentence elements that are grammatically equal.

Be sure to balance one prepositional phrase with another. For example:

**Faulty:** Flight 82 travels first to Boise, then to Denver, then Salt Lake City. (*To* precedes only the first two of the three cities in this list.)

**Parallel:** Flight 82 travels first to Boise, then Denver, then Salt Lake City.

**Parallel:** Flight 82 travels first to Boise, then to Denver, then to Salt Lake City.

Do not mix gerunds with other constructions:

**Faulty:** Being understaffed, lack of funding, and being outpaced by competitors soon resulted in the fledgling company's going out of business.

**Parallel:** Understaffed, underfunded, and outpaced by competitors, the fledgling company soon went out of business.

**Parallel:** As a result of understaffing, insufficient funding, and outpacing on the part of its competitors, the fledgling company soon went out of business.

Apply articles and modifying words consistently:

**Faulty:** Among *the* mountains, *the* sea, and desert, we humans have yet to explore fully only the sea.

**Parallel:** Among *the* mountains, sea, and desert, we humans have yet to explore fully only the sea.

**Parallel:** Among *the* mountains, *the* sea, and *the* desert, we humans have yet to explore fully only the sea.

In some instances, restating the modifier for each element results in confusion and unnecessary wordiness. In other instances, repeating the modifier might be necessary to achieve clarity. For example:

**Awkward:** Some pachyderms can go for days at a time without water or without food or sleep.

**Better:** Some pachyderms can go for days at a time without water, food, or sleep.

**Unclear:** Going for broke and broke usually carry identical consequences.

**Clear:** Going for broke and going broke usually carry identical consequences.

Pay particular attention to parallelism when dealing with *correlatives* such as the following:

- Either . . . or . . .

- Neither . . . nor . . .

- Both . . . and . . .

- Not only . . . but also . . .

The element immediately following the first correlative term should be parallel in construction to the element following the second term. For example:

**Faulty:** Those wishing to participate should *either* contact us by telephone *or* should send e-mail to us.

**Parallel (but repetitive):** Those wishing to participate *either should* contact us by telephone *or should* send e-mail to us.

**Parallel:** Those wishing to participate should *either* contact us by telephone *or* send e-mail to us.

## SHIFTS IN MOOD, VOICE, TENSE, AND PERSPECTIVE

An effective sentence is internally consistent in mood, voice, tense, and perspective. Avoid shifts between the *indicative* and *subjunctive* moods. For example:

**Inconsistent:** If the rally *were to turn* violent, many innocent bystanders *will be* injured.

**Consistent (subjunctive):** If the rally *were to turn* violent, many innocent bystanders *would* be injured.

**Consistent (indicative):** If the rally *turns* violent, many innocent bystanders *will be* injured.

Also avoid shifts between the active and passive voices. For example:

**Inconsistent:** The theater-goers were entertained by the first act of the play, but the second act offended them.

**Consistent (passive):** The theater-goers were entertained by the first act of the play, but were offended by the second act.

**Consistent (active):** The play's first act entertained the theater-goers, but the second act offended them.

Also avoid needless shifts in tense. For example:

**Inconsistent:** The king's generosity *extends* to his family, but it *did not extend* to his subjects.

**Consistent (present):** The king's generosity *extends* to his family, but it *does not extend* to his subjects.

**Consistent (past):** The king's generosity *extended* to his family, but it *did not extend* to his subjects.

Finally, avoid confusing shifts in time perspective by reconstructing the sentence chronologically. For example:

**Confusing:** Softco *is anticipating* strong sales during the fourth business quarter and *increased* its rate of production last quarter.

**Clear:** Softco *increased* its rate of production last quarter and *is anticipating* strong sales during the fourth quarter.

## WORD USAGE—THE GMAT "HIT" LIST

In GMAT sentence correction problems, words might be used improperly in the context of the sentence or clause in which they appear. A sentence might misuse a word by doing one of the following:

- Confusing the word with another word (often because the two words sound or look similar)

- Distorting the meaning of the word by misapplying it

It is impossible to predict specific words that the GMAT sentence correction problems will "misuse." The best that you can do is to learn those words that are most frequently used (and misused) as well as those that appear most frequently on the GMAT.

### Words Involving Number and Size

Words describing and comparing size, number, and quantity are often misused. Distinguish words used to describe *degree* from those used to describe *number*. The following sentences illustrate the proper use of key words such as *amount, quantity, more, greater, fewer,* and *less*:

- The *amount* (or *quantity*) of salt used in the stew recipe is *greater* (not *more*) than that used in the soup recipe.

- *Less* (or *a smaller amount or quantity of*) salt is used in the soup recipe than in the stew recipe.

- The *size* (not *amount*) of Bigville's population is *greater* (not *more*) than that of Smallville's population.

- The *number* (not *amount*) of people in Smallville is *less* (or *smaller,* not *fewer*) than the number of people in Bigville.

- *Fewer* (not *less*) people reside in Smallville than in Bigville.

- *More* people reside in Bigville than in Smallville.

- A *larger number* (not *a greater amount*) of people reside in Bigville than in Smallville.

## Two-Word Phrases Often Confused with Single Words

**all right**—entirely correct

**alright**—improper; no such word

**all together**—in a body or close group

**altogether**—entirely

**a lot**—many

**alot**—improper; no such word

**any one**—any specific person or thing in a group

**anyone**—any person at all

**a while** (article and noun)—a period of time

**awhile** (adverb)—for a period of time

**every one**—each person or item in a group

**everyone**—all people

**may be**—might be; could be

**maybe**—possibly

**some one**—improper

**someone**—one person

# IDIOMS—THE GMAT "HIT" LIST

The GMAT also tests for proper use of *idioms*, or *idiomatic phrases*, which are particular phrases (not single words) used commonly to express ideas. An idiomatic phrase is either proper (standard) or improper (nonstandard) simply based on whether it has been accepted over time as conventional and standard.

Non-native English speakers find idioms particularly troublesome, because they often don't make sense and because the English language includes more idiomatic expressions than any other language. Native English speakers usually can easily recognize an improper idiom because it doesn't *sound* right. Nevertheless, even native English speakers misuse idioms.

As with word usage, it is impossible to predict what specific idioms will appear in GMAT sentence correction problems. The best you can do here is to prepare for those that are most frequently used (and misused) as well as those that appear most frequently on the GMAT.

## Problematic Prepositions and Phrases with Prepositions

**Among/between.** Use *among* for three or more items (as in "*among* the many stars"). Use *between* for two items (as in "*between* a rock and a hard place").

**Like/as, as if, as though.** Use *like* as a preposition, not as a conjunction:

He looks exactly *like* Fred (not like Fred looks).

Use *as though* or *as if* (not *like*) as conjunctions:

He looked *as though* (or) *as if* (not *like*) he were about to cry.

Use *as*, not *like*, as a conjunction for similes:

The television news reporter spoke about the election *as* (not *like*) a nonpartisan journalist should.

**Differ, different, from/with/on/in.** *Differ* is a verb, and *different* is an adjective. The prepositions that you use with these terms differs according to the context.

The positions of Smith and Adams *differ from* (not *with*) those of all other candidates.

Smith and Adams *differ with* each other as to who the best candidate is.

Smith and Adams *differ on* (not *about*) their positions on the issues.

Smith's position on the issue is *different from* (not *than*) that of all other candidates.

The candidates are *different in* party membership but not in ideology.

The candidates *differ in* party membership but not in ideology.

**Other idiomatic prepositional phrases**

- Doug will surely *die from* excessive smoking.

  Doug will surely *die of* pneumonia.

- It is not always easy to *distinguish* good art *from* (not *with* or *and*) bad art.

  The university *distinguished* the alumnus *with* an honorary doctoral degree.

  Fluffy the cat can be *distinguished by* her unique markings.

- Gary was *disappointed in* his son.

  Gary was *disappointed with* (not *in* or *by*) his son's test results.

- The runner grew *impatient with* (not *about* or *at*) the slow pace of the race.

  Sprinters are often *impatient in* (not *with* or *about*) waiting for the final lap of longer races.

- The two analysts *agreed with* each other.

The two analysts *agreed to* examine the numbers further.

The two analysts *agreed on* (not *about*) only one conclusion.

- John *confided in* his older brother.

  John *confided to* his older brother that he stole the bicycle.

- No reasonable jury could *concur in* (not *about*) finding the defendant guilty.

  The jury members have decided to *concur with* one another regarding the defendant's guilt.

- Susan's former boyfriend plans to *interfere with* (not *in*) the wedding reception.

  Susan's former boyfriend *interfered in* (not *by*) spiking the punch at the wedding reception.

- The Cougars will *prevail over* (not *against*) the Panthers in the upcoming game.

  The Cougars' coach must *prevail on* his team to play more aggressively during the second half of the game.

In each of the following idiomatic phrases, only one preposition is proper:

- Acquiesce *in* (not *to*) illegal activity

- Alarmed *at* (not *about*) the news

- Apologize *for* (not *about*) a mistake

- Ignorant *of* (not *about*) the facts

- Independent *of* (not *from*) parental assistance

- Insist *on* (not *in*) a course of action

- Oblivious *of* (not *about* or *to*) the time

- Preferable *to* (not *than* or *over*) the other choice

- Required *of* (not *from*) all students

- Rich *in* (not *with*) resources

- Short *of* (not *on*) cash

- Succeed *in* (not *with*) an attempt

- Superior *to* (not *over*) the alternatives

- *Aside from* (not *outside of*) one particular instance

- *Within* (not *inside of*) a few minutes

## Necessary Prepositions and Improper Uses of Prepositions

The following commonly used idiomatic expressions all include prepositions:

- It is *of* no use to continue to struggle against oppression.

- The other children couldn't help (not help *from*) laughing at the girl with mismatching shoes.

- This discovery was made (not made *in*) about December of last year.

- The meeting will adjourn (not adjourn *at*) about two o'clock.

- The team could *have* (not could *of*) won the game with a better pitcher.

- All the residents are still *inside* (not inside *of*) the building.

## Other Nonstandard Idioms

- The waiter brought *half a* (or) *a half* (not *half of a, a half a,* or *a half of a*) loaf of bread to the table.

- *Being that* (not *being as*) the sky is gray and cloudy, the camp director should cancel the hike.

- Richard consulted his accountant *as to, about, regarding, in regard to,* or *as regards* (not *in regards to*) the income-tax consequences of the sale.

- **Improper:** Calcification *is when* (or) *is where* calcium deposits form around a bone.

- **Preferable:** Calcification *occurs when* calcium deposits form around a bone.

# Sentence Correction Lesson 3: Mini-Test and Review

## Today's Topics:

Today you will apply what you learned on Days 9 and 10 to 16 sentence correction problems. After taking this mini-test under timed conditions, review the explanations that follow.

## MINI-TEST (SENTENCE CORRECTION)

**Number of questions:** 16
**Suggested time:** 20 minutes
**Directions (as provided on the test):**
"In each of the following sentences, some part of the sentence or the entire sentence is underlined. Beneath each sentence you will find five ways of phrasing the underlined part. The first of these repeats the original; the other four are different. If you think the original is the best of these responses, choose the first response; otherwise, choose one of the others. Select the best version.

"This is a test of correctness and effectiveness of expression. In choosing answers, follow the requirements of standard written English; that is, pay attention to grammar, choice of words, and sentence construction. Choose the answer that produces the most effective sentence; this answer should be clear and exact, without awkwardness, ambiguity, redundancy, or grammatical error."

1. <u>History shows that while simultaneously attaining</u> global or even regional dominance, a country generally succumbs to erosion of its social infrastructure.

   (A) History shows that while simultaneously attaining

   (B) History would show that, while attaining

   (C) History bears out that, in the course of attaining

   (D) During the course of history, the attainment of

   (E) Throughout history, during any country's attaining

2. According to Newtonian physics, <u>the greater the resistance between two particles, given the so-called "gravitational constant," the less will be the gravitational force between them.</u>

   (A) the greater the distance between two particles, given the so-called "gravitational constant," the less will be the gravitational force between them.

   (B) the greater the distance the less the gravitational force between two particles, given the so-called "gravitational constant."

(C) given the so-called "gravitational constant," more distance between two particles will result in a lesser gravitational force between them.

(D) the less of a gravitational force between two objects, the more of a distance between them, given the so-called "gravitational constant."

(E) given the so-called "gravitational constant," the greater the distance between two particles, the smaller the gravitational force between them.

3. For generations after Napoleon posed for his portrait with hand in vest, men, especially Civil War generals, similarly posed for their portraits.

(A) For generations after Napoleon posed for his portrait with hand in vest, men, especially Civil War generals

(B) Generations of men after Napoleon, who posed for his portrait with hand in vest, especially Civil War generals,

(C) After Napoleon posed for his portrait with hand in vest, generations of men, especially Civil War generals,

(D) For generations after Napoleon posed for his portrait with hand in vest, Civil War generals especially, and men in general

(E) Generations of men after Napoleon, especially Civil War generals, who posed for his portrait with hand in vest

4. To ensure the integrity of fossil evidence found at climatically unstable archeological sites, the immediate coating of newly exposed fossils with a specially formulated alkaline solution is as crucial, if not more crucial than, the prompt removal of the fossil from the site.

(A) if not more crucial than,

(B) as, if not more crucial than,

(C) as if not more than

(D) if not more crucial, than

(E) if not more crucial, as

5. In 19th century Europe, a renewed interest in Middle Eastern architecture was kindled not only by increased trade but also by increased tourism and improved diplomatic relations.

(A) not only by increased trade but also by

(B) by not only increased trade but also by

(C) not only by increased trade but also

(D) not only by increased trade but

(E) by increased trade and also by

6. Upon man-made toxins invading the human body, special enzymes are deployed rebuilding any DNA strands damaged resulting from it.

(A) Upon man-made toxins invading the human body, special enzymes are deployed rebuilding any DNA strands damaged resulting from it.

(B) Upon man-made toxins, invasion of the human body, special enzymes are deployed that rebuild any damaged DNA strands resulting from the invasion.

(C) When man-made toxins invade the human body, special enzymes are deployed to rebuild any DNA strands damaged as a result.

(D) Special enzymes are deployed whenever man-made toxins invade the human body; they rebuild any damage that results to DNA strands.

(E) Damage to DNA strands that results when man-made toxins invade the human body are repaired by deployed special enzymes.

7. The California gold rush, the historical development instilling the greatest sense of manifest destiny in the populace, wore not the clothing of political ideology but rather a suit spun of gold and greed.

(A) The California gold rush, the historical development instilling the greatest sense of manifest destiny in the populace, wore not the clothing of political ideology but rather a suit spun of gold and greed.

(B) The historical development which most greatly instilled a sense of manifest destiny in the populace wore not the clothing of political ideology but instead a suit spun of gold and greed; it was the California gold rush.

(C) The historical development most instilling in the populace a sense of manifest destiny was the California gold rush, wearing a suit of greed and gold, not the clothing of political ideology.

(D) It was the California gold rush, not the clothing of political ideology, but rather a suit of gold and greed, that most greatly instilled in the populace a sense of manifest destiny.

(E) The greatest sense of manifest destiny in the populace was instilled by the California gold rush, which wore a suit of gold and greed rather than the clothing of political ideology.

8. The government's means of <u>disposal of war sur-</u>plus following World War II met with vociferous objections by industrialists, prominent advisors, and many others.

(A) of disposal of

(B) in disposing

(C) to dispose

(D) used in disposing

(E) of disposing

9. Too many naive consumers <u>hasty and happily provide</u> credit information to unscrupulous "merchants," who provide nothing in exchange but a credit fraud nightmare.

(A) hasty and happily provide

(B) hastily and happily provide

(C) hasty and happy providing

(D) hastily and happily providing

(E) providing hastily and happily

10. <u>Despite sophisticated computer models for assessing risk, such a model is nevertheless limited in their ability to define what risk is.</u>

(A) Despite sophisticated computer models for assessing risk, such a model is nevertheless

(B) Sophisticated computer models, which assess risk, are nevertheless

(C) Despite their sophistication, computer models for assessing risk are

(D) Assessment of risk can be achieved with computer models; but their sophistication is

(E) Assessing risk with sophisticated computer models is limited because such models are

11. <u>That which is self-evident cannot be disputed, and that in</u> itself is self-evident.

(A) That which is self-evident cannot be disputed, and that in

(B) That that is self-evident cannot be disputed, of which

(C) It is self-evident that which cannot be disputed, and this fact

(D) The self-evident cannot be disputed, and this fact

(E) That which is self-evident cannot be disputed, a fact which

12. If the corporate bureaucracy persists in its discriminatory hiring and job advancement practices, <u>its chief executives will expose themselves</u> to class-action litigation by the groups prejudiced thereby.

(A) its chief executives will expose themselves

(B) its chief executives would expose themselves

(C) their chief executives will expose themselves

(D) its chief executives themselves would become exposed

(E) the chief executives will, by themselves, be exposed

13. Of the 1,000 chemicals in coffee, <u>less than 30 have been tested, most of which produce cancer in laboratory rats.</u>

(A) less than 30 have been tested, most of which produce cancer in laboratory rats.

(B) most of which produce cancer in laboratory rats, fewer than 30 have been tested.

(C) fewer than 30 have been tested, and most of these produce cancer in laboratory rats.

(D) less than 30 of which have been tested, most of them produce cancer in laboratory rats.

(E) most of the less than 30 tested produced cancer in laboratory rats.

14. Elvis Presley <u>was, and always will be considered by many, as</u> the indisputable king of rock-and-roll.

   (A) was, and always will be considered by many, as

   (B) was and always will be considered by many as being

   (C) was, and always will be by many, considered

   (D) was, and always will be considered by many as,

   (E) was considered by many and always will be by many

15. <u>The volatility of the "fabulous 15" stock index, less than 80% of broader stock indices.</u>

   (A) The volatility of the "fabulous 15" stock index, less than 80% of broader stock indices.

   (B) The "fabulous 15" stock index is less than 80% as volatile as broader stock indices.

   (C) The "fabulous 15" stock index is less than 80% as volatile as that of broader market indices.

   (D) Volatility is less than 80% for the "fabulous 15" stock index compared to broader stock indices.

   (E) The volatility of the "fabulous 15" stock index is less than 80% of broader stock indices.

16. The media often hastens to malign celebrities who have come into sudden and unexpected prominence, whether <u>they be actors, musicians, or some other high-profile vocation.</u>

   (A) they be actors, musicians, or some other high-profile vocation.

   (B) their vocation be acting, music, or some other high-profile vocation.

   (C) they be actors, music, or some other high profile vocation.

   (D) their vocation is that of actor, musician, or otherwise a high-profile one.

   (E) they are actors, are musicians, or in some other high-profile vocation.

# Quick Answer Guide

## Mini-Test: Sentence Correction

| | | | |
|---|---|---|---|
| 1. | C | 9. | B |
| 2. | E | 10. | C |
| 3. | C | 11. | D |
| 4. | B | 12. | A |
| 5. | A | 13. | C |
| 6. | C | 14. | D |
| 7. | A | 15. | B |
| 8. | E | 16. | B |

## EXPLANATIONS

**1. (moderate). Answer: C.**

Response A is confusing in its intended meaning; the use of the word "simultaneously" suggests that two or more items are attained. If the sentence had continued with the phrase "global and regional dominance," the use of the word "simultaneously" would have made more sense.

B confuses the perspective (tense) of the sentence with the use of the word "would." The present tense is preferable here to convey the sentence's intended meaning.

C excludes the confusing word "simultaneously" and properly sets off the prepositional phrase beginning with "in the course" with commas to clarify the sentence's meaning.

D creates a nonsensical sentence by failing to set up a subordinate modifying clause before "a country."

E includes the awkward phrase "during any country's attaining." Also, the use of "a country" twice is unnecessarily wordy and redundant.

**2. (easier). Answer: E.**

Response A creates confusion by separating the two parallel clauses "the greater . . . " and "the less . . . ." Also, "will be" is unnecessary and undermines the parallel structure of the two clauses.

B improperly omits "between two particles" immediately following "distance," thereby creating confusion as to what the word "distance" refers to.

C creates a faulty parallel between the two main clauses; "a lesser" should be replaced with "less" to parallel "more" in the preceding clause.

D includes two related idiomatic problems: "the less of a" and "the more of a" are both idiomatically improper. Both phrases should exclude the word "of."

E remedies both problems with the original sentence. The words "smaller" and "lesser" are properly used interchangeably here, because both refer to amount rather than quantity.

### 3. (easier). Answer: C.

The original sentence A, while not grammatically incorrect *per se*, awkwardly sets off "men" by itself with commas, improperly suggesting that "men" is one item in a series of items.

B misplaces the modifying clause "especially Civil War generals"; this clause should appear closer to its antecedent ("men").

C remedies the original sentence's problem, clarifying the sentence's meaning by positioning "generations" immediately before "men."

D includes the awkwardly constructed phrase "Civil War generals especially, and men in general." Not only is the phrase clumsy and unnecessarily wordy, the word "general" carries a different meaning the second time that the sentence uses it, creating further confusion.

E misplaces the modifier "especially Civil War generals," suggesting that Napoleon was a Civil War general, as well as presenting an apparent pronoun disagreement between "generals" and "his."

### 4. (moderate). Answer: B.

The original sentence A presents an incomplete form of the idiomatic comparative phrase " . . . as [adjective] as . . . ." Removing the second comparison (set off by commas) reveals the omission of "as" ("is as crucial . . . *as*").

B completes the form of the idiomatic phrase by including the word "as."

C presents an incomplete form, omitting "crucial" in the second comparison.

D improperly uses "than" instead of "as" in the first comparison ("as crucial . . . then"). At the same time, the second comparison is incomplete; the comparative clause set off by commas must embrace "than."

E corrects only the first of the two problems with D, as well as creating a new problem: The word "as" should precede (not follow) the parenthetical comparison.

### 5. (moderate). Answer: A.

The original sentence A properly uses the modifying pair "not only . . . but also." The two modifying phrases ("not only by increased" and "but also by increased") are grammatically parallel.

B suffers from faulty parallelism. The second use of "by" is redundant.

C also suffers from faulty parallelism: The word "by" is improperly omitted after "but also."

D improperly uses the modifying pair "not only . . . but" instead of the idiomatically proper "not only . . . but also."

E is awkwardly phrased; it should exclude "also."

### 6. (moderate). Answer: C.

The original sentence A is faulty in two respects. First, to clarify the sentence's meaning, a comma should set off the modifying phrase beginning with "rebuilding." Second, it is unclear what "it" refers to in the modifying prepositional phrase "from it."

B improperly uses "that" instead of "which." Also, it is unclear what "resulting" refers to here—DNA strands or damage to the DNA strands.

C improves on the awkward use of a noun clause in the first part of the original sentence. The infinitive "to rebuild" and the phrase "as a result" clarify the meaning of the second part of the sentence. In spite of its use of the passive voice ("enzymes are deployed"), C is the best response.

D uses the plural verb form "result" in reference to the singular noun "damage." D also separates the pronoun "they" from its intended antecedent "enzymes."

E improperly uses the plural "are repaired" and "result" in reference to the singular "damage." Also, the phrase "deployed special enzymes" awkwardly strings together a verb (used as an adjective) and another adjective.

### 7. (challenging). Answer: A.

The original sentence A is the best choice; it contains no errors in grammar, diction, or usage.

B improperly uses "which" instead of "that." Also, "but rather" is idiomatically preferable to "but instead" in this sentence. Finally, this sentence's overall construction, especially considering the final clause, is somewhat awkward.

C includes the awkward phrase "most instilling." Placing the phrase "in the populace" between the verb "instilling" and the direct object "a sense . . . " confuses the sentence's meaning.

D is awkwardly constructed. The modifying phrase "a suit of gold and greed" should appear immediately after the subject to which it refers—the California gold rush.

E uses the awkward passive construction ("was instilled by") instead of the preferred active construction ("gold rush instilled").

## 8. (challenging). Answer: E.

Response A uses "of" twice; the result is wordy and arguably improper idiomatically.

B and C are idiomatically improper; a person is said to dispose *of* something.

D is redundant in its use of the word "used"; The word "means" adequately conveys the meaning.

E is idiomatically proper.

## 9. (easier). Answer: B.

The original sentence A improperly uses the adjective "hasty" instead of the adverb "hastily" to modify the verb "provide."

B remedies the problem in the original sentence.

C fails to correct the error in the original sentence and commits a similar error in its use of "happy" instead of "happily." C also creates two successive modifying phrases ("providing . . . " and "who . . . ") but no predicate; the result is a long sentence fragment.

D also creates a long but incomplete sentence.

E creates confusion by separating the verb "providing" from its object "credit information." Also, like C and D, E establishes a long but incomplete sentence.

## 10. (moderate). Answer: C.

The original sentence A is faulty in two respects. First, the singular "model" disagrees with the plural "their" (which logically refers to "models"). Second, the first clause is inconsistent in grammatical construction with the second clause, making for an awkward and confusing sentence.

B improperly uses the modifying phrase "which assess risk" to describe computer models in general, thereby distorting the sentence's probable meaning.

C remedies both problems in the original sentence. The plural "models" agrees with the pronoun "their," and the construction of the first clause is grammatically consistent with that of the second clause.

D improperly modifies "sophistication" with the possessive pronoun "their." It is unclear whether "their ability" refers to "computer models" or " sophistication."

E improperly uses the phrase "is limited" to describe "assessing risk." The computer models' ability, not assessing risk, is limited.

## 11. (challenging). Answer: D.

A contains a vague pronoun reference. It is unclear what the second "that" refers to.

B improperly uses "That that" instead of the idiomatically proper "That which" in the main clause that begins the sentence. Also, the phrase "of which" leaves it unclear as to what "itself" refers.

C reverses the subject and predicate of the main clause, resulting in a confusing and awkward sentence.

D restates the idea of the first clause of the original sentence more succinctly and clearly, as well as making it clear by the use of "and this fact" that the idea in the latter part of the sentence refers to the earlier statement itself.

E creates a vague and ambiguous modifying clause (following the comma). It is unclear what "a fact" refers to here.

## 12. (easier). Answer: A.

The original sentence A correctly uses the singular pronoun "its" in referring to the singular "bureaucracy." Also, A is consistent in its future tense and perspective.

B confuses the sentence's time perspective (tense). The use of "would" calls for the use of the subjunctive in the beginning of the sentence: "should the corporate bureaucracy persist . . . ."

C improperly uses the plural pronoun "their" in referring to the singular "bureaucracy."

D confuses the sentence's tense in the same manner as B. Also, the placement of "themselves" obscures the sentence's meaning.

E uses an ambiguous syntax that suggests (perhaps improperly) that *only* chief executives will be exposed to class-action litigation.

## 13. (moderate). Answer: C.

The original sentence A improperly uses "less" instead of "fewer" in reference to a numerical quantity (the number of chemicals tested). Also, the modifier "most of which" is separated from its antecedent ("30"), resulting in confusion as to whether "most of which" refers to the 30 chemicals tested or the tests themselves.

B confuses the meaning of the sentence by placing "most of which" immediately after "1,000 chemicals in coffee." This construction improperly suggests that 1,000 chemicals produce cancer in laboratory rats.

C remedies both problems in the original sentence.

D improperly uses "less" instead of "fewer." Also, it is unclear whether "most of them" refers to "1,000 chemicals" or to "less than 30"; the construction is ambiguous and confusing.

E improperly uses "less" instead of "fewer." Also, the phrase "most of the less than" is awkward and confusing.

## 14. (moderate). Answer: D.

Answer A is faulty in two respects. First, the placement of the commas sets up a faulty parallel structure between the progressive verbs "was considered" and "will be considered." Second, the idiom "considered as" is questionable here. A person is *considered* or *considered to be,* not *considered as,* at least in the broader context of this sentence.

B improperly uses the idiom "considered . . . as being" rather than the preferred *considered* or *considered to be.*

C sets up a faulty parallel structure in which the phrase "was considered" is intended as a grammatical parallel to "will be by many, considered." The latter phrase is nonsensical.

D remedies both problems with the original sentence.

E omits "considered" between "be" and "by," resulting in the nonsensical phrase "will be by many." The use of only a single comma contributes to the confusing construction and faulty parallel between what "was" and what "will be."

## 15. (easier). Answer: B.

The original sentence A is not a complete sentence.

B completes the sentence without committing any errors in grammar or diction.

C improperly uses "that of," which in this construction refers to nothing (it is a dangling modifier).

D is nonsensical; the basis for comparison as well as what is being compared is ambiguous.

E improperly (and nonsensically) suggests that volatility is less than 80% of "broader stock indices" (instead of "the volatility of broader stock indices").

## 16. (moderate). Answer: B.

The original sentence A suffers from faulty parallelism. Each of the three items in the underlined clause should be similar in grammatical construction. Although "actors" and "musicians" both describe the celebrities themselves, "some other high-profile vocation" does not.

B establishes a consistent (parallel) grammatical construction among the three items in the series. In B, each of the three items refers clearly to a vocation.

C fails to establish parallel grammatical construction among the three items in the series; "music" is a vocation and does not describe a person.

D also fails to establish parallel grammatical construction; "otherwise a high profile one" refers to a vocation, not a person.

E creates a new faulty parallel structure by including "are" in only two of the three items in the series.

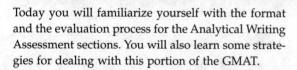

## Day 12

# Analytical Writing Assessment Lesson 1: Essay Format and Strategies

## Today's Topics:

1. The GMAT Analytical Writing Assessment at a glance
2. What's the difference between the two essay types?
3. Anatomy of the Analysis of an Issue question
4. Anatomy of the Analysis of an Argument question
5. How writing samples are evaluated
6. General strategies for writing your essays
7. Managing your time

Today you will familiarize yourself with the format and the evaluation process for the Analytical Writing Assessment sections. You will also learn some strategies for dealing with this portion of the GMAT.

## THE GMAT ANALYTICAL WRITING ASSESSMENT AT A GLANCE

**Number of questions:** 2
**Time allowed:** 30 minutes per question
**Types of questions:**

- Analysis of an Issue

- Analysis of an Argument

**Number of sections:** 2
**Appearance relative to other exam sections:** First

**Basic format:**

- Analysis of an Issue: a brief passage outlining an issue followed by a question and instructions

- Analysis of an Argument: a brief passage containing an argument followed by instructions

**The analytical writing sections test your ability to:**

- Think critically about arguments

- Analyze issues

- Argue persuasively and cogently

- Use language effectively and follow the conventions of standard written English

**Skills required:**

- College-level writing

- College-level reasoning

**Ground rules:**

• Scratch paper is provided.

• Two questions (one Analysis of an Issue, one Analysis of an Argument) randomly selected by the CAT from the prepublished topics on the official Graduate Management Admission Council®Website (http://www.gmat.org)

• Essay answers are word processed, not handwritten. Only basic word processing functions are available. No spell-checker is available. Also, the Tab key is not available; to start a new paragraph, skip a line.

• There is no "correct" response for an Analysis of an Issue question, but you are expected to demonstrate general knowledge of the topic.

• There is no set response for an Analysis of an Argument question, but you are expected to analyze important features of the argument.

## What's the Difference Between the Two Essay Types?

The Analytical Writing Assessment section consists of two essay questions. One type of question asks you to discuss an issue and take a position on it. This type is called an *Analysis of an Issue* question. The other type of question asks you to evaluate an argument critically and write a critique of it. This type of question is called an *Analysis of an Argument* question. Although the two types of questions have similar names, the similarity stops there.

Analysis of an Argument questions test your *critical reasoning and analytic* skills. In this type of problem, the passage presents an argument followed by a question asking you to evaluate the cogency of the argument and analyze its line of reasoning and use of evidence. In most cases, the problem asks you to discuss what is required to make the argument more persuasive. Your analysis of the argument *must* focus strictly on important *logical features* of the argument. In *no* case does a problem ask you to present your own views on the topic. General knowledge of

the *issue* of the argument is *not* a prerequisite for doing well on this type of question.

Analysis of an Issue questions test your ability to *communicate* your opinion on an issue effectively and persuasively. In this type of problem, the passage presents an issue, and the question stem asks you to take a position on the issue. Typically, the question stem instructs you to explain your position using reasons or examples drawn from your own experiences, observations, or readings. Your analysis of the issue *must* demonstrate that you *understand* the issue and recognize its complexity, and in *every* case the question asks you to present your *own views and opinions* on the issue. General knowledge of the *issue* presented in the passage *is a prerequisite* for doing well on this type of question.

## Anatomy of an Analysis of an Issue Question

The directions for the Analysis of an Issue section are as follows:

> In this section, you will need to analyze the issue presented below and explain your views on it. The question has no "correct" answer. Instead you should consider various perspectives as you develop your own position on the issue.

Analysis of an Issue questions have two elements:

• A passage that contains a brief discussion of an issue or that states a position on an issue

• A question about the issue in the passage and instructions about the scope and content of your essay

Here are a couple of typical examples:
**Example 12-1**

> One of the primary reasons cited by the government for requiring that all children be vaccinated against infectious diseases such as mumps, measles, and smallpox is to protect them from the debilitating, and sometimes fatal, effects of these diseases. Parent groups contend, however, that most children will not even be exposed to these diseases in the first place. Moreover, they contend

that some children have adverse reactions to the vaccines and some of them die as a result of being vaccinated.

Do you believe that the benefits of the government's mandated vaccination program for children outweigh the disadvantages? Explain your position, using reasons and/or examples drawn from your experience or reading.

### Example 12-2

Everyone agrees that a college education is necessary to live and work in our complex society, and yet the cost of higher education increases every year. Many people maintain that the government should help students meet these rising costs because, in the long run, society will benefit. But others assert that students reap the benefits of a college education and should pay for it themselves.

Which do you find more compelling, the case for government assistance to students, or the opposing viewpoint? Explain your position using reasons or examples drawn from your own experience, observations, or reading.

## ANATOMY OF AN ANALYSIS OF AN ARGUMENT QUESTION

The directions for the Analysis of an Argument section as follows:

In this section, you will be asked to write a critique of the argument presented below. *You are NOT being asked to present your own views on the subject.*

Analysis of an Argument questions have two elements:

- A passage that contains an argument

- Instructions about the scope and content of your essay

Here are a couple of typical examples:

### Example 12-3

Most environmentalists believe that the "information superhighway" does not pose a serious threat to the environment. But what they fail to see is that the information superhighway will enable millions of people to work at home, far from the office. In other words, it will enable them to flee the cities and the suburbs and take up residence in areas that have hitherto been unpopulated and unspoiled. This dispersal of the populace portends an environmental disaster of the first magnitude.

Discuss how logically convincing you find this argument. In discussing your viewpoint, be sure to analyze the line of reasoning and the use of evidence in the argument. Also, discuss what, if anything, would make the argument more convincing or help you to better evaluate its conclusion.

### Example 12-4

Persons who do not control their cholesterol levels are more likely to have heart disease than those who do. However, even among those who do not control their cholesterol levels, the majority do not have heart disease. Therefore, to avoid heart disease, there is no need to adopt a diet that is low in cholesterol rather than one that is high in cholesterol.

How well reasoned do you find this argument? In your discussion, be sure to consider the line of reasoning and use of evidence in the argument. For example, you might need to consider what assumptions underlie the reasoning in the argument and what additional information would be required to strengthen or weaken the argument. You can also discuss what would make the argument more persuasive.

## HOW WRITING SAMPLES ARE EVALUATED

### How Are Your Essays Graded?

Each of your essays is graded by readers trained in the evaluation of writing. They employ a holistic grading method in which they read your papers quickly and assign a score from 0–6 based on the overall quality of your writing. Each essay is read by two readers who are not informed of the other's score. Both readers employ the same scoring criteria. If the scores assigned by the first two readers differ by more than two points, a third reader grades your essay. The three scores are then averaged. After each of your essays is assigned a score, the two scores are averaged, and the result is your final Analytical Writing Assessment score—a single score ranging from 0–6 (in half-point intervals).

## What Do the Scores Mean?

To understand the meaning of the scores, first consider what they don't mean. Usually, minor spelling errors or small errors in English grammar or diction do not adversely affect your score. In Analysis of an Issue questions, the side of the issue that you choose to defend or criticize is irrelevant to your score. In Analysis of an Argument questions, there is no set answer to which your essay must conform.

**Scoring: Analysis of an Issue.** Here are the official grading criteria readers use when scoring your essay.

*Score of 6: Outstanding.* A 6 paper presents a cogent, well-articulated analysis of the issue's complexities and demonstrates mastery of the elements of effective writing. A typical paper in this category does the following:

- Explores ideas and develops a position on the issue with insightful reasons and/or persuasive examples

- Is clearly well organized

- Demonstrates superior control of language, including diction and syntactic variety

- Demonstrates superior facility with the conventions (grammar, usage, and mechanics) of standard written English but might have minor flaws

*Score of 5: Strong.* A 5 paper presents a well-developed analysis of the issue's complexities and demonstrates a strong control of the elements of effective writing. A typical paper in this category does the following:

- Develops a position on the issue with well-chosen reasons and/or examples

- Is generally well organized

- Demonstrates clear control of language, including diction and syntactic variety

- Demonstrates facility with the conventions of standard written English but might have minor flaws

*Score of 4: Adequate.* A 4 paper presents a competent analysis of the issue and demonstrates adequate control of the elements of writing. A typical paper in this category does the following:

- Develops a position on the issue with relevant reasons and/or examples

- Is adequately organized

- Demonstrates adequate control of language, including diction and syntax, but might lack syntactic variety

- Displays control of the conventions of standard written English but might have some flaws

*Score of 3: Limited.* A 3 paper demonstrates some competence in its analysis of the issue and in its control of the elements of writing, but is clearly flawed. A typical paper in this category exhibits *one or more* of the following characteristics:

- Is vague or limited in developing a position on the issue

- Is poorly organized

- Is weak in the use of relevant reasons or examples

- Uses language imprecisely or lacks sentence variety

- Contains occasional major errors or frequent minor errors in grammar, usage, and mechanics

*Score of 2: Seriously flawed.* A 2 paper demonstrates serious weaknesses in analytical writing skills. A typical paper in this category exhibits *one or more* of the following characteristics:

- Is unclear or seriously limited in presenting or developing a position on the issue

- Is disorganized

- Provides few, if any, relevant reasons or examples

- Has serious and frequent problems in the use of language and in sentence structure

- Contains numerous errors in grammar, usage, or mechanics that interfere with meaning

*Score of 1: Fundamentally deficient.* A 1 paper demonstrates fundamental deficiencies in analytical writing skills. A typical paper in this category exhibits *one or more* of the following characteristics:

- Provides little evidence of the ability to develop or organize a coherent response to the topic

- Has severe and persistent errors in language and sentence structure

- Contains a pervasive pattern of errors in grammar, usage, and mechanics that severely interferes with meaning

*Score of 0.* Any paper that is obviously not written on the assigned topic receives a score of zero.

*Score of NR.* Any nonverbal response receives a score of NR.

**Scoring: Analysis of an Argument.** Here are the official grading criteria readers use when scoring your essay.

*Score of 6: Outstanding.* A 6 paper presents a cogent, well-articulated critique of the argument and demonstrates mastery of the elements of effective writing. A typical paper in this category does the following:

- Clearly identifies and insightfully analyzes important features of the argument

- Develops ideas cogently, organizes them logically, and connects them smoothly with clear transitions

- Effectively supports the main points of the critique

- Demonstrates control of language, including diction and syntactic variety

- Demonstrates facility with the conventions of standard written English but might have some minor flaws

*Score of 5: Strong.* A 5 paper presents a well-developed critique of the argument and demonstrates good control of the elements of effective writing. A typical paper in this category does the following:

- Clearly identifies important features of the argument and analyzes them in a generally thoughtful way

- Develops ideas clearly, organizes them logically, and connects them with appropriate transitions

- Sensibly supports the main points of the critique

- Demonstrates control of language, including diction and syntactic variety

- Demonstrates facility with the conventions of standard written English but might have occasional flaws

*Score of 4: Adequate.* A 4 paper presents a competent critique of the argument and demonstrates adequate control of the elements of writing. A typical paper in this category does the following:

- Identifies and capably analyzes important features of the argument

- Develops and organizes ideas satisfactorily but might not connect them with transitions

- Supports main points of the critique

- Demonstrates sufficient control of language to convey ideas with reasonable clarity

- Generally follows the conventions of standard written English but might have some flaws

*Score of 3: Limited.* A 3 paper demonstrates some competence in its critique of the argument and in its control of the elements of writing, but is clearly flawed. A typical paper in this category exhibits *one or more* of the following characteristics:

- Does not identify or analyze most of the important features of the argument, although some analysis is present

- Is limited in the logical development and organization of ideas

- Offers support of little relevance and value for points of the critique

- Uses language imprecisely

- Contains occasional major errors or frequent minor errors in grammar, usage, and mechanics

*Score of 2: Seriously flawed.* A 2 paper demonstrates serious weaknesses in analytical writing skills. A typical paper in this category exhibits *one or more* of the following characteristics:

- Does not identify or analyze the main features of the argument, but might instead present the writer's own views on the subject

- Does not develop ideas or is disorganized

- Provides little, if any, relevant or reasonable support

- Has serious and frequent problems in the use of language and in sentence structure

- Contains numerous errors in grammar, usage, and mechanics that interfere with meaning

*Score of 1: Fundamentally deficient.* A 1 paper demonstrates deficiencies in analytical writing skills. A typical paper in this category exhibits *one or more* of the following characteristics:

- Provides little evidence of the ability to understand and analyze the argument or to develop an organized response to it

- Has severe and persistent errors in language and sentence structure

- Contains a pervasive pattern of errors in grammar, usage, and mechanics that results in incoherence

*Score of 0.* Any paper that is obviously not written on the assigned topic receives a score of zero.

*Score of NR.* Any nonverbal response receives a score of NR.

## "Scorecards" for Self-Evaluation

The following scorecards are based on the official scoring criteria.

**Analysis of an Issue scorecard.** Answer yes, no, or maybe to each of the following questions:

- Do you clearly indicate that you understand and appreciate the complexities of the issue?

- Is your essay well organized?

- Do you use persuasive examples and/or insightful reasons to support your position?

- Do you present a well-reasoned, clearly articulated analysis of the issue?

- Do you cover all the tasks mentioned in the instructions?

- Do you demonstrate a superior command of standard written English?

For each "yes" answer to the preceding questions, give yourself a mark of 1; for each "no" answer, give yourself a mark of 0; for each "maybe" answer, give yourself a mark of .5. Total the marks to calculate your score.

**Analysis of an Argument scorecard.** Answer yes, no, or maybe to each of the following questions:

- Do you clearly indicate that you understand the argument, and analyze important features of the argument?

- Do you develop and organize your ideas logically and connect them smoothly with clear transitions?

- Do you provide relevant and reasonable support to the main points of your critique?

- Is your essay well organized?

- Do you cover all the tasks mentioned in the instructions?

- Do you demonstrate a superior command of standard written English?

For each "yes" answer to the preceding questions, give yourself a mark of 1; for each "no" answer, give yourself a mark of 0; for each "maybe" answer, give yourself a mark of .5. Total the marks to calculate your score.

# GENERAL STRATEGIES FOR WRITING YOUR ESSAYS

Writing essays under timed conditions can be a trying experience and can raise your anxieties to a point where you find it difficult to perform well. You can effectively eliminate the main sources of anxiety by having a clear plan in mind as to how you will approach the GMAT's Analytical Writing Assessment section. The following general strategies will help you do your best on the essay portion of your exam. Specific strategies and templates for writing Analysis of an Issue and Analysis of an Argument essays will be explored on days 13 and 14.

## Pretest Preparation Strategy

Here is a brief checklist of things that you should know or do *before* you take the GMAT's Analytical Writing Assessment portion:

- Study the Analysis of an Issue topics and the Analysis of an Argument topics published on the official Graduate Management Admission Council®Website (http://www.gmat.org)

- Know the difference between Analysis of an Issue questions and Analysis of an Argument questions

- Know what is required to get a score of 5 or 6 for each essay type

- Know how to organize your essay for each type of essay question

- Practice writing an essay of each type (taken from the topics published on the GMAT Website (http://www.gmat.org) and evaluate them using the scorecards. Write practice essays on a *computer* using *only* basic word processing functions.

## Test-Taking Strategy

Use this six-step approach on both the Analysis of an Issue and Analysis of an Argument questions:

1. *Read the passage carefully.* Unlike Critical Reasoning questions, where you are advised to read the question stem first, essay questions require that you start by reading the passage carefully. For the Analysis of an Issue question, you first want to identify the *issue* that the passage is discussing. For the Analysis of an Argument question, you first want to identify the argument's conclusion, the reasons given to support the conclusion, and the major assumptions that underlie the argument's reasoning.

2. *Read the instructions carefully.* Be sure you understand the scope of the assignment specified in the instructions. Make a checklist itemizing the requirements that the instructions specify.

3. *Think about your response.* With the itemized checklist from step 2 in mind, think about the main ingredients of your response. Use the planning checklist (discussed on days 13 and 14) as a guide to identify your essay's components. For the Analysis of an Issue question, think about your position on the issue and think about the reasons and examples you will use to support your position. For the Analysis of an Argument question, think about the passage's argument, focusing your attention on the deficiencies or strengths of the reasoning and the assumptions required to infer the conclusion. Make brief notes, but don't spend time organizing your ideas at this point.

4. *Outline your essay.* Using the organizational templates for each essay type as a guide (see days 13 and 14), organize the ingredients that you developed in step 3.

5. *Write your essay.* Using the outline developed in step 4 as a guide, write complete sentences expressing your ideas. Pay attention to your diction, grammar, usage, and mechanics as you write. Vary sentence length; this helps ensure syntactic variety. Use transitional phrases to indicate the direction of your thought and use indicator words and phrases to signal your reasons and your conclusion.

6. *Proofread your essay.* Read your essay looking for errors in diction, usage, or grammar. Rewrite any sentences that are syntactically similar to each other. Check the flow of your essay. Pay particular attention to transitions and to sentences that express reasons and conclusions. Make sure each is signaled with an appropriate transition or indicator word or phrase.

## MANAGING YOUR TIME

Thirty minutes is plenty of time to fashion your response if you use your time wisely. The six-step approach outlined in the preceding section can serve as a convenient guide to time management. Here's a breakdown of the amount of time that you should spend on each step for each type of question.

### Breakdown for Analysis of an Issue Question

- Step 1: 1 minute
- Step 2: 1 minute
- Step 3: 5 minutes
- Step 4: 3 minutes
- Step 5: 18 minutes
- Step 6: 2 minutes

### Breakdown for Analysis of an Argument Question

- Step 1: 3 minutes
- Step 2: 1 minute
- Step 3: 5 minutes
- Step 4: 3 minutes
- Step 5: 16 minutes
- Step 6: 2 minutes

# Analytical Writing Assessment Lesson 2: Analysis of an Issue

## Today's Topics:

1. Writing a high-scoring Analysis of an Issue essay
2. A planning checklist for your Analysis of an Issue essay
3. A sample template for your Analysis of an Issue essay
4. An example question with a model response
5. Mini-test and review your response

Today you will learn how to write a high-scoring Analysis of an Issue essay. You will also write an Analysis of an Issue essay under timed conditions.

## WRITING A HIGH-SCORING ANALYSIS OF AN ISSUE ESSAY

Here are the basic components of a high-scoring Analysis of an Issue essay:

**Content.** Your essay should include the following:

- Recognition of the issue and its complexity
- A clear statement of your position on the issue
- Reasons or examples to support your position
- A conclusion based on the reasons and examples

**Length.** Your essay should be at least four paragraphs long.

**Organization.** Your essay should consist of the following elements (not necessarily in this order):

- A paragraph acknowledging the issue, its complexity, and your position

- At least two separate paragraphs discussing each reason or example in support of your position
- A paragraph summing up your position

**Style.** Your writing style should be each of the following:

- Concise
- Correct in its grammar, mechanics, and usage
- Persuasive
- Varied in its sentence length and structure

## A PLANNING CHECKLIST FOR YOUR ANALYSIS OF AN ISSUE ESSAY

The following checklist is *not* intended as an outline for your essay, but rather as a guide to the elements that your essay should ideally include. Basically, it is a planning tool to help you develop your essay's content.

Here are the questions that you want to consider as you read the passage:

- What is the *issue*?

- What is *your position* on the issue?

- What are *your reasons* in support of your position on the issue? (Try to think of at least two.)

- What *examples* drawn from your experience and/or reading support your position? (Try to think of at least one.)

- What is *your evidence* in support of the truth of your reasons or examples? (Try to think of evidence that supports each reason or example.)

## A SAMPLE TEMPLATE FOR YOUR ANALYSIS OF AN ISSUE ESSAY

The following sample template is intended as a guide to aid you in organizing your analysis of an issue essay. Determine the *number* of paragraphs in your essay from the number of elements that you have identified using the planning checklist and the amount of time that it takes you to write the essay. The *order* of the paragraphs in your essay can vary depending on your own writing style. The *transitional devices* in the sample template are purposely simplistic; you should not copy them. The following paragraphs are necessary (but not sufficient) for a high-scoring essay.

### The First Paragraph

In the first paragraph, your goal is threefold: State the issue clearly, explore some of the complexities of the issue, and state your position on the issue.

Here's a sample template for the first paragraph that accomplishes these three goals. Write at least four sentences.

Whether or not _____
_____is a complex issue.

On the one hand, _____
_____
_____.

On the other hand,_____
_____
_____.

My view is that _____
_____
_____.

### The Second Paragraph

In the second paragraph, your goal is twofold: State *one* of your reasons, and if possible, provide evidence or examples that support it.

Here's a sample template for the second paragraph that accomplishes these two goals. Write at least three sentences.

The main reason in favor of my view is
_____
_____.

To my way of thinking, this is a good reason because
_____
_____
_____.

### The Third Paragraph

In the third paragraph, your goal is once again twofold: State *another* reason, and if possible, provide evidence or examples that support it.

Here's a sample template for the third paragraph that accomplishes these two goals. Write at least three sentences.

Another reason in favor of my view is
_____
_____
_____.

In my mind, this is a good reason because
_____
_____
_____.

### The Final Paragraph

In the final paragraph, your goal is to provide the reader with a "snapshot" overview of your position.

Here's a sample template for the final paragraph that accomplishes this goal. Write at least two sentences.

Based on the reasons stated above, I conclude that_____

_____

_____.

## AN EXAMPLE QUESTION WITH A MODEL RESPONSE

Now let's apply what you've learned today to Example 12-1 from Day 12:

One of the primary reasons cited by the government for requiring by law that all children be vaccinated against infectious diseases such as mumps, measles, and smallpox is to protect them from the debilitating, and sometimes fatal, effects of these diseases. Parent groups contend, however, that most children will not even be exposed to these diseases in the first place. Moreover, they contend that some children have adverse reactions to the vaccines and some of them die as a result of being vaccinated.

Do you believe that the benefits of the government's mandated vaccination program for children outweigh the disadvantages? Explain your position, using reasons and/or examples drawn from your experience or reading.

The following is an excellent response for this example question:

Whether or not the government should require by law that all children be vaccinated against infectious diseases is a complex issue. On the one hand, the government has a responsibility to ensure that proper steps are taken to safeguard the health of the public. On the other hand, parents have a responsibility to ensure the health of their children. Ultimately, the issue in this case is whether the government's obligation to protect the public from harm should take precedence over the parent's obligation to protect their children from potential harm. My view is that the government's obligation in this case should take precedence.

The main reason in favor of my view is the fact that infectious diseases can spread very rapidly. Because of this, hundreds of children can be infected from a single infected child. The idea of putting hundreds of children at risk to keep from putting one child at risk is not a good trade-off in my estimation. To my way of thinking, the advantage clearly outweighs the disadvantage in this instance.

Another reason in favor of my view is the fact that many parents lack the knowledge and the money to protect their children adequately from disease. The advantage of a government-mandated vaccination program is that it ensures that all children, regardless of the education and wealth of their parents, will be protected from infectious diseases. In my mind, this advantage offsets the disadvantage of potential harm to children who have adverse reactions or die from being vaccinated.

Based on the reasons stated above, I conclude that the advantages of a government-mandated vaccination program for children outweigh the disadvantages expressed by the parent groups.

## MINI-TEST AND REVIEW

### Directions

Write an essay on the following topic, applying what you learned today and on Day 12. Take 30 minutes to write your essay. After completing your essay, evaluate it using the scorecard from Day 12 and read the sample response included here to evaluate your writing ability further.

### Sample Question

Reacting to recent statistics that show an increase in highway fatalities, some people have argued that the 65 miles per hour (mph) speed limit should be repealed and the 55 mph law reinstated. However, others, citing statistics that show reductions in the cost of transporting goods due to savings in travel time, argue that the speed limit should be raised to 70 mph.

Which do you find more compelling—the call for the reinstatement of the 55 mph speed limit or the opposing view? Explain your position, using examples and/or reasons drawn from your experience and reading.

### Sample Response

The issue of whether the current speed limit law should be repealed and replaced by a lower or a higher speed limit is a controversial one. On one side, economic factors dictate that the speed limit should be raised. On the other side, safety factors dictate that the speed limit should be lowered. Ultimately, the issue is which of these factors is deemed most important. My view is that the 55 mph speed law should be reinstated for the simple reason that saving lives is more important than saving dollars.

To begin with, I agree that raising the speed limit to 70 mph will save time in transporting goods and hence tend to reduce costs. But it is unlikely that this will result in significant overall cost reductions, because driving at higher speeds consumes considerably more fuel. At best, the reduction in costs due to reduced travel time will be offset by the increases in the costs of fuel. The net result is that the dollar savings will be minimal.

Another reason against raising the speed limit to 70 mph is that cars emit more air pollutants when they are driven at higher rates of speed. When coupled with the fact that thousands of people die every year from lung disease brought on by air pollution, this reason presents a strong case against raising the current speed limit and an even stronger case for lowering it. It also provides a strong rationale for repealing the current speed limit.

Finally, numerous studies have shown that the higher the speed limit, the higher the death rate. Even critics of the 55 mph speed limit concede that it helped to reduce the number of deaths and injuries in automobile accidents. This fact shows against the current speed limit as well as the proposal to raise the limit to 70 mph. Given the vast amount of money spent each year on health care, there is little doubt that saving lives is more important to most of us than saving money.

The 55 mph speed limit saves lives, and the economic advantages of retaining the current speed limit or increasing it are dubious. For these reasons, the current speed limit should be repealed and the 55 mph speed limit reinstated.

## Day 14

# Analytical Writing Assessment Lesson 3: Analysis of an Argument

## Today's Topics:

1. Writing a high-scoring Analysis of an Argument essay
2. A planning checklist for your Analysis of an Argument essay
3. A sample template for your Analysis of an Argument essay
4. An example question with a model response
5. Mini-test and review

Today you will learn how to write a high-scoring Analysis of an Argument essay. You will also write an Analysis of an Argument essay under timed conditions.

## WRITING A HIGH-SCORING ANALYSIS OF AN ARGUMENT ESSAY

Here are the basic components of a high-scoring Analysis of an Argument essay:

**Content:** Your essay should include the following:

- A clear statement of the author's argument

- A critique of important features of the author's argument

- Effective support of the main points of critique

**Length:** Your essay should be at least four indented paragraphs long.

**Organization:** The essay should include the following contents (not necessarily in this order):

- A paragraph outlining the main features of the author's argument

- Paragraphs analyzing the argument's reasoning, premises, and/or assumptions

- A paragraph summing up your critique of the argument

**Style:** Your writing style should be each of the following:

- Concise

- Correct in grammar, mechanics, and usage

- Logical

- Varied in sentence length and structure

- Full of smooth transitions

## A PLANNING CHECKLIST FOR YOUR ANALYSIS OF AN ARGUMENT ESSAY

The following checklist is *not* intended as an outline for your essay, but rather as a guide to the elements that your essay should ideally include. Basically, it is a planning tool to help you develop your essay's content.

Here are the questions that you want to consider as you read the passage:

- What is the *conclusion* of the argument?

- What *reasons* does the author offer in support of the conclusion?

- On what *assumptions* does the author's argument depend? (Try to think of at least one.)

- Is the argument logically *convincing*? If you think that it is convincing, why? If you find the argument unconvincing, why?

- What additional information or evidence would *strengthen* the argument?

- What additional information or evidence would *weaken* the argument?

## A SAMPLE TEMPLATE FOR YOUR ANALYSIS OF AN ARGUMENT ESSAY

The following sample template is intended as a guide to aid you in organizing your Analysis of an Argument essay. Determine the *number* of paragraphs in your essay from the number of elements that you have identified using the planning checklist and the amount of time that it takes you to write the essay. The *order* of the paragraphs in your essay can vary depending on your own writing style. The *transitional devices* in the sample template are purposely simplistic; you should not copy them. The following paragraphs are necessary (but not sufficient) for a high-scoring essay.

### The First Paragraph

In the first paragraph, your goal is twofold: Briefly restate the passage's argument and clearly indicate whether you find the argument logically convincing. Here's a sample template for the first paragraph that accomplishes these goals. Write at least two sentences.

The author concludes that_____

_____

because_____

_____

_____.

This argument is convincing/not convincing for several reasons.

### The Second Paragraph

In the second paragraph, your goal is to critique *one* of the following: the argument's reasoning, one of the argument's premises, or one of the argument's assumptions.

Here's a sample template for the second paragraph that accomplishes this goal. Write at least three sentences.

In the first place,_____

_____

_____.

### The Third Paragraph

In the third paragraph, your goal is to critique *one* of the following: the argument's reasoning, one of the argument's premises, or one of the argument's assumptions.

Here's a sample template for the third paragraph that accomplishes this goal. Write at least three sentences.

In the second place,_____

_____

_____.

### The Fourth Paragraph

In the fourth paragraph, your goal is to critique *one* of the following: the argument's reasoning, one of the argument's premises, or one of the argument's assumptions.

Here's a sample template for the fourth paragraph that accomplishes this goal. Write at least three sentences.

Finally,_____
_____
_____.

## The Final Paragraph

In the final paragraph, your goals are to summarize your critique of the argument and discuss how the author could improve or strengthen the argument.

Here's a sample template for the final paragraph that accomplishes these goals.

In conclusion, to further convince me that _____
_____, the author would
have to _____
_____.

Until this evidence is forth coming, I am not completely convinced that _____
_____.

---

## AN EXAMPLE QUESTION WITH A MODEL RESPONSE

---

Now apply what you've learned today to Example 12-3 from Day 12:

Most environmentalists believe that the "information superhighway" does not pose a serious threat to the environment. But what they fail to see is that the information superhighway will enable millions of people to work at home, far from the office. In other words, it will enable them to flee the cities and the suburbs and take up residence in areas that have hitherto been unpopulated and unspoiled. This dispersal of the populace portends an environmental disaster of the first magnitude.

Discuss how logically convincing you find this argument. In discussing your viewpoint, be sure to analyze the line of reasoning and the use of evidence in the argument. Also, discuss what, if anything, would make the argument more convincing or help you to better evaluate its conclusion.

The following is an excellent response to this example question:

The author concludes that the information highway poses a serious threat to the environment because it will emancipate millions of people from traditional workplaces. The author reasons that once emancipated, these workers will migrate into previously unpopulated and unspoiled areas and predicts that the result of this migration will be an environmental disaster of the first magnitude. This argument is not convincing for several reasons.

In the first place, the author's prediction of environmental disaster is based on the questionable assumption that most people would prefer to live in unpopulated and remote areas. Nowhere in the passage does the author offer evidence to support this assumption. In fact, given the gregariousness of most people, it is highly unlikely that this claim is true.

In the second place, the author assumes that most people live in cities and suburbs only because of the proximity to work and that given the opportunity they would move. Again, the argument offers no evidence to support this questionable assumption. It seems equally reasonable to assume that people live in cities and suburbs for other reasons as well, such as the proximity to entertainment and cultural events.

Finally, the author fails to consider the benefits to the environment that this technology might bring. For example, transmitting information uses much less energy than transporting commuters, so it will save precious natural resources and be less polluting. It may turn out that the environmental advantages of this technology to the environment far outweigh the disadvantages. Lacking a complete analysis of the situation, the author's forecast of environmental disaster cannot be taken seriously.

In conclusion, to convince me that the information superhighway poses a threat to the environment, the author would have to provide evidence that, given the opportunity, most people would in fact move to remote and unspoiled areas and that the adverse effects of this migration would outweigh the benefits of this technology.

Until this evidence is forthcoming, I am not con-vinced that the information superhighway poses a serious threat to the environment.

---

## MINI-TEST AND REVIEW

Write an essay on the following topic, applying what you learned today and on Day 12. Take 30 minutes to write your essay. After completing your essay, evaluate it using the scorecard from Day 12, and then read the sample response included here to evaluate your writing ability further.

### Sample Topic

Eighty percent of the homeless people interviewed in a recent survey said that they prefer to eat and sleep on the streets rather than go to shelters. Sur-prisingly, this survey proves that contrary to popu-lar opinion, homeless people prefer the discomfort and uncertainty of life on the streets to the comfort and security afforded by shelters.

How convincing do you find this argument? In your discussion, be sure to consider the argument's line of reasoning and use of evidence. For example, you might need to consider what assumptions un-derlie the argument's reasoning and what additional information would be required to strengthen or weaken the argument. You can also discuss what would make the argument more persuasive.

### Sample Response

Based on a survey in which 80% of the homeless re-spondents said that they prefer to eat and sleep on the streets rather than go to shelters, the author con-cludes that all homeless people share this preference. This argument is not convincing for several reasons.

To begin with, the conclusion that the author reaches goes beyond the evidence. Only 80% of the respondents indicated a preference for eating and sleeping on the streets. Yet, the author concludes that all homeless people share this preference. The evi-dence does not warrant this conclusion.

Second, it is not clear from the passage whether the homeless people interviewed are representative of the entire population of homeless people. If, for example, the survey were conducted in a small rural community rather than a large metropolitan one, the findings would be highly questionable. Or, if it turned out that the survey was conducted during the summer rather than the winter, this fact would raise doubts about the survey's reliability.

Third, the argument does not mention how many homeless people were interviewed for the sur-vey, nor how the people were selected. If, for ex-ample, only 10 people were interviewed, this would be too small a sample to support the conclusion in this case. Lacking information about the sampling method used in the survey, it is impossible to assess the argument's persuasiveness.

Finally, the author assumes that shelters are more comfortable and secure than the streets. The ar-gument offers no evidence to support this assump-tion. Perhaps the shelters are overcrowded and crime-ridden. If this were so, it would go a long way toward explaining the survey's results.

As it stands, the argument is unconvincing. To make the argument more persuasive, the author would have to restate the conclusion to bring it into line with the evidence and provide information that would ensure that the survey was reliable. Addition-ally, the author would need to provide evidence to support the assumption that shelters are more secure and comfortable than the streets.

# Quantitative Ability Lesson 4: Algebra—Basic Concepts

## Today's Topics:

1. Basic terminology
2. Manipulating algebraic expressions
3. Solving linear equations
4. Solving quadratic equations
5. Solving algebraic inequalities
6. Algebra exercises

Today's lesson covers the "building blocks" that you need to handle GMAT algebra problems. After reviewing the rules for combining and simplifying algebraic expressions, you learn how to solve both linear and factorable quadratic equations.

## BASIC TERMINOLOGY

*Algebra* involves the use of *variables* (such as $x$ or $a$) in mathematical expressions to represent unknown values. An *algebraic expression* is any mathematical expression that includes one or more variables. Here is an example of an algebraic expression with two variables ($a$ and $b$):

$$a - 2b + 5$$

Every algebraic expression includes either one *term* or a series of two or more terms separated by + or – signs. The preceding expression includes three terms: $a$, $2b$, and $5$. $a$ and $2b$ are called *variable terms* (because their values can vary); $5$ is called a *constant term* (because its value does not vary). In the second term, $2$ is called the *coefficient* of $b$. $5$ is the coefficient of the constant third term. Algebraic expressions

with more than one term are usually called *polynomials*. *Binomials* and *trinomials* are polynomials with two and three terms, respectively:

$7x + 15yz$ (binomial)

$-\dfrac{2}{3}p - 9q + 17$ (trinomial)

Algebraic expressions without exponents (variables raised to a power) are called *linear* algebraic expressions. Those with variables raised to the second power are called *quadratic* expressions:

$2x + 3y$ (linear)

$2x^2 + 3y$ (quadratic)

$2x^2 + 3y^2$ (quadratic)

## MANIPULATING ALGEBRAIC EXPRESSIONS

Many GMAT Quantitative questions require you to manipulate algebraic expressions—that is, to restate them in some other form. Keep in mind that all the rules for arithmetical operations and for exponents and roots (see Day 7) apply to algebraic terms and expressions. In manipulating algebraic expressions, you might possibly do the following:

- Simplify a particular term by combining or canceling:

$$4x^2 \cdot 2x^3 = 8x^5$$

$$(x^2)^3 = x^6$$

$$\frac{a^4b^3}{a^2bc} = \frac{a^2b^2}{c}$$

$$\frac{b^2}{ab^3} = \frac{1}{ab^2}$$

$$\frac{\sqrt{16x^3y^2}}{\sqrt{4x^2y^2}} = \frac{4xy\sqrt{x}}{2xy} = 2\sqrt{x}$$

- Combine two (or more) terms having the same variable and same exponent:

$$a + a = 2a$$

$$\frac{1}{3}y - 6y = -\frac{17}{3}y$$

$$2\sqrt{x^2+y} + \sqrt{x^2+y} = 3\sqrt{x^2+y}$$

You cannot, however, combine these expressions:

$a^2 + a$ (the exponents are different)

$2a + 2b$ (the variables are different)

- Factor out numbers and variables common to all terms:

$$2x + 4xy + 10x^2y^2 = 2x(1 + 2y + 5xy^2)$$

(each term includes the coefficient 2 and the variable $x$)

- Distribute a term among two or more other terms (the reverse of factoring out numbers and variables common to all terms):

$$-3b(-8x - bx + 3) = 24bx + 3b^2x - 9b$$

($-3b$ is distributed among three other terms)

## SOLVING LINEAR EQUATIONS

Algebraic expressions are usually used in algebra to form equations. An equation sets two expressions equal to each other. An equation whose variables are in the first power only and whose graph is a straight line is a **linear equation**. For example,

$$11s - \frac{12}{11}t = 75 \text{ (a linear equation)}$$

### Solving Linear Equations with One Variable

To solve a linear equation (that is, to find the value of the variable that satisfies the equation), isolate the variable on one side of the equation. To accomplish this, perform the same operation on both sides of the equation, as the following paragraphs describe.

**Add or subtract the same term from both sides of the equation.** Doing so does not change the equality; it merely restates the equation in a different form.

$$2x - 6 = x - 9$$

First, place $x$-terms on the same side by subtracting $x$ from both sides:

$$2x - 6 - x = x - 9 - x$$
$$x - 6 = -9$$

Next, isolate $x$ by adding 6 to both sides:

$$x - 6 + 6 = -9 + 6$$
$$x = -3$$

**Multiply or divide both sides of the equation by the same non-zero term.** Doing so does not change the equality; it merely restates the equation in a different form. Here's an example:

$$-12 = \frac{11}{x}$$

multiply both sides by $x$:

$$(-12)(x) = \frac{11}{x}(x)$$

isolate $x$ by dividing both sides by $-12$:

$$\frac{-12x}{-12} = \frac{11}{-12}$$

$$x = -\frac{11}{12}$$

Here's another example:

$$15x + \frac{1}{3} = 3$$

isolate the $x$-term on one side:

$$15x = 2\frac{2}{3} \text{ or } \frac{8}{3}$$

$$\frac{15x}{15} = \frac{\frac{8}{3}}{15}$$

multiply $\frac{8}{3}$ by reciprocal of 15:

$$x = \left(\frac{8}{3}\right)\left(\frac{1}{15}\right) = \frac{8}{45}$$

**Where the original equation involves fractions, use** *cross-multiplication* **to eliminate the fractions.** Multiply the numerator from one side of the equation times the denominator from the other side. (In effect, cross-multiplication is a shortcut method of multiplying both sides of the equation by both denominators.) Set the product equal to the product of the other numerator and denominator:

$$\frac{7a}{8} \diagup\hspace{-1.2em}\diagdown \frac{a+1}{3}$$

$(3)(7a) = 8(a + 1)$ (result of cross-multiplication)

$21a = 8a + 8$ (distributing 8 to both $a$ and 1)

$21a - 8a = 8a + 8 - 8a$ (isolating $a$-terms on one side)

$$13a = 8$$

$$\frac{13a}{13} = \frac{8}{13} \text{ (isolating } a \text{ by dividing both sides by 13)}$$

$$a = \frac{8}{13}$$

**Square both sides of the equation to eliminate radical signs.** Where the variable is indicated under a radical sign (square root), remove the radical sign by squaring both sides of the equation. (Use a similar technique for cube or other roots.)

$$2 = \frac{11}{3}\sqrt{2x}$$

$$\frac{6}{11} = \sqrt{2x}$$

Square both sides and solve for x:

$$\frac{36}{121} = 2x$$

$$\frac{18}{121} = x$$

In some instances, however, squaring both sides of what appears to be a linear equation might reveal that the equation is nonlinear. The following example is a quadratic equation that has two possible values (or roots):

$$6x = \sqrt{3x}$$

$$36x^2 = 3x$$

$$36x^2 - 3x = 0$$

$$x(36x - 3) = 0$$

$$x = 0 \text{ or } 36x - 3 = 0$$

$$x = 0, \frac{1}{12}$$

You will examine quadratic equations in more detail a bit later.

## Linear Equations with More Than One Variable

A single linear equation with more than one variable cannot be solved. That is to say, you cannot determine the value of any variable. Consider the following equation:

$$4x - 9 = \frac{3}{2}y$$

Because this equation includes more than one variable, it is impossible to determine the value of either $x$ or $y$. You *can*, however, express either $x$ or $y$ in terms of the other variable. In fact, GMAT problems often call for you to do just that. Referring to the preceding equation, you can solve for $x$ in terms of $y$:

$$4x = \frac{3}{2}y + 9$$

$$x = \frac{3}{8}y + \frac{9}{4}$$

You can also solve for $y$ in terms of $x$:

$$\frac{4x - 9}{\frac{3}{2}} = y$$

$$\frac{8}{3}x - 6 = y$$

## Solving a System of Two Linear Equations with Two Variables

A *system of equations* involves two or more equations with one or more common variables. Here is a system of two equations with two variables:

$$\frac{2}{5}x + y = 3y - 10$$

$$y = 10 - x$$

Solving (determining a number value) for either of two variables requires at least *two distinct* equations (that is, two equations and two unknowns).

**Equivalent equations.** In some cases, what appears to be a system of two equations with two variables is actually one equation expressed in two different ways. The following two equations are really the same equation and are said to be *equivalent* to each other:

$$a + b = 30$$
$$2b = 60 - 2a$$

Why? Although these two equations appear different, you can manipulate the second equation so that it looks exactly the same as the first equation:

$$2b = 60 - 2a$$
$$2b = 2(30 - a)$$
$$b = 30 - a$$
$$a + b = 30$$

*Important:* A common ploy used in GMAT data sufficiency problems is to provide (as statements

1 and 2) two identical equations with two variables, but to "disguise" one of them so that it does not appear at first glance to be identical to the other one. In one equation with two variables, it is not possible to determine the value of either variable. Thus, the correct response to this type of Data Sufficiency question would be E.

**The substitution method.** If you are dealing with two linear equations that are *not* equivalent, you can determine the values for the two variables that satisfy both equations (in other words, you can solve for $x$ and $y$). One way to solve for the two variables is to express one of them in terms of the other using one of the equations, and then *substitute* that value in the other equation. Consider the system of equations introduced earlier in this section:

**Equation 1:** $\frac{2}{5}x + y = 3y - 10$

**Equation 2:** $y = 10 - x$

The value of $y$ in equation 2 can be substituted for $y$ in Equation 1 (first combine the two $y$-terms in equation 1) to solve for $x$:

$$\frac{2}{5}x = 2y - 10$$

$$\frac{2}{5}x = 2(10 - x) - 10$$

$$\frac{2}{5}x = 20 - 2x - 10$$

$$\frac{2}{5}x = 10 - 2x$$

$$\frac{2}{5}x + 2x = 10$$

$$\frac{12}{5}x = 10$$

$$x = \frac{50}{12} \text{ or } \frac{25}{6}$$

You can then substitute this $x$-value for $x$ in either Equation 1 or 2 to determine the value of $y$. Using Equation 2:

$$y = 10 - \frac{25}{6}$$

$$y = \frac{60}{6} - \frac{25}{6}$$

$$y = \frac{35}{6}$$

**The addition-subtraction method.** Another way to solve for $x$ and $y$ is to make the coefficients of one of the variables the same (disregarding the sign) in both equations and either add the equations or subtract one equation from the other. Here's an example:

$$3x + 4y = -8$$

$$x - 2y = \frac{1}{2}$$

In the second equation, multiply both sides by 2 (to make the $y$-coefficients the same) to solve for $x$ by adding the equations:

$$
\begin{aligned}
3x + 4y &= -8 \\
2x - 4y &= 1 \\
\hline
5x + 0 &= -7
\end{aligned}
$$

$$x = -\frac{7}{5}$$

Similarly, to solve for $y$, multiply both sides of the second equation by 3 (to make the $x$-coefficients the same), then subtract the second equation from the first:

$$
\begin{aligned}
3x + 4y &= -8 \\
3x - 6y &= \frac{3}{2} \\
\hline
0 + 10y &= -9\frac{1}{2}
\end{aligned}
$$

$$10y = -\frac{19}{2}$$

$$y = -\frac{19}{20}$$

You can also combine the addition-subtraction and substitution methods. Simply solve for one variable using the former method, then substitute the value of that variable in either equation to determine the other variable's value.

## SOLVING QUADRATIC EQUATIONS

A *quadratic equation* is an equation that you can express in the general form $ax^2 + bx + c = 0$, where $a$, $b$, and $c$ are real numbers and $a \neq 0$. Note that the $b$-term and $c$-term are not essential—that is, $b$ and/or $c$ can equal zero. (A quadratic equation has *at most* two real-number solutions, but might have only one or no real-number solutions.)

You can solve any quadratic equation by using the following formula:

$$x = \frac{-b \pm \sqrt{b^2 - 4ac}}{2a}$$

However, the GMAT does not require that you apply this formula. GMAT problems involving quadratic expressions are almost always *factorable,* and thus you can simplify and solve them without resorting to the preceding formula, as discussed in the following sections.

### Factoring Quadratic Expressions

Solving quadratic equations on the GMAT usually calls for the following three-step process:

1. Put the equation into the *standard form* ($ax^2 + bx + c = 0$).

2. Factor the terms of the left side of the equation into two linear expressions (roots) whose product is zero.

3. Independently set each linear expression (root) equal to zero and solve for the variable in each.

You will find that equations in which the coefficient of either the $b$-term or $c$-term is zero are easier to factor, whereas equations with coefficients other than 0 and 1 are usually more difficult to factor. To illustrate this process, consider the following three quadratic equations in turn:

**Equation 3:** $3x^2 = 10x$ (easier)

**Equation 4:** $-3y = 4 - y^2$ (tougher)

**Equation 5:** $-7z = 15 - 2z^2$ (toughest)

**Equation 3.** In Equation 3 (which does not include a $c$-term), it is easy to recognize that you can factor out an $a$-term as one of the two roots:

$3x^2 = 10x$ [the original equation]

$3x^2 - 10x\ (+\ 0) = 0$ [general form $(ax^2 + bx + c = 0)$]

$x(3x - 10) = 0$ [the two roots are $x$ and $(3x - 10)$]

$x = 0, 3x - 10 = 0$ [each root is set equal to zero]

$x = 0, \dfrac{10}{3}$ [two possible values of $x$ (two roots)]

**Equation 4 and the FOIL method.** Solving more complex quadratic equations is a bit trickier. For example, in Equation 4, after putting the equation into the general form, you can see that there are no common variables or coefficients that you can factor out of all three terms:

$-3y = 4 - y^2$ [the original equation]

$y^2 - 3y - 4 = 0$ [general form $(ax^2 + bx + c = 0)$]

Instead, you must factor the quadratic expression into two linear *binomial* expressions, using the *FOIL (first-outer-inner-last)* method. Under the FOIL method, the sum of the following four terms is equivalent to the original (nonfactored) quadratic expression:

- F, the product of the *first* terms of the two binomials

- O, the product of the *outer* terms of the two binomials

- I, the product of the *inner* terms of the two binomials

- L, the product of the *last (second)* terms of the two binomials

Note the following relationships:

- F is the $ax^2$ term (the first term) of the quadratic expression.

- O + I is the $bx$ term (the second term) of the quadratic expression.

- L is the $c$ term (the third term) of the quadratic expression.

Applying the FOIL method to Equation 4, you can first set up the following equation with two binomial factors:

$(y + ?)\ (y + ?) = 0$

To determine the missing values of the two second terms, find two numbers for which the product is $c$ (in this case, $-4$) and the sum of which is $b$ (in this case, $-3$). Those two numbers are $-4$ and $1$:

$(y - 4)\ (y + 1) = 0$

$y - 4 = 0, y + 1 = 0$

$y = 4, -1$

To check your work, reverse the process, using the FOIL method to multiply the two binomials together:

$y^2$ (first) $+ y$ (outer) $- 4y$ (inner) $- 4$ (last) $= 0$

$y^2\ (\ + y - 4y\ ) - 4 = 0$

$y^2 - 3y - 4 = 0$

**Equation 5 and the FOIL method.** In Equation 5, $z^2$ has a coefficient of 2. This complicates the process of factoring into two binomials. A bit of trial and error might be required to determine all coefficients in both binomials. Restate the equation in the general form and set up two binomial roots:

$$-7z = 15 - 2z^2$$

$$2z^2 - 7z - 15 = 0$$

$$(2z + ?)(z + ?) = 0$$

One of the two missing constants must be negative, because their product (the "L" term under the FOIL method) is $-15$. The possible integral pairs for these constants are $(1, -15)$, $(-1, 15)$, $(3, -5)$, and $(-3, 5)$. Substituting each value pair for the two ?s in Equation 5 reveals that 3 and $-5$ are the missing constants (remember to take into account that the first $x$-term includes a coefficient of 2):

$$(2z + 3)(z - 5) = 0$$

Check your work by reversing the process:

$2z^2\ (-\ 10z + 3z) - 15 = 0$ [FOIL]

$2z^2 - 7z - 15 = 0$

Now, solve for $z$:

$(2z + 3)(z - 5) = 0$

$2z + 3 = 0, x - 5 = 0$

$z = -\dfrac{3}{2}, 5$

## Nonlinear Expressions with Two Variables

On the GMAT, if you encounter nonlinear expressions with two variables, you probably don't have to determine numerical values for the variables. Instead, your task is to factor and simplify the expression. Two related nonlinear expressions that appear over and over again on the GMAT are worth noting (use the FOIL method to verify these equations):

$x^2 + y^2 = x^2 + 2xy + y^2$

$(x - y)^2 = x^2 - y^2$

Memorize each of these two expressions in both factored and nonfactored forms. When you see either form on the exam, in all likelihood the problem will require you to convert it to the other form.

## SOLVING ALGEBRAIC INEQUALITIES

You solve algebraic inequalities in the same manner as you solve equations. Isolate the variable on one side of the equation, factoring and canceling wherever possible. However, one important rule distinguishes inequalities from equations: Whenever you *multiply or divide by a negative number,* you must *reverse* the order of the inequality—that is, the inequality symbol. (This rule does not apply, however, to other operations.)

$12 - 4x < 8$

Subtract 12 from each side; inequality unchanged:

$-4x < -4$

Divide both sides by –4; reverse inequality:

$x > 1$

## PUTTING IT ALL TOGETHER: ALGEBRA EXERCISES

On the GMAT, whenever you encounter a complex and intimidating algebraic expression or equation, always ask yourself the following questions about each expression contained in the problem:

- Do the terms include common variables or coefficients that I can factor out?

- Can I combine common variables and coefficients within a term?

- Do any of the variables include exponents? If so, can a quadratic expression be isolated and factored into two binomials?

Before you move ahead to tomorrow's advanced algebra lesson, make sure that you are competent in applying the basic algebraic concepts covered today by attempting the following 10 questions (answers and explanations immediately follow):

1. If $\dfrac{2y}{9} = \dfrac{y-1}{3}$, then $y =$

   (A) $\dfrac{1}{3}$    (B) $\dfrac{4}{9}$    (C) $\dfrac{9}{15}$    (D) $\dfrac{9}{4}$    (E) 3

2. If $x + y = a$, and $x - y = b$, then $x =$

   (A) $a + b$    (B) $a - b$    (C) $\dfrac{1}{2}(a + b)$    (D) $\dfrac{1}{2}ab$

   (E) $\dfrac{1}{2}(a - b)$

3. If $x^2 - 4x = 21$, then $x =$

   (A) 7 or 3    (B) –7 or –3    (C) –7 or 3    (D) 7 or –3
   (E) 7 only

4. If $\sqrt{4x+4} - 4 = 8$, then $x =$

   (A) 15    (B) 35    (C) 39    (D) 47    (E) 51

5. Which of the following is a factor of $x^2 - x - 20$?

   (A) $x - 4$    (B) $x - 10$    (C) $x + 4$    (D) $x - 2$    (E) $x + 5$

6. If $x + y = 16$, and if $x^2 - y^2 = 48$, then $x - y$ equals

   (A) 3    (B) 4    (C) 6    (D) 32    (E) 36

7. If $\dfrac{\dfrac{3x-1}{3}}{x} = 10$ , then $x =$

(A) $-9$ or $-\dfrac{3}{10}$  (B) $\dfrac{3}{5}$ or $-2$  (C) $9$ or $-\dfrac{10}{3}$

(D) $\dfrac{10}{3}$ or $-3$  (E) $10$ or $-3$

8. If $-2x > -5$, then

(A) $x > \dfrac{5}{2}$  (B) $x < \dfrac{5}{2}$  (C) $x > -\dfrac{2}{5}$  (D) $x < \dfrac{2}{5}$

(E) $x > -\dfrac{5}{2}$

9. If $3x + 2y = 5a + b$ and $4x - 3y = a + 7b$, then $x =$

(A) $a + b$   (B) $a - b$   (C) $2a + b$
(D) $4a - 6b$   (E) $17a + 17b$

10. If $x + y = 8$, $x + z = 7$, and $y + z = 6$, what is the value of $x$?

(A) 3   (B) 3.5   (C) 4   (D) 4.5   (E) 5

## Answers and Explanations to the Algebra Exercises

1. The correct response is E.
$$9(y - 1) = 2y(3)$$
$$9y - 9 = 6y$$
$$3y = 9$$
$$y = 3$$

2. The correct response is C. Add the two equations:
$$x + y = a$$
$$x - y = b$$
$$2x = a + b$$
$$x = \dfrac{1}{2}(a + b)$$

3. The correct response is D.
$$x^2 - 4x - 21 = 0$$
$$(x - 7)(x + 3) = 0$$
$$x - 7 = 0, x + 3 = 0$$
$$x = 7, -3$$

4. The correct response is B.
$$2\sqrt{x+1} = 12$$
$$\sqrt{x+1} = 6$$
$$x + 1 = 36$$
$$x = 35$$

5. The correct response is C.
$$x^2 - x - 20 =$$
$$x^2 - 5x + 4x - 20 =$$
$$(x - 5)(x + 4)$$

6. The correct response is A.
$$x^2 - y^2 = (x + y)(x - y) = 48$$
Substituting 16 for $x + y$:
$$16(x - y) = 48$$
$$x - y = 3$$

7. The correct response is D. Invert the denominator fraction and multiply it by the numerator. Set the quadratic expression equal to 0, then find the two root values of x:
$$\dfrac{3x^2 - x}{3} = 10$$
$$3x^2 - x = 30$$
$$3x^2 - x - 30 = 0$$
$$(3x - 10)(x + 3) = 0$$
$$3x - 10 = 0, x + 3 = 0$$
$$x = \dfrac{10}{3}, -3$$

8. The correct response is B. Multiply both sides of the equation by $-1$ and reverse the order of the inequality:
$$2x < 5$$
$$x < \dfrac{5}{2}$$

9. The correct response is A. Multiply the first equation by 3, the second by 2, then add the following:

$$9x + 6y = 15a + 3b$$
$$8x - 6y = 2a + 14b$$
$$\overline{17x + 0y = 17a + 17b}$$
$$x = a + b$$

10. The correct response is D. This problem involves a system of three equations with three variables. The following solution employs both the substitution and addition-subtraction methods.

Express $x$ in terms of $y$: $x = 8 - y$. Substitute this expression for $x$ in the second equation: $(8 - y) + z = 7$ or $-y + z = -1$. Add this equation to the third equation in the system.

$$-y + z = -1$$
$$y + z = 6$$
$$\overline{2z = 5}$$
$$z = 2.5$$

Substitute $z$'s value for $z$ in the second equation to find the value of $x$:

$$x + 2.5 = 7$$
$$x = 4.5$$

## Day 16

# Quantitative Ability Lesson 5: Algebra Word Problems

## Today's Topics:

1. Work problems
2. Motion problems
3. Mixture problems
4. Age problems
5. Overlapping set problems
6. Fraction problems
7. Weighted average problems
8. Currency problems
9. Investment problems

Today you will learn how to handle the various types of quantitative word problems appearing commonly on the GMAT and that involve setting up and solving algebraic equations.

## WORK PROBLEMS

Work problems involve one or more "workers" (people or machines) accomplishing a task or job. In work problems, there is an inverse relationship between the number of workers and the time that it takes to complete the job—in other words, the more workers, the quicker the job gets done. A GMAT work problem might specify the rates at which certain workers work alone and ask you to determine the rate at which they work together, or vice versa. Here is the basic formula for solving a work problem:

$$\frac{1}{x} + \frac{1}{y} = \frac{1}{A}$$

In this formula, $x$ and $y$ represent the time needed for each of two workers—$x$ and $y$—to complete the job alone, and $a$ represents the time it takes for both $x$ and $y$ to complete the job working aggregately (together). The reasoning is that in one unit of time (that is, one hour) $x$ performs $\frac{1}{x}$ of the job, $y$ performs $\frac{1}{y}$ of the job, and $x$ and $y$ perform $\frac{1}{A}$ of the job.

*Note:* In the real world, if two workers can perform a given task in the same amount of time working alone, they might not be capable of performing that same task in half that time working together. However, in GMAT work problems, you can assume that there is no individual efficiency gained or lost by two or more workers working together.

Now look at two work problems, one requiring you to determine the aggregate rate of the workers (working together), the other requiring you to determine an individual worker's rate (working alone).

**Example 16-1: Individual rates given**

One printing press can print a daily news-paper in 12 hours, while another press can print it in 18 hours. How long will the job take if both presses work simultaneously?

The rate of the faster press is $\frac{1}{12}$ (it can print $\frac{1}{12}$ of the paper in one hour), and the rate of the slower press is $\frac{1}{18}$:

$$\frac{1}{12} + \frac{1}{18} = \frac{1}{A}$$

$$\frac{3}{36} + \frac{2}{36} = \frac{1}{A}$$

$$\frac{5}{36} = \frac{1}{A}$$

$$5A = 36$$

$$A = \frac{36}{5}$$

It takes both presses $\frac{36}{5}$ hours, or 7 hours and 12 minutes, to print the daily paper working together.

**Example 16-2: Aggregate rate given**

Petra and Belinda can make a particular quilt in two days when working together. If Petra requires six days to make the quilt alone, how many days does Belinda need to make the quilt alone?

Petra can complete one-sixth of the quilt in one day. The aggregate rate of Belinda and Petra working together is $\frac{1}{2}$ (together they can complete one half of the quilt in one day):

$$\frac{1}{6} + \frac{1}{b} = \frac{1}{2}$$

$$\frac{b+6}{6b} = \frac{1}{2}$$

$$2(b + 6) = 6b$$

$$2b + 12 = 6b$$

$$4b = 12$$

$$b = 3$$

It takes Belinda three days working alone to make the quilt.

In some cases, a second worker might slow or impede the other worker's progress, contributing a negative rate of work. Nevertheless, your approach should be basically the same, as in Example 16-3.

**Example 16-3: Negative rate of work**

A certain tank holds a maximum of 450 cubic meters of water. If a hose can fill the tank at a rate of 5 cubic meters per minute, but the tank has a hole through which a constant $\frac{1}{2}$ cubic meters of water escapes each minute, how long does it take to fill the tank to its maximum capacity?

In this problem, the hole is the "second worker" but is acting counterproductively, so that you must subtract its rate from the hose's rate to determine the aggregate rate of the hose and the hole. The hose alone takes 90 minutes to fill the tank. The hole alone empties a full tank in 900 minutes. Thus, the hose and the hole, "working" together, fill the tank as follows:

$$\frac{1}{90} - \frac{1}{900} = \frac{1}{A}$$

$$\frac{10}{900} - \frac{1}{900} = \frac{1}{A}$$

$$\frac{9}{900} = \frac{1}{A}$$

$$9A = 900$$

$$A = 100$$

It takes 100 minutes to fill the tank to its maximum capacity.

## MOTION PROBLEMS

Motion problems involve the linear movement of persons or objects over time. Fundamental to all GMAT motion problems is the following simple and familiar formula:

distance = rate × time

You can also express this formula as follows:
$d = (r)(t)$

Some GMAT motion problems track two objects (or persons) that move either in the same direction or in opposite directions. Others involve one moving object (or person), tracking two parts or "legs" of a trip (for example, away and back during a round trip). In any case, one of the three variables—distance, rate, or time—is *constant* (that is, the same for both moving objects or both legs of a trip). This feature enables you to set up an equation and to solve for the missing value. Don't confuse *motion* problems with *work* problems. Although both involve rate, work problems do not involve movement over a distance but rather rate of work and results of production.

Nearly every GMAT motion problem falls into one of three categories:

- Two objects moving in opposite directions

- Two objects moving in the same direction

- One object making a round trip

(A fourth type of motion problem involves perpendicular (right-angle) motion—for example, where one object moves in a northerly direction while another moves in an easterly direction. However, this type is really just as much a geometry as an algebra problem, because you determine the distance between the two objects by applying the Pythagorean Theorem to determine the length of a hypotenuse. See Day 21.)

Now take a look at one example of each of the three types of motion problems.

**Example 16-4: Motion in opposite directions (time constant)**

A passenger train and a freight train leave at 10:30 a.m. from stations that are 405 miles apart. The trains travel toward each other, with the rate of the passenger train 45 miles per hour (mph) faster than that of the freight train. If they pass each other at 1:30 p.m., how fast is the passenger train traveling?

Notice in this problem that each train traveled exactly three hours—in other words, time is the constant in this problem. Let $x$ equal the rate (speed) of the freight train. You can express the rate of the passenger train as $x + 45$. Substitute these values for time and rate into the motion formula for each train:

Passenger: $(x + 45)(3) = 3x + 135$

Freight: $(x)(3) = 3x$ (rate × time = distance)

The total distance that the two trains cover is given as 405 miles. Express this algebraically and solve for $x$:

$$(3x + 135) + (3x) = 405$$

$$6x = 270$$

$$x = 45$$

Accordingly, the rate of the passenger train was $45 + 45$, or 90 mph.

**Example 16-5: Motion in same direction (distance constant)**

Janice left her home at 11 a.m., traveling along Route 1 at 30 mph. At 1 p.m., her brother Richard left home and started after her on the same road at 45 mph. At what time did Richard catch up to Janice?

Notice that the distance that Janice covered is equal to that of Richard—that is, distance is constant. Letting $x$ equal Janice's time, you can express Richard's time as $x - 2$. Substitute these values for time and the values for rate given in the problem into the motion formula for Richard and Janice:

Janice: $(30)(x) = 30x$

Richard: $(45)(x - 2) = 45x - 90$

Because the distance is constant, Janice's distance as expressed algebraically can be equated with Richard's distance, and you can determine the value of $x$ as follows:

$$30x = 45x - 90$$

$$15x = 90$$

$$x = 6$$

Janice had traveled six hours when Richard caught up with her. Because Janice left at 11:00 a.m., Richard caught up with her at 5:00 p.m.

**Example 16-6: Motion involving a round trip (distance constant)**

How far can Scott drive into the country if he drives out at 40 mph, returns over the same road at 30 mph, and spends eight hours away from home including a one-hour stop for lunch?

Scott's actual driving time is seven hours, which you must divide into two parts: his time spent driving into the country and his time spent returning. Letting the first part equal $x$, the return time is what remains of the seven hours, or $7 - x$. Substitute these expressions into the motion formula for each of the two parts of Scott's journey:

Going: $(40)(x) = 40x$

Returning: $(30)(7 - x) = 210 - 30x$

Because the journey is round trip, the distance going equals the distance returning. Accordingly, you can determine the value of $x$ algebraically:

$40x = 210 - 30x$

$70x = 210$

$x = 3$

If Scott traveled 40 mph for three hours, he traveled 120 miles.

## MIXTURE PROBLEMS

In mixture problems, you combine substances with different characteristics, resulting in a particular mixture or proportion. There are really two types of mixture problems:

- *Wet mixture problems* involve liquids, gases, or granules, which are measured and mixed by volume or weight, not by number (quantity).

- *Dry mixture problems* involve a number of discreet objects, such as coins, cookies, or marbles, that are measured and mixed by number (quantity) as well as by relative weight, size, value, and so on.

Your approach toward wet and dry mixture problems should be similar. Take a look at an example of each type:

### Example 16-7: Wet mixture

How many quarts of pure alcohol must you add to 15 quarts of a solution that is 40% alcohol to strengthen it to a solution that is 50% alcohol?

The original amount of alcohol is 40% of 15. Letting $x$ equal the number of quarts of alcohol that you

must add to achieve a 50% alcohol solution, $.4(15) + x$ equals the amount of alcohol in the solution after adding more alcohol. You can express this amount as 50% of $(15 + x)$. Thus, you can express the mixture algebraically as follows:

$(.4)(15) + x = (.5)(15 + x)$

$6 + x = 7.5 + .5x$

$.5x = 1.5$

$x = 3$

You must add three quarts of alcohol to achieve a 50% alcohol solution.

If you have difficulty expressing mixture problems algebraically, use a table such as the following to indicate amounts and percentages, letting $x$ equal the amount or percentage that you are asked to solve for:

|  | # of quarts | X % alcohol = | amount of alcohol |
|---|---|---|---|
| original | 15 | 40% | 6 |
| added | $x$ | 100% | $x$ |
| new | $15 + x$ | 50% | $.5(15 + x)$ |

### Example 16-8: Dry mixture

How many pounds of nuts selling for 70 cents per pound must you mix with 30 pounds of nuts selling at 90 cents per pound to make a mixture that sells for 85 cents per pound?

The cost (in cents) of the nuts selling for 70 cents per pound can be expressed as $70x$, letting $x$ equal the number that you are asked to determine. You then add this cost to the cost of the more expensive nuts ($30 \times 90 = 2,700$) to obtain the total cost of the mixture, which you can express as $85(x + 30)$. You can state this algebraically and solve for $x$ as follows:

$70x + 2700 = 85(x + 30)$

$70x + 2700 = 85x + 2550$

$150 = 15x$

$x = 10$

You must add 10 pounds of 70-cent-per-pound nuts to make a mixture that sells for 85 cents per pound.

As with wet mixture problems, if you have trouble formulating an algebraic equation needed to solve the problem, indicate the quantities and values in a table such as the one shown in the below figure letting $x$ equal the value that you are asked to determine.

| | # of pounds $\times$ | price per pound $=$ | total value |
|---|---|---|---|
| less expensive | $x$ | 70 | $70x$ |
| more expensive | 30 | 90 | 2,700 |
| mixture | $x + 30$ | 85 | $85(x + 30)$ |

## AGE PROBLEMS

Age problems ask you to compare ages of two or more people at different points in time. In solving age problems, you might have to represent a person's age at the present time, several years from now, or several years ago. Any age problem allows you to set up an equation to relate the ages of two or more people, as in the following examples:

- If X is 10 years younger than Y at the present time, you can express the relationship between X's age and Y's age as $x = y - 10$ (or $x + 10 = y$).

- Five years ago, if A was twice as old as B, you can express the relationship between their ages as $2(a - 5) = b - 5$, where $a$ and $b$ are the present ages of A and B, respectively.

### Example 16-9

Eva is 24 years older than her son Frank. In eight years, Eva will be twice as old as Frank will be then. How old is Eva now?

Letting $x$ equal Frank's present age, you can express Frank's age eight years from now as $x + 8$. Similarly, you can express Eva's present age as $(x + 24)$, and her age eight years from now as $(x + 32)$. Set up the following equation relating Eva's age and Frank's age eight years from now:

$$x + 32 = 2(x + 8)$$
$$x + 32 = 2x + 16$$
$$16 = x$$

Jack's present age is 16, and Eva's present age is 40.

## OVERLAPPING SET PROBLEMS

Overlapping set problems involve distinct sets that share some number of members. Do not confuse these problems with the set problems that you examined on day 7, which involve combinations of set members. GMAT overlapping set problems come in one of two varieties: single overlap and double overlap (the latter type is more complex). Now look at an example of each.

### Example 16-10: Single overlap

Each of the 24 people auditioning for a community-theater production is either an actor, a musician, or both. If 10 of the people auditioning are actors and 19 of the people auditioning are musicians, how many of the people auditioning are musicians but not actors?

This problem presents three mutually exclusive sets: actors who are not musicians, musicians who are not actors, and actors who are also musicians. The total number of people among these three sets is 24. You can represent this scenario with the following algebraic equation ($n$ = number of actors/musicians), solving for $19 - n$ to respond to the question:

$$(10 - n) + n + (19 - n) = 24$$
$$29 - n = 24$$
$$n = 5$$
$$19 - n = 14$$

There are 14 musicians auditioning who are not actors. With problems such as this one, it might be helpful to use a Venn diagram in which overlapping circles represent the set of musicians and the set of actors, as shown in the next figure.

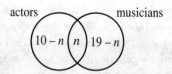

You can, of course, approach this problem less formally as well. The number of actors plus the number of musicians equals 29 (10 + 19 = 29); however, only 24 people are auditioning. Thus, 5 of the 24 are actor-musicians, so 14 of the 19 musicians must not be actors.

### Example 16-11: Double overlap

Adrian owns 48 neckties, each of which is either 100% silk or 100% polyester. Forty percent of his ties are striped, and 13 of his ties are silk. How many ties does Adrian own that are polyester but are not striped?

This double overlap problem involves four distinct sets: striped silk ties, striped polyester ties, nonstriped silk ties, and nonstriped polyester ties. The number of ties among these four discreet sets totals 48. Although you can approach this problem formally, the best way to handle it is to set up a table representing the four sets, filling in the information given in the problem as shown in the figure (the value required to answer the question is indicated by the question mark).

|  | silk | polyester |  |
|---|---|---|---|
| striped |  |  | 40% |
| non-striped |  | ? | 60% |
|  | 13 | 35 |  |

Given that 13 ties are silk (see the left column), 35 ties must be polyester (see the right column). Also, given that 40% of the ties are striped (see the top row), 60% must be nonstriped (see the bottom row). Thus, 60% of 35 ties, or 19 ties, are polyester and nonstriped.

---

## FRACTION PROBLEMS

Fraction problems can be deceptively confusing if you are not ready for them. A fraction is really a *ratio*

between two numbers. If the *value* of a fraction is $\frac{3}{4}$, for instance, this does not necessarily mean that the numerator is 3 and the denominator is 4. The numerator and denominator can be 6 and 8, 1.5 and 3, −900 and −1,200, or an infinite number of other possible combinations. All you know is that the ratio of the two numbers is 3 to 4, or 3:4. Thus, you can express the numerator generally by $3x$ and the denominator by $4x$, and the fraction by $\frac{3x}{4x}$. With this in mind, consider Example 16-12.

### Example 16-12

At the beginning of the day, a small grocery store carried exactly three times as many cans of chicken soup as cans of tomato soup. During the day, the store sold six cans of chicken soup but no cans of tomato soup. The store receives a shipment of eight new cans of tomato soup but no new cans of chicken soup during the day. If at the end of the day the store carried eight cans of tomato soup and nine cans of chicken soup, how many cans of chicken soup did it carry at the beginning of the day?

You can represent the original ratio of tomato soup to chicken soup by the fraction $\frac{x}{3x}$. Both quantities change during the day, resulting in a new ratio. You can represent this algebraically:

$$\frac{x+8}{3x-6} = \frac{8}{9}$$

To solve for $x$, use this formula:

$$9x + 72 = 24x - 48 \text{ (cross-multiplication)}$$
$$120 = 15x$$
$$x = 8$$
$$3x = 24$$

The grocery store carried 24 cans of chicken soup (and eight cans of tomato soup) at the beginning of the day.

---

## WEIGHTED AVERAGE PROBLEMS

On Day 7, you examined the concept of simple average (arithmetic mean). Recall the formula for determining the average ($A$) of a series of terms (numbers), where $n$ equals the number of terms (numbers) in the series:

$$A = \frac{a+b+c...}{n}$$

Thus, the arithmetic mean of –2, 7, 22, and 19 is 11.5:

$$A = \frac{-2+7+22+19}{4} = \frac{46}{4} = 11.5$$

When some numbers among the terms to be averaged are given greater "weight" than others, however, the foregoing formula is inadequate. In such problems, you must adjust the various terms to reflect differing weights. As a simple illustration, suppose that a student receives grades of 80 and 90 on two exams, but the former grade receives three times the weight of the latter exam. The student's weighted-average grade is not 85 but rather some number closer to 80 than 90. One way to approach this problem is to think of the first grade (80) as three scores of 80, which added to the score of 90 and divided by 4 (not 2) results in the weighted average:

$$WA = \frac{80+80+80+90}{4} = \frac{330}{4} = 82.5$$

You can also approach this problem more intuitively (less formally). You are looking for a number between 80 and 90 (a range of 10). The simple average would obviously lie midway between the two. Given that the score of 80 receives three times the weight of the score of 90, the weighted average is three times closer to 80 than to 90, or three-fourths of the way from 90 to 80. Dividing the range into four segments, it is clear that the weighted average is 82.5. Similarly, if 80 received twice the weight of 90, the weighted average is $83\frac{1}{3}$, and if 80 received four times the weight of 90, the weighted average is 82. Apply both the formal algebraic and less formal approaches to the following examples:

### Example 16-13: Weighted average is given

Mike's average monthly salary for the first four months that he worked was $3,000. What must his average monthly salary be for each of the next eight months, so that his average monthly salary for the year is $3,500?

In this relatively easy example, the $3,000 salary receives a weight of 4, while the unknown salary receives a weight of 8. You can approach this problem in a strict algebraic manner as follows:

$$3,500 = \frac{4(3,000)+8x}{12}$$
$$(12)(3,500) = 12,000 + 8x$$
$$30,000 = 8x$$
$$x = 3,750$$

Mike's salary for each of the next eight months must be $3,750 for Mike to earn an average of $3,500 a month during the entire 12 months. You can also approach this problem more intuitively. One-third of the monthly salary payments are "underweighted" (less than the desired $3,500 average) by $500. Thus, to achieve the desired average with 12 salary payments, you must overweight the remaining two-thirds of the payments (exceeding $3,500) by half that amount—that is, by $250.

### Example 16-14: Terms to be averaged are given

Cynthia drove for seven hours at an average rate of 50 mph and for one hour at an average rate of 60 mph. What was her average rate for the entire trip?

As in the exam-grade illustration earlier, think of Cynthia's average rate as the average of eight equally-weighted one-hour trips. Seven of those trips receive a weight of 50, and one of the trips receives a weight of 60. You can express this algebraically as follows:

$$AR = \frac{7(50)+60}{8} = \frac{350+60}{8} = \frac{410}{8} = 51.25$$

Cynthia's average rate during the entire trip was 51.25 mph. Of course, you can approach this problem more intuitively. The single faster hour of the eight-hour trip boosts what would otherwise have been a 50-mph average rate up one-eighth of the way to 60—that is, up by 1.25 to 51.25.

## CURRENCY PROBLEMS

Currency problems are really quasi-weighted-average problems, because each item (bill or coin) in a problem is weighted according to its monetary value. Unlike weighted average problems, however, the "average" value of all the bills or coins is not at issue. In solving currency problems, remember the following:

- You must formulate algebraic expressions involving both *number* of items (bills or coins) and *value* of items.

- You should convert the value of all moneys to a common unit (that is, cents or dollars) before formulating an equation. If converting to cents, for example, you must multiply the number of nickels by 5, dimes by 10, and so forth.

### Example 16-15

Jim has $2.05 in dimes and quarters. If he has four fewer dimes than quarters, how much money does he have in dimes?

Letting $x$ equal the number of dimes, $x + 4$ represents the number of quarters. The total value of the dimes (in cents) is $10x$, and the total value of the quarters (in cents) is $25(x + 4)$ or $25x + 100$. Given that Jim has $2.05, the following equation emerges:

$$10x + 25x + 100 = 205$$
$$35x = 105$$
$$x = 3$$

Jim has three dimes, so he has 30 cents in dimes.

---

## INVESTMENT PROBLEMS

GMAT investment problems usually involve interest and require more than simply calculating interest earned on a given principal amount at a given rate. They usually call for you to set up and solve an algebraic equation.

### Example 16-16

Dr. Kramer plans to invest $20,000 in an account paying 6% interest annually. How many additional dollars must she invest at the same time at 3% so that her total annual income during the first year is 4% of her entire investment?

Letting $x$ equal the amount invested at 3%, you can express Dr. Kramer's total investment as 20,000 + $x$. The interest on $20,000 plus the interest on the additional investment equals the total interest from both investments. You can state this algebraically as follows:

$$.06(20,000) + .03x = .04(20,000 + x)$$

Multiplying all terms by 100 to eliminate decimals, solve for $x$:

$$6(20,000) + 3x = 4(20,000 + x)$$
$$120,000 + 3x = 80,000 + 4x$$
$$40,000 = x$$

She must invest $40,000 at 3% for her total annual income to be 4% of her total investment ($60,000).

In solving GMAT investment problems, remember the following:

- It's best simply to eliminate percentage signs (or multiply terms by 100 to eliminate decimals).

- Don't try to solve these problems intuitively; interest problems can be misleading on their face. (For instance, in Example 16-16, you might have guessed or "intuited" that Dr. Kramer would have to invest more than *twice* as much at 3% than at 6% to lower the overall interest rate to 4%. Not true!)

## Quantitative Ability Lesson 6:
## Mini-Test and Review (Algebra)

### Today's Topics:

Today you apply what you learned from the previous two days to a 20-question mini-test, which includes Problem Solving questions as well as Data Sufficiency questions.

## MINI-TEST (ALGEBRA)

**Number of questions:** 20
**Suggested time:** 40 minutes

**Directions:** Attempt the following 20 Quantitative questions under simulated exam conditions. After completing the mini-test, review the explanations that follow. Preceding the explanation for each question, the question type and difficulty level are indicated.

1. ABC Company pays an average of $140 per vehicle each month in outdoor parking fees for three of its eight vehicles. The company pays garage parking fees for the remaining five vehicles. If ABC pays an average of $240 per vehicle overall each month for parking, how much does ABC pay per month in garage parking fees for its vehicles?

   (A) $300
   (B) $420
   (C) $912
   (D) $1,420
   (E) $1,500

2. If $\frac{9b^3 - 15b^2 - 6b}{18b^2 + 6b} = 13b - 17$, then $b =$

   (A) $\frac{-14}{5}$
   (B) $\frac{5}{16}$
   (C) $\frac{32}{25}$
   (D) 3
   (E) $\frac{7}{2}$

3. Each computer in a computer lab is equipped with either a modem, a sound card, or both. What percentage of the computers are equipped with modems but not sound cards?

   1. Twenty percent of the computers are equipped with both modems and sound cards.
   2. Twenty-five percent of the computers are equipped with sound cards but not with modems.

   (A) Statement 1 alone is sufficient to answer the question, but statement 2 alone is not sufficient
   (B) Statement 2 alone is sufficient to answer the question, but statement 1 alone is not sufficient

(C) Both statements together are needed to answer the question, but neither statement alone is sufficient to answer the question

(D) Either statement by itself is sufficient to answer the question

(E) Not enough facts are given to answer the question

4. An investor wants to sell some of the stock that he owns in MicroTron and Dynaco Corporations. He can sell MicroTron stock for $36 per share, and he can sell Dynaco stock for $52 per share. If he sells 300 shares altogether at an average price per share of $40, how many shares of Dynaco stock has he sold?

(A) 52

(B) 75

(C) 92

(D) 136

(E) 184

5. Dan drove home from college at an average rate of 60 miles per hour. On his trip back to college, his rate was 10 miles per hour slower and the trip took him one hour longer than the drive home. How far is Dan's home from the college?

(A) 65 miles

(B) 100 miles

(C) 200 miles

(D) 280 miles

(E) 300 miles

6. The denominator of a certain fraction is twice as large as the numerator. If you add 4 to both the numerator and denominator, the value of the new fraction is $\frac{5}{8}$. What is the denominator of the original fraction?

(A) 3

(B) 6

(C) 9

(D) 12

(E) 13

7. How long would it take five typists to type 30 pages if all five typists type at the same speed?

1. One typist can type four pages in 30 minutes.

2. Three typists can type eight pages in 20 minutes.

(A) Statement 1 alone is sufficient to answer the question, but statement 2 alone is not sufficient

(B) Statement 2 alone is sufficient to answer the question, but statement 1 alone is not sufficient

(C) Both statements together are needed to answer the question, but neither statement alone is sufficient to answer the question

(D) Either statement by itself is sufficient to answer the question

(E) Not enough facts are given to answer the question

8. If $x$ is a nonzero integer, what is the value of $x$?

1. $-4x - 7 > -14$

2. $5x + 3 > -2(x + 1)$

(A) Statement 1 alone is sufficient to answer the question, but statement 2 alone is not sufficient

(B) Statement 2 alone is sufficient to answer the question, but statement 1 alone is not sufficient

(C) Both statements together are needed to answer the question, but neither statement alone is sufficient to answer the question

(D) Either statement by itself is sufficient to answer the question

(E) Not enough facts are given to answer the question

9. If a portion of $10,000 is invested at 6% and the remaining portion is invested at 5%, and if $x$ represents the amount invested at 6%, what is the annual income in dollars from the 5% investment?

(A) $5(x - 10,000)$

(B) $.05(x + 10,000)$

(C) $.05(10,000 - x)$

(D) $5(10,000 - x)$

(E) $.05(x - 10,000)$

10. Jill is now 20 years old and her brother Gary is now 14 years old. How many years ago was Jill three times as old as Gary was at that time?

   (A) 3

   (B) 8

   (C) 9

   (D) 11

   (E) 13

11. If $|a| > |b|$ and if $a$ and $b$ are both integers, is $\sqrt{a^2 - b^2}$ an integer?

   1. $a^2 + 1 = \dfrac{a^2}{b^2}$

   2. $a - b$ is an odd integer.

   (A) Statement 1 alone is sufficient to answer the question, but statement 2 alone is not sufficient

   (B) Statement 2 alone is sufficient to answer the question, but statement 1 alone is not sufficient

   (C) Both statements together are needed to answer the question, but neither statement alone is sufficient to answer the question

   (D) Either statement by itself is sufficient to answer the question

   (E) Not enough facts are given to answer the question

12. In a group of $m$ workers, if $b$ workers earn $D$ dollars per week and the rest earn half that amount each, which of the following represents the total number of dollars paid to the entire group of workers in a week?

   (A) $bD + b - m$

   (B) $bD + \dfrac{1}{2}mD$

   (C) $\dfrac{3}{2}bD + mD$

   (D) $\dfrac{3}{2}D(b + m)$

   (E) $\dfrac{1}{2}D(b + m)$

13. Lisa has 45 coins, which are worth a total of $3.50. If the coins are all nickels and dimes, how many more dimes than nickels does she have?

   (A) 5

   (B) 10

   (C) 15

   (D) 20

   (E) 25

14. If a train travels $r + 2$ miles in $h$ hours, which of the following represents the number of miles the train travels in one hour and 30 minutes?

   (A) $\dfrac{3r+6}{2h}$

   (B) $\dfrac{3r}{h+2}$

   (C) $\dfrac{\frac{r+2}{h+3}}{2}$

   (D) $\dfrac{r}{h+6}$

   (E) $2h + 6r$

15. How many ounces of soy sauce must you add to 18 ounces of a peanut sauce and soy sauce mixture consisting of 32% peanut sauce to create a mixture that is 12% peanut sauce?

   (A) $38\dfrac{2}{5}$

   (B) 30

   (C) $26\dfrac{2}{3}$

   (D) $24\dfrac{3}{4}$

   (E) 21

16. What is the numerical value of the second term in the following sequence: $x, x + 1, x + 3, x + 6, x + 10, x + 15 \ldots$?

   1. The sum of the first and second terms is one-half the sum of the third and fourth terms.

   2. The sum of the sixth and seventh terms is 43.

   (A) Statement 1 alone is sufficient to answer the question, but statement 2 alone is not sufficient

(B) Statement 2 alone is sufficient to answer the question, but statement 1 alone is not sufficient

(C) Both statements together are needed to answer the question, but neither statement alone is sufficient to answer the question

(D) Either statement by itself is sufficient to answer the question

(E) Not enough facts are given to answer the question

17. Among all sales staff at Listco Corporation, college graduates and those without college degrees are equally represented. Each sales staff member is either a level 1 or level 2 employee. How many sales staff members without college degrees are level 2 employees?

1. Level 1 college graduates account for 15% of Listco's sales staff.

2. Listco employs 72 level 1 employees, 30 of whom are college graduates.

(A) Statement 1 alone is sufficient to answer the question, but statement 2 alone is not sufficient

(B) Statement 2 alone is sufficient to answer the question, but statement 1 alone is not sufficient

(C) Both statements together are needed to answer the question, but neither statement alone is sufficient to answer the question

(D) Either statement by itself is sufficient to answer the question

(E) Not enough facts are given to answer the question

18. Two buses are 515 miles apart. At 9:30 a.m., they start traveling toward each other at rates of 48 and 55 miles per hour. At what time will they pass each other?

(A) 1:30 p.m.

(B) 2:00 p.m.

(C) 2:30 p.m.

(D) 3:00 p.m.

(E) 3:30 p.m.

19. During the first three weeks of his 10-week diet program, Bob lost an average of five pounds per week. During the final seven weeks of the program, he lost an average of two pounds per week. How much weight had Bob lost after the seventh week of the diet program?

1. Bob lost an average of one pound per week during the fifth and sixth weeks of the program.

2. Bob lost the same amount of weight during the first three weeks of the program as during the last three weeks of the program.

(A) Statement 1 alone is sufficient to answer the question, but statement 2 alone is not sufficient

(B) Statement 2 alone is sufficient to answer the question, but statement 1 alone is not sufficient

(C) Both statements together are needed to answer the question, but neither statement alone is sufficient to answer the question

(D) Either statement by itself is sufficient to answer the question

(E) Not enough facts are given to answer the question

20. Two water hoses feed a 40-gallon tank. If one of the hoses dispenses water at the rate of 2 gallons per minute, and the other hose dispenses water at the rate of 5 gallons per minute, how many minutes does it take to fill the 40-gallon tank, if the tank is empty initially?

(A) $2\frac{5}{8}$

(B) $5\frac{2}{7}$

(C) 7

(D) $8\frac{4}{9}$

(E) 28

# Quick Answer Guide

## Mini-Test: Algebra

| | | | |
|---|---|---|---|
| 1. | E | 11. | A |
| 2. | C | 12. | E |
| 3. | C | 13. | A |
| 4. | B | 14. | A |
| 5. | E | 15. | B |
| 6. | D | 16. | D |
| 7. | D | 17. | C |
| 8. | C | 18. | C |
| 9. | C | 19. | B |
| 10. | D | 20. | B |

## EXPLANATIONS

### 1. Weighted average (easier). Answer: E.

The total parking fee that ABC pays each month is $1,920 ($240 × 8). Of that amount, $420 is paid for outdoor parking for three cars. The difference ($1,920 − $420 = $1,500) is the total garage parking fee that the company pays for the other five cars.

### 2. Factorable quadratic equations (moderate). Answer: C.

Here are the steps required to solve for $b$:

$$\frac{3b\left(3b^2 - 5b - 2\right)}{6b(3b+1)} = 13b - 17$$

$$\frac{3b(3b+1)(b-2)}{6b(3b+1)} = 13b - 17$$

$$\frac{b-2}{2} = 13b - 17$$

$$b - 2 = 26b - 34$$

$$25b = 32$$

$$b = \frac{32}{25}$$

### 3. Overlapping sets, single overlap (easier). Answer: C.

Neither statement 1 nor 2 alone suffices to answer the question. You still do not know what portion of the remaining computers are equipped only with modems. However, both statements together establish that 55% (100−20−25) are equipped only with modems.

### 4. Dry mixture (challenging). Answer: B.

The value of Dynaco shares sold plus the value of MicroTron shares sold must be equal to the value of all shares sold (that is, the "mixture"). Letting $x$ represent the number of shares of Dynaco sold, you can represent the number of shares of MicroTron sold by $300 - x$. The figure on page 147 represents all values algebraically.

| | # of shares | X price per share | = total value |
|---|---|---|---|
| Dynaco | $x$ | 52 | $52x$ |
| MicroTron | $300-x$ | 36 | $36(300-x)$ |
| mixture | 300 | 40 | 12,000 |

Set up an equation in which the value of Dynaco shares sold plus the value of MicroTron shares sold equals the total value of all shares sold, and solve for $x$:

$$\$52(x) + \$36(300 - x) = \$40(300)$$
$$52x + 10,800 - 36x = 12,000$$
$$16x = 1,200$$
$$x = 75$$

The investor has sold 75 shares of Dynaco stock. Checking your work:

$$\$52(75) + \$36(300 - 75) = \$12,000$$
$$\$3,900 + \$36(225) = \$12,000$$
$$\$3,900 + \$8,100 = \$12,000$$

## 5. Motion, round trip (challenging). Answer: E.

You can express the distance both in terms of Dan's driving time going home and going back to college. Letting $x$ equal the time (in hours) it took Dan to drive home, you can express the distance between his home and his workplace both as $60x$ and as $50(x + 1)$. Equate the two distances (because distance is constant) and solve for $x$ as follows:

$$60x = 50(x + 1)$$
$$60x = 50x + 50$$
$$10x = 50$$
$$x = 5$$

It took Dan five hours at 60 miles per hour to drive from college to home, so the distance is 300 miles.

## 6. Fractions (moderate). Answer: D.

Represent the original fraction by $\frac{x}{2x}$, and add 4 to both the numerator and denominator:

$$\frac{x+4}{2x+4} = \frac{5}{8}$$
$$8x + 32 = 10x + 20 \text{ (cross-multiplication)}$$
$$12 = 2x$$
$$x = 6$$

The original denominator is $2x$, or 12.

## 7. Work problem (easier). Answer: D.

To answer the question, you must determine the speed (or rate) at which a typist types, in terms of pages per unit of time. Each of the two statements provides that information. Although it is not necessary to work any further (the correct response is D), you can set up a general equation to express the time required by a typist to type one page:

$$\frac{(\text{\# of typists})(\text{time})}{\text{\# of pages}} = \text{time per page}$$

Based on the values provided in either statement 1 or 2, the typing rate of a single typist is $7\frac{1}{2}$ minutes per page:

$$\frac{(1 \text{ typist})(30 \text{ minutes})}{4 \text{ pages}} = 7\frac{1}{2} = \frac{(3 \text{ typist})(20 \text{ minutes})}{8 \text{ pages}}$$

Accordingly, five typists could type 30 pages in 45 minutes:

$$\frac{(5 \text{ typists})(45 \text{ minutes})}{30 \text{ pages}} = 7\frac{1}{2}$$

## 8. Solving algebraic inequalities (moderate). Answer: C.

You can solve for $x$ in statement 1:

$$14x - 7 > x - 14$$
$$-5x - 7 > -14$$
$$-5x > -7$$
$$-x > -\frac{7}{5}$$
$$x < \frac{7}{5}$$

You can solve for $x$ in statement 2:

$$5x + 3 > -2(x + 1)$$
$$5x + 3 > -2x - 2$$
$$7x + 3 > -5$$
$$x > -\frac{5}{7}$$

Neither statement 1 nor 2 alone suffices to determine the value of $x$. However, considering both statements together, $-\frac{5}{7} < x < \frac{7}{5}$. Only two integral $x$-values—0 and 1—fall within this range. Given that $x$ is a nonzero integer, $x = 1$. Both statements 1 and 2 together suffice to determine the value of $x$, which is 1.

## 9. Investment (moderate). Answer: C.

The amount invested at 5% is $10,000 - x$ dollars. Thus, the income from that amount is $.05(10,000 - x)$ dollars.

## 10. Age (easier). Answer: D.

Jill's age $x$ years ago can be stated algebraically as $20 - x$. At that time, Gary's age was $14 - x$. The following equation emerges:

$$20 - x = 3(14 - x)$$
$$20 - x = 42 - 3x$$
$$2x = 22$$
$$x = 11$$

Jill was three times as old as Gary 11 years ago. (Jill was 9 and Gary was 3.)

## 11. Equations with radicals (challenging). Answer: A.

Manipulate the equation in statement 1 to isolate a term that bears a clear relationship to $\sqrt{a^2 - b^2}$ :

$$a^2 + 1 = \frac{a^2}{b^2}$$
$$b^2 ( a^2 + 1 ) = a^2$$
$$b^2 a^2 + b^2 = a^2$$
$$b^2 a^2 = a^2 - b^2$$
$$(ab)^2 = a^2 - b^2$$
$$ab = \sqrt{a^2 - b^2}$$

Given that $a$ and $b$ are both integers, $ab$ must be an integer. Accordingly, $\sqrt{a^2 - b^2}$ must be an integer, and statement 1 suffices alone to answer the question. Turning to statement 2, given that $a - b$ is an integer, whether $\sqrt{a^2 - b^2}$ is also an integer depends on the values of $a$ and $b$. For example; if $a = 5$ and

$b = 4$, $5 - 4 = 1$ (an odd integer), and $\sqrt{5^2 - 4^2} = \sqrt{9} = 3$ (an integer). However if $a = 5$ and $b = 2$, $5 - 2 = 3$ (an integer), but $\sqrt{5^2 - 2^2} = \sqrt{21}$ (not an integer). Thus, statement 2 alone is insufficient to answer the question.

## 12. Weighted average (moderate). Answer: E.

The money earned by $b$ workers at $D$ dollars per week is $bD$. The number of workers remaining is $(m - b)$, and because they earn $\frac{1}{2} D$ dollars per week, the money they earn is $\frac{1}{2} D(m - b) = \frac{1}{2} mD - \frac{1}{2} bD$. Thus, the total amount earned is $bD + \frac{1}{2} mD - \frac{1}{2} bd = \frac{1}{2} bd + \frac{1}{2} mD = \frac{1}{2} D(b + m)$.

## 13. Currency (moderate). Answer: A.

Let $x$ equal the number of nickels:

$$45 - x = \text{the number of dimes}$$
$$5x = \text{the value of all nickels (in cents)}$$
$$450 - 10x = \text{the value of all dimes (in cents)}$$

Given a total value of 350 cents:

$$5x + 450 - 10x = 350$$
$$-5x = -100$$
$$x = 20$$

Lisa has 20 nickels and 25 dimes; thus, she has five more dimes than nickels.

## 14. Motion (moderate). Answer: A.

Given that the train travels $r + 2$ miles in $h$ hours, you can express its rate in miles per hour as $\frac{r+2}{h}$. In $1\frac{1}{2}$ hours, the train would travel $\frac{3}{2}$ this distance, or $\left(\frac{3}{2}\right)\left(\frac{r+2}{h}\right) = \frac{3r+6}{2h}$.

## 15. Wet mixture (challenging). Answer: B.

Letting $x$ equal the number of ounces of soy sauce added to the mixture, $18 + x$ equals the total amount of the mixture after you add the soy sauce. You can represent all values algebraically as shown in the figure on page 149.

| | # of ounces | × % peanut sauce | = amount of peanut sauce |
|---|---|---|---|
| original | 18 | 32 | 5.76 |
| added | $x$ | 0 | 0 |
| new | $x + 18$ | 12 | $12x + 216$ |

The amount of peanut sauce (5.76 ounces) must equal 12% of the new total amount of the mixture, which is $18 + x$. You can express this as an algebraic equation and solve for $x$:

$$5.76 = .12(x + 18)$$
$$576 = 12(x + 18)$$
$$576 = 12x + 216$$
$$360 = 12x$$
$$x = 30$$

You must add 30 ounces of soy sauce to achieve a mixture that includes 12% peanut sauce.

## 16. Linear equations, one variable (easier). Answer: D.

Statement 1 establishes a linear equation with one variable: $x + (x + 1) = \frac{1}{2} [(x + 3) + (x + 6)]$. You can determine the second term by solving for $x$, and statement 1 suffices to answer the question. [The second term is 4.5 ($x = 3.5$); however, you need not determine these values.] Statement 2 also establishes a linear equation with one variable: $(x + 15) + (x + 21) = 43$. The seventh term is $(x + 21)$ because each successive term in the sequence adds to $x$ a number that is one greater than the number that the previous term added to $x$. Statement 2 alone suffices to answer the question. (Again, $x = 3.5$ and the second term is 4.5, although you need not determine either value.)

## 17. Overlapping sets, double overlap (moderate). Answer: C.

You can organize the information in this problem as shown in the following figure.

| | Level 1 | Level 2 | |
|---|---|---|---|
| cg | | | 50% |
| non-cg | | | 50% |

Statement 1 provides no information about the number of sales staff members. Thus, you can easily eliminate answers A and D. Statement 2, although providing the number of level 1 sales employees of each type, is insufficient alone to determine the numbers of the level 2 employees. However, statements 1 and 2 together suffice to answer the question. You can fill in the table as follows:

| | Level 1 | Level 2 | |
|---|---|---|---|
| cg | 30(15%) | 70(35%) | 50% |
| non-cg | 42(21%) | 58(29%) | 50% |
| | 72(36%) | 128(64%) | |

## 18. Motion, opposite directions (moderate). Answer: C.

The total distance is equal to the distance that one bus traveled plus the distance that the other bus traveled (to the point where they pass each other). Letting $x$ equal the number of hours traveled, you can express the distances that the two buses travel in that time as $48x$ and $55x$. Equate the sum of these distances with the total distance and solve for $x$:

$$48x + 55x = 515$$
$$103x = 515$$
$$x = 5$$

The buses will pass each other five hours after 9:30 a.m.—at 2:30 p.m.

## 19. Weighted average (challenging). Answer: B.

Statement 1 alone is insufficient to answer the question, because you cannot determine Bob's weight loss during the fourth through seventh weeks. Statement 2 alone, however, suffices to answer the question. Given that Bob lost an average of 5 pounds per week during the first three weeks, his total weight loss during that period was 15 pounds. With statement 2, his total weight loss during all but the fourth through seventh weeks was 30 pounds. Given that he lost 29 pounds altogether during the week $[(3 \times 5) + (7 \times 2)]$, he must have gained 1 pound during the fourth through seventh week. Accordingly, he had lost 14 pounds $(-15 + 1)$ after the first seven weeks.

## 20. Work problem (moderate). Answer: B.

The first hose can perform $\frac{1}{20}$ of the job in one minute. The second hose can perform $\frac{1}{8}$ of the job in one minute. You can add the two rates together to obtain the aggregate rate per minute:

$$\frac{1}{20} + \frac{1}{8} = \frac{1}{A}$$

$$\frac{2}{40} + \frac{5}{40} = \frac{1}{A}$$

$$\frac{7}{40} = \frac{1}{A}$$

$$7A = 40$$

$$A = 5\frac{2}{7}$$

It takes $5\frac{2}{7}$ minutes for both hoses together to fill the tank.

# Day 18

## Reading Comprehension Lesson 1: Strategies and Techniques

### Today's Topics:

1. GMAT Reading Comprehension at a glance
2. Questions and answers about Reading Comprehension
3. Anatomy of a Reading Comprehension set
4. Techniques to help you read more actively
5. Techniques to help you follow the author's train of thought

Today you will familiarize yourself with the format of the Reading Comprehension portions of the Verbal section and learn basic strategies for reading the passages quickly and effectively.

## GMAT READING COMPREHENSIVE AT A GLANCE

**Number of questions:** 12–13 (9–10 scored, 3–4 unscored)
**Number of question sets:** 4
**Suggested time:** 20–24 minutes total, 5–6 minutes per question set
**Basic format:**

- The questions are divided into four *sets*.

- Each set involves a different reading *passage*.

- Each passage is accompanied by three or four questions (usually three)

**Directions (as indicated on the test):** "Each passage is followed by a group of questions based on its content. After reading the passage, choose the best answer to each question and fill in the corresponding oval. Answer all questions on the basis of what is stated or implied in the passage."

**Ground rules:**

- Scratch paper is provided.

- Pencils are permitted and provided.

- Consider each question independently of all others.

**This section tests your ability to:**

- Read carefully and accurately

- Determine the relationships among the various parts of the passage

- Draw reasonable inferences from the material in the passage

## QUESTIONS AND ANSWERS ABOUT READING COMPREHENSION

**Can I really improve my reading skills in a few weeks?** Although a few weeks is probably not sufficient time to alter your reading habits drastically, it is enough time to train yourself to read more actively and efficiently and to learn how to choose between "best" and "second-best" responses to GMAT Reading Comprehension questions.

**Is it worthwhile to increase my vocabulary by learning as many new words as possible before exam day?** No. Reading Comprehension questions are not designed to test your vocabulary. Where a passage introduces but does not define a technical term, the passage supplies all that you need to know about the term to respond to the questions.

**From what sources are the Reading Comprehension passages taken?** Passages draw from a variety of subjects, including the humanities, social sciences, the physical sciences, ethics, philosophy, and law. Specific sources include professional journals and periodicals, dissertations, as well as periodicals and books that deal with sophisticated subjects of intellectual interest. Most passages have been written within the last 10 or 20 years. Almost all passages are excerpted from larger works and have been edited to increase their "density."

**Am I at an advantage if a passage involves a topic that is familiar to me?** Probably not. The testing service is careful to ensure that all questions are answerable based solely on the information that the passage provides. Also, the exam includes passages from a variety of disciplines, so it is unlikely that any particular test-taker knows enough about two or more of the areas included on the test to hold a significant advantage over other test-takers. You might nevertheless be at a *slight* advantage if you have some familiarity with the general area that a passage treats. If the terminology is familiar, you might find the passage more interesting, be more relaxed and at ease with it, and find it easier to concentrate.

## ANATOMY OF A READING COMPREHENSION SET

### The Passage

Each of the four Reading Comprehension sets in the Verbal section includes a passage and three or four questions (usually three). Three of the four passages will include about 200 words each. The remaining

passages may include as many as 350 words. Passages vary somewhat in difficulty and complexity. Most test-takers would consider the following passage, which is about 200 words in length, to be of average complexity. Read this passage, limiting your time to two minutes.

The encounter that a portrait records is most tangibly the sitting itself. The sitting may be brief or extended, collegial or confrontational. Cartier-

(5) Bresson has expressed his passion for portrait photography by characterizing it as "a duel without rules, a delicate rape." Such metaphors contrast quite sharply with Richard Avedon's conception of a sitting. While Cartier-Bresson

(10) reveals himself as an interloper and opportunist, Avedon confesses—perhaps uncomfortably— to a role as diagnostician and (by implication) psychic healer: not as someone who necessarily transforms his subjects, but as someone who re-

(15) veals their essential nature. Both photographers, however, agree that the fundamental dynamic in this process lies squarely in the hands of the artist.

A quite-different paradigm has its roots not in

(20) confrontation or consultation but in active collaboration between the artist and sitter. This very different kind of relationship was formulated most vividly by William Hazlitt in his essay entitled "On Sitting for One's Picture" (1823). To

(25) Hazlitt, the "bond of connection" between painter and sitter is most like the relationship between two lovers. Hazlitt fleshes out his thesis by recalling the career of Sir Joshua Reynolds. According to Hazlitt, Reynold's sitters were

(30) meant to enjoy an atmosphere that was both comfortable for them and conducive to the enterprise of the portrait painter, who was simultaneously their host and their contractual employee.

### The Questions

Reading Comprehension questions are not designed simply to measure your ability to remember what you read. Rather, they are designed to gauge your ability to assimilate and understand the ideas presented. For example, consider the three following

question stems, all of which relate to the foregoing passage and require you to go beyond merely memorizing or recalling what you have read:

1. Which of the following best expresses the passage's main idea?

2. The author quotes Cartier-Bresson in order to

3. Which of the following best characterizes the portraiture experience as viewed by Avedon?

Keep in mind the following general observations about the Reading Comprehension questions:

- Although it might be possible to analyze *some* questions based on an isolated sentence or two, for most questions you need to bring together information from various parts of the passage to formulate an informed response.

- Questions focusing on information appearing early in the passage are usually posed before other questions. (This is not a hard-and-fast rule, however.)

- Questions vary somewhat in difficulty. Some require close judgment calls, whereas for others the "best" response is far better than any other choice. Questions requiring you simply to recall one or two specific bits of information are usually easier than those requiring you to assimilate and assess an entire paragraph or the entire passage. However, the type that you find easiest depends on your particular strengths and weaknesses. For example, you might be quite good at understanding abstract concepts but not as proficient at remembering details.

## The Answer Choices

Now consider question 1 along with its five answer choices:

1. Which of the following best expresses the passage's main idea?

   (A) The success of a portrait depends largely on the relationship between artist and subject.

   (B) Portraits, more than most other art forms, provide insight into the artist's social relationships.

   (C) The social aspect of portraiture sitting plays an important part in the sitting's outcome.

   (D) Photographers and painters differ in their views regarding their role in portrait photography.

   (E) The paintings of Reynolds provide a record of his success in achieving a social bond with his subjects.

In handling Reading Comprehension questions, your job is to determine the "best" response among the five choices. In doing so, you must make qualitative distinctions among the answer choices. The two or three "worst" choices might jump out at you as obviously incorrect responses.

However, the qualitative distinctions among the remaining choices can be subtle. Determining the best answer usually requires comparing the quality of the two (or three) best choices.

**The worst responses (B and E).** In question 1, B and E are qualitatively the "worst" responses among the five choices. B distorts the information in the passage and departs from the topic at hand. Although the passage does support the notion that a portrait might reveal something about the relationship between the artist and the sitter, the author neither states nor implies that a portrait reveals anything about the artist's other relationships. Moreover, nowhere in the passage does the author compare portraiture with other art forms. E is too narrow and refers to information that the passage does not mention. The passage is not just about Reynolds, but about the portraiture encounter in general. Also, the author does not comment on Reynold's "success" or about how his relationship with his sitters might have contributed to his success.

**Responses that have merit but are nevertheless incorrect (D and A).** Answer-choice D has merit in that the author does claim that the Reynolds paradigm (described in the second paragraph) is "quite different" from the two paradigms that the first paragraph discusses, and the latter does indeed involve a painter (Reynolds) whereas the other two paradigms involve photographers (Cartier-Bresson and Avedon). However, the author does not generalize from this fact that a portrait artist's approach or view depends on whether the artist is a painter or a photographer. Thus, D is a bit off focus as well as calling for an unwarranted generalization. Answer choice A also has merit. In fact, but for C, A would be the best response because it embraces the passage as a whole and properly focuses on the author's primary concern with exploring the relationship between the artist and the sitter. However, the passage does not discuss how or whether this relationship results in a "successful" portrait; thus, A distorts the passage's information.

**The best response (C).** Although it is difficult to articulate a single "main idea" or thesis of this passage, the author seems to be most concerned with emphasizing that a portrait sitting is a social encounter, not just an artistic exercise, and that artists consider their relationship with their sitters to be somehow significant. Thus, response C is a good statement of the author's primary point.

## Questions 2 and 3

To round out your first look at a Reading Comprehension question set, consider the remaining two questions (and answer choices) accompanying the previous portraiture passage. An analysis of both questions follows. (Tomorrow, you take a closer look at question types and wrong-answer ploys that the testing service uses.)

2. The author quotes Cartier-Bresson in order to
   (A) refute Avedon's conception of a portrait sitting.
   (B) provide one perspective of the portraiture encounter.
   (C) support the claim that portrait sittings are, more often than not, confrontational encounters.
   (D) show that a portraiture encounter can be either brief or extended.
   (E) distinguish a sitting for a photographic portrait from a sitting for a painted portrait.

3. Which of the following best characterizes the portraiture experience as viewed by Avedon?
   (A) a collaboration
   (B) a mutual accommodation

   (C) a confrontation
   (D) an uncomfortable encounter
   (E) a consultation

**Question 2: Analysis.** This question is a typical "purpose-of-detail" question (you learn more about question types tomorrow). B is the best response. In the passage, the author compares and contrasts three different perspectives of the portraiture encounter: Avedon's view, Cartier-Bresson's view, and Reynold's view as interpreted and reflected by Hazlitt. Response B properly expresses the function that the author's discussion of Cartier-Bresson (including the quote) serves in the author's overall discussion.

The second-best response is probably A. Admittedly, the author is explicit that Cartier-Bresson's conception is quite different from that of Avedon. However, A exaggerates the author's purpose as well as the meaning of the information in the passage. The author is not concerned with "refuting" Avedon's conception—the author neither states nor implies that Avedon's conception is wrong or inaccurate in some way. The author is not arguing for one view over another, but is rather simply presenting different personal perspectives of the portraiture encounter.

C distorts the author's point. According to the passage, Cartier-Bresson's conception of the portraiture encounter can be characterized as confrontational. However, the author does not claim that this conception is either the prevailing or better view of the portraiture encounter. D also confuses the information in the passage. The author states earlier in the paragraph that a sitting can either be "brief or extended, collegial or confrontational." The views of Cartier-Bresson and Avedon, discussed immediately thereafter, differ from each other in that Cartier-Bresson conceives his relationship with his sitters as confrontational, whereas Avedon views it as collegial. However, the author makes no further mention of the length of the sitting, either when describing the views of Avedon and Cartier-Bresson or in any other part of the passage. E distorts the author's purpose and is unsupported by the passage. Nowhere in the passage does the author, either explicitly or implicitly, seek to distinguish between portrait photography and portrait painting.

**Question 3: Analysis.** This is a typical example of an "assessment" question—one in which your job is to assimilate and interpret specific information in the passage. E is the best response. In the first sentence of the second paragraph, the author distinguishes a "quite-different paradigm" (that is, the case of Reynolds) from the conceptions of Cartier-Bresson and Avedon in that the Reynolds paradigm "has its roots not in confrontation or consultation but in active collaboration between artist and sitter." It is rather obvious from the third sentence of the passage that Cartier-Bresson conceives the encounter as "confrontational"; thus, the author seems to be characterizing an Avedon sitting as a "consultation."

B is also a good response but nevertheless not as good as E. But for E, B would be the best response. Although the term "mutual accommodation," which does not appear in the passage, is not altogether inconsistent with Avedon's view, the term suggests a relationship in which both artist and painter allow for the other's needs or desires. Such a description is closer to Hazlitt's analogy of two lovers than to Avedon's view of the artist as diagnostician and psychic healer.

Response A also has merit, yet it is not as good a response as either B or E. Admittedly, the idea of "a collaboration" is not in strong opposition to the idea of "a consultation." However, the author explicitly ascribes this characterization to the Reynolds paradigm, not to Avedon's view. Thus, A confuses the passage's information.

C and D are the qualitatively worst responses among the five. C confuses the passage's information. The quotation in the first paragraph makes it clear that Cartier-Bresson (not Avedon) conceives the encounter as "confrontational." D also confuses the passage's information. According to the passage, Avedon confesses "uncomfortably" to his role as diagnostician and psychic healer. It does not necessarily follow, however, that Avedon finds his encounters with his sitters to be uncomfortable.

# TECHNIQUES TO HELP YOU READ MORE ACTIVELY

Most Reading Comprehension questions are designed to measure your ability to understand the ideas presented rather than simply to recall the information stated. The first skill is a higher one in that it requires independent thinking. This fact should drive your approach to the Reading Comprehension passages. To understand a passage, you must be able to identify the thesis (or main idea) and the author's primary purpose, and follow the author's line of reasoning. Both require an active frame of mind in which you are constantly interacting with the material as you read.

Here are GMAT test-takers' most common problems with the Reading Comprehension passages:

- Poor concentration

- Slow reading speed

- The need to search the passage again and again for the information needed to respond to each question

- Difficulty narrowing down the answer choices to one answer that is clearly the best

All these problems result from the same bad habit: *passive* reading. Begin right now to develop a more active approach. You can start by keeping the following goal in mind as you read each passage: *Understand the passage well enough so that you can briefly explain the main point and line of reasoning to someone who has not read the passage.*

## Avoid the Passive Reading Mode

Most test-takers take a rather passive approach toward the Reading Comprehension passages. They give equal time and attention to every sentence in the passage, reading the passage from beginning to end without interruption, with very little thought as to what particular information is most important to respond to the specific questions. This strategy is actually better characterized as a *non*strategy. What is the probable result of this approach? The reader might remember some scattered factual information and ideas, thereby enabling him or her to respond correctly to some easier questions. However, the reader is not likely to respond effectively to most questions, which require some insight and assessment of the passage's information.

## Pause Midway Through the Passage to Sum Up and Anticipate

After reading the first logical "block" of the passage (perhaps the first third or half of the passage), pause for a moment to evaluate that material. Try to summarize, answering the following questions for yourself:

- How would I sum up the passage to this point?

- At what point is the discussion now?

- What basic points is the author trying to get across in this portion? Do these ideas continue a line of thought, or do they begin a new one?

- Where is the discussion likely to go from here?

In the previous portraiture passage, after reading the first paragraph, you might engage yourself in the following mental dialogue:

> The passage discusses two artists—Cartier-Bresson and Avedon. Their views about the artist-subject relationship are different (duel/rape versus doctor-patient) but also similar—the artist establishes the social dynamic. The first sentence looks like a possible "thesis" statement.

## Consider the First Question as You Read

Don't wait until you've read the entire passage to begin considering the first question posed. If the initial question relates at all to that first portion of the passage, try responding to it at this point, at least tentatively. The passage's first half will most certainly provide enough information for you to respond (tentatively) to any question that asks about the author's overall thesis, topic, or purpose. Return to the passage and read the next logical "chunk" (in this case, the second paragraph). Reconsider the first question in light of this additional information. Have you changed your mind about your tentative

response after reading the second paragraph? Or has the second paragraph confirmed that your initial response was correct?

The first paragraph of the portraiture passage probably provides sufficient information to eliminate at least one or two answer choices in question 1. Based on the first paragraph, B seems to be off focus. It appears from the first paragraph that the author is concerned not about artist's social relationships generally but rather with the portrait artist-subject relationship particularly. D seems to distort the author's focus, at least as revealed in the first paragraph. Cartier-Bresson and Avedon are both photographers, and one of the main points made in this paragraph is that they differ with one another in their views. D doesn't take this fact into account. It's too early to tell about the other responses, though. They each look viable, but you need to find out how the passage will continue. Tentatively eliminate B and D and keep the other responses in mind as you read on.

## Always Read the Entire Passage Before Confirming Your Response to the First Question

Even if the first question posed seems clearly to involve the early portion of the passage, do not confirm your response to that question without first reading the entire passage. It is always possible that information relevant to the first question will appear at the end of the passage.

## Summarize the Passage After Reading It

After reading the entire passage on portraiture, take a few seconds to recap the passage in your mind. What was the author's main point and what were the major supporting points? Just remind yourself at this point about the flow of the discussion; don't be concerned with remembering all the detailed factual information.

For example, after reading the entire passage, you might recap the discussion and formulate a thesis as follows:

> The first paragraph contrasts the views of Cartier-Bresson and Avedon—the former views the

portrait encounter as a confrontation, the latter as a consultation. The second paragraph contrasts Reynold's view (via Hazlitt) to those of the first two artists—Reynold's relationship with subjects was collaborative.

This passage as a whole states that different portrait artists view the artist-subject relationship differently.

## Try to Minimize Vertical Scrolling

Some vertical scrolling will be necessary to read an entire passage. Try to minimize scrolling by taking notes and by responding to the first question posed as you read. Also, do not dwell on questions too long; otherwise, you might be tempted to reread the passage in its entirety, thereby using up valuable time and adding to the eye strain associated with scrolling up and down text on the screen.

## Should You Preview Before Reading the Passage?

Test-preparation publications usually recommend that, before reading a passage straight through (from beginning to end), you should *preview* the passage by reading the first (and perhaps last) sentence of each paragraph. This technique supposedly provides clues about the passage's scope, the author's thesis or major conclusions, and the argument's structure and flow. Although this technique makes sense *in theory*, it is rarely helpful *in practice* on the GMAT, for several reasons:

- These techniques call for you to read the same material twice. Does that sound efficient to you?

- Previewing takes time—time that you probably cannot afford under timed conditions. It also involves rapid vertical scrolling, which adds to eye strain.

- Although reading the beginning and end of each paragraph might be helpful for some passages, for others this technique will be of little or no help.

# TECHNIQUES TO HELP YOU FOLLOW THE AUTHOR'S TRAIN OF THOUGHT

## Look for Common Organization Patterns

How the author has organized a passage reveals the flow of the author's argument. Focusing on structure will help you to do the following:

- Understand the author's main idea and primary purpose

- Identify major evidence in support of the thesis

- Understand the author's purpose in mentioning various details

- Distinguish main points from minor details

You can probably respond correctly to all the more general questions (that is, the questions regarding the main idea, the primary purpose, and the author's attitude) just by determining the passage's basic structure and the materials' organization.

No two passages reflect identical patterns of organization; however, three general organizational patterns appear most often among the passages: theory and critique, historical influence, and classification. (The portraiture passage is a good example of the third pattern.)

Familiarizing yourself with these patterns will help you to anticipate the flow of the discussion in a passage. As you examine these patterns, bear in mind that not all passages fall neatly into one of these common patterns. A particular passage might reflect two patterns, present a variation of one of the three common patterns, or reflect some other less common pattern.

### Pattern 1: Theory and Critique

*Introductory sentences.* The author identifies the conventional (older, established, or traditional) view, theory, or explanation of a phenomenon. The introduction also either implies or states that the conventional view is flawed. (If the conventional view could not be criticized, the author probably would not be interested in writing about the topic in the first place.)

*The body.* Look for one of the following patterns:

- The author focuses on one (or perhaps two) newer, more enlightened view. The author might attribute the new view either to a particular individual (such as a scientist, author, or sociologist) or to a school of thought in general (such as the leaders of the feminist movement of the 1970s).

- The author points to specific examples, observations, data, or other evidence that support a different theory. The author might also point out that the evidence is conflicting (and so no firm conclusions can be reached).

*Final sentences.* Look for one of the following typical patterns:

- The author admits that both views have their merits and shortcomings.

- The author suggests that all views are incomplete in their understanding and insight and that we need to study the subject further.

- The author introduces (but does not describe in detail) a new piece of evidence that suggests yet another view, an explanation for conflicting views, or a synthesis of numerous views.

In any case, the author will almost always have an opinion on the subject.

### Pattern 2: Historical Influence

*Introductory sentences.* The author describes the state of affairs either currently or at a relatively recent time in history; the author asserts that this state of affairs has directly or indirectly resulted from certain previous historical phenomena.

*The body.* Look for one of the following typical patterns:

- The author discusses alternative theories regarding historical cause and effect (for example, some historians believe $X$ was the primary contributing cause of $Y$, whereas other historians disagree and believe instead that $Z$ was the cause). However, if this discussion turns out to be the author's primary concern, you are dealing with a theory and critique pattern rather than a historical influence pattern.

- The author traces chronologically the events leading up to and contributing to a phenomenon.

*Final sentences.* Look for one of the following typical patterns:

- The author recaps by concluding that the current phenomenon is rooted in one or more particular ideology, movement, school of thought, event, or such.

- The author concludes that no single influence adequately explains the course of events; instead, we should recognize all contributing factors.

### Pattern 3: Classification

*Introductory sentences.* The author might identify two or three basic types, categories, or classes of a phenomenon.

*The body.* Look for the author to accomplish one or more of the following:

- Describe each class in some detail

- Compare and contrast characteristics of members of the different classes (for example, the Cartier-Bresson, Avedon, and Reynolds paradigms in the portraiture passage)

- Further divide one or more classes into subclasses

*Final sentences.* Look for one of the following patterns (the first pattern is the most common):

- The discussion concludes simply by finishing the description of the classes and subclasses; in other words, the passage makes no conclusions or arguments. (For example, the portraiture passage simply ends with a discussion of the Reynolds paradigm.)

- The author points out new evidence that suggests an additional class or subclass.

- The author explains briefly how practitioners use the classification system to observe and test theories.

- The author points out a problem with the current classification system and suggests that some modification might be appropriate.

## Look for Structural Clues or "Triggers"

"Triggers" are key words and phrases that provide clues as to the structure and organization of the passage and the direction in which the discussion is flowing. The following common trigger words and phrases precede an item in a list (such as examples, classes, reasons, or characteristics):

- first, second (and so on)
- also
- in addition
- another

These words signal that the author is contrasting two phenomena:

- alternatively
- rather than
- by contrast
- while
- however
- yet
- on the other hand

These words signal a logical conclusion based on preceding material:

- consequently
- therefore
- in conclusion
- as a result
- then
- accordingly
- thus

These words signal that the author is comparing (identifying similarities between) two phenomena:

- similarly
- just as
- in the same way
- to
- analogous
- also
- parallel
- as
- likewise

These words signal evidence (factual information) used to support the author's argument:

- because
- in light of
- since

These words signal an example of a phenomenon:

- for instance
- such as
- e.g.
- is an illustration of

## Don't Be Overly Concerned with the Details as You Read

GMAT Reading Comprehension passages are packed with details. If you try to absorb all the details as you read, you will lose sight of the main points and sacrifice reading speed. Don't get bogged down in the details; gloss over them. Instead, just keep in mind where such things as examples, lists, and other details are located. Then, if a particular question involves those details, you can quickly and easily locate them and read them in more detail.

## Develop Notes and Outlines

It can be helpful to make shorthand notes to summarize paragraphs or to indicate the flow of the passage's discussion. Effective notes can also help you locate details more quickly and recap the passage more effectively. Keep your notes as brief as possible—two or three words should suffice to indicate a particular idea or component of the passage. For certain high-density passages, a "mini-outline" might be necessary to organize information and to keep particular details straight in your mind. The following scenarios typically call for the mini-outline:

- If the passage categorizes or classifies various phenomena, notes can help clarify which phenomena belong in which categories.

- If the passage mentions numerous individual names (for example, of authors, artists, political figures, and so on), use notes to link them according to influence, agreement or disagreement, and so forth.

# Day 19

## Reading Comprehension Lesson 2: Question Types

### Today's Topics:

1. A sample question set
2. Question types and wrong-answer ploys
3. Recognizing the main idea or primary purpose
4. Recalling explicit information
5. Inferring from or interpreting specific information
6. Recognizing the function of specific information
7. Extrapolating from or applying passage ideas
8. The GMAT's favorite wrong-answer ploys
9. Tips for responding to GMAT's Reading questions

Today you will examine and learn to handle the various question types that appear in reading comprehension sets, focusing particularly on common wrong-answer "ploys."

## A SAMPLE QUESTION SET

Before examining question types and wrong-answer ploys, take 5–6 minutes to read the following passage and to respond to the three accompanying questions. These questions help illustrate the materials that follow.

The decline of the Iroquois Indian nations began during the American Revolution of 1776. Disagreement as to whether they should become involved in the war began to divide the Iroquois.
*(5)* Because of the success of the revolutionaries and the encroachment upon Iroquois lands that followed, many Iroquois resettled in Canada, while those who remained behind lost the respect they had enjoyed among other Indian nations. The in-
*(10)* troduction of distilled spirits resulted in widespread alcoholism, leading in turn to the rapid decline of both the culture and population. The influence of the Quakers impeded, yet in another sense contributed, to this decline. By establishing
*(15)* schools for the Iroquois and by introducing them to modern technology for agriculture and husbandry, the Quakers instilled in the Iroquois some hope for the future yet undermined the Iroquois' sense of national identity.
*(20)* Ironically, it was Handsome Lake who can be credited with reviving the Iroquois culture. Lake, the alcoholic half-brother of Seneca Cornplanter, perhaps the most outspoken proponent among

the Iroquois for assimilation of white customs and institutions, was a former member of the Great Council of Iroquois nations. Inspired by a near-death vision in 1799, Lake established a new religion among the Iroquois which tied the more useful aspects of Christianity to traditional Indian beliefs and customs.

(25)

1. The passage mentions all the following events as contributing to the decline of the Iroquois culture *except:*

    (A) New educational opportunities for the Iroquois people

    (B) Divisive power struggles among the leaders of the Iroquois nations

    (C) Introduction of new farming technologies

    (D) Territorial threats against the Iroquois nations

    (E) Discord among the nations regarding their role in the American Revolution

2. Among the following reasons, it is most likely that the author considers Handsome Lake's leading a revival of the Iroquois culture to be "ironic" because

    (A) he was a former member of the Great Council.

    (B) he was not a full-blooded relative of Seneca Cornplanter.

    (C) he was related by blood to a chief proponent of assimilation.

    (D) Seneca Cornplanter was Lake's alcoholic half-brother.

    (E) his religious beliefs conflicted with traditional Iroquois beliefs.

3. Assuming that the reasons asserted in the passage for the decline of the Iroquois culture are historically representative of the decline of cultural minorities, which of the following developments would most likely contribute to the demise of a modern-day ethnic minority?

    (A) A bilingual education program in which children who are members of the minority group learn to read and write in both their traditional language and the language prevalent in the present culture

    (B) A tax credit for residential-property owners who lease their property to members of the minority group

    (C) Increased efforts by local government to eradicate the availability of illegal drugs

    (D) A government-sponsored program to assist minority-owned businesses in using computer technology to improve efficiency

    (E) The declaration of a national holiday commemorating a past war in which the minority group played an active role

## QUESTION TYPES AND WRONG-ANSWER PLOYS

The Iroquois question set includes examples of three of the five types of questions that you will encounter in GMAT reading comprehension sets, distinguished by the skill that is being tested:

- Recognizing the passage's main idea or primary purpose

- Recalling explicit information in the passage

- Inferring from or interpreting specific passage information

- Recognizing the function of specific information in the passage

- Extrapolating from or applying passage ideas (this type appears less frequently than the others)

The wrong-answer choices in the Iroquois question set illustrate many of the test maker's favorite wrong-answer types, which include answer choices that do the following:

- Distort, understate, or overstate the ideas presented in the passage

- Are mentioned in the passage but do not respond to the question at hand

- Call for speculation or unsupported inference

- Are contrary to or contradicted by the passage or are stated "backward" (a backward answer might confuse cause with effect or author argument with author disagreement)

- Confuse one opinion or position with another

- Are too narrow or specific

- Are too broad, general, or vague

- Bring in extrinsic information that the passage does not include

Now take a closer look at each of the five question types, focusing on the proper approach and wrong-answer ploys commonly used with each type. As you do so, you will revisit the three questions accompanying the Iroquois passage as well as the three questions accompanying the portraiture passage in Day 18.

## QUESTION TYPE 1: RECOGNIZING THE MAIN IDEA OR PRIMARY PURPOSE

Some questions test whether you recognize the author's main point or overall concern or purpose. These questions require you to discern between the forest and the trees—that is, to distinguish broader and larger ideas and points from supporting evidence and details. Here's how to approach these questions:

- After reading the entire passage, formulate your own thesis statement and a statement of author's purpose—*before* considering the answer choices. By knowing what sort of response to look for, you will be far less tempted by the other (wrong) responses. Ask yourself two questions:

  Toward what point is the author's effort primarily directed?

  What does the author spend most of his or her time discussing? (This question might sound simplistic, but it helps to keep your thinking straight for this type of question.)

- Every passage has a "main idea" (thesis) and primary purpose. You *might* find a particular sentence or two, perhaps at the beginning or end of the passage, that sums up the passage. However, don't expect every passage to be so helpful; many passages do not include *explicit* thesis statements or primary-purpose statements.

- There should be a consistency between the passage's main idea and the author's primary purpose. If both question types appear in the question set, your responses to these two questions should be consistent with each other.

- As you read the passage, pay particular attention to all words and phrases that indicate or suggest the author's *attitude* (tone, opinion, perspective, and so on). The best response must reflect or at least show consistency with the author's attitude.

### Look for These Wrong Answer Ploys

- **The response that is *too narrow* in scope.** The response focuses on one element of the passage, ignoring other important elements. If the passage discusses a particular topic in only one of three or four paragraphs, you can pretty safely conclude that the author's primary concern is not with that specific topic. Be particularly suspicious of a response that refers to a single *specific person, event, idea,* or *work* (such as a book or composition). For example:

  If the passage is concerned with comparing two phenomena, a response that ignores this concern and focuses on only one of the two phenomena is too narrow to be a viable best response.

  If the author uses specific examples to support an argument, a response that ignores the author's larger point and focuses on one of the examples is too narrow to be a viable best response.

  If the author describes two existing theories and goes on to propose and describe a new and better theory, the author's primary purpose is not to examine, describe, or criticize current theories; the best response would go further and include the author's concern with proposing a new theory.

- **The response that is *too broad* in scope.** The response encompasses the author's main concern or idea but extends that concern or idea beyond the author's intended scope. For example, the response's scope might extend beyond the topic, geographic region, or time frame that the passage discusses.

- **The response that *distorts* the author's position.** For example, if the author's ultimate concern is to argue for a particular position or to propose a new and better explanation for some phenomenon, any response that ignores the author's opinion and instead implies objectivity on the author's part is not a viable best response.

### An Example from Yesterday's Question Set

Referring to Day 18's portraiture reading comprehension passage, consider this example question:

1. Which of the following best expresses the passage's main idea?

   (A) The success of a portrait depends largely on the relationship between artist and subject. *(This response distorts the passage's information.)*

   (B) Portraits, more than most other art forms, provide insight into the artist's social relationships. *(This response distorts the passage's information.)*

   (C) The social aspect of portraiture sitting plays an important part in the outcome of the sitting. *(This is the correct response.)*

   (D) Photographers and painters differ in their views regarding their role in portrait photography. *(This response distorts the passage's information.)*

   (E) The paintings of Reynolds provide a record of his success in achieving a social bond with his subjects. *(This response is too narrow.)*

   (For a more detailed analysis of this question, see Day 18.)

---

## QUESTION TYPE 2: RECALLING EXPLICIT INFORMATION

---

Some questions are designed to measure your ability to assimilate details—more specifically, your ability to process detailed information accurately as well as your efficiency in looking up information. The

question might either ask which choice (among the five) *is* mentioned or which choice (among the five) is *not* mentioned. Here's how to approach these questions:

- Effective notes or a mini-outline will help you locate the relevant information quickly. Wherever some sort of list is included in the passage—a list of characteristics, a list of examples, or some other list—take note of it. You can be sure that there will be an explicit detail question that focuses on that list.

- Do not insist that answer choices repeat word-for-word what the passage states. Answer choices are usually not expressed exactly as they are in the passage, but instead paraphrase the language used in the passage.

- Do not rely on your memory for details to answer these questions. Always go to the relevant portion of the passage, and read around (from the preceding sentence to the following sentence) the particular excerpt referred to in the question stem.

### Look for These Wrong-Answer Ploys

- **The response that confuses the information in the passage by referring to unrelated details.** These questions are quite specific in the information to which they refer. For example, consider question 1 from the Iroquois question set:

  The passage mentions all the following events as contributing to the decline of the Iroquois culture *except*:

  An answer choice that is mentioned in the passage but is nevertheless not mentioned specifically as a contributing factor to the decline of the Iroquois culture would be incorrect. Accordingly, look out for answer choices that involve unrelated details.

- **The response that is not mentioned in the passage.** One or more answer choices might provide information completely unsupported by or not mentioned anywhere in the passage. These wrong answers can be quite tempting; your natural reaction is that the information appeared some-where in the passage, but you missed it. Well, probably not! Don't fall for this ploy.

- **The response that contradicts the information in the passage.** The response might at first glance appear to be a viable response, but it actually contradicts what the passage states. This ploy will trap you if you fail to read each answer choice carefully.

### An Example from Today's Question Set

1. The passage mentions all the following events as contributing to the decline of the Iroquois culture *except*:

   (A) new educational opportunities for the Iroquois people. *(The passage explicitly mentions this.)*

   (B) divisive power struggles among the leaders of the Iroquois nations. *(This is the correct response.)*

   (C) introduction of new farming technologies. *(The passage explicitly mentions this.)*

   (D) territorial threats against the Iroquois nations. *(The passage explicitly mentions this.)*

   (E) discord among the nations regarding their role in the American Revolution. *(The passage explicitly mentions this.)*

   B is the best response. Nowhere in the passage does the author mention any power struggles among the leaders of the Iroquois nations. Although the first paragraph does refer to a dispute among the Iroquois leaders, the dispute involved the role that the Iroquois should play in the American Revolution. Thus, B confuses the information in the passage by referring to unrelated details. The passage explicitly refers to the events mentioned in choices A, C, D, and E as factors contributing to the decline of the Iroquois culture.

---

## QUESTION TYPE 3: INFERRING FROM OR INTERPRETING SPECIFIC INFORMATION

---

Some questions require you to draw simple inferences or to recognize somewhat broader points by interpreting specific passage information. Here's how to approach these questions:

- Don't overlook the obvious! Questions calling for inference require you to make only very "tight" inferences; in other words, the passage will suggest the inference so strongly that no other interpretation is really reasonable. Do not fight the passage by looking for a more subtle or deeper interpretation.

- An author inference usually requires that you piece together (logically speaking) no more than two consecutive sentences. To analyze the question, locate the relevant line or lines in the passage, read around those lines—the sentence preceding and the sentence following. The inference should be clear enough to you.

- The question stem might refer to specific lines or a specific paragraph in the passage. In any event, you will discover that, based on the information in the question stem, you can locate the relevant portion of the passage within 5 to 10 seconds (which is quite helpful if you are short of time).

### Look for These Wrong-Answer Ploys

- **The unwarranted or unsupported inference or interpretation.** This response will leap to a conclusion not supported by the part of the passage that makes the inference. Such a response might bring in material that is outside of the passage or might exaggerate or distort the author's relatively narrow inference.

- **The response that is either backward or runs contrary to the passage.** You might be surprised how easily you can turn around certain facts or, perhaps confusing cause with effect, confuse author agreement with author disagreement. The test maker knows this and typically includes an answer choice that is contradicted by, runs contrary to, or states backward some information in the passage.

- **The response that confuses one thing with another.** The response might mention details that the passage mentions elsewhere but which do not respond to the question at hand.

- **The response that distorts the meaning of the information in the passage.** This response might either twist or exaggerate the author's intended meaning.

## An Example from Yesterday's Question Set

3. Which of the following best characterizes the portraiture experience as viewed by Avedon?

(A) a collaboration *(This answer confuses information from the passage.)*

(B) a mutual accommodation *(This response distorts information from the passage.)*

(C) a confrontation *(This response confuses information from the passage.)*

(D) an uncomfortable encounter *(This response distorts information from the passage.)*

(E) a consultation *(This is the correct answer.)*

(For a more detailed analysis of this question, see Day 18.)

## An Example from Today's Question Set

2. Among the following reasons, it is most likely that the author considers Handsome Lake's leading a revival of the Iroquois culture to be "ironic" because

(A) he was a former member of the Great Council. *(This response confuses details from the passage.)*

(B) he was not a full-blooded relative of Seneca Cornplanter. *(This response confuses details from the passage.)*

(C) he was related by blood to a chief proponent of assimilation. *(This is the correct answer.)*

(D) Seneca Cornplanter was Lake's alcoholic half-brother *(This response states information from the passage backward.)*

(E) his religious beliefs conflicted with traditional Iroquois beliefs. *(This response is contrary to the passage's information.)*

C is the best response. The passage states that Cornplanter was an outspoken proponent of assimilation and that Handsome Lake was related to Cornplanter as a half-brother. The fact that Lake was responsible for the Iroquois reasserting their national identity is ironic, then, in light of Lake's blood relationship to Cornplanter.

A and B are both accurate statements, based on the information in the passage. However, they confuse passage information by referring to unrelated details, thereby failing to respond to the question. D gets the information in the passage backward; it was Lake, not Cornplanter, who was alcoholic.

E runs contrary to the information in the passage and is unresponsive to the question. Lake emphasized the similarities between Christianity and his brand of Iroquois religion; the passage does not deal with the differences between Christianity and the Iroquois' traditional beliefs. Moreover, even if the passage did support E, it is not the irony to which the author refers.

## QUESTION TYPE 4: RECOGNIZING THE FUNCTION OF SPECIFIC INFORMATION

Some questions are designed to determine whether, in immersing yourself in the details, you lost sight of the author's reason for including the details. To avoid falling into this trap, be sure to interact with the passage at all times, asking yourself what role or function specific information plays in the context in which the passage mentions it. Here's how to approach these questions:

- Maintain an active mind set as you read. When you come across detailed information in the passage, ask yourself what role these details play in the discussion. Is the author trying to support his or her point with several specific examples? Is the author observing similarities and differences between two things? As you read, remember that it is more important for you to understand *why* the author mentions details than to remember the details themselves (you can always look them up later).

- Some inference is required. You will not find an explicit answer to this question in the passage. In other words, the author is not going to state outright that the reason that he or she is mentioning a particular detail is to support a particular assertion. Instead, you must infer the author's purpose in mentioning the detail.

- As with inference questions, these questions call for you to make only very "tight" inferences; in other words, the passage will suggest the author's purpose so strongly that no other interpretation is really reasonable.

## Look for These Wrong-Answer Ploys

- **The response that is unsupported.** This response infers a purpose that the passage's information does not support, possibly by bringing in extrinsic material from outside the passage.

- **The response that exaggerates or distorts the author's purpose.** As noted earlier, you must make only narrow or tight inferences when inferring the author's purpose in mentioning details. A wrong answer might distort or exaggerate the author's relatively narrow inference.

- **The response that confuses the information in the passage.** Such a response restates a point made elsewhere in the passage. This response will tempt you if you recall reading the statement and are confident that the statement is true or accurately states the author's position. Don't let such responses fool you. By focusing your attention on only the relevant portion of the passage, you can be confident that this response, while possibly an accurate statement, is a wrong answer.

- **The response that confuses the author's position with that of another, possibly contradicting the information in the passage.** The author might mention certain details to support his or her argument against a position or theory. Be sure not to confuse the author's argument with opposing views.

## An Example from Yesterday's Question Set

2. The author quotes Cartier-Bresson in order to

(A) refute Avedon's conception of a portrait sitting. *(This response exaggerates the passage's information.)*

(B) provide one perspective of the portraiture encounter. *(This is the correct response.)*

(C) support the claim that portrait sittings are, more often than not, confrontational encounters. *(This response distorts the passage's information.)*

(D) show that a portraiture encounter may be either brief or extended. *(This response confuses the passage's information.)*

(E) distinguish a sitting for a photographic portrait from a sitting for a painted portrait *(The passage does not support this response.)*

(For a more detailed analysis of this question, see Day 18.)

---

## QUESTION TYPE 5: EXTRAPOLATING FROM OR APPLYING PASSAGE IDEAS

---

These questions are not nearly as common as the other types. Such questions ask you either to apply passage information to new situations or to speculate as to how the passage would continue. The approach here is similar to that of handling inference and interpretation questions.

## Common Wrong-Answer Ploys

- **The response that the ideas referred to in the question stem do not support.** Such a response might require an unwarranted inference, or might depart from the topic or be irrelevant to the ideas presented in the passage.

- **The response that runs contrary to the ideas to which the question stem refers.** This answer choice can fool you, because it might include all the right words and phrases. However, the answer turns around the idea presented in the passage, possibly by including or excluding a key word.

- **The response that covers old ground when the question asks for a logical continuation of the passage.** The author's discussion is unlikely to reverse its "flow" and rehash material already treated in the earlier parts of the passage. However, don't rule out this possibility. For example, the author might continue by examining in more detail one of two or three points made in the passage. If this is the case, the final sentences probably will provide a clue that this is the next area of discussion.

## An Example from Today's Question Set

3. Assuming that the reasons that the passage asserts for the decline of the Iroquois culture are historically representative of the decline of cultural minorities, which of the following developments would most likely contribute to the demise of a modern-day ethnic minority?

   (A) A bilingual education program in which children who are members of the minority group learn to read and write in both their traditional language and the language prevalent in the present culture. *(The passage does not fully support this response.)*

   (B) A tax credit for residential-property owners who lease their property to members of the minority group. *(This response is too general and the passage does not support it.)*

   (C) Increased efforts by local government to eradicate the availability of illegal drugs. *(This response is contrary to the passage's information.)*

   (D) A government-sponsored program to assist minority-owned businesses in using computer technology to improve efficiency. *(This is the correct response.)*

   (E) The declaration of a national holiday commemorating a past war in which the minority group played an active role. *(The passage's information does not support this response; in fact, this response contradicts the passage's information.)*

   D is the best response. According to the passage, the Quakers' introduction of new technology to the Iroquois was partly responsible for the decline of the Iroquois culture in that it contributed to the tribe's loss of national identity. D presents a similar situation.

   A is probably the second-best response. Insofar as the children referred to in response A learn the language of the prevailing culture, assimilation and a resulting loss of ethnic identity might tend to occur. However, this sense of identity might be reinforced by their learning to read and write in their traditional language as well. Therefore, A is not as likely to lead to the demise of the minority group as D, at least based on the Iroquois' experience as discussed in the passage.

   B is too vague, and the passage does not support it. Whether a government incentive to provide housing for members of the minority group actually undermines the group's sense of ethnic identity would probably depend on whether the incentives result in integration or segregation. Moreover, because the passage does not address whether the Iroquois became geographically integrated (assimilated), it does not support B.

   C runs contrary to the result called for in the question. The scenario posed in C would actually contribute to the minority group's retaining its ethnic identity, at least based on the information in the passage. According to the passage, the introduction of spirits to the Iroquois population led to rampant alcoholism, which in turn contributed to the culture's decline. Similarly, widespread drug abuse might have a similar effect today. Accordingly, any effort to curb such abuse—as response C suggests—would tend to impede a decline rather than contribute to it.

   E, like C, runs contrary to the result of that called for in the question. Also, the passage does not support E. Any ceremony or holiday calling attention to the ethnic population as a distinct group and helping to bring the population together as a group under a shared experience would tend to reinforce a sense of identity. Moreover, the passage does not refer to any developments during the time of the Iroquois decline that might be similar in any way to scenario E; accordingly, the passage does not support E.

# THE GMAT'S FAVORITE WRONG-ANSWER PLOYS

Keep a mental list of the wrong-answer types or ploys. When you have trouble narrowing down the answer choices to the best response, review this list in your mind, and the remaining wrong answers should reveal themselves. Here is a checklist, in order of frequency of use on the GMAT:

- **The response distorts the information in the passage.** It might understate, overstate, or twist the passage's information or the author's point in presenting that information.

- **The response uses information from the passage, but does not respond to the question.** Such a response might include information found in the passage but not respond appropriately to the question posed.

- **The response relies on speculation or an unsupported inference.** It calls for some measure of speculation in that the statement is not readily inferable from the information given.

- **The response is contrary to the passage or stated backward.** Such a response contradicts the passage's information or gets information backward.

- **The response confuses one opinion or position with another.** Such a response incorrectly represents the position or opinion of one person or group as that of another.

- **The response is too narrow (specific).** It focuses on particular information in the passage that is too specific or narrowly focused in terms of the question posed.

- **The response is too broad (general).** It embraces information or ideas that are too general or widely focused in terms of the question posed.

- **The response relies on information that the passage does not mention.** Such a response brings in extrinsic information not found anywhere in the passage.

# TIPS FOR RESPONDING TO GMAT'S READING QUESTIONS

## Tip 1: Don't Second-Guess the Test Maker

The directions for the GMAT reading comprehension sets instruct you to choose the "best" response among the five choices. Isn't this awfully subjective? True, there is an element of subjective judgment involved in reading comprehension. However, these questions are tested and revised several times before they appear as scored questions on an actual GMAT. *Do not second-guess the test maker's judgment or command of standard written English.* If you think that there are two or more viable "best" responses, *you* have either misread or misinterpreted the passage, the question, or the answer choices.

## Tip 2: Read Every Answer Choice in Its Entirety

As noted in tip 1, you are looking for the "best" response. Often, more than one answer choice is viable. Don't hastily select or eliminate answer choices without reading them all. *GMAT test-takers miss more questions for this reason than for any other!*

## Tip 3: Don't Over-Analyze Questions or Second-Guess Yourself

If you believe that you understood the passage fairly well but a particular answer choice seems confusing or a bit nonsensical, do not assume that it's your fault. Many wrong-answer choices simply don't make much sense. If an answer choice strikes you this way, don't examine it further; eliminate it. Similarly, if you've considered all five choices, and one response strikes you as the best one, *more often than not, your initial response will be the correct one.*

## Tip 4: Don't Overlook the Obvious

Reading Comprehension questions vary in difficulty level, which means that some of the questions will be pretty easy. If a particular response seems obviously correct or incorrect, don't assume that you are missing something.

## Tip 5: Eliminate Responses That Run Contrary to the Thesis

Regardless of the type of question that you are dealing with, keep in mind the overall thesis, main idea, or point that the author is making in the passage as a whole. You can eliminate any answer choice to any question that runs contrary to or is inconsistent with that thesis. You might be surprised how many questions you can answer correctly using only this technique.

## Tip 6: Keep in Mind Common Wrong-Answer Ploys to Avoid Falling into the Test Maker's Traps

Be assured: The test makers will try again and again to bait you with their favorite wrong-answer ploys. Learn to recognize these ploys, and keep them in mind as you take tomorrow's mini-test as well as the Verbal Section of the practice test later in this book.

# Reading Comprehension Lesson 3: Mini-Test and Review

## Today's Topics:

Today you will apply what you learned on Days 18 and 19 to three reading comprehension passages. After taking this mini-test under timed conditions, review the explanations that follow. Preceding the explanation for each question, the question type and difficulty level are indicated.

## MINI-TEST (READING COMPREHENSION)

**Number of questions:** 9
**Suggested time:** 18 minutes

**Directions (as indicated on the test):** "Each passage is followed by a group of questions based on its content. After reading the passage, choose the best answer to each question and fill in the corresponding oval. Answer all questions on the basis of what is stated or implied in the passage."

*Questions 1–3 are based on the following passage:*

Dorothea Lange was perhaps the most notable of the photographers commissioned during the 1930s by the Farm Security Administration (FSA), part of a federal plan to revitalize the nation's
(5) economy and to communicate its human and social dimensions. The value of Lange's photographs as documents for social history is enhanced by her technical and artistic mastery of the medium. Her well-composed, sharp-focus images reveal a wealth
(10) of information about her subjects and show historical evidence that would scarcely be known but for her camera. Her finest images, while according with conditions of poverty that prompted political response, portray people who appear indomitable,
(15) unvanquished by their reverses. "Migrant Mother," for example, portrays a sense of the innocent victim, of perseverance, of destitution as a temporary aberration calling for compassion, solutions, and politics to alter life for the better. The power of that photo-
(20) graph, which became the symbol of the photographic file of the FSA, endures today.

The documentary book was a natural genre for Lange and her husband Paul Taylor, whose narrative accompanied Lange's FSA photographs. In *An*
(25) *American Exodus*, produced by Lange and Taylor, a sense of the despair of Lange's subjects is heightened by the captioned quotations of the migrants. Taken from 1935 to 1940, the *Exodus* pictures became the accepted vision of the migration of Dust Bowl farm
(30) workers into California.

1. According to the passage, the photograph entitled "Migrant Mother"

   (A) appeared in the documentary book *An American Exodus*.

   (B) was accompanied by a caption written by Lange's husband.

   (C) was taken by Lange in 1935.

   (D) portrays the mother of a Dust Bowl farm worker.

   (E) is considered by the author to be one of Lange's best photographs.

2. The passage provides information for responding to all the following questions *except*:

   (A) What was the FSA's purpose in compiling the photographic file to which Lange contributed?

   (B) How did the FSA react to the photographs taken by Lange under its commission?

   (C) In what areas of the United States did Lange take the photographs that appear in *An American Exodus*?

   (D) Why did Lange agree to work for the FSA?

   (E) What qualities make Lange's photographs noteworthy?

3. Among the following characterizations, the passage is best viewed as

   (A) a survey of the great photographers of the Depression era.

   (B) an examination of the photographic techniques of Dorothea Lange.

   (C) an argument for the power of pictures to enact social change.

   (D) a discussion of the goals and programs of the FSA's photographic department.

   (E) an explanation of Lange's interest in documenting the plight of Depression victims.

*Questions 4–6 are based on the following passage:*

   Those who criticize the United States government today for not providing health care to all citizens equate health-care provision with medical insurance coverage. By this standard, 17th and 18th
(5) Century America lacked any significant conception of public health law. However, despite the general paucity of bureaucratic organization in preindustrial America, the vast extent of health regulation and provision stands out as remarkable.
(10)  Of course, the public role in the protection and regulation of 18th Century health was carried out in ways quite different from those today. Organizations responsible for health regulation were less stable than modern bureaucracies, tending to appear
(15) in crises and wither away in periods of calm. The focus was on epidemics that were seen as unnatural and warranting a response, not to the many endemic and chronic conditions that were accepted as part and parcel of daily life. Additionally, religious

influence was significant, especially in the 17th
(20) Century. Finally, in an era that lacked sharp demarcations between private and governmental bodies, many public responsibilities were carried out by what we would now consider private associations.
(25) Nevertheless, the extent of public health regulation long before the dawn of the welfare state is remarkable and suggests that the founding generation's assumptions about the relationship between government and health were more complex than is commonly assumed.

4. Which of the following statements about the United States government's role in the provision of health care finds the least support in the passage?

   (A) The government today addresses health concerns that formerly were not considered serious enough to warrant government involvement.

   (B) What were once public health-care functions are now served by the private sector.

   (C) Philosophical considerations play a less significant role today in the formulation of public health-care policies than in previous centuries.

   (D) Public health care today is guided largely by secular rather than religious values.

   (E) Modern public health-care agencies are typically established not as temporary measures but as permanent establishments.

5. Which of the following best expresses the author's point of contention with "those who criticize the United States government for not providing health care to all citizens"?

   (A) Their standard for measuring such provision is too narrow.

   (B) They underestimate the role that insurance plays in the provision of health care today.

   (C) They fail to recognize that government plays a more significant role today in health care than in previous eras.

   (D) They misunderstand the intent of the founding generation with respect to the proper role of the government in the area of health care.

   (E) They lack any significant conception of public health law.

6. Which of the following best expresses the passage's main point?

(A) The government's role in health care has not expanded over time to the extent that many critics have asserted.

(B) The government should limit its involvement in health care to epidemiological problems.

(C) Health problems plaguing preindustrial America resulted largely from inadequate public health care.

(D) History suggests that the United States government has properly played a significant role in provision of health care.

(E) Private insurance is an inadequate solution to the problem of health care.

*Questions 7–9 are based on the following passage:*

Radiative forcings are changes imposed on the planetary energy balance; radiative feedbacks are changes induced by climate change. Forcings can arise from natural or anthropogenic causes. For
(5) example, the concentration of sulfate aerosols in the atmosphere can be altered by volcanic action or by the burning of fossil fuels. The distinction between forcings and feedbacks is sometimes arbitrary; however, forcings are quantities normally specified
(10) in global climate model simulations, whereas feedbacks are calculated quantities. Examples of radiative forcings are greenhouse gases (such as carbon dioxide and ozone), aerosols in the troposphere, and surface reflectivity. Radiative feedbacks include
(15) clouds, water vapor in the troposphere, and sea-ice cover.

The effects of forcings and feedbacks on climate are complex and uncertain. For example, clouds trap outgoing radiation and thus provide a warming
(20) influence. However, they also reflect incoming solar radiation and thus provide a cooling influence. Current measurements indicate that the net effect of clouds is to cool the Earth. However, scientists are unsure whether the balance will shift in the future as
(25) the atmosphere and cloud formation are altered by the accumulation of greenhouse gases. Similarly, the vertical distribution of ozone affects both the amount of radiation reaching the Earth's surface and of reradiated radiation that is trapped by the greenhouse
(30) effect. These two mechanisms affect the Earth's temperature in opposite directions.

7. You can infer from the information in the passage that "burning of fossil fuels" (see line 7)

(A) is an anthropogenic cause of radiative forcings

(B) results in both radiative forcings and radiative feedbacks

(C) does not affect atmospheric forcings or feedbacks

(D) is a significant type of radiative forcing

(E) is an anthropogenic cause of radiative feedbacks

8. According to the passage, radiative forcings and radiative feedbacks can usually be distinguished in which of the following ways?

(A) Whether the radiative change is global or more localized

(B) The precision with which the amounts of radiative change can be determined

(C) That altitude at which the radiative change occurs

(D) Whether the amount of radiative change is specified or calculated

(E) Whether the radiative change is directed toward or away from the Earth

9. The author discusses the effect of clouds on atmospheric temperature probably to show that

(A) radiative feedbacks can be more difficult to isolate and predict than radiative forcings.

(B) the climatic impact of some radiative feedbacks is uncertain.

(C) some radiative feedbacks cannot be determined solely by global climate model simulations.

(D) the distinction between radiative feedbacks and radiative forcings is somewhat arbitrary.

(E) the effects of radiative forcings on planetary energy balance are both complex and uncertain.

# Quick Answer Guide

## Mini-Test: Reading Comprehension

1. E

2. D

3. C

4. C

5. A

6. D

7. A

8. D

9. B

## EXPLANATIONS

### 1. Explicit detail (moderate). Answer: E.

The author cites "Migrant Mother" as an example of "(h)er finest images"—that is, as an example of her best photographs.

A calls for speculation. The photograph might have appeared in Lange's book; however, the passage does not explicitly say so.

B calls for speculation. Lange's husband wrote narrative captions for the photographs appearing in *Exodus*. However, the passage does not indicate that "Migrant Mother" was accompanied by a caption or even that the photograph appeared in the book.

C provides information not mentioned in the passage. Although it is reasonable to assume that Lange took the photograph during the 1930s, the passage neither states nor implies what year she took the photo.

D calls for speculation. According to the passage, the photographs appearing in *Exodus* "became the accepted vision of the migration of Dust Bowl farm workers to California." However, the author does not indicate either that "Migrant Mother" appeared in the book or that the woman portrayed in the photograph was indeed the mother of a Dust Bowl farm worker.

### 2. Explicit detail (moderate). Answer: D.

The passage provides absolutely no information about Lange's motives or reasons for accepting her FSA commission.

The passage's first sentence answers A implicitly: " . . . the FSA, part of a federal plan to revitalize the economy and to communicate its human and social dimensions." Thus, the photographic file was compiled in furtherance of that purpose.

The first paragraph's last sentence answers B implicitly. The FSA thought highly enough of one of Lange's photographs to use it as a symbol for its photographic file.

The second paragraph answers C implicitly. According to the passage, the *Exodus* pictures recorded the migration of Dust Bowl farm workers into California. Thus, some (and probably all or nearly all) of these photographs were taken in the Dust Bowl region of the U.S. or in California.

The passage answers E in the first paragraph, where the author mentions Lange's "well-composed, sharp-focus" images.

### 3. Primary purpose (moderate). Answer: C.

Admittedly, C is not an ideal characterization of the passage, which seems more concerned with Lange's work than with making a broader argument about the power of pictures. Nevertheless, the author does allude to Lange's ability to convey a need for social change through her photographs. Accordingly, the passage can be characterized as presenting one example (Lange) to support the broader point suggested by choice C.

Response A is far too broad. Lange is the only photographer that the passage discusses.

B is too narrow. Although the author mentions some of Lange's techniques (for example, her "well-composed, sharp-focus images"), the author does not examine them in any detail.

D distorts the passage and is too broad. First, the passage does not indicate that a distinct photographic department within the FSA existed; in this sense, D distorts the passage's information. Second, although the first sentence alludes to the FSA's overall purpose, the passage offers no further discussion of the agency's goals or program, other than the discussion of Lange's involvement in compiling its photographic file; in this sense, D is far too broad.

E distorts the passage. The author does not discuss Lange's motive or reasons for photographing Depression victims other than that the FSA commissioned her to do so.

### 4. Explicit detail (challenging). Answer: C.

The passage does not support statement C; nowhere does the author suggest that the government policies today regarding health care are guided less by philosophical considerations than in previous eras. The term "philosophical" should not be equated with the term "religious" (otherwise, C and D would be essentially the same responses).

Answer A is the second-best response. Support for A is less explicit than for any other incorrect answer choice. Nevertheless, A finds support from the author's point that the government did not formerly address many nonepidemic diseases because they were considered part and parcel of daily life. You can reasonably infer from this excerpt that epidemic diseases were considered a greater threat (that is, more serious), thereby warranting government's attention.

B restates the author's assertion that "many public responsibilities were carried out by what we would now consider private associations."

D is readily inferable. The author asserts that the public role in health care is carried out in different ways today than it was in prior centuries. The author then points out that "religious influence was significant, especially in the 17th Century." It is reasonably inferable, then, that religion does not play a significant role today in public health-care decisions.

E restates the author's point that government health-care organizations in previous eras were less stable than modern bureaucracies.

### 5. Interpretation (moderate). Answer A.

According to the author, the critics equate the degree (extent) of health-care provision with insurance coverage. The author contends that by this standard of measurement, public health care during the 18th Century was practically nonexistent. In fact, however, the government played a significant role in health care during that century in ways other than providing insurance to its citizens. Thus, the critics' standard for measuring the extent of the government's role in health care is far too narrow in that it ignores all the other possible ways in which government can play a role in health care.

The passage does not support B. Nowhere does the author state or imply that insurance plays a larger role in health care than the critics contend. Also, statement B makes no distinction between private and public insurance.

C is not well supported. Based on the information in the second paragraph, it appears that the United States government has played a significant role in health care throughout history; the author does not contend that the government's role in health care is greater today than in previous eras (implicitly, some of the evidence in the second paragraph supports this contention, whereas other evidence undermines it). Moreover, even if the passage strongly supported C, the statement is nevertheless not the author's point of contention with the critics.

D is unsupported and does not respond to the question. The author makes no attempt to evaluate the critics' understanding of the founding generation's intent. Even if the passage supported statement D, it is nevertheless not the author's point of contention with the critics.

E confuses the details in the second paragraph. It was America that, by the critics' standards, "lacked any significant conception of public health law." Statement E asserts, however, that the critics were the ones who lacked such conception.

## 6. Interpretation (moderate). Answer: D.

In the passage, the author rebuts the critics' argument that government is not providing health care to all citizens and implies, at the close of the passage, that the founding generation probably intended that government play a significant ("complex") role in health care.

Answer A is unsupported and runs contrary to the passage. The passage's evidence is conflicting as to whether the government's role has in fact expanded over time, and the author does not really address this issue. Also, according to the passage, the critics assert that the government plays too small a role in health care; thus, A actually tends to run contrary to the critics' contention.

The passage does not support B, which calls for an unwarranted inference. Although acknowledging that the government in fact has expanded its health concerns from epidemics to chronic and endemic disorders, the author does not take a position on whether such expansion is desirable or proper.

C is wholly unsupported. The author makes no attempt in the passage to identify the health problems of preindustrial America or their causes.

E distorts the main idea. Although statement E is consistent with the author's implicit argument that the government should play a significant role in health care, it fails to express the broader point that the author seeks to make.

## 7. Inference (easier). Answer: A.

The author states in the first paragraph that "(f)orcings can arise from natural or anthropogenic causes." In the following sentence, the author describes two specific causes of forcings, presumably to illustrate the point of the previous sentence. By considering both sentences together, you can reasonably infer that the first example (volcanic activity) is a natural cause, whereas the second (the burning of fossil fuels) is an anthropogenic cause.

The passage only partly supports B. Although you can infer that the burning of fossil fuels causes radiative forcings, the author neither states nor suggests that this activity also causes radiative feedbacks.

C contradicts the information in this part of the passage. The passage states explicitly that the concentration of sulfate aerosols is affected ("can be altered") by burning of fossil fuels. Thus, although burning of fossil fuels might not affect radiative feedbacks, you can infer that such activity does affect radiative forcings.

D is nonsensical. The burning of fossil fuels is a cause, not a type, of radiative forcing.

E confuses forcings with feedbacks.

## 8. Explicit detail (moderate). Answer: D.

According to the passage, radiative "forcings are quantities normally specified in global climate model situations, whereas feedbacks are calculated quantities."

Answer A is wholly unsupported by the passage. The author never discusses the geographic extent of radiative changes in any context.

The passage does not support B. The fact that feedbacks are "calculated quantities" whereas forcings are "specified" quantities does not in itself suggest that one can be more precisely determined than the other.

C and E confuse the information in the passage in a similar way. The second paragraph discusses altitude as a factor influencing the relative effects on ozone changes (a radiative forcing) of radiation directed toward Earth and radiation directed away from Earth. This area of discussion involves forcings only, not feedbacks.

## 9. Purpose of detail (moderate). Answer: B.

B restates the author's point in the first sentence of the second paragraph. Immediately thereafter, the author discusses clouds as an example of this point—it is difficult to predict the impact of greenhouse gases on clouds and thus on temperature.

The passage does not support A. In the second paragraph, the author discusses two particular examples of radiative changes: one involving radiative forcings and the other involving radiative feedbacks.

The author's purpose in discussing these two phenomena is to illustrate the author's previous point that "(t)he effects of some forcings and feedbacks on climate are complex and uncertain." However, the author makes no attempt to compare the relative complexity or uncertainty of these two effects.

C confuses the information in the passage and is somewhat nonsensical. The global climate model simulations specifies (do not determine) forcings (not feedbacks). Moreover, C is wholly unsupported by the information in the second paragraph; nowhere does the author discuss or mention global climate simulations in relation to the effects of clouds on atmospheric temperatures.

The passage supports D, but that answer does not respond to the question. In the first paragraph, the author attempts to distinguish between forcings and feedbacks and does indeed mention that the distinction can be somewhat arbitrary. However, this point is completely unrelated to the discussion in the second paragraph.

E is the second-best response. The passage's first sentence defines radiative forcings as "changes imposed on the planetary energy balance." E is indeed one of the author's points in the second paragraph. However, E does not respond to the question, which deals with feedbacks rather than forcings.

## Quantitative Ability Lesson 7: Geometry, Part 1

### Today's Topics:

1. Lines and angles
2. Triangles
3. Quadrilaterals
4. Geometry exercises

Today you learn how to handle GMAT geometry problems involving intersecting lines, triangles, and quadrilaterals. Then you test your competency with the concepts covered by attempting the exercises at the end of the lesson.

## LINES AND ANGLES

Lines and line segments are the basic building blocks of all GMAT geometry problems. In fact, some GMAT geometry problems involve nothing more than intersecting lines (and the angles created thereby). Two types are most common on the GMAT:

- Problems involving *wheel spokes*

- Problems involving *parallel lines* and *transversals*

Before examining these two problems types, review some basic terminology and some fundamental rules. Referring to the figure, to the right, the following symbols are used on the GMAT to denote lines, line segments, and angles that result from intersecting lines:

- $l_1$ identifies line *AC,* and $l_2$ identifies line *BD.* On the GMAT, lines and line segments are always assumed to be straight.

- *AB* and $\overline{AB}$ are used interchangeably to identify line segment *AB;* you can also use them to denote the *length* of line segment *AB.*

- Point *E* is the *vertex* of any of the angles formed by the intersection of $l_1$ and $l_2$.

- $\angle AED$ denotes the angle having point *E* as its vertex and *EA* and *ED* as the two *rays* leading away from the vertex and forming the angle. The size of $\angle AED$ is $x°$—that is, $\angle AED$ has a degree measure of $x$.

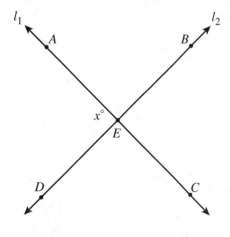

- *Opposite* angles are the same size, or *congruent* (≅), or equal in degree measure. In the above figure, the following are true:

$$\angle AED \cong \angle BEC$$
$$\angle AEB \cong \angle DEC$$

- *Supplementary* angles form a straight line when added together; their degree measures total 180. In fact, a straight line is actually a 180° angle. In the above figure, the following are true:

$$\angle AED + \angle AEB = 180° \text{ (a straight line)}$$
$$\angle AEB + \angle BEC = 180° \text{ (a straight line)}$$
$$\angle BEC + \angle CED = 180° \text{ (a straight line)}$$
$$\angle CED + \angle AED = 180° \text{ (a straight line)}$$

### Wheel Spokes

Building on the foregoing rules, the sum of all angles where two or more lines intersect at the same point is 360° (regardless of how many angles are involved). Thus, in the above figure the following is true:

$$\angle AEB + \angle BEC + \angle CED + \angle AED = 360°$$

A *right angle* is an angle measuring 90°. The intersection of two *perpendicular* lines results by definition in a right angle. If you know that one angle formed by two intersecting lines is a right (90°) angle, then you know that the two lines are perpendicular and that all four angles formed by the intersection are right angles, as shown below.

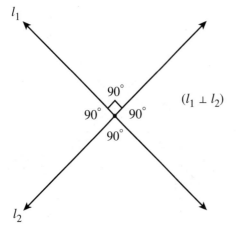

Combining all the foregoing rules, the following relationships among the angles in the diagram below emerge (the last two are less obvious and therefore more "testworthy" for the GMAT):

- $y + v = 180$ ($y$ and $v$ form a straight line; they are supplementary)

- $x + w = 180$ ($x$ and $w$ form a straight line; they are supplementary)

- $v + z + w = 180$ ($v$, $z$, and $w$ form a straight line; they are supplementary)

- $x + y - z = 180$ ($x + y$ exceed 180 by the amount of their overlap, which equals $z$, the angle opposite to the overlapping angle)

- $x + y + v + w = 360$ (the sum of all angles, excluding $z$, is 360°; $z$ is excluded because it is already accounted for by the overlap of $x$ and $y$)

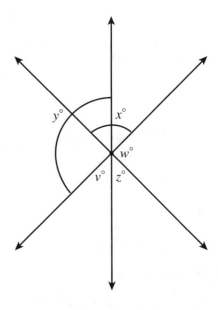

### Parallel Lines and Transversals

Parallel lines are lines that never intersect, even continuing infinitely in both directions. A GMAT problem would denote two parallel lines, 1 and 2, as follows:

$$l_1 \parallel l_2$$

GMAT problems involving parallel lines also involve at least one *transversal*, which is a line that intersects each of two (or more) parallel lines. In the below figure, $l_1 \parallel l_2$, and $l_3$ *transverses* (is a transversal of) $l_1$ and $l_2$.

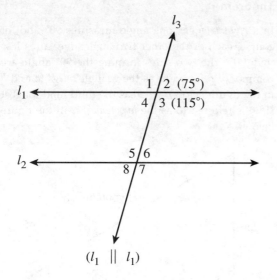

$(l_1 \parallel l_1)$

In the above figure, because $l_1 \parallel l_2$, the upper "cluster" of angles (created by the intersection of $l_1$ and $l_3$) looks identical to, or "mirrors," the lower "cluster" (created by the intersection of $l_2$ and $l_3$). For example, $\angle 1$ is congruent (equal in size or degree measure) to $\angle 5$ ($\angle 1$ and $\angle 5$ are said to be *corresponding* angles). Because opposite angles are congruent, the following relationships among the eight angles in the foregoing diagram emerge:

- All the *odd*-numbered angles are congruent (equal in size) to one another.

- All the *even*-numbered angles are congruent (equal in size) to one another.

Moreover, if you know the size of just one of the eight angles, you can determine the size of all eight angles. For example, if $\angle 2$ measures 75°, then angles 4, 6, and 8 also measure 75° each, whereas angles 1, 3, 5, and 7 each measure 105° (75° + 105° = 180° which forms a straight line). If you add a second transversal paralleling the first one, the resulting four-sided figure is a *parallelogram*—a quadrilateral

with two pairs of parallel sides. Applying the transversal analysis to parallelogram *ABCD* shown below, the following are evident:

- $\angle 1 \cong \angle 4$

- $\angle 2 \cong \angle 3$

- $\angle 1 + \angle 2 = 180°$, $\angle 1 + \angle 3 = 180°$

- $\angle 2 + \angle 4 = 180°$, $\angle 3 + \angle 4 = 180°$

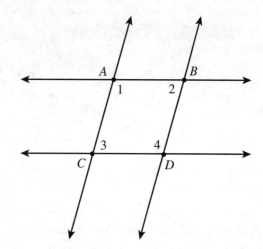

In fact, all four "clusters" of angles (defined by vertices *A*, *B*, *C*, and *D*) mirror one another in their corresponding angle measures. If you know the size of just one angle, you can determine the size of all 16 angles!

## TRIANGLES

The *triangle* (defined as a three-sided polygon) is the GMAT's favorite geometric figure. Triangle problems appear in a variety of scenarios—by themselves in a pure mathematical setting, as word problems, and in "hybrid" geometry problems involving triangular components of quadrilaterals and circles. To score high on the GMAT, you must know all the following properties and rules involving triangles.

### Properties of All Triangles

Referring to the triangle shown on page 180, the following properties apply to *all* triangles.

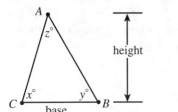

**Length of the sides.** Each side is shorter than the sum of the lengths of the other two sides:

$AC < AB + BC$

$BC < AB + AC$

$AB < BC + AC$

**Angle measures.** The sum of the three angles = 180°:

$x + y + z = 180$

$180 - x = y + z$

$180 - y = x + z$

$180 - z = x + y$

Accordingly, the sum of the measures of any two (of the three) angles must be less than 180°:

$x + y < 180$ ($x < 180 - y$, $y < 180 - x$)

$x + z < 180$ ($x < 180 - z$, $z < 180 - x$)

$y + z < 180$ ($y < 180 - z$, $z < 180 - y$)

**Angles and opposite sides.** The relative angle sizes correspond to the relative lengths of the sides opposite those angles. In other words, the smaller the angle, the smaller the side opposite the angle, and vice versa. In the above triangle, for example:

If $x > y > z$, then $AB > AC > BC$

Accordingly, if two angles are equal in size, the sides opposite those angles are of equal length (and vice versa).

*Caution:* Do not take this rule too far. The sizes of angle measures do *not* correspond precisely to lengths of opposite sides! For example, if a certain triangle has angle measures of 30°, 60°, and 90°, the ratio of the angles is 1:2:3. However, this does *not* mean that the ratio of the opposite sides is also 1:2:3 (it is *not*, as you will soon learn!).

**Area.** The area of any triangle is equal to one-half the product of its base and its height (altitude)—that is, $A_t = \frac{1}{2}(b)(h)$. You can use any side as the base to calculate area.

### Right Triangles and the Pythagorean Theorem

In a *right triangle*, one angle measures 90° and, of course, each of the other two angles measures less than 90°. The two sides forming the 90° angle are commonly referred to as the triangle's *legs* (*a* and *b* in the figure below), whereas the third (and longest side) is referred to as the *hypotenuse* (*c* in the figure below).

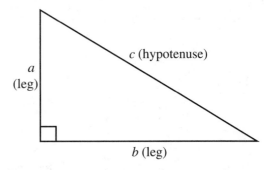

The *Pythagorean Theorem* expresses the relationship among the sides of any right triangle (*a* and *b* are the two legs, and *c* is the hypotenuse):

$$a^2 + b^2 = c^2 \quad or \quad \sqrt{a} + \sqrt{b} = \sqrt{c}$$

The Pythagorean Theorem is the single most useful formula in GMAT geometry problems. With any right triangle, if you know the length of two sides, you can determine the length of the third side with the theorem. *Remember:* The Pythagorean Theorem applies only to *right* triangles, not to any others.

**Pythagorean side triplets.** These are sets of numbers that satisfy the Pythagorean Theorem. In each of the following triplets, the first two numbers represent the relative lengths of the two legs, whereas the third—and largest—number represents the relative length of the hypotenuse:

- $1:1:\sqrt{2}\ \left(1^2+1^2=\left(\sqrt{2}\right)^2\right)$

- $1:\sqrt{3}:2\ (1^2+\left(\sqrt{3}\right)^2=2^2)$

- $3:4:5\ (3^2+4^2=5^2)$

- $5:12:13\ (5^2+12^2=13^2)$

- $8:15:17\ (8^2+15^2=17^2)$

- $7:24:25\ (7^2+24^2=25^2)$

Each of the preceding triplets is expressed as a *ratio* because it represents the relative proportion of the triangle's sides. All right triangles with sides having the same ratio or proportion have the same shape (they are *similar* to one another). For example, a right triangle with sides 5, 12, and 13 units long is smaller but exactly the same shape (proportion) as one with sides 15, 36, and 39 units long. Learn to recognize given numbers (lengths of triangle sides) as multiples of Pythagorean triplets to save valuable time in solving GMAT right-triangle problems.

Now look at some examples. All three squares in the figure below include two $1:1:\sqrt{2}$ triangles.

 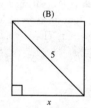 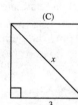

(A) indicates the basic triplet. In (B), the hypotenuse is given as 5. To calculate either leg's length, divide 5 by $\sqrt{2}$, *or* multiply 5 by $\frac{\sqrt{2}}{2}$: $x=\frac{5\sqrt{2}}{2}$. In (C), the leg's length is given as 3. To calculate the hypotenuse, multiply 3 by $\sqrt{2}$: $x=3\sqrt{2}$.

In the next figure, all three triangles are $1:\sqrt{3}:2$ triangles.

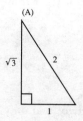 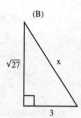 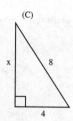

(A) indicates the basic triplet. In (B), the length of the legs are given as 3 and $\sqrt{27}$ (or $3\sqrt{3}$), and the ratio of $3\sqrt{3}$ to 3 is $\sqrt{3}:1$. Thus, this is a $1:\sqrt{3}:2$ triangle. Calculate the hypotenuse from either leg:

- $x=3\times2=6$

- $x=3\sqrt{3}\times\dfrac{2}{\sqrt{3}}=6$

In (C), the lengths of the hypotenuse and of one leg are given as 8 and 4. This ratio is 2:1. Thus, this is a $1:\sqrt{3}:2$ triangle. Calculate the length of leg $x$ from either the other leg or the hypotenuse:

- $x=(4)\left(\sqrt{3}\right)=4\left(\sqrt{3}\right)$

- $x=(8)\left(\dfrac{\sqrt{3}}{2}\right)=4\sqrt{3}$

In the below figure, all three triangles are 3:4:5 triangles.

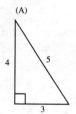 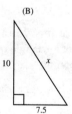 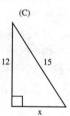

(A) indicates the basic triplet. (B) gives the length of the legs. The ratio of 10 to 7.5 is 4:3. Thus, this is a 3:4:5 triangle. Calculate the hypotenuse from either leg:

- $x=(7.5)\left(\dfrac{5}{3}\right)=12.5$

- $x=(10)\left(\dfrac{5}{4}\right)=12.5$

(C) gives the length of the hypotenuse and of one leg as 15 and 12. This ratio is 5:4. Thus, this is a 3:4:5 triangle. Calculate the length of leg $x$ from either the other leg or the hypotenuse:

- $x = (15)\left(\dfrac{3}{5}\right) = 9$

- $x = (12)\left(\dfrac{3}{4}\right) = 9$

**Pythagorean angle triplets.** In two (and only two) of the unique triangles identified in the preceding section as Pythagorean triplets, *all degree measures are integers*:

- The corresponding angles opposite the sides of a $1:1:\sqrt{2}$ triangle are 45°, 45°, and 90°.

- The corresponding angles opposite the sides of a $1:\sqrt{3}:2$ triangle are 30°, 60°, and 90°.

The figure below shows these angle triplets and their corresponding leg triplets.

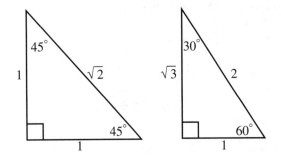

Thus, to determine *all* angle measures and lengths of *all* sides of a triangle quickly, all you need to know is the following:

- that the triangle is a right triangle

- that one of the angles is either 30°, 45°, or 60°

- the length of any one of the three sides

## Isosceles Triangles

An isosceles triangle is one in which two sides are equal in length and, accordingly, two angles are equal in size. In any isosceles triangle, an *altitude* line from the angle formed by the equal sides always bisects the opposite side. Thus, if you know the lengths of the sides, you can easily determine the triangle's area by applying the Pythagorean

Theorem. Consider, for example, isosceles triangle *ABC* in the figure below.

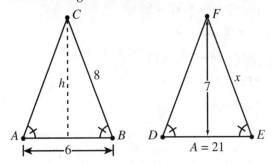

You can determine the height by applying the Pythagorean Theorem:

$$3^2 + h^2 = 8^2$$
$$h^2 = 64 - 9 = 55$$
$$h = \sqrt{55}$$

Thus, the area of triangle *ABC* $= \dfrac{1}{2}(6)\left(\sqrt{55}\right) = 3\sqrt{55}$. If you knew $h$ but not the length of *CB* or *AC*, you could determine these lengths. The altitude line ($h$) bisects the base *AB*, creating two "mirror-image" right triangles, each with legs of length 3 and $\sqrt{55}$. Apply the Pythagorean Theorem:

$$x^2 = 3^2 + (\sqrt{55})^2$$
$$x^2 = 9 + 55 = 64$$
$$x = 8$$

In isosceles triangle *DEF* above, the area is given as 21, and the height is 7. To find $x$, first determine $b$:

$$A = \dfrac{1}{2}(b)(h)$$

$$21 = \dfrac{1}{2}(b)(7)$$

$$b = 6$$

Now use $\dfrac{1}{2}b$ as a leg of a right triangle, and apply the Pythagorean Theorem to find $x$.

$$x^2 = 3^2 + 7^2$$
$$x^2 = 9 + 49 = 58$$
$$x = \sqrt{58}$$

## Equilateral Triangles

An equilateral triangle is a special triangle in which all three sides are the same length and, accordingly, all three angles are the same size (60°). Any line bisecting one of the 60° angles will divide an equilateral triangle into two right triangles with angle measures of 30, 60, and 90°—that is, two $1:\sqrt{3}:2$ triangles.

The area of an equilateral triangle = $\dfrac{s^2}{4}\sqrt{3}$, where $s$ is the length of a side. In the lefthand figure below, if $s = 6$, the area of the triangle = $9\sqrt{3}$.

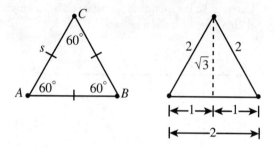

To confirm this formula, bisect the triangle into two 30-60-90 ($1:\sqrt{3}:2$) triangles (as in the righthand figure above). The area of this equilateral triangle is $\frac{1}{2}(2)(\sqrt{3})$ or $\sqrt{3}$. The area of each smaller right triangle is $\dfrac{\sqrt{3}}{2}$.

On the GMAT, you are most likely to encounter equilateral triangles in problems involving *circles* (one of tomorrow's lesson topics).

## QUADRILATERALS

A quadrilateral is a four-sided figure. The specific types of quadrilaterals that appear most frequently on the GMAT include the following:

- A *square*, which is a special type of rectangle

- A *rectangle*, which is a special type of parallelogram

- A *parallelogram*, which is a special type of quadrilateral

Although the following two types of quadrilaterals appear less frequently on the GMAT, you should also be familiar with them:

- *Rhombus*

- *Trapezoid*

Each of these five types of quadrilaterals has its own properties (characteristics) that should be second nature to you as you approach the GMAT. The following are the two most important properties:

- *Area* (the surface covered by the figure on a plane)

- *Perimeter* (the total length of all sides)

The figure below indicates the area (A) and perimeter (P) formulas for each of these five quadrilaterals. Memorize these formulas!

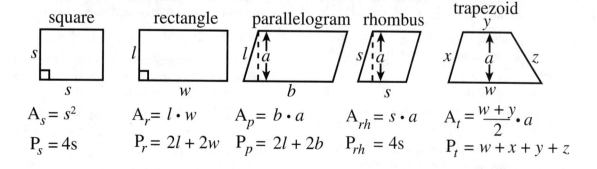

## The Properties of a Square

This next figure shows a square. All squares have the following properties:

- All four sides are equal in length
- All four angles are right angles (90°)
- The perimeter = 4s
- The area = $s^2$

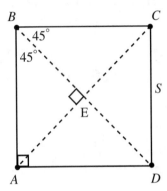

*Diagonals* are line segments connecting opposite corners of a quadrilateral. When you add diagonals to a square, the following are true:

- The area of the square = $\frac{(AC)^2}{2}$ or $\frac{(BD)^2}{2}$ (diagonal squared, divided by 2; this formula applies only to squares, not to other quadrilaterals!).
- The diagonals are equal in length ($AC = BD$).
- The diagonals are perpendicular; their intersection creates four right angles.
- The diagonals *bisect* each 90° angle of the square; that is, they split each angle into two equal (45°) angles.
- You create four distinct *congruent* (the same shape and size) triangles, each having an area of one-half that of the square: *ABD, ACD, ABC,* and *BCD*.
- You create four distinct congruent triangles, each having an area of one-fourth that of the square: *ABE, BCE, CDE,* and *ADE*.
- All eight triangles created are *right isosceles* triangles (with angle measures of 45º, 45º, and 90º.)

## The Properties of a Rectangle

This next figure shows a rectangle. All rectangles have the following properties:

- The opposite sides are equal in length.
- All four angles are right angles (90°).
- The perimeter = $2l + 2w$.
- The area = $l \times w$.
- The maximum area of a rectangle with a given perimeter is a square.
- Conversely, the minimum perimeter of a rectangle with a given area is a square.

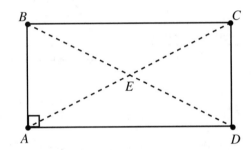

When you add diagonals to a rectangle, the following are true:

- The diagonals are equal in length ($AC = BD$).
- The diagonals are *not* perpendicular (unless the rectangle is a square).
- The diagonals do *not* bisect each 90° angle of the rectangle (unless the rectangle is a square).
- $AE = BE = CE = DE$.
- You create four distinct congruent triangles, each having an area of one-half that of the rectangle: *ABD, ACD, ABC,* and *BCD*.
- *ABE* is congruent to *CDE*; both triangles are isosceles (but they are right triangles *only* if the rectangle is a square).
- *BEC* is congruent to *AED*; both triangles are isosceles (but they are right triangles *only* if the rectangle is a square).

## The Properties of a Parallelogram

The next figure shows a parallelogram. All parallelograms have the following properties:

- Opposite sides are parallel.

- Opposite sides are equal in length.

- Opposite angles are the same size (equal in degree measure).

- All four angles are equal in size *only* if the parallelogram is a rectangle—that is, if the angles are right angles.

- The perimeter = $2l + 2w$.

- The area = base ($b$) × altitude ($a$).

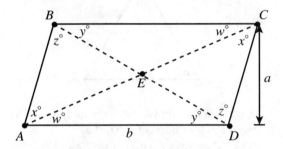

When you add diagonals to a parallelogram, the following are true (referring to the above figure):

- The diagonals ($AC$ and $BD$) are *not* equal in length (unless the figure is a rectangle).

- The diagonals are *not* perpendicular (unless the figure is a square or rhombus).

- The diagonals do *not* bisect each angle of the parallelogram (unless it is a square or rhombus).

- The diagonals bisect each other ($BE = ED$, $CE = AE$).

- You create two pairs of congruent triangles, each having an area of one-half that of the parallelogram: $ABD$ is congruent to $BCD$, and $ACD$ is congruent to $ABC$.

- The triangle $ABE$ is congruent to $CED$ (they are mirror-imaged horizontally *and* vertically); the triangles are isosceles only if the quadrilateral is a rectangle.

- The triangle $BEC$ is congruent to $AED$ (they are mirror-imaged horizontally *and* vertically); the triangles are isosceles only if the quadrilateral is a rectangle.

## The Properties of a Rhombus

The next figure shows a rhombus. All rhombuses have the following properties:

- All sides are equal in length.

- Opposite sides are parallel.

- No angles are right angles (angle measures ≠ 90°).

- The perimeter = $4s$.

- The area = side ($s$) × altitude ($a$).

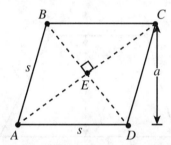

If you add diagonals ($AC$ and $BD$) to a rhombus, the following are true:

- The area = $\frac{AC \times BD}{2}$ (one-half the product of the diagonals; this formula applies to a rhombus and a square, but not to any other quadrilaterals!).

- The diagonals bisect each other ($BE = ED$, $AE = EC$).

- The intersection of diagonals creates four right angles (diagonals are perpendicular).

- The diagonals are *not* equal in length ($AC \neq BD$).

- The diagonals bisect each angle of the rhombus.

- You create two pairs of *congruent* (the same shape and size) isosceles triangles, each triangle having an area of one-half that of the rhombus, (triangle $ABD$ is congruent to $BCD$, and triangle $ACD$ is congruent to $ABC$); none of these four triangles are right triangles.

- Triangle *ABE* is congruent to *CED*; both are right triangles (but not isosceles).

- Triangle *BEC* is congruent to *AED*; both are right triangles (but not isosceles).

## The Properties of a Trapezoid

This next figure shows a trapezoid. All trapezoids have the following properties:

- Only one pair of opposite sides are parallel (*BC* ‖ *AD*)

- The perimeter = *AB* + *BC* + *CD* + *AD*

- The area = $\frac{BC+AD}{2}$ × altitude (*a*) (one-half the sum of the two parallel sides multiplied by the altitude)

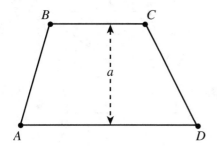

No predictable patterns emerge from the addition of two diagonals to a trapezoid.

---

## GEOMETRY EXERCISES

---

Before you move ahead to tomorrow's advanced geometry lesson, make sure that you understand the basic geometry concepts covered today by attempting the following 10 questions. Answers and explanations immediately follow.

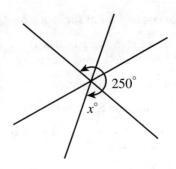

1. In the above figure, *x* =
   (A) 50  (B) 55  (C) 60  (D) 70  (E) 80

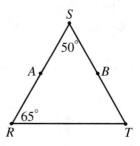

2. In triangle *RST* above, if *A* is the midpoint of *RS*, and if *B* is the midpoint of *ST*, then

   (A) *SA* > *ST*  (B) *BT* > *BS*  (C) *BT* = *SA*
   (D) *SR* > *ST*  (E) *RT* > *ST*

3. What is the perimeter of an equilateral triangle whose area is 16 √3 ?
   (A) 16 (B) 24 (C) 24 √3 (D) 48 (E) 48 √3

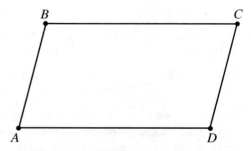

4. In parallelogram *ABCD* above, ∠*A* measures 60°. The sum of the degree measures ∠*B* and ∠*D* is
   (A) 60°  (B) 120°  (C) 180°  (D) 240°  (E) 300°

5. If you double both a rectangle's length and width, you increase the area by what percent?

   (A) 50  (B) 100  (C) 200  (D) 300  (E) 400

6. What is the perimeter of a square whose diagonal is 8?

   (A) 16  (B) $16\sqrt{2}$  (C) 32  (D) $32\sqrt{2}$  (E) $32\sqrt{3}$

7. A rectangular door measures 5′ by 6′8″. What is the distance from one corner of the door to the diagonally opposite corner?

   (A) 8′3″  (B) 8′4″  (C) 9′  (D) 9′4″  (E) 9′6″

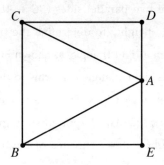

8. Isosceles triangle $ABC$ is inscribed in square $BCDE$ as shown above. If the area of $BCDE$ is 4, what is the perimeter of $ABC$?

   (A) $2 + \sqrt{5}$  (B) $2 + \sqrt{10}$  (C) 8
   (D) $2 + 2\sqrt{5}$  (E) 12

9. In a parallelogram with an area of 15, the base is represented by $x + 7$ and the altitude is $x - 7$. What is the length of the parallelogram's base?

   (A) 1  (B) 5  (C) 8  (D) 15  (E) 34

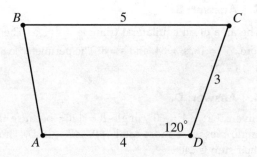

10. What is the area of trapezoid $ABCD$ in the above figure?

   (A) $5\sqrt{2}$  (B) $\dfrac{9\sqrt{3}}{2}$  (C) $\dfrac{27\sqrt{3}}{4}$  (D) $13\dfrac{1}{2}$  (E) 16

---

## EXERCISE ANSWERS AND EXPLANATIONS

---

**1.  Answer: D.**

Referring to the figure below, the total degree measure of all angles is 360. Given that all angles but $a$ and $b$ total 250, $a + b = 110$. $a + b + x = 180$ (they form a straight line). Thus, $x = 70$.

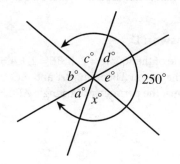

**2.  Answer: C.**

$\angle T = 65°$, so triangle $RST$ is isosceles, and $RS = ST$. $BT = \dfrac{1}{2} ST$, and $SA = \dfrac{1}{2} SR$. Thus, $BT = SA$.

**3.  Answer: B.**

The area of an equilateral triangle $= \frac{s^2}{4}\sqrt{3}$. There-fore, $\frac{s^2}{4} = 16$. $s^2 = 64$, and $s = 8$. The perimeter is $8 + 8 + 8 = 24$.

**4.  Answer: D.**

Given that $\angle A = 60°$, angle $B = 120°$, because the angle measures must total 180. $\angle B = \angle D$. Thus, their sum is 240°.

**5.  Answer: D.**

If the dimensions are doubled, the area is multiplied by $2^2$, or 4. The new area is four times as great as the original area—that is, it has been increased by 300%.

**6.  Answer: B.**

The diagonal of a square is the hypotenuse of a $1:1:\sqrt{2}$ isosceles right triangle, where the two legs are sides of the square. Thus, given that the hypotenuse is 8, each side is $\frac{8}{\sqrt{2}}$, and the perimeter of the square is $4 \times \frac{8}{\sqrt{2}} = \frac{32}{\sqrt{2}} = 16\sqrt{2}$.

**7.  Answer: B.**

The width of the door is 60″ (5′), and its length is 80″ (6′8″). This is a 6:8:10 triangle (conforming to the 3:4:5 Pythagorean triplet), with a diagonal of 100″, or 8′4″.

**8.  Answer: D.**

Each side of the square = 2. If $BE = 2$, $EA = 1$, then by the Pythagorean Theorem, $BA$ and $AC$ each equals $\sqrt{5}$. Thus, the perimeter of triangle $ABC = 2 + 2\sqrt{5}$.

**9.  Answer: D.**

The area of a parallelogram $= (b)(h)$:

$$(x + 7)(x - 7) = 15$$
$$x^2 - 49 = 15$$
$$x^2 = 64$$
$$x = 8$$
$$\text{base} = x + 7 = 15$$

**10. Answer: C.**

The area of a trapezoid is one-half the product of the sum of the two parallel sides $(BC + AD)$ and the trapezoid's height. To determine the trapezoid's height, form a right triangle, as shown in the figure below. This right triangle conforms to the 30-60-90 Pythagorean angle triplet. Thus, the ratio of the three sides is $1:\sqrt{3}:2$. The hypotenuse is given as 3, so the height is $3\frac{\sqrt{3}}{2}$. The area of the trapezoid $=$

$$\frac{1}{2}(4 + 5) \cdot \frac{3\sqrt{3}}{2} = \frac{9}{2} \cdot \frac{3\sqrt{3}}{2} = \frac{27\sqrt{3}}{4}.$$

# Quantitative Ability Lesson 8:
# Geometry, Part 2

## Today's Topics:

1. Circles
2. Solids
3. Cylinders
4. Pyramids
5. Coordinate geometry
6. Data interpretation

Today you complete your review of geometry by examining circles, geometric solids, and coordinate geometry. You also learn some tips for handling GMAT data interpretation (charts and graphs) problems.

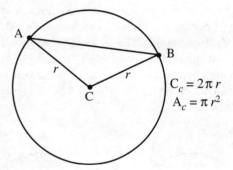

$$C_c = 2\pi r$$
$$A_c = \pi r^2$$

## CIRCLES

### Radius, Area, and Circumference

A *circle* is the set of all points that lie equidistant from the same point (the circle's *center*) on a plane. The distance from the center to any point on the circle is the *radius*, and the greatest distance from one point to another on the circle is the *diameter*. A circle's diameter is twice the length of its radius ($d = 2r$). A *chord* is a line segment connecting two points on the circle; the longest possible chord of a circle passes through its center and is the circle's diameter ($AB$ in the figure to the right). The distance around the circle (its "perimeter") is called the *circumference*. An *arc* is a segment of a circle's circumference.

Here are the formulas for determining a circle's *circumference* and *area*:

- Circumference = $2\pi r$ or $\pi d$

- Area = $\pi r^2$

With these two formulas, you can determine a circle's area, circumference, diameter, and radius, as long as you know just one of these values. Consider the following examples:

- A circle whose radius is 4 has a diameter of 8, a circumference of $8\pi$, and an area of $16\pi$

- A circle whose area is 9 has a radius of $\dfrac{3}{\sqrt{\pi}}$ $(9 = \pi r^2, r = \dfrac{\sqrt{9}}{\sqrt{\pi}})$, a diameter of $\dfrac{6}{\sqrt{\pi}}$, and a circumference of $6\sqrt{\pi}$ $[C = 2\pi(\dfrac{3}{\sqrt{\pi}})]$

The value of $\pi$ is approximately 3.14 or $\dfrac{22}{7}$ (on the GMAT, you probably won't have to work with a value for $\pi$ any more precise than "a little over 3"). In fact, in most GMAT circle problems, the solution is expressed in terms of $\pi$ rather than numerically.

## Hybrid Problems (Circles and Other Geometric Figures)

More complex GMAT circle problems typically involve other geometric figures as well. Most common are "hybrid" problems involving circles and triangles. Any triangle with one vertex at the circle's center and the other two vertices on the circle must be isosceles, because the sides forming the vertex at the circle's center are each equal to the circle's radius. If the angle at the circle's center is 90°, the length of the triangle's hypotenuse (chord) must be $r\sqrt{2}$, because the ratio of the triangle's sides is $1:1:\sqrt{2}$ (see triangle $ABC$ in Fig (A) below). If the angle at the circle's center is 60°, the length of the triangle's hypotenuse (chord) must be $r$, because the triangle is equilateral (see triangle $CDE$ in Figure (A) below):

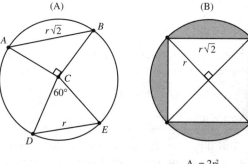

(A)

$A_s = 2r^2$
$A_s : A_c = 2 : \pi$

Assuming the two circles are the same size the length of chord $AB$ in figure, (A) is equal to the length of each side of the *inscribed* square in

figure, (B). Accordingly, the area of a square inscribed in a circle is $(\sqrt{2}\,r)^2$ or $2r^2$. The ratio of the inscribed square's area to the circle's area is $2:\pi$. The *difference* between the two areas—that is, the total shaded area in the above figure (B)—is $\pi r^2 - 2r$. [Accordingly, the area of each crescent-shaped shaded area is $\dfrac{1}{4}(\pi r^2 - 2r)$.]

Distinguish the circle/inscribed-square relationship in the above figure from the square/inscribed-circle relationship illustrated in the figure below. Each side of the square is $2r$. Thus, the square's area is $(2r)^2$, or $4r^2$. The ratio of the square's area to that of the inscribed circle is $\dfrac{4}{\pi}:1$. The *difference* between the two areas—that is, the total shaded area in the below figure—is $4r^2 - \pi r^2$, or $(4 - \pi)r^2$. (Accordingly, the area of each separate, smaller shaded area is one-fourth of that difference.)

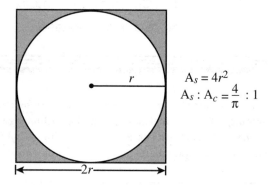

$A_s = 4r^2$
$A_s : A_c = \dfrac{4}{\pi} : 1$

## Concentric Circles

A GMAT circle problem might involve *concentric* circles, which are two or more circles with the same center but unequal radii (creating a "bulls-eye" effect). The relationship between the areas of concentric circles depends, of course, on the relative lengths of their radii. The corresponding relationship is exponential, not linear. For example, if the larger circle's radius is *twice* that of the smaller circle's radius, as in figure (A) below, the ratio of the circles' areas is 1:4 $[(\pi r^2 : \pi(2r)^2)]$. If the larger circle's radius is *three* times the length of that of the smaller circle, as in the below figure (B) below, the ratio is 1:9 $[(\pi r^2 : \pi(3r)^2)]$. A 1:4 ratio between radii results in a 1:16 area ratio (and so forth).

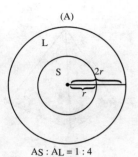

(A)

AS : AL = 1 : 4

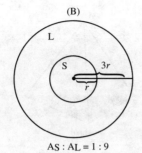

(B)

AS : AL = 1 : 9

## Arcs

An *arc* is a segment of a circle's circumference. You can express an arc's size in terms of its degree measure, its length, or both. The length of an arc (as a fraction of the circle's circumference) is directly proportional to the degree measure of the arc (as a fraction of the circle's total degree measure of 360°). Accordingly, an arc of 60° would have a length of $\frac{60}{360}$, or $\frac{1}{6}$ the circle's circumference. Given $C = 2\pi r$, that arc is $\frac{1}{6}(2\pi r)$, or $\frac{\pi r}{3}$ (as illustrated by arc *AB* in the figure below).

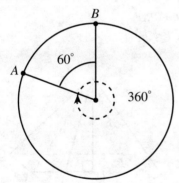

Similarly, the length of a 100° arc is $\frac{100}{360}$ or $(\frac{5}{18})$ of the circle's circumference ($2\pi r$), or $\frac{5\pi r}{9}$.

---

## RECTANGULAR SOLIDS

---

A *rectangular solid* is formed by six rectangular surfaces, or *faces*, connecting at right angles at eight corners (see the below figure). The volume of any rectangular solid is the product of its three dimensions—that is, length × width × height.

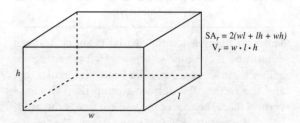

$SA_r = 2(wl + lh + wh)$
$V_r = w \cdot l \cdot h$

In any rectangular solid, the three pairs of opposing faces are each identical; they have the same dimensions and area. Accordingly, the surface area of any rectangular solid is $2(lw + lh + wh)$.

A *cube* is a rectangular solid in which all six faces (surfaces) are square. Because all six faces of a cube are identical in dimension and area, given a length *s* of one of a cube's edges, its surface area is six times the square of *s*:

$$SA_c = 6s^2$$

Given a *length s* of one of a cube's edges, the *volume* of the cube is *s* cubed. Conversely, given the volume *V* of a cube, the length of one edge *s* is the cube root of *V*:

$$V = s^3$$
$$S = \sqrt[3]{V}$$

Given the area *A* of one face of a cube, you can determine the cube's *volume* by cubing the square root of *A*. Conversely, given the volume *V* of a cube, you can determine the area by squaring the cube root of *V*:

$$V_c = \left(\sqrt{A}\right)^3$$
$$A_f = \left(\sqrt[3]{V_c}\right)^2$$

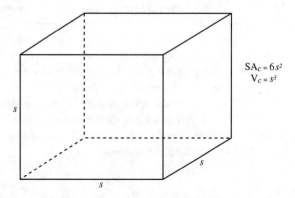

$SA_c = 6s^2$
$V_c = s^3$

## CYLINDERS

This next figure is a right circular cylinder. You can determine a cylinder's *surface area* by adding together three areas: the circular base, the circular top, and the rectangular surface around the cylinder's vertical face. The area of the vertical face is the product of the circular base's circumference (that is, the rectangle's width) and the cylinder's height. Thus, given a radius $r$ and height $h$ of a cylinder, the following is true:

Surface Area $(SA) = 2\pi r^2 + (2\pi r)(h)$

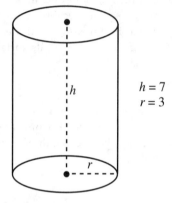

$h = 7$
$r = 3$

Accordingly, the surface area of the cylinder in the above figure is $18\pi + 42\pi$, or $60\pi$.

Given a cylinder's radius and height, you can determine its *volume* by multiplying the area of its circular base by its height:

$V_c = \pi r^2 \times h$

Accordingly, the volume of the cylinder in the above figure is $(9\pi)(7)$, or $63\pi$.

## PYRAMIDS

GMAT problems involving pyramids are uncommon; nevertheless, they are "fair game" according to the testing service, so you should be ready for them—just in case. There are two distinct types of pyramids: a three-sided pyramid with a triangular base [see figure (A)] and a four-sided pyramid with a square base [see figure (B)]. In either type, all triangular faces are the same shape and size.

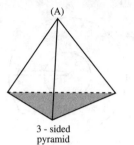

(A)

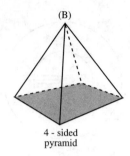

(B)

3 - sided pyramid

4 - sided pyramid

GMAT problems involving pyramids usually involve the *altitude* and/or *surface area* of the four-sided type. The altitude of a four-sided pyramid is the pyramid's height—a line segment running from the pyramid's apex down to the center of the square base ($PQ$ in the figure below). Given the altitude and the dimensions of the square base, you can determine the area of each triangular face by applying the Pythagorean Theorem. For example, if the altitude $PQ = 6$, and the area of the square base is 36, you can determine the length of $PX$ as follows:

Each side of square $ABCD$ is $\sqrt{36}$, or 6; thus, $QX = 3$

$6^2 + 3^2 = (PX)^2$

$36 + 9 = (PX)^2$

$PX = 3\sqrt{5}$

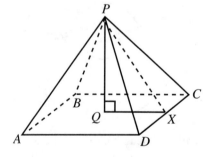

$PX$ ($3\sqrt{5}$) is the (sloping) height of each of the pyramid's triangular faces. The base of each triangle is 6 (because the area of the square base is 36). Thus, the area of triangle $PCD = (\frac{1}{2})(6)(3\sqrt{5})$, or $9\sqrt{5}$. Accordingly, the total surface area of all four triangular sides is four times this amount, or $36\sqrt{5}$.

# COORDINATE GEOMETRY

On the GMAT, you are likely to encounter one or two *coordinate geometry* questions, which involve the rectangular *coordinate plane* defined by two axes—a horizontal *x-axis* and a vertical *y-axis*. You can define any point on the coordinate plane by using two co-ordinates: an *x-coordinate* and a *y-coordinate*. A point's *x*-coordinate is its horizontal position on the plane, and its *y*-coordinate is its vertical position on the plane. You denote the coordinates of a point with (*x,y*), where *x* is the point's *x*-coordinate and *y* is the point's *y*-coordinate.

## Coordinate Signs and the Four Quadrants

The center of the coordinate plane—the intersection of the *x* and *y* axes—is called the *origin*. The coordinates of the origin are (0,0). Any point along the *x*-axis has a *y*-coordinate of 0 (*x*,0), and any point along the *y*-axis has an *x*-coordinate of 0 (0,*y*). The coordinate signs (positive or negative) of points lying in the four quadrants I–IV in this next figure are as follows:

- Quadrant I (+,+)

- Quadrant II (−,+)

- Quadrant III (−,−)

- Quadrant IV (+,−)

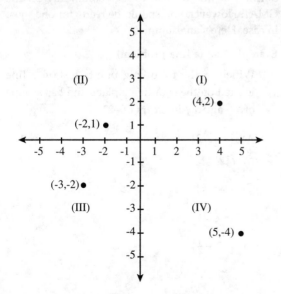

## GMAT Coordinate Plane Problems

Most GMAT coordinate geometry problems involve either triangles, circles, or both. In triangle problems, your task is usually to determine the length of a sloping line segment (by forming a right triangle and applying the Pythagorean Theorem). In circle problems, your task is usually to determine the circumference or area of a circle lying on the plane. Here's an example of each type:

**Example 22-1 (triangle problem)**

> On the coordinate plane, what is the length of a line segment with the end points (−5,9) and (4,−3)?

> On the coordinate plane, construct a right triangle with the line segment as the hypotenuse (see the below figure). The length of the horizontal leg is 9 (the horizontal distance from −5 to 4), and the length of the vertical leg is 12 (the vertical distance from −3 to 9). Conforming to the 3:4:5 Pythagorean triplet, 9 and 12 are multiples of 3 and 4. Thus, without calculating the length of the line segment using the theorem, you can quickly determine that the length is 15 (the Pythagorean triplet 3:4:5 is equivalent to 9:12:15).

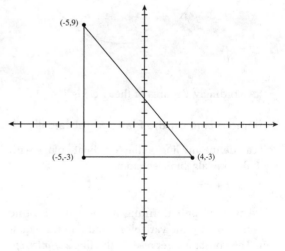

**Example 22-2 (circle problem)**

> On the coordinate plane, what is the area of a circle whose center is located at (2,−1), if the point (−3,3) lies on the circle's perimeter?

Construct a right triangle with the circle's radius as the hypotenuse (see the figure below). The length of the triangle's horizontal leg is 5 (the horizontal distance from −3 to 2), and the length of its vertical leg is 4 (the vertical distance from −1 to 3). *Be careful:* These numbers do *not* conform to the Pythagorean triplet 3:4:5, because 4 and 5 are the lengths of the two *legs* here! Instead, you must calculate the length of the hypotenuse (the circle's radius) by applying the Pythagorean Theorem:

$$4^2 + 5^2 = r^2$$
$$16 + 25 = r^2$$
$$41 = r^2$$
$$r = \sqrt{41}$$

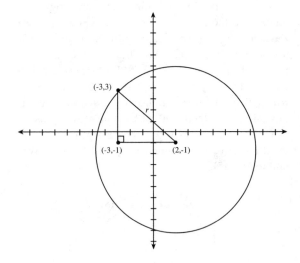

Accordingly, the area of the circle is 41π.

## Defining a Line on the Plane Algebraically

You can define any line on the coordinate plane with the following algebraic equation:

$$y = mx + b$$

Any $(x,y)$ pair defining a point on the line can substitute for the variables $x$ and $y$ in this equation. The constant $b$ represents the line's *y-intercept* (the point on the y-axis where the line crosses that axis). The constant $m$ represents the line's *slope*. The slope is best thought of as a fraction in which the

numerator indicates the vertical change from one point to another on the line (moving left to right) corresponding to a given horizontal change, which the fraction's denominator indicates. The common term used for this fraction is "rise-over-run." Keep in mind the following characteristics of certain slopes (*m*-values):

- A line sloping *upward* from left to right has a positive slope (*m*).

- A line sloping *downward* from left to right has a negative slope (*m*).

- A *horizontal* line has a slope of zero (*m* = 0, and *mx* = 0).

- A *vertical* line has an undefined slope (the *m*-term in the equation is ignored).

- A line with a slope of 1 (−1) slopes upward (downward) from left to right at a 45° angle in relation to the *x*-axis.

- A line with a fractional slope between 0 and 1 (−1) slopes upward (downward) from left to right but at *less* than a 45° angle in relation to the *x*-axis.

- A line with a slope greater than 1 (less than −1) slopes upward (downward) from left to right at *more* than a 45° angle in relation to the *x*-axis.

Problems involving the algebraic equation for defining a line do *not* appear commonly on the GMAT. However, you should be ready for one—just in case. Here's an example:

### Example 22-3 (a line problem)

Which of the following points lies on a line located on the coordinate plane and has a slope of $-\frac{3}{2}$ and a *y*-intercept of −2?

(A) $\left(-\frac{3}{2}, -2\right)$

(B) $(4,6)$

(C) $\left(\frac{3}{8}, -\frac{3}{2}\right)$

(D) $\left(-\frac{8}{3}, 2\right)$

(E) $\left(-2, -\frac{3}{2}\right)$

Substitute each value pair into the equation $y = -\frac{3}{2}x - 2$. The only $(x,y)$ pair that satisfies the equation is $\left(-\frac{8}{3}, 2\right)$, which is response D. On the coordinate plane, the line appears as shown in the figure below.

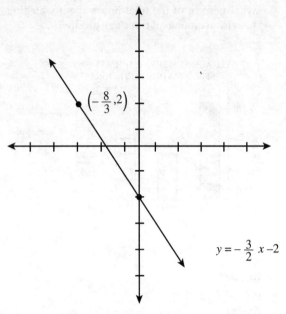

## DATA INTERPRETATION

*Data interpretation* questions require you to analyze information presented graphically in statistical charts and graphs. Four types of charts and graphs are most common on the GMAT:

- Tables
- Bar graphs
- Pie charts
- Line graphs

You are likely to encounter two or three data interpretation questions in the GMAT Quantitative section. Here's a typical GMAT "table" problem:

### Example 22-4 (a table problem)

According to the following table, of the total number of product units sold to the institutions during January, which of the following most closely approximates the percentage that were *not* standard product versions?

PRODUCT VERSION

| | | Basic | Standard | Deluxe |
|---|---|---|---|---|
| PURCHASER CATEGORY | domestic institutions | 3.6 | 8.5 | 1.9 |
| | domestic non-institutions | 7.5 | 11.4 | 2.0 |
| | foreign institutions | 1.7 | 4.9 | 2.2 |
| | foreign non-institutions | 1.0 | 5.1 | 0.8 |

(A) 24

(B) 37

(C) 41

(D) 59

(E) 68

The total number of product units sold to institutions = $(3.6 + 8.5 + 1.9) + (1.7 + 4.9 + 2.2) = 22.8$. The number of these units that were not standard versions = $(3.6 + 1.9) + (1.7 + 2.2) = 9.4$. This number is approximately 41% of 22.8. (*Approximation tip:* As a fraction of 22.8, 9.4 is more than one-third but is less than one-half. Thus, you can eliminate A, D, and E. By rounding down both numerator and denominator $\frac{9}{22.5}$, it is evident that the total [22.5] is $2\frac{1}{2}$ times greater than 9; in other words, 9 is 40% of 22.5, and C is the answer.)

Data interpretation questions are not *conceptually* difficult. Nevertheless, it is surprisingly easy to trip yourself up by committing careless errors. Heed the following three tips to ensure that you respond correctly to data interpretation questions.

**Tip 1: Don't confuse percentages and raw numbers.** Most data interpretation questions involve raw data as well as *proportion*—in terms of either percent, fraction, or ratio (usually percent). Always ask yourself whether the solution to a problem is a *raw* number or a *proportional* number (such as a percentage). You can be sure that the GMAT will bait you with appropriate incorrect answer choices!

**Tip 2: Be careful to read the proper column, axis, line, or bar.** This point of advice might seem obvious; nevertheless, reading the wrong data is probably the leading cause of incorrect responses to data interpretation questions. To ensure that you don't commit this careless error, point your finger to the proper line, column, or bar on the screen; *put your finger right on the screen,* and don't move it until you're sure that you've got the right data.

**Tip 3: Approximate numbers appropriately.** Most data interpretation questions call for approximation. Avoid committing careless computational errors and doing more pencil-work than needed by keeping in mind the following:

- Rounding numbers up or down to the nearest appropriate unit or half-unit often suffices to respond correctly to the question. Be sure to round off numerators and denominators of fractions in the same direction (either both up or both down).

- Don't split hairs when interpreting line charts and bar graphs. If a point appears to be about $\frac{4}{10}$ of the distance from one hash mark to the next, do not hesitate to round up to $\frac{5}{10}$. For example, in the figure, (A) below, round the 1990 price down to $25 and the 1991 price up to $30. In the figure, (B) below, the number of requests per minute peaks at *about* 1:00 p.m., whereas the lowest per-minute rate during the afternoon occurs at *about* 5:00.

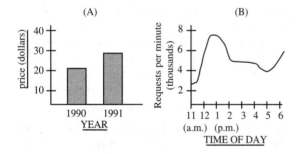

(A)   (B)

- Formulate a clear idea as to the overall size of the number that the question calls for. For example, is it a double-digit number? Is it a percentage that is obviously greater than 50 percent? Is it a large raw number in the thousands?

**Example 22-5 (bar chart)**

According to the chart in the figure below, the two age groups other than the group that spent the greatest number of hours per week watching sports on television accounted for approximately what percent of the total hours spent watching television among all three age groups?

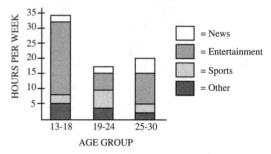

(A) 27

(B) 36

(C) 60

(D) 74

(E) 85

The group that spent the most time per week watching sports on television was the 19–24 year olds (who spent an average of approximately six hours per week watching sports programming). The average hours for all three groups totals approximately 74 (33 + 19 + 22). Of that total, the two groups other than the 19–24 age group accounted for 55 hours, or $\frac{55}{74}$, or about 74% of the total hours for all three age groups.

## Quantitative Ability Lesson 9:
## Mini-Test and Review (Geometry)

### Today's Topics:

Today you will apply what you learned on Days 21 and 22 to a 20-question mini-test, which includes both Problem Solving and Data Sufficiency questions.

## MINI-TEST (GEOMETRY)

**Number of questions:** 20
**Suggested time:** 40 minutes

**Directions:** Solve the following 20 Quantitative questions under simulated exam conditions. After completing the mini-test, review the explanations that follow. Preceding the explanation for each question, the question type and difficulty level are indicated.

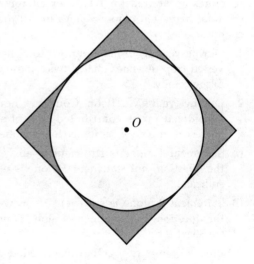

1. If the area of circle $O$ in the figure above is $64\pi$, what is the perimeter of the square?
   (A)  16
   (B)  32
   (C)  64
   (D)  $32\pi$
   (E)  $64\pi$

HARVESTED CROP REVENUES (YEAR X)
(Percent of total revenue among four counties)

| | non - subsidized farms | subsidized farms |
|---|---|---|
| Willot County | 7% | |
| Tilson County | | 12% |
| Stanton County | | |
| Osher County | 8% | |
| (Total Percentages) | 30% | |

2. Based on the table above, if the total harvested crop revenues for Willot and Tilson counties combined equaled those for Stanton and Osher counties combined, then Stanton County's subsidized farm revenues accounted for what percentage of the total harvested crop revenues for all four counties?

1.  During year $X$, Osher County's total harvested crop revenues totaled twice those of Tilson county.

2.  During year $X$, Tilson County's non-subsidized farms contributed 18% of all harvested crop revenues for the four counties.

(A) Statement 1 alone is sufficient to answer the question, but statement 2 alone is not sufficient

(B) Statement 2 alone is sufficient to answer the question, but statement 1 alone is not sufficient

(C) Both statements together are needed to answer the question, but neither statement alone is sufficient to answer the question

(D) Either statement by itself is sufficient to answer the question

(E) Not enough facts are given to answer the question

3. If the diameter of a circle is increased by 50%, by how much is the area increased?

(A) 75%

(B) 100%

(C) 125%

(D) 150%

(E) 200%

4. On the coordinate plane, what is the area of a right triangle, one side of which is defined by the points (2,3) and (–4,0)?

1.  The triangle's sides cross the $y$-axis at exactly two points altogether.

2.  The $y$-coordinate of the third vertex of the triangle is zero.

(A) Statement 1 alone is sufficient to answer the question, but statement 2 alone is not sufficient

(B) Statement 2 alone is sufficient to answer the question, but statement 1 alone is not sufficient

(C) Both statements together are needed to answer the question, but neither statement alone is sufficient to answer the question

(D) Either statement by itself is sufficient to answer the question

(E) Not enough facts are given to answer the question

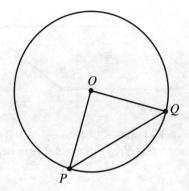

5. In the above figure, if point $O$ lies at the center of the circle, what is the area of triangle $OPQ$?

   1. The radius of the circle is 3.

   2. $PO = PQ$.

   (A) Statement 1 alone is sufficient to answer the question, but statement 2 alone is not sufficient

   (B) Statement 2 alone is sufficient to answer the question, but statement 1 alone is not sufficient

   (C) Both statements together are needed to answer the question, but neither statement alone is sufficient to answer the question

   (D) Either statement by itself is sufficient to answer the question

   (E) Not enough facts are given to answer the question

6. A certain cylindrical pail has a diameter of 14 inches and a height of 10 inches. Approximately how many gallons will the pail hold, if there are 231 cubic inches to a gallon?

   (A) 4.8

   (B) 5.1

   (C) 6.7

   (D) $14\frac{2}{3}$

   (E) 44

7. In triangle $ABC$, $AB = BC$. If the size of $\angle B$ is $x°$, which of the following represents the degree measure of $\angle A$?

   (A) $x$

   (B) $180 - x$

   (C) $180 - \dfrac{x}{2}$

   (D) $90 - \dfrac{x}{2}$

   (E) $90 - x$

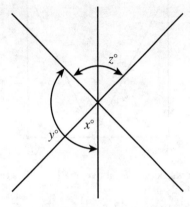

8. In the above figure, what is the value of $x$?

   1. $y = 130$

   2. $z = 100$

   (A) Statement 1 alone is sufficient to answer the question, but statement 2 alone is not sufficient

   (B) Statement 2 alone is sufficient to answer the question, but statement 1 alone is not sufficient

   (C) Both statements together are needed to answer the question, but neither statement alone is sufficient to answer the question

   (D) Either statement by itself is sufficient to answer the question

   (E) Not enough facts are given to answer the question

9. If a circle whose radius is $x$ has an area of 4, what is the area of a circle whose radius is $3x$?

   (A) $\sqrt{13}$

   (B) $4\sqrt{13}$

   (C) 12

   (D) 36

   (E) 144

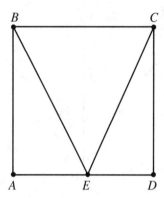

10. In rectangle $ABCD$ above, if $AE = ED$, is rectangle $ABCD$ a square?

    1. The length of $AE$ multiplied by $\sqrt{5}$ is equal to the length of $BE$.

    2. The area of triangle $BCE$ is exactly half that of rectangle $ABCD$.

    (A) Statement 1 alone is sufficient to answer the question, but statement 2 alone is not sufficient

    (B) Statement 2 alone is sufficient to answer the question, but statement 1 alone is not sufficient

    (C) Both statements together are needed to answer the question, but neither statement alone is sufficient to answer the question

    (D) Either statement by itself is sufficient to answer the question

    (E) Not enough facts are given to answer the question

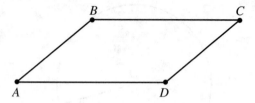

11. In parallelogram $ABCD$ (above), $\angle B$ is five times the size of $\angle C$. What is the measure in degrees of $\angle B$?

    (A) 30

    (B) 60

    (C) 100

    (D) 120

    (E) 150

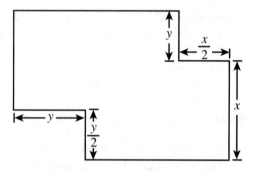

12. A carpet in the shape of a rectangle must be trimmed into the shape shown in the above figure. What is the minimum possible area of the carpet before it is trimmed?

    1. $y = 4$

    2. $x = 5$

    (A) Statement 1 alone is sufficient to answer the question, but statement 2 alone is not sufficient

    (B) Statement 2 alone is sufficient to answer the question, but statement 1 alone is not sufficient

    (C) Both statements together are needed to answer the question, but neither statement alone is sufficient to answer the question

    (D) Either statement by itself is sufficient to answer the question

    (E) Not enough facts are given to answer the question

13. If the volume of one cube is eight times greater than that of another, what is the ratio of the surface area of the larger cube to that of the smaller cube?

(A) $\sqrt{2}$ :1

(B) $2\sqrt{2}$ :1

(C) 2:1

(D) 4:1

(E) 8:1

PRICE OF COMMON STOCK OF
XYZ CORP. AND ABC CORP.
(YEAR X)

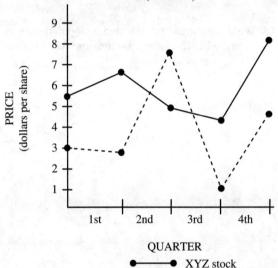

14. Based on the chart above, at the time during year X when the difference between the price of ABC common stock and the price of XYZ common stock was at its greatest, the price of ABC common stock was approximately what percent of the price of XYZ common stock and ABC common stock combined?

(A) 16%

(B) 31%

(C) 36%

(D) 42%

(E) 103%

15. Eight square window panes of equal size are to be pieced together to form a rectangular French door. What is the perimeter of the door, excluding framing between and around the panes?

1. Each pane is one square foot in area.

2. The area of the door, excluding framing between and around the panes, is eight square feet.

(A) Statement 1 alone is sufficient to answer the question, but statement 2 alone is not sufficient

(B) Statement 2 alone is sufficient to answer the question, but statement 1 alone is not sufficient

(C) Both statements together are needed to answer the question, but neither statement alone is sufficient to answer the question

(D) Either statement by itself is sufficient to answer the question

(E) Not enough facts are given to answer the question

16. The length of an arc of a certain circle is one-fifth the circumference of the circle. If the length of the arc is $2\pi$, what is the radius of the circle?

(A) 1

(B) 2

(C) $\sqrt{10}$

(D) 5

(E) 10

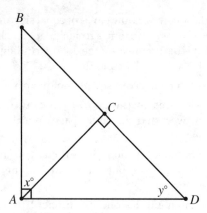

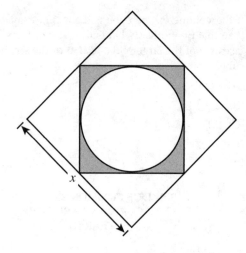

17. In the above figure, does $x = y$?

   1. Triangle $ACD$ is an isosceles triangle.

   2. Triangle $ABC$ is an isosceles triangle.

   (A) Statement 1 alone is sufficient to answer the question, but statement 2 alone is not sufficient

   (B) Statement 2 alone is sufficient to answer the question, but statement 1 alone is not sufficient

   (C) Both statements together are needed to answer the question, but neither statement alone is sufficient to answer the question

   (D) Either statement by itself is sufficient to answer the question

   (E) Not enough facts are given to answer the question

18. What is the area of the shaded region in the above figure, which contains one circle and two squares?

   (A) $\dfrac{\pi x}{2} - 4$

   (B) $x^2 - 2\pi$

   (C) $\dfrac{x(2 - \pi x)}{4}$

   (D) $\dfrac{7x^2}{4}$

   (E) $\dfrac{x^2(4 - \pi)}{8}$

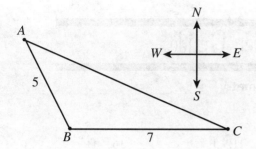

19. Once a month, a crop duster sprays a triangular area defined by three farm houses—A, B, and C—as indicated in the above figure. Farmhouse B lies due west of Farmhouse C. Given the compass directions and distances (in miles) indicated in the above figure, what is the total area that the crop duster sprays?

1. Farmhouse C is located 4 miles further south than farmhouse A.

2. Farmhouse C is located 10 miles further east than farmhouse A.

(A) Statement 1 alone is sufficient to answer the question, but statement 2 alone is not sufficient

(B) Statement 2 alone is sufficient to answer the question, but statement 1 alone is not sufficient

(C) Both statements together are needed to answer the question, but neither statement alone is sufficient to answer the question

(D) Either statement by itself is sufficient to answer the question

(E) Not enough facts are given to answer the question

20. On the coordinate plane, two points $P$ and $Q$, defined by the coordinates $(-1,0)$ and $(3,3)$, respectively, are connected to form a chord of a circle that also lies on the plane. If the area of the circle is $\frac{25}{4}\pi$, what are the coordinates of the center of the circle?

(A) $\left(\frac{1}{2}, \frac{1}{2}\right)$

(B) $\left(1, 1\frac{1}{2}\right)$

(C) $(0,1)$

(D) $\left(\frac{1}{2}, 1\right)$

(E) $\left(-1\frac{1}{2}, \frac{1}{2}\right)$

# Quick Answer Guide

## Mini-Test: Geometry

| | | | |
|---|---|---|---|
| 1. C | 6. C | 11. E | 16. D |
| 2. C | 7. D | 12. E | 17. D |
| 3. C | 8. C | 13. D | 18. E |
| 4. B | 9. D | 14. B | 19. D |
| 5. C | 10. A | 15. E | 20. B |

## EXPLANATIONS

### 1. Area of circle/perimeter of square (easier). Answer: C.

The area of the circle = $64\pi = r^2\pi$. Thus, the radius of the circle = 8. The side of the square is twice the circle's radius, or 16. Therefore, the perimeter of the square is $4 \times 16 = 64$.

### 2. Data interpretation (challenging). Answer: C.

Statement 1 establishes the total contributions of Willot and Tilson counties relative to those of Stanton and Osher counties, but the statement provides no additional information about Stanton County's specific percentage contribution. Statement 1 alone is therefore insufficient to answer the question. Based on statement 2 alone, Tilson County's nonsubsidized farms must have accounted for 6% of all revenues (18–12%). Accordingly, Stanton County's nonsubsidized farms must have accounted for 9% of all revenues (the percentages in the leftmost column must total 30). However, this information is insufficient to determine Stanton County's subsidized farm contribution. With both statements 1 and 2 together, Osher County's revenues must

total 36% (because statement 2 stipulates that Osher county contributed twice the revenues of Tilson county, which you now know contributed 18% of all revenues). At this point, you have partially completed the table as shown in the below figure.

| | non -<br>subsidized<br>farms | subsidized<br>farms | | |
|---|---|---|---|---|
| Willot County | 7% | | | |
| Tilson County | (6%) | 12% | (18%) | } 50% |
| Stanton County | (9%) | | | |
| Osher County | 8% | (28%) | (36%) | } 50% |
| (Total Percentages) | 30% | (70%) | | |

It is now evident that Stanton County's subsidized farms contributed 6% of the total revenues (Stanton and Osher county revenues must account for 50% of the total). Thus, statements 1 and 2 together suffice to answer the question.

## 3. Area of a circle (challenging). Answer: C.

This question is deceptively difficult. The area of a circle is $\pi r^2$. Thus, if $d$ (and thus $r$) were increased by .5, the linear ratio of the original diameter (and radius) to the larger diameter (and radius) is 1:1.5. Accordingly, the ratio of the original area to the larger area is $(1)^2:(1.5)^2$, or 1:2.25. The increase is 1.25 or 125% of the original area. Confirm this increase by substituting a simple number such as 2 for the original radius. The area ratio is $2^2:3^2$, or 4:9, an increase of 125% (from 4 to 9).

## 4. Coordinate geometry (challenging). Answer: B.

Statement 1 alone allows for more than one possible area, as illustrated in this next figure.

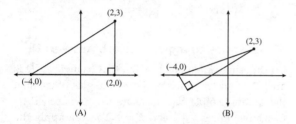

    (A)               (B)

Statement 2 alone, however, allows for only one possible area (and shape and position) of the triangle: the above figure, (A). Thus, statement 2 alone suffices to answer the question.

## 5. Equilateral triangles (moderate). Answer: C.

Statement 1 provides no information about the area of triangle $OPQ$ relative to the area of the circle. Thus, that statement alone is insufficient to answer the question. The information in statement 2 establishes that triangle $OPQ$ is an equilateral triangle (all three sides are equal in length, and all three angles are 60°). However, no specific values are provided to determine the area. Thus, statement 2 alone is insufficient to answer the question. Adding that the radius of the circle is 3, however, enables you to compute the area of the equilateral triangle. The base is 3 and the height is $1.5\sqrt{3}$ (an equilateral triangle consists of two $1:\sqrt{3}:2$ right triangles). Thus, statements 1 and 2 together suffice to answer the question. (The area of triangle $OPQ$ is $2.25\sqrt{3}$.)

## 6. Cylinders (easier). Answer: C.

The volume of the cylindrical pail is equal to the area of its circular base multiplied by its height:

$$V = \pi r^2 h = \left(\frac{22}{7}\right)(49)(10) = 1{,}540 \text{ cubic inches}$$

The gallon capacity of the pail $= \frac{1{,}540}{231}$, or about 6.7.

## 7. Isosceles triangles (moderate). Answer: D.

The triangle is isosceles, so $\angle A = \angle C$. Letting $a$, $c$, and $x$ represent the degree measures of $\angle A$, $\angle C$, and $\angle B$, respectively, solve for $a$:

$$a + c + x = 180$$
$$2a + x = 180 \ [a = c]$$
$$2a + x = 180$$
$$2a = 180 - x$$
$$a = \frac{180}{2} - \frac{x}{2}$$
$$a = 90 - \frac{x}{2}$$

## 8. Lines and angles (moderate). Answer: C.

It is obvious that neither statement 1 nor 2 alone provides sufficient information to determine the angle measure of $x$. Thus, you can easily eliminate A, B, and D. Next, consider statement 1 and 2 together. Notice that $\angle y$ and $\angle z$ together form a degree measure that exceeds 180° (a straight line) by $x°$. Thus, $y + z - x = 180$. Statements 1 and 2 provide the values of $y$ and $z$ and thus suffice to answer the question ($x = 50$).

## 9. Area of a circle (easier). Answer: D.

The area of a circle is $\pi r^2$. The area of a circle with a radius of $x$ is $\pi x^2$, which is given as 4. The area of a circle with radius $3x$ is $\pi(3x)^2 = 9\pi x^2 = (9)(4) = 36$.

## 10. Rectangles/right triangles (challenging). Answer: A.

Given $(AE)(\sqrt{5}) = BE$ (statement 1), $AB$ must be exactly twice the length of $AE$. Why? Because triangle $ABE$ is a right triangle, the Pythagorean Theorem establishes that $(AE)^2 + (AB)^2 = (BE)^2$, or $1^2 + 2^2 = \sqrt{5}$.

Given that $AE = ED$, $AB = AD$, and the rectangle is indeed a square. Statement 1 alone suffices to answer the question. Considering statement 2, a bit of visualization reveals that the area of triangle $BCE$ is always exactly half that of rectangle $ABCD$, regardless of where point $E$ lies along line segment $AD$. Thus, statement 2 alone is insufficient to answer the question.

## 11. Parallelograms (easier). Answer: E.

The sum of the angles in a parallelogram is 360°. Angles $B$ and $C$ account for half, or 180°. Letting $x$ equal the degree measure of angle $C$, angle B = 5x.

$$5x + x = 180$$
$$6x = 180$$
$$x = 30$$
$$\angle B = 5x = (5)(30) = 150$$

## 12. Rectangles: area (easier). Answer: E.

You can determine the height of the rectangular carpet with the information provided by statements 1 and 2 together (height = $x + y$ = 9). However, even considering both statements 1 and 2, you cannot determine the width of the rectangle carpet, and accordingly, you cannot determine its area (minimum or otherwise).

## 13. Rectangular solids: cubes (challenging). Answer: D.

The ratio of the two volumes is 8:1; thus, the linear ratio of the cubes' edges is the cube root of this ratio: $\sqrt[3]{8} : \sqrt[3]{1}$, or 2:1. The area ratio is the square of the linear ratio, or 4:1.

## 14. Data interpretation (easier). Answer: B.

The price difference was at its maximum at the end of the 1st quarter, when the price of ABC stock was about $28 and the price of XYZ stock was about $66. The total price of both was about $94. $28 is $\left(\frac{28}{94}\right)$ or about 31% of $94.

## 15. Rectangles: area and perimeter (moderate). Answer: E.

You could piece together the panes into either a single column (or row) of eight panes or into two adjacent columns (or rows) of four panes each. In the first case, the door's perimeter would be 18. In the second case, the door's perimeter would be 12. Thus, statement 1 alone is insufficient to answer the question. Statement 2 alone is insufficient for the same reason. Both statements together still fail to provide sufficient information to determine the shape (or perimeter) of the door.

## 16. Circles: arcs (moderate). Answer: D.

The circumference is five times the length of the arc:
$$5(2\pi) = 10\pi = \pi d$$
$$d = 10, \text{ and } r = 5$$

## 17. Isosceles triangles (easier). Answer: D.

Considering statement 1, given that triangle $ACD$ is a right isosceles triangle, the two angles other than the 90° angle must each measure 45°. Because $\angle BAD$ measures 90°, $x = 45$, and $x = y$. You can apply the same analysis to statement 2, and either statement suffices to answer the question.

## 18. Circles/squares/right triangles (challenging). Answer: E.

To determine the area of the shaded region, subtract the area of the circle from the area of the smaller of the two squares. First, determine the area of the smaller square. Each of the four outside triangles is a $1:1:\sqrt{2}$ right triangle, with a side of the smaller square as the hypotenuse. Each leg of these triangles is $\frac{x}{2}$ long; thus, each side of the smaller square is $\frac{x\sqrt{2}}{2}$ long. Accordingly, the area of the smaller square is $(\frac{x\sqrt{2}}{2})^2$, or $\frac{x^2}{2}$. Next, determine the area of the circle. Its diameter is $\frac{x\sqrt{2}}{2}$ (the length of each side of the smaller square). Thus, its radius is half that amount, or $\frac{x\sqrt{2}}{4}$. The circle's area $= \pi\left(\frac{x\sqrt{2}}{4}\right)^2 =$ $\pi\left(\frac{2x^2}{16}\right)=\frac{\pi x^2}{8}$. Subtract this area from the square's area: $\frac{x^2}{2}-\frac{\pi x^2}{8}=\frac{4x^2-\pi x^2}{8}=\frac{x^2(4-\pi)}{8}$.

### 19. Right triangles (easier). Answer: D.

The area of any triangle equals $\frac{1}{2}$(base)(height). Using seven miles as the base of the triangle in this problem, the triangle's height is the north-south (vertical) distance from $A$ to an imaginary line extending westerly from $B$. Statement 1 explicitly provides the triangle's height. Statement 2 also provides sufficient information to determine this height. As indicated in this next figure, the triangle's height is four miles ($3^2 + 4^2 = 5^2$, per the Pythagorean Theorem). Accordingly, either statement alone suffices to determine the triangle's area.

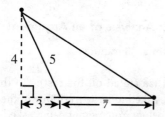

(The area $= \frac{1}{2}(7)(4) = 14$.)

### 20. Coordinate geometry (challenging). Answer: B.

Given that the area of the circle is $\frac{25\pi}{4}$, you can determine the circle's radius and diameter:

$$A = \pi r^2$$

$$\frac{25\pi}{4} = \pi r^2$$

$$\frac{25}{4} = r^2$$

$$r = \frac{5}{2}$$

$$d = 5$$

On the coordinate plane, the distance between the points whose coordinates are $(-1,0)$ and $(3,3)$ is 5 (the chord forms the hypotenuse of a 3:4:5 right triangle, as illustrated in the figure below). Because these two points are five units apart, chord $PQ$ must be the circle's diameter. The circle's center lies on chord $PQ$ midway between $P$ and $Q$. The $x$-coordinate of the center is midway between the $x$-coordinates of $P$ and $Q$ ($-1$ and 3), whereas the $y$-coordinate is midway between the $y$-coordinates of $P$ and $Q$ (0 and 3)—that is, the center of the circle is the point $(1, 1\frac{1}{2})$.

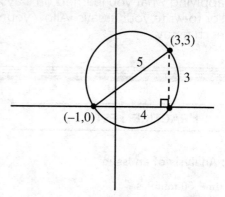

# Analytical Writing Assessment Practice Test

## Today's Topics:

Today you will take an Analytical Writing Assessment practice test applying what you learned on Days 12, 13, and 14. Use a word processor to write your essays. Allow yourself exactly 30 minutes to complete each essay.

---

## PRACTICE TEST

### Section 1: Analysis of an Issue

**Suggested time:** 30 minutes

**Directions (as stated on the test):** "In this section, you will need to analyze the issue presented below and explain your views on it. The question has no 'correct' answer. Instead you should consider various perspectives as you develop your own position on the issue."

> Animal rights activists argue that zoos should be abolished because they are cruel to animals and do not provide the educational and conservation benefits to the public that they promise. Their opponents assert that zoos are necessary if certain species of animals are to survive extinction and if the public is to learn about the natural world.
>
> Which argument do you find more compelling: the case for the abolishment of zoos or the opposing viewpoint? Explain your position using reasons and/or examples drawn from your own experience and reading.

### Section 2: Analysis of an Argument

**Sugested time:** 30 minutes

**Directions (as stated on the test):** "In this section, you will be asked to write a critique of the argument presented below. You are not being asked to present your own views on the subject."

> During the peak air-travel period this year, 2,000 airline pilots from the Pilots Association refused to report for work, and instead, converged at the nation's capitol to protest against the lack of funding for improvements in airport security. The remaining 22,000 airline pilots in the association evidently weren't concerned with airport security because they reported to work as usual. Since the protesters account for less than one-tenth of the entire Pilots Association membership, their concerns about airport security are hardly representative of the views of the association. For this reason, the legislature need not concern itself with the demands of the protesting pilots.
>
> How well reasoned do you find this argument? In your discussion, be sure to consider the line of reasoning and use of evidence in the argument. For

example, you might need to consider what assumptions underlie the reasoning in the argument and what additional information would be required to strengthen or weaken the argument. You can also discuss what would make the argument more persuasive.

# Analytical Writing Assessment: Review of the Practice Test

## Today's Topics:

1. Your Analysis of an Issue essay
2. Your Analysis of an Argument essay

Today you will evaluate the Analytical Writing Assessment practice test that you took on Day 24. Also, you will read sample responses to each of the questions on the test to evaluate your writing ability further.

## THE ANALYSIS OF AN ISSUE QUESTION

Using the following scorecard, evaluate your response to the Analysis of an Issue question that you wrote on Day 24. Better yet, have a friend evaluate your essay using the scorecard.

### Analysis of an Issue Scorecard.

• Do you clearly indicate that you understand and appreciate the complexities of the issue?

• Is your essay well organized?

• Do you use persuasive examples or insightful reasons to support your position?

• Do you present a well-reasoned, clearly articulated analysis of the issue?

• Do you cover all the tasks mentioned in the instructions?

• Do you demonstrate a superior command of standard written English?

For each "yes" answer to these questions, give yourself a mark of 1; for each "no" answer, give yourself a mark of 0; for each "maybe" answer, give yourself a mark of .5. Total the marks to calculate your score.

## Sample response.

Read the following sample response to the Analysis of an Issue question on the practice test to evaluate your writing ability further:

Whether or not zoos should be abolished is a controversial and complex issue. It is controversial because of the problem of animal rights; it is complex because of the educational and conservation questions that this issue raises. The animal rights issue in this case focuses mainly on the question of whether animals have a fundamental right to liberty. The educational and conservation questions deal mainly with the accuracy of the information about animals conveyed in this setting and the effectiveness of breeding animals in captivity. On the basis of the following reasons, my view is that zoos should be abolished.

To begin with, although the question of whether animals have rights might not be answerable, there is significant observational evidence that animals are adversely affected by captivity. Anyone who has visited a zoo has experienced first hand the pathetic sight of animals pacing up and down their cages hoping to find an opening to escape. This experience alone should suffice to convince one to abolish zoos.

Second, the educational benefits of zoos are highly suspect simply because the public learns nothing about wild animals in their natural habitat from watching animals in cages. The animals in zoos are domesticated. The public can learn nothing about the natural world by observing domesticated animals in unnatural settings.

Third, the conservation programs at zoos are highly ineffective. There are two reasons for this. In the first place, breeding animals in captivity is difficult. In the second place, the offspring, if there are any, are inbred. This leads to inferior animals that eventually die out, thus thwarting the goal of conservation.

Given the dubious educational and conservation benefits and the obvious fact that captivity is detrimental to animals, I conclude that zoos should be abolished.

# THE ANALYSIS OF AN ARGUMENT QUESTION

Using the following scorecard, evaluate your response to the Analysis of an Argument question that you wrote on Day 24. Better yet, have a friend score your essay using the scorecard.

**Analysis of an Argument scorecard.**

- Do you clearly indicate that you understand the argument and analyze important features of the argument?

- Do you develop and organize your ideas logically and connect them smoothly with clear transitions?

- Do you provide relevant and reasonable support for the main points of your critique?

- Is your essay well organized?

- Do you cover all the tasks mentioned in the instructions?

- Do you demonstrate a superior command of standard written English?

For each "yes" answer to these questions, give yourself a mark of 1; for each "no" answer, give yourself a mark of 0; for each "maybe" answer, give yourself a mark of .5. Total the marks to calculate your score.

**Sample response.**

Read the following sample response to the Analysis of an Argument question on the practice test to evaluate your writing ability further.

The author concludes that the legislature need not concern itself with the demands of the protesting pilots on the grounds that their views are not representative of the entire association. The evidence cited for this claim is that the protesting pilots make up less than one-tenth of entire Pilots Association membership. The reasoning in this argument is flawed for several reasons.

First, the author assumes that the fact that only one-tenth of the pilots took part in the protest is sufficient to conclude that their views are unrepresentative of the entire association. This assumption is clearly mistaken. For example, if it turns out that the protesting pilots were randomly selected from the entire membership, their views would reflect the views of the entire association. Without information regarding the way in which the protesting pilots were selected, it is presumptuous to conclude that their opinions fail to reflect the opinions of their colleagues.

Second, the author cites the fact that the remaining 22,000 pilots reported to work as usual as evidence that they are not concerned about improvements in airport security. One obvious rejoinder to this line of reasoning is that the pilots who reported to work did so with the knowledge that the protesting pilots would express their concerns. In any case, the author has failed to demonstrate a logical connection between their alleged lack of concern and the fact that they reported to work as usual. Lacking this, the conclusion reached by the author that the remaining 22,000 pilots are not concerned about airport security is unacceptable.

As it stands, the argument is not well reasoned. To make it logically acceptable, the author would have to demonstrate that the protesting pilots had some characteristic in common that biases their views and thereby nullifies their protest as representative of the entire membership of the association.

## Practice Test, Section 3: Quantitative Ability

### Today's Topics:

Today you take a full-length practice test on Quantitative Ability. After completing the test, check your answers with the quick answer guide at the end of this lesson.

## PRACTICE TEST

**Number of questions:** 37
**Time allowed:** 75 minutes

**Directions:** If you are not already familiar with the directions and assumptions for Problem Solving and Data Sufficiency questions, review the relevant materials (Day 6). Tomorrow you assess your performance and review the explanations for this practice test.

1. Which of the following equations is equivalent to $x = \sqrt{25y^2 - 10xy}$?

   (A) $x = 5y + 1$

   (B) $x = -5y$

   (C) $x = 5y\sqrt{y} - 2$

   (D) $x = \dfrac{2y}{5}$

   (E) $x = \dfrac{\sqrt{5}}{2y}$

2. The sum of Alan's age and Bob's age is 40. The sum of Bob's age and Carl's age is 34. The sum of Alan's age and Carl's age is 42. How old is Bob?

   (A) 12

   (B) 16

   (C) 18

   (D) 20

   (E) 24

3. If $x$ and $y$ are integers, is $x + y - 1$ divisible by 3?

   1. When $x$ is divided by 3, the remainder is 2.

   2. When $y$ is divided by 6, the remainder is 5.

   (A) Statement 1 alone is sufficient to answer the question, but statement 2 alone is not sufficient

   (B) Statement 2 alone is sufficient to answer the question, but statement 1 alone is not sufficient

   (C) Both statements together are needed to answer the question, but neither statement alone is sufficient to answer the question

   (D) Either statement by itself is sufficient to answer the question

   (E) Not enough facts are given to answer the question

4. Four knots—A, B, C, and D—appear in that order along a straight length of rope. Does $BD$ equal $AB$?

  1. $AC < BD$

  2. $\dfrac{AD}{2} = CD$

(A) Statement 1 alone is sufficient to answer the question, but statement 2 alone is not sufficient

(B) Statement 2 alone is sufficient to answer the question, but statement 1 alone is not sufficient

(C) Both statements together are needed to answer the question, but neither statement alone is sufficient to answer the question

(D) Either statement by itself is sufficient to answer the question

(E) Not enough facts are given to answer the question

5. At the beginning of a five-day trading week, the price of a certain stock was $10 per share. During the week, four of the five closing prices of the stock exceeded $10. Did the average closing price of the stock during the week exceed its price at the beginning of the week?

  1. The stock's closing price on Tuesday was the same as its closing price on Thursday.

  2. The sum of the stock's highest and lowest closing prices during the week was 20.

(A) Statement 1 alone is sufficient to answer the question, but statement 2 alone is not sufficient

(B) Statement 2 alone is sufficient to answer the question, but statement 1 alone is not sufficient

(C) Both statements together are needed to answer the question, but neither statement alone is sufficient to answer the question

(D) Either statement by itself is sufficient to answer the question

(E) Not enough facts are given to answer the question

6. What is the value of $x$?

  1. $4x^2 - 4x = -1$

  2. $2x^2 + 9x = 5$

(A) Statement 1 alone is sufficient to answer the question, but statement 2 alone is not sufficient

(B) Statement 2 alone is sufficient to answer the question, but statement 1 alone is not sufficient

(C) Both statements together are needed to answer the question, but neither statement alone is sufficient to answer the question

(D) Either statement by itself is sufficient to answer the question

(E) Not enough facts are given to answer the question

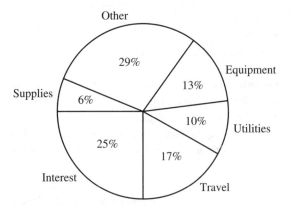

7. The chart above shows expenditures of XYZ Company during the year. How much did XYZ Company spend on travel during the year?

  1. XYZ Company's expenditures for supplies during the year totaled $18,000.

  2. XYZ Company's expenditures for legal services during the year totaled $31,300.

(A) Statement 1 alone is sufficient to answer the question, but statement 2 alone is not sufficient

(B) Statement 2 alone is sufficient to answer the question, but statement 1 alone is not sufficient

(C) Both statements together are needed to answer the question, but neither statement alone is sufficient to answer the question

(D) Either statement by itself is sufficient to answer the question

(E) Not enough facts are given to answer the question

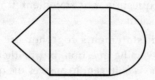

8. Three carpet pieces—in the shapes of a square, a triangle, and a semicircle—are attached to one another, as shown in figure above, to cover the floor of a room. If the area of the square is 144 and the perimeter of the triangle is 28, what is the perimeter of the room's floor?

(A) $32 + 6\pi$

(B) $40 + 6\pi$

(C) $34 + 12\pi$

(D) $52 + 6\pi$

(E) $52 + 12\pi$

9. $c$ is $83\frac{1}{3}\%$ of what number?

(A) $\dfrac{2c}{3}$

(B) $\dfrac{5c}{6}$

(C) $\dfrac{7c}{8}$

(D) $\dfrac{8c}{7}$

(E) $\dfrac{6c}{5}$

10. A family of two adults and two children are going together to the local zoo, which charges exactly twice as much for each adult admission ticket as for each child's admission ticket. If the total admission price for the family of four is $12.60, what is the price of a child's ticket?

(A) $1.60

(B) $2.10

(C) $3.20

(D) $3.30

(E) $4.20

11. If $(b*a*c)$ is defined as being equal to $ab - c$, what does $(4*3*5) + (6*5*7)$ equal?

(A) 6

(B) 11

(C) 15

(D) 30

(E) 40

12. Two ships leave from the same port at 11:30 a.m. If one sails due east at 24 miles per hour and the other due south at 10 miles per hour, how many miles apart are the ships at 2:30 p.m.?

(A) 45

(B) 62

(C) 68

(D) 78

(E) 84

13. Which of the following fractions is equal to $\frac{1}{4}\%$?

(A) $\dfrac{1}{400}$

(B) $\dfrac{1}{40}$

(C) $\dfrac{1}{25}$

(D) $\dfrac{4}{25}$

(E) $\dfrac{1}{4}$

14. It takes Paul $m$ minutes to mow the lawn. Assuming that he mows at a constant rate, after Paul mows for $k$ minutes, what part of the lawn remains unmowed?

(A) $\dfrac{k}{m}$

(B) $\dfrac{m}{k}$

(C) $\dfrac{m-k}{k}$

(D) $\dfrac{k-m}{m}$

(E) $\dfrac{m-k}{m}$

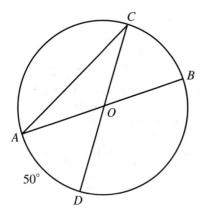

15. $AB$ and $CD$ are diameters of circle $O$. What is the number of degrees in angle $CAB$?

(A) $12\dfrac{1}{2}$

(B) 25

(C) 50

(D) 100

(E) 130

16. If $a = \sqrt{b}$, what is the value of $a - b$?

1. $b = 3a$

2. $ab = 27$

(A) Statement 1 alone is sufficient to answer the question, but statement 2 alone is not sufficient

(B) Statement 2 alone is sufficient to answer the question, but statement 1 alone is not sufficient

(C) Both statements together are needed to answer the question, but neither statement alone is sufficient to answer the question

(D) Either statement by itself is sufficient to answer the question

(E) Not enough facts are given to answer the question

17. A county animal shelter houses two different types of animals: dogs and cats. If $d$ represents the number of dogs, and if $c$ represents the number of cats, which of the following expresses the portion of animals at the shelter that are dogs?

(A) $\dfrac{d+c}{d}$

(B) $\dfrac{d+c}{c}$

(C) $\dfrac{d}{c}$

(D) $\dfrac{c}{d}$

(E) $\dfrac{d}{d+c}$

18. If $\left(\dfrac{a}{b}\right)\left(\dfrac{b}{c}\right)\left(\dfrac{c}{d}\right)\left(\dfrac{d}{e}\right)(x) = 1$, then what must $x$ equal?

(A) $\dfrac{a}{e}$

(B) $\dfrac{e}{a}$

(C) $e$

(D) $\dfrac{1}{a}$

(E) $\dfrac{be}{a}$

19. Two competitors battle each other in each match of a tournament with nine participants. What is the minimum number of matches that must occur for every competitor to battle every other competitor?

(A) 27

(B) 36

(C) 45

(D) 64

(E) 81

20. On the coordinate plane, how far is the point (–4,–3) from the origin?

(A) 2

(B) 2.5

(C) $4\sqrt{2}$

(D) $4\sqrt{3}$

(E) 5

21. If $a \neq 0$ or 1, which of the following fractions is equivalent to $\dfrac{\left(\dfrac{1}{a}\right)}{2-\dfrac{2}{a}}$ ?

(A) $\dfrac{1}{2a-2}$

(B) $\dfrac{2}{a-2}$

(C) $\dfrac{1}{a-2}$

(D) $\dfrac{1}{a}$

(E) $\dfrac{2}{2a-1}$

22. If a jewelry merchant bought a particular ring for $10,000 and sold the ring to Judith, how much did Judith pay for the ring?

1. The merchant's profit from the sale was 50%.

2. The amount that the merchant paid for the ring was two-thirds of the amount that Judith paid for the ring.

(A) Statement 1 alone is sufficient to answer the question, but statement 2 alone is not sufficient

(B) Statement 2 alone is sufficient to answer the question, but statement 1 alone is not sufficient

(C) Both statements together are needed to answer the question, but neither statement alone is sufficient to answer the question

(D) Either statement by itself is sufficient to answer the question

(E) Not enough facts are given to answer the question

23. Is $x > y$?

1. $x$ is the arithmetic mean of all two-digit prime numbers less than 23.

2. $y$ is the sum of all factors of 60 that are greater than –1 and less than 6.

(A) Statement 1 alone is sufficient to answer the question, but statement 2 alone is not sufficient

(B) Statement 2 alone is sufficient to answer the question, but statement 1 alone is not sufficient

(C) Both statements together are needed to answer the question, but neither statement alone is sufficient to answer the question

(D) Either statement by itself is sufficient to answer the question

(E) Not enough facts are given to answer the question

24. A certain cylindrical tank set on its circular base is 7.5 feet in height. If the tank is filled with water, and if the water is then poured out of the tank into smaller cube-shaped tanks, how many cube-shaped tanks are required to hold all the water?

1. The length of a cube-shaped tank's side is equal to the radius of the cylindrical tank's circular base.

2. If you stack three cube-shaped tanks on top of one another, the top of the third cube stacked is the same distance above the ground as the top of the cylindrical tank.

(A) Statement 1 alone is sufficient to answer the question, but statement 2 alone is not sufficient

(B) Statement 2 alone is sufficient to answer the question, but statement 1 alone is not sufficient

(C) Both statements together are needed to answer the question, but neither statement alone is sufficient to answer the question

(D) Either statement by itself is sufficient to answer the question

(E) Not enough facts are given to answer the question

25. Is $xyz < 0$?

1. $x^3y^2z < 0$

2. $z^3yx < 0$

(A) Statement 1 alone is sufficient to answer the question, but statement 2 alone is not sufficient

(B) Statement 2 alone is sufficient to answer the question, but statement 1 alone is not sufficient

(C) Both statements together are needed to answer the question, but neither statement alone is sufficient to answer the question

(D) Either statement by itself is sufficient to answer the question

(E) Not enough facts are given to answer the question

26. In a boat race between David and Jeff, when Jeff had covered half the 30-mile race distance, David was two miles ahead of Jeff. How long did it take David to travel the entire 30-mile distance?

1. David traveled the last 15 miles of the race distance in 40 minutes.

2. Jeff traveled the first 15 miles of the race distance in 45 minutes.

(A) Statement 1 alone is sufficient to answer the question, but statement 2 alone is not sufficient

(B) Statement 2 alone is sufficient to answer the question, but statement 1 alone is not sufficient

(C) Both statements together are needed to answer the question, but neither statement alone is sufficient to answer the question

(D) Either statement by itself is sufficient to answer the question

(E) Not enough facts are given to answer the question

27. During one complete revolution of a circular gear, a wheel driven directly by the gear completes $2\frac{1}{2}$ revolutions. After the wheel rolls across the ground 20 feet, how many revolutions has the gear completed?

1. The diameter of the gear is 10 inches.

2. The radius of the wheel is 12.5 inches.

(A) Statement 1 alone is sufficient to answer the question, but statement 2 alone is not sufficient

(B) Statement 2 alone is sufficient to answer the question, but statement 1 alone is not sufficient

(C) Both statements together are needed to answer the question, but neither statement alone is sufficient to answer the question

(D) Either statement by itself is sufficient to answer the question

(E) Not enough facts are given to answer the question

28. $3 + [12 - a(-3 - a)(a + 6)](-2) - 2a =$

    (A) $-2a^2 + 4a - 21$

    (B) $2a^3 - 12a^2 + 34a + 15$

    (C) $-2a^3 - 18a^2 - 38a - 21$

    (D) $-a^3 - 3a^2 - a + 27$

    (E) $a^3 - 9a^2 - 19a + 15$

29. If $q$ workers can paint a house in $d$ days, how many days will it take $q + 2$ workers to paint the same house, assuming all workers paint at the same rate?

    (A) $d + 2$

    (B) $d - 2$

    (C) $\dfrac{q+2}{qd}$

    (D) $\dfrac{qd}{q+2}$

    (E) $\dfrac{qd + 2d}{q}$

30. In an election between two candidates—Lange and Sobel—70% of the voters voted for Sobel. Of the election's voters, 60% were male. If 35% of the female voters voted for Lange, what percentage of the male voters voted for Sobel?

    (A) 14

    (B) 16

    (C) 26

    (D) 44

    (E) 65

31. If a building $b$ feet high casts a shadow $f$ feet long, then, at the same time of day, a tree $t$ feet high will cast a shadow how many feet long?

    (A) $\dfrac{ft}{b}$

    (B) $\dfrac{fb}{t}$

    (C) $\dfrac{b}{ft}$

    (D) $\dfrac{tb}{f}$

    (E) $\dfrac{t}{fb}$

32. What is the difference between the sum of the integers 15 through 33, inclusive, and the sum of the integers 11 through 31, inclusive?

    (A) 11

    (B) 15

    (C) 26

    (D) 32

    (E) 41

33. A solution of 60 ounces of sugar and water is 20% sugar. How much water must you add to make a solution that is 5% sugar?

    (A) 180 ounces

    (B) 120 ounces

    (C) 100 ounces

    (D) 80 ounces

    (E) 20 ounces

STATE SCHOLARSHIP FUNDS AWARDED (1980-95)

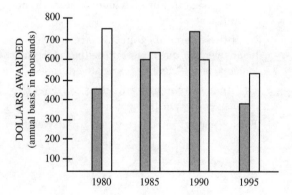

34. Based on the information in the graph above, during the greatest 10-year change in nonminority scholarship funds awarded, what is approximately the greatest five-year percentage change in minority scholarship funds awarded?

    (A) 15

    (B) 25

    (C) 27

    (D) 33

    (E) 43

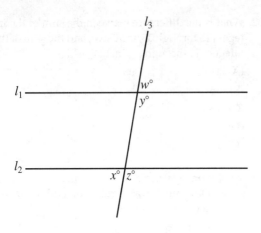

35. In the figure above, is $l_1$ parallel to $l_2$?

    1. $x + 90 = 270 - y$

    2. $z + w = 180$

    (A) Statement 1 alone is sufficient to answer the question, but statement 2 alone is not sufficient

    (B) Statement 2 alone is sufficient to answer the question, but statement 1 alone is not sufficient

    (C) Both statements together are needed to answer the question, but neither statement alone is sufficient to answer the question

    (D) Either statement by itself is sufficient to answer the question

    (E) Not enough facts are given to answer the question

36. If a total of 55 books were sold at a community book fair, and if each book was either hardback or paperback, how many hardback books were sold at the book fair?

    1. The total proceeds from the sale of paperback books, each of which was sold for 75 cents, was $19.50.

    2. The proceeds from the book fair totaled $48.50.

    (A) Statement 1 alone is sufficient to answer the question, but statement 2 alone is not sufficient

    (B) Statement 2 alone is sufficient to answer the question, but statement 1 alone is not sufficient

    (C) Both statements together are needed to answer the question, but neither statement alone is sufficient to answer the question

    (D) Either statement by itself is sufficient to answer the question

    (E) Not enough facts are given to answer the question

37. If $p$ pencils cost $2q$ dollars, how many pencils can you buy for $c$ cents?

    (A) $\dfrac{pc}{2q}$

    (B) $\dfrac{pc}{200q}$

    (C) $\dfrac{50pc}{q}$

    (D) $\dfrac{2pq}{c}$

    (E) $200pcq$

# Quick Answer Guide

**Practice Test: Quantitative Ability**

| | | | |
|---|---|---|---|
| 1. B | 11. D | 21. A | 31. A |
| 2. B | 12. D | 22. D | 32. B |
| 3. C | 13. A | 23. C | 33. A |
| 4. D | 14. E | 24. C | 34. D |
| 5. B | 15. B | 25. B | 35. D |
| 6. A | 16. D | 26. E | 36. A |
| 7. A | 17. E | 27. D | 37. B |
| 8. B | 18. B | 28. C | |
| 9. E | 19. B | 29. D | |
| 10. B | 20. E | 30. D | |

# Practice Test: Review of Section 3 (Quantitative Ability)

## Today's Topics:

Today you will review yesterday's Quantitative Ability practice test. Preceding each explanation, the question type and difficulty level are indicated.

## 1. Quadratic equations (moderate). Answer: B.

To solve this problem, first remove the radical by squaring both sides of the equation. Then set the result equal to 0. Simplify by factoring and express $x$ in terms of $y$:

$$x = \sqrt{-25\,y^2 - 10xy}$$
$$x^2 = -25y^2 - 10xy$$
$$x^2 + 10xy + 25y^2 = 0$$
$$(x + 5y)^2 = 0$$
$$x + 5y = 0$$
$$x = -5y$$

## 2. System of linear equations (moderate). Answer: B.

The question presents three equations:

$$A + B = 40$$
$$B + C = 34$$
$$A + C = 42$$

To solve for $B$, first subtract the second equation from the third equation. The result is $A - B = 8$. Then subtract this resulting equation from the first equation. This result is $2B = 32$, or $B = 16$.

## 3. Integers (easier). Answer: C.

Neither statement 1 nor 2 alone provides any information about the second variable or, in turn, about the value of $x + y - 1$. Thus, you can easily eliminate A, B, and D. Next, consider statements 1 and 2 together. Given a remainder of 2 when $x$ is divided by 3, the value of $x$ must be greater than a multiple of 3 by exactly 2: $x = \{5, 8, 11, 14 \ldots\}$. Given a remainder of 5 when $y$ is divided by 6, the value of $y$ must be greater than a multiple of 6 by exactly 5: $y = \{11, 17, 23, 29 \ldots\}$. Adding together any $x$-value and any $y$-value always results in a sum that exceeds a multiple of 3 by exactly 7 (or by exactly 1). Accordingly, subtracting 1 from that sum always results in a multiple of 3. Thus, given statements 1 and 2, $x + y - 1$ is divisible by 3.

## 4. Linear ordering (easier). Answer: D.

Statement 1 alone suffices to answer the question. Given $AC < BD$, $AB$ (which is smaller than $AC$) must be smaller than $BD$. $BD > AB$, and the answer to the question is no. Statement 2 also suffices alone to answer the question. Given $\frac{AD}{2} = CD$, C bisects $AD$, and $AC = CD$. Thus, $AB$ (which is smaller than $AC$) must be smaller than $CD$. Because $CD$ is smaller than $BD$, $AB < BD$, and the answer to the question is no.

## 5. Arithmetic mean (moderate). Answer: B.

Statement 1 provides no information about any of the closing prices relative to the stock's initial price of $10. Thus, statement 1 alone is insufficient to answer the question. Statement 2 establishes that the average of the highest and lowest closing prices during the week was $10. In other words, the lowest closing price was less than the stock's initial price by the same amount as the amount by which the highest closing price exceeded the stock's initial price. Given that the three remaining closing prices were all greater than $10, the average of all five closing prices must be greater than $10. Thus, statement 2 alone suffices to answer the question.

## 6. Quadratic equations (challenging). Answer: A.

Both equations are quadratic. For each one, you can determine the possible values of $x$ by setting the quadratic expression equal to 0 (zero) and factoring that expression. Considering statement 1 alone, solve for $x$:

$$4x^2 - 4x = -1$$
$$4x^2 - 4x + 1 = 0$$
$$(2x - 1)(2x - 1) = 0$$
$$(2x - 1)^2 = 0$$
$$2x - 1 = 0$$
$$x = \frac{1}{2}$$

Based on the equation given in statement 1, the only possible value of $x$ is $\frac{1}{2}$. Thus, statement 1 alone suffices to answer the question. Considering statement 2, solve for $x$:

$$2x^2 + 9x = 5$$
$$2x^2 + 9x - 5 = 0$$
$$(x + 5)(2x - 1) = 0$$
$$x + 5 = 0 \text{ or } 2x - 1 = 0$$
$$x = -5 \text{ or } \frac{1}{2}$$

Based on the equation given in statement 2, there are two possible values of $x$: $-5$ and $\frac{1}{2}$. Thus, statement 2 alone is insufficient to answer the question.

## 7. Data interpretation (easier). Answer: A.

Given expenditures of $18,000 for supplies, you can determine the total expenditures of XYZ Company during the year. The $18,000 is 6% of the total; thus, the total is $300,000. Travel expenditures accounted for 17% of $300,000, or $51,000. Statement 1 alone suffices to answer the question. Considering statement 2 alone, the chart does not specifically indicate "legal services." These expenses are probably a portion of "other," but the specific percentage or amount of expenditures for legal services is unknown. Statement 2 alone is insufficient to answer the question.

## 8. Geometry: circles, quadrilaterals, triangles (moderate). Answer: B.

Each side of the square = 12. The length of the remaining two sides of the triangle totals 16. The perimeter of the semicircle = $\frac{1}{2}\pi d = \frac{1}{2}\pi(12) = 6\pi$. The length of the two sides of the square included in the overall perimeter totals 24. The total perimeter of the floor = $16 + 6\pi + 24 = 40 + 6\pi$.

## 9. Percent (easier). Answer: E.

$$83\frac{1}{3}\% = \frac{5}{6}$$
$$c = \frac{5}{6}x$$
$$6c = 5x$$
$$\frac{6c}{5} = x$$

## 10. Algebraic formulas: dry mixture (moderate). Answer: B.

The price of two children's tickets together equals the price of one adult ticket. The total admission price is therefore equivalent to the price of three adult tickets.

$$3a = 12.60$$
$$a = 4.20$$

Price of a child's ticket = $\left(\frac{1}{2}\right)(4.20) = \$2.10$

## 11. Hypothetical operations (easier). Answer: D.

$(4*3*5) = 12 - 5 = 7$

$(6*5*7) = 30 - 7 = 23$

$7 + 23 = 30$

## 12. Geometry: triangles (moderate). Answer: D.

In three hours, one ship traveled 72 miles, while the other traveled 30 miles. The ratio of these two distances is 30:72 or 5:12, suggesting a 5:12:13 triangle in which the hypotenuse is the distance between the two ships at 2:30 p.m. That distance is 78 miles.

## 13. Equivalent forms of numbers (easier). Answer: A.

$$\frac{1}{4}\% = \frac{\frac{1}{4}}{100} = \left(\frac{1}{4}\right)\left(\frac{1}{100}\right) = \frac{1}{400}$$

## 14. Algebraic formulas: rate (challenging). Answer: E.

In $k$ minutes, $\frac{k}{m}$ of the lawn is mowed. Still unmowed, then, is $(1 - \frac{k}{m})$ or $(\frac{m-k}{m})$.

## 15. Geometry: circles (easier). Answer: B.

Given that arc $AD = 50°$; $\angle AOD = 50°$. $\angle AOC$ is supplementary; thus $\angle AOC = 130°$. Triangle $AOC$ is isosceles ($AO$ and $CO$ are both radii). Therefore $\angle CAB = 25°$.

## 16. System of equations (moderate). Answer: D.

To answer this question, it suffices to recognize that *either* statement 1 or 2, together with $a = \sqrt{b}$, establishes a system of two equations in two variables. Because neither statement 1 nor 2 is equivalent to $a = \sqrt{b}$, either statement 1 or 2 suffices alone to solve for $a$ and $b$ and, in turn, to determine the value of $a - b$ ($a = 3$, $b = 9$).

## 17. Proportion (easier). Answer: E.

The shelter houses $d + c$ animals altogether. Of these animals, $d$ are dogs. You can express that portion as the fraction $\frac{d}{d+c}$.

## 18. Operations on variables (easier). Answer: B.

$$\left(\frac{a}{b}\right)\left(\frac{b}{c}\right)\left(\frac{c}{d}\right)\left(\frac{d}{e}\right)(x) = 1$$

$$\left(\frac{a}{e}\right)(x) = 1$$

$$x = \frac{e}{a}$$

## 19. Sets (moderate). Answer: B.

Competitor 1 must engage in eight matches. Competitor 2 must engage in seven matches not already accounted for (the match between competitors 1 and 2 has already been tabulated). Similarly, competitor 3 must engage in six matches other than those accounted for, and so on. The minimum number of total matches $= 8 + 7 + 6 + 5 + 4 + 3 + 2 + 1 = 36$.

## 20. Coordinate geometry (easier). Answer: E.

Plotting the point reveals a 3-4-5 triangle ($3^2 + 4^2 = 5^2$), in which the $x$-axis and $y$-axis serve as the two legs of the triangle.

## 21. Complex fractions (easier). Answer: A.

Simplify this complex fraction by multiplying *every* term by $a$:

$$\frac{\frac{a}{a}}{2a - \frac{2a}{a}} =$$

$$\frac{1}{2a-2}$$

## 22. Percent (easier). Answer: D.

Given that the merchant paid $10,000 for the ring, if the merchant earned a 50% profit from the sale to Judith, she paid $15,000 for the ring ($10,000 + 50% of $10,000). Statement 1 alone suffices to answer the question. If the merchant paid two-thirds what Judith paid, then $10,000 = ($\frac{2}{3}$)(Judith's price). Again, you can determine the price that Judith paid ($10,000 $\times \frac{3}{2}$ = $15,000). Thus, statement 2 alone also suffices.

### 23. Integers (moderate). Answer: C.

Neither statement 1 nor 2 suffices alone to determine the values of both $x$ and $y$. Thus, you can easily eliminate A, B, and D. Next, consider both statements together. The two-digit prime numbers less than 23 include 11, 13, 17, and 19. Their sum is 60, and the average of the four numbers is 15 $\left(\frac{60}{4}\right)$. $x = 15$. Considering statement 2, the positive factors of 60 that are less than 6 include 1, 2, 3, 4, and 5. Their sum is 15. $y = 15$. $x = y$, and the answer to the question, based on statements 1 and 2 together, is no.

### 24. Geometry: solids (challenging). Answer: C.

To answer the question, you must determine the relative volumes of the cylindrical tank and a cube-shaped tank. Statement 1 fails to provide sufficient information to determine these volumes. The volume of the cylindrical tank is $7.5\pi r^2$, and, given statement 1, you can express the cube's volume as $r^3$. The ratio of the two volumes, then, is $7.5\pi r^2 : r^3$ or $7.5\pi : r$. Accordingly, the relative volumes of the containers vary depending on the value of $r$. Statement 2 is also insufficient to answer the question. Given statement 2, the length of a cube's side is 2.5 feet, and you can determine its volume ($s^3$). However, you cannot determine the cylindrical tank's volume, because the size of its circular base remains unknown. Statement 1 provides this missing information. Thus, statements 1 and 2 together suffice to answer the question. (Given statements 1 and 2, the ratio of $V$ [cylinder] to $V$ [cube] is $3\pi : 1$, so 10 cube-shaped tanks are required.)

### 25. Exponents (moderate). Answer: B.

Given $x^3 y^2 z < 0$, neither $x$, $y$, nor $z$ can equal zero, and either all three terms ($x^3$, $y^2$, and $z$) are negative or exactly one of the three terms is negative [$(-)(-)(-) < 0$, $(-)(+)(+) < 0$]. However, whether $y$ is negative or positive, $y^2$ is positive; thus, either $x$ or $z$ (but not both) must be negative. Accordingly, $xyz$ could be either positive or negative, depending on the value of $y$. Statement 1 alone is insufficient to answer the question. Given $z^3 yx < 0$, either $z$, $y$, and $x$ are all negative or exactly one of the three variable is negative. In either case, $xyz < 0$. Thus, statement 2 alone suffices to answer the question.

### 26. Rate (moderate). Answer: E.

Statement 1 alone provides no information about how long it took David to travel the first 15 miles, and is therefore insufficient by itself to answer the question. Statement 2 alone provides even less information about how long it took David to travel the entire distance. Although you can determine from statement 2 that David traveled the first 17 miles in 45 minutes, you cannot determine how long it took David to travel the remaining 13 miles. Statement 1 and 2 together establish that David traveled 32 miles (17 + 15) in 85 minutes (45 + 40). However, 2 of the 32 miles are accounted for twice. Without knowing either the time that it took David to travel the 16th and 17th miles of the race or his average speed over those two miles, you cannot determine David's total time for the 30 mile race. Thus, statements 1 and 2 together are insufficient to answer the question.

### 27. Geometry: circles, ratios (challenging). Answer: D.

Given that the wheel has rolled 20 feet, you must first determine the wheel's circumference to calculate the number of revolutions that the wheel has made and, in turn, the number of revolutions that the gear has made. Either statement provides sufficient information to determine the wheel's circumference. Given statement 1, the gear's circumference is $10\pi$ inches, and the wheel's circumference is 2.5 times that amount, or $25\pi$ inches. Given statement 2 (alone), the wheel's circumference, again, is $25\pi$ inches. To find the number of revolutions completed by the wheel after 20 feet, divide 20 feet by $25\pi$ inches. To find the corresponding number of gear revolutions; divide the result by $2\frac{1}{2}$.

### 28. Laws of arithmetic (easier). Answer: C.

$$3 + [12 - a\,(-3 - a)(a + 6)](-2) - 2a =$$
$$3 + [12 - a(-3a - a^2 - 18 - 6a)]\,(-2) - 2a =$$
$$3 + [12 + 3a^2 + a^3 + 18a + 6a^2]\,(-2) - 2a =$$
$$3 - 24 - 6a^2 - 2a^3 - 36a - 12a^2 - 2a =$$
$$-2a^3 - 18a^2 - 38a - 21$$

## 29. Algebraic formulas: work (challenging). Answer: D.

The number of days ($d$) that it takes $q$ workers to paint a house varies inversely with the number of days that it takes $q + 2$ workers to paint a house. You can express the relationship with the following equation: $(q)(d) = (q + 2)(x)$, where $x$ = the number of days that it takes $q + 2$ workers to paint a house. You can solve for $x$ as follows: $x = \frac{qd}{q+2}$.

## 30. Proportion (moderate). Answer: D.

You can organize this problem's information in a table, as shown in this next figure.

|  | male | female |  |
|---|---|---|---|
| Lange |  | 14% | 30% |
| Sobel | ? |  | 70% |
|  | 60% | 40% |  |

Because 35% of 40% of the voters (female voters) voted for Lange, 14% (.40 × .35) of all voters were females who voted for Lange. You can now fill in the entire table (the total of all four percentages must be 100%), as shown in the below figure.

|  | male | female |  |
|---|---|---|---|
| Lange | 16% | 14% | 30% |
| Sobel | 44% | 26% | 70% |
|  | 60% | 40% |  |

## 31. Algebraic formulas: ratio (moderate). Answer: A.

The ratio of height to the shadow is constant. Thus, you can set the ratio of $b$ to $f$ equal to the ratio of $t$ to $x$, where $x$ represents the length of the tree's shadow:

$$\frac{b}{f} = \frac{t}{x}$$

$$bx = ft$$

$$x = \frac{ft}{b}$$

## 32. Integers (easier). Answer: B.

You need not add all the terms of each sequence. Instead, notice that the two sequences have in common integers 15 through 31, inclusive. Thus, those terms cancel out, leaving 32 + 33 = 65 in the first sequence and 11 + 12 + 13 + 14 = 50 in the second sequence. The difference is 15.

## 33. Algebraic formulas: wet mixture (challenging). Answer: A.

You can express the amount of sugar after you add water as .05(60 + $x$), where 60 + $x$ represents the total amount of solution after you add the additional water. This amount of sugar is the same as (equal to) the original amount of sugar (20% of 60). Set up an equation, multiply both sides by 100 to remove the decimal point, and solve for $x$:

$$5(60 + x) = 1{,}200$$

$$300 + 5x = 1{,}200$$

$$5x = 900$$

$$x = 180$$

## 34. Data interpretation (moderate). Answer: D.

The greatest 10-year change in nonminority scholarship funds awarded occurred from 1980 to 1990: $750,000 to $600,000 (approximately). During this period, the greatest change in funds awarded occurred from 1980 to 1985—an increase from $450,000 to $600,000 (approximately). This increase of approximately $150,000 is 33% of $450,000 (the amount in 1980).

## 35. Geometry: lines and angles (easier). Answer: D.

You can express the equation in statement 1 as $x + y = 180$; thus, $x$ and $y$ are supplementary angles. This information suffices to establish that the angles created by the intersection of $l_1$ and $l_3$ are identical to those created by the intersection of $l_2$ and $l_3$. Accordingly, $l_1 \parallel l_2$, and statement 1 alone suffices to answer the question. Statement 2 establishes that $z = y$, because $w + y = 180$. This information suffices to establish that the degree measures of the angles created by the intersection of $l_1$ and $l_3$ are identical to those created by the intersection of $l_2$ and $l_3$. Accordingly, $l_1 \parallel l_2$, and statement 2 alone suffices to answer the question.

## 36. Algebraic formulas: dry mixture (moderate). Answer: A.

Given statement 1, you can determine the total number of paperbacks sold: ($.75)(P) = $19.50, or $P = 26$. Given that 55 books were sold altogether, 29 hardback books were sold, and statement 1 alone suffices to answer the question. Statement 2 provides no information about the prices of either type of book, and is therefore insufficient to answer the question.

## 37. Algebraic formulas: ratio (moderate). Answer: B.

Use a proportion comparing pencils to cents. Expressing $2q$ dollars as $200q$ cents, solve for the number of pencils (represented by $x$) that you can buy for $c$ cents:

$$\frac{p}{200q} = \frac{x}{c}$$

$$\frac{pc}{200q} = x$$

## Practice Test, Section 4:
## Verbal Ability

### Today's Topics:

Today you take a full-length Verbal Ability practice test. After completing the test, check your answers with the Quick Answer Guide at the end of this lesson.

---

### PRACTICE TEST

**Number of questions:** 41
**Time allowed:** 75 minutes

**Directions:** If you are not already familiar with the directions for Sentence Correction, Critical Reasoning, and Reading Comprehension questions, review the introductory materials in the first lesson for each type (Days 3, 9, and 18, respectively). Tomorrow you will assess your performance and review the explanations for this test.

1. On this issue, this state's elected officials ignored the wishes of their electorate, which cannot reasonably be disputed in light of the legislative record.

   (A) On this issue, this state's elected officials ignored the wishes of their electorate, which

   (B) This state's elected officials, ignoring on this issue the wishes of their electorate,

   (C) That this state's elected officials ignored the wishes of their electorate

   (D) On this issue, the wishes of the electorate were ignored by this state's elected officials, and

   (E) That the wishes of the electorate on this issue were ignored by this state's elected officials

2. *The Reluctant Monarch,* which Francis Craig wrote as her third in a series of books about the British Monarchy.

   (A) *The Reluctant Monarch,* which Francis Craig wrote as her third

   (B) *The Reluctant Monarch,* written by Francis Craig, is her third

   (C) Written by Francis Craig, *The Reluctant Monarch,* which is her third book

   (D) Francis Craig wrote *The Reluctant Monarch,* which book is her third

   (E) *The Reluctant Monarch* is the third book written by Francis Craig

3. Either interest rates or the supply of money can,
   along with the level of government spending, be
   factors contributing to the amount of inflation.

   (A) can, along with the level of government
       spending, be factors contributing to

   (B) along with the level of government spend-
       ing, can one or the other be contributing
       factors in

   (C) can, along with the level of government
       spending, contribute as factors to

   (D) can contribute, along with the level of
       government spending, to

   (E) can be a contributing factor to, along with
       the level of government spending

4. Contrary to popular belief, there are cases in which
   wearing a seat belt can actually endanger one's
   life rather than protect it. In one recent accident,
   for example, a car hit a tree and, except for a small
   space on the floor, was completely crushed. Luck-
   ily, the driver was not wearing a seat belt and was
   thrown to the floor on impact. Had he been wearing a seat belt, he would surely have been killed.
   Cases like this lead me to conclude that we should
   not be required by law to wear seat belts.

   Which of the following is an assumption on which
   the preceding argument depends?

   (A) Laws should not require an individual to
       engage in an act that might endanger his or
       her life.

   (B) Most people believe that the mandatory
       seat-belt law saves lives.

   (C) Obeying the mandatory seat-belt law does
       not necessarily protect the wearer in
       automobile accidents.

   (D) People should not obey the mandatory seat-
       belt law.

   (E) Obeying the seat-belt law isn't always a
       good idea.

5. *Democratic senator:* The fact that the Republicans
   have not articulated one good reason in support
   of their opposition to cuts in social security payments to the elderly shows that they are obviously
   in favor of them.

Which of the following best describes the flaw in
the senator's reasoning?

(A) Arguing that there are only two possible
    alternatives from which to choose, and
    because one can be eliminated, the other
    must be true

(B) Arguing that a claim is true because of the
    lack of evidence that it is false

(C) Arguing that what is true of some members
    of a group must also be true of all members
    of the group

(D) Inferring a conclusion from unrepresenta-
    tive or biased data

(E) Drawing a general conclusion from too
    small a sample of cases

**Questions 6–8 refer to the following passage:**

The arrival in a new location of a nonindigenous
plant or animal species might be either intentional
or unintentional. Rates of species movement
driven by human transformations of natural
(5) environments as well as by human mobility—
through commerce, tourism, and travel—
dwarf natural rates by comparison. Although
geographic distributions of species naturally
expand or contract over historical time intervals
(10) (tens to hundreds of years), species' ranges rarely
expand thousands of miles or across physical
barriers such as oceans or mountains.

A number of factors confound quantitative
evaluation of the relative importance of various
(15) entry pathways. Time lags often occur between
establishment of nonindigenous species and their
detection, and tracing the pathway for a long-
established species is difficult. Experts estimate
that nonindigenous weeds are usually detected
(20) only after having been in the country for 30 years
or having spread to at least 10,000 acres. In addition, federal port inspection, although a major
source of information on nonindigenous species
pathways, especially for agricultural pests, pro-
(25) vides data only when such species enter via
scrutinized routes. Finally, some comparisons between pathways defy quantitative analysis—for
example, which is more "important": the entry
pathway of one very harmful species or one by
(30) which many but less harmful species enter the
country?

6. Which of the following statements about species movement is best supported by the passage's information?

(A) Species movement is affected more by habitat modifications than by human mobility.

(B) Human-driven factors affect the rate at which species move more than they affect the long-term amount of such movements.

(C) Natural expansions in the geographic distribution of species account for less species movement than do natural contractions.

(D) Natural environments created by commerce, tourism, and travel contribute significantly to species movement.

(E) Movement of a species within a continent depends largely on the geographic extent of human mobility within the continent.

7. Which of the following best expresses the second paragraph's primary purpose?

(A) To identify the problems in assessing the relative significance of various entry pathways for nonindigenous species

(B) To describe the events usually leading to the detection of a nonindigenous species

(C) To discuss the role that time lags and geographic expansion of nonindigenous species play in species detection

(D) To point out the inadequacy of the federal port inspection system in detecting the entry of nonindigenous species

(E) To explain why it is difficult to trace the entry pathways for long-established nonindigenous species

8. Based on the information in the passage, whether the entry pathway for a particular nonindigenous species can be determined is *least* likely to depend on which of the following?

(A) Whether the species is considered to be a pest

(B) Whether the species gains entry through a scrutinized route

(C) The rate at which the species expands geographically

(D) How long the species has been established

(E) The size of the average member of the species

9. The atmospheric study reported last month in the *Journal of the Environment* would not <u>have been taken seriously by the scientific community if they were</u> cognizant of the questionable methodology employed.

(A) have been taken seriously by the scientific community if they were

(B) be taken seriously by the scientific community in the event that it had become

(C) have been taken seriously by the scientific community were they

(D) have been taken seriously by the scientific community when the scientific community became

(E) have been taken seriously by the scientific community had scientists been

10. Residential water use has been severely restricted in response to the current drought in our state. However, current reservoir levels are the same as they were during the drought that occurred here eight years ago. Because residential water use was not restricted then, it should not be restricted now.

Which of the following, if true, would most seriously undermine the author's contention?

(A) No new reservoirs have been constructed in the state since the last drought.

(B) The population of the state has grown at a steady rate of over 2 million people a year since the last drought.

(C) Residential water use makes up over 50 percent of the total water use.

(D) The restrictions on residential water use are projected to last for only two months during the summer.

(E) Since the last drought, water conserving devices are required by law to be installed in all new residential construction.

11. According to modern science, everything in the universe is composed of atoms that are exceedingly small. They are so small, in fact, that they cannot be seen even with the most powerful microscopes because they do not provide sufficient stimulus for the optic nerve even when magnified. But, if it is true that everything in the universe is composed of invisible atoms, surely it follows that everything in the universe is invisible. The patent absurdity of this, however, is clearly evidenced by the fact that tables, chairs, and everyday objects are visible. So it follows that modern science must be mistaken in claiming that everything is composed of atoms.

Which of the following best describes a flaw in the author's reasoning?

(A) The author's reasoning depends on the mistaken belief that just because something occurred prior to something else it must be the cause of it.

(B) The author's reasoning depends on the mistaken belief that what is true of the parts is necessarily true of the whole.

(C) The author uses the word "invisible" in two different senses.

(D) The author's reasoning depends on the mistaken belief that the origin of a view is relevant to its truth or falsity.

(E) The author's reasoning depends on the mistaken belief that whatever cannot be proven to be true must be false.

12. The rules of etiquette for formal dinner parties with foreign diplomats require citizens from both the host and from the diplomat's countries to be seated across from each other.

(A) citizens from both the host and from the diplomat's countries to be seated across from each other.

(B) citizens of the host country and of the diplomat's party to sit opposite each other.

(C) that the host country and diplomat's country seat their citizens opposite one another.

(D) that citizens of the host country be seated opposite those of the diplomat's country.

(E) the host country's citizens to be seated opposite to the diplomat's country's citizens.

13. Health professionals widely concur that, beyond a certain point, the benefits that an individual can expect to derive by further exercise is negligible.

(A) by further exercise is negligible.

(B) from further exercise are negligible.

(C) in furthering exercise are negligible.

(D) by exercising further would be negligible.

(E) by exercising even more would be negligible.

14. After bounty hunters turn over their captives to the authorities, they often are denied due process of law.

(A) After bounty hunters turn over their captives to the authorities, they often are denied due process of law.

(B) After turning over bounty hunters' captives to the authorities, the authorities often deny them due process of law.

(C) The authorities often deny captives due process of law after bounty hunters turn the captives over to the authorities.

(D) Bounty hunters turn over their captives to the authorities, often being denied due process of law.

(E) A captive, when turned over by bounty hunters to the authorities, is often denied due process of law.

**Questions 15–17 refer to the following passage:**

Scientists in the post-1917 Soviet Union occupied an ambiguous position. While the government encouraged and generally supported scientific research, it simultaneously thwarted the scientific (5) community's ideal: freedom from geographic and political boundaries. A strong nationalistic emphasis on science led at times to the dismissal of all non-Russian scientific work as irrelevant to Soviet science. A 1973 article in *Literatunaya* (10) *Gazeta*, a Soviet publication, insisted: "World science is based upon national schools, so the weakening of one or another national school in-evitably leads to stagnation in the development of world science." According to the Soviet re-

(15) gime, socialist science was to be consistent with, and in fact grow out of, the Marxism-Leninism political ideology. Toward this end, some scien-tific theories or fields, such as relativity and ge-netics, were abolished. Where scientific work

(20) conflicted with political criteria, the work was often disrupted. During the Stalinist purges of the 1930s, many Soviet scientists simply disap-peared. In the 1970s, Soviet scientists who were part of the refusenik movement lost their jobs

(25) and were barred from access to scientific re-sources. Nazi Germany during the 1930s and, more recently, Argentina, imposed strikingly similar, though briefer, constraints on scientific research.

15. Which of the following best characterizes the "am-biguous position" (see the first sentence) in which Soviet scientists were placed during the decades that followed the Bolshevik Revolution?

(A) The Soviet government demanded that their research result in scientific progress, although funding was insufficient to accomplish this goal.

(B) They were exhorted to strive toward scientific advancements, while at the same time the freedoms necessary to make such advancements were restricted.

(C) While required to direct their research entirely toward military defense, most advancements in this field were being made by non-Soviet scientists with whom the Soviet scientists were prohibited contact.

(D) They were encouraged to collaborate with Soviet colleagues but were prohibited from any discourse with scientists from other countries.

(E) The Soviet government failed to identify those areas of research that it deemed most worthwhile, but punished those scientists with whose work it was not satisfied.

16. The author quotes an article from *Literatunaya Gazeta* most probably to do which of the following?

(A) Illustrate the general sentiment among members of the international scientific community during the time period

(B) Underscore the point that the Soviet government sanctioned only those notions about science that conformed to the Marxist-Leninist ideal

(C) Show the disparity of views within the Soviet intellectual community regarding the proper role of science

(D) Underscore the Soviet emphasis on the notion of a national science

(E) Support the author's assertion that the Marxist-Leninist impact on Soviet scientific freedom continued through the decade of the 1970s

17. What is the author's primary purpose in the passage?

(A) Examine the events leading up to the suppression of the Soviet refusenik move-ment of the 1970s

(B) Define and dispel the notion of a national science as promulgated by the post-revolution Soviet regime

(C) Describe specific attempts by the modern Soviet regime to suppress scientific freedom

(D) Examine the major 20th Century challenges to the normative assumption that science requires freedom and that it is inherently international

(E) Point out the similarities and distinctions between scientific freedom and scientific internationalism in the context of the Soviet Union

18. Lying is morally justified only if it is done to save a person's life. But most people lie not because a life is in danger but only to avoid the unpleasant consequences of telling the truth. Thus, most lies that are told are morally unjustified.

In which of the following is the pattern of reasoning most parallel to that in the preceding argument?

(A) Capital punishment is justified if it deters people from taking another's life. But it has been demonstrated conclusively that capital punishment is not an effective deterrent. Thus, capital punishment is not justified.

(B) Capital punishment is justified only if we are certain that the convicted offender is actually guilty of the crime. But there are many cases in which persons who are not guilty are convicted of capital offenses. Therefore, in many cases capital punishment is unjustified.

(C) Capital punishment is morally wrong only if it does not promote the greatest good for the greatest number of people. But sacred religious texts do not condemn capital punishment as being morally wrong. Thus, capital punishment promotes the greatest good for the greater number of people.

(D) If the defendant in a murder trial is determined to be guilty beyond a reasonable doubt, the maximum penalty allowed under the law can be imposed. But most defendants in murder trials are not determined to be guilty beyond a reasonable doubt. Therefore, the maximum penalty is seldom imposed.

(E) Corporal punishment for persons who commit violent crimes is justified only if the punishment will alter the persons' behavior in the future. But most persons who commit violent crimes are corporally punished not to alter their future behavior but only to exact revenge. Therefore, most instances of corporal punishment are unjustified.

19. A recipe for cooking potatoes states that potatoes should be cooked in boiling water for 20 minutes to be properly prepared. This holds only for potatoes that have been diced into one-inch cubes; smaller cubes would require proportionately less cooking time and larger ones proportionately more. It is important that potatoes not be overcooked, since this greatly diminishes their food value. Undercooking also should be avoided because undercooked potatoes cannot be properly digested.

If the preceding statements are true, which of the following conclusions does the passage most strongly support?

(A) Whole potatoes, when properly cooked, cannot be properly digested.

(B) Potatoes that are diced into one-half-inch cubes and cooked in boiling water for 20 minutes will likely have little food value.

(C) Potatoes that are properly digestible must be cooked in boiling water for at least 20 minutes.

(D) Boiling in water is the only method of cooking potatoes that will ensure high food value and proper digestibility.

(E) To be prepared properly, potatoes must be boiled in water for at least 20 minutes.

20. The Earth-moon system, the satellites of Jupiter, and the satellites of Saturn are all examples of planetary systems in which a satellite moves in the gravitational field of a much more massive body. In every one of these systems, the satellite moves in an elliptical orbit.

If the preceding statements are true, they provide the most support for which one of the following ?

(A) The more massive a body, the more gravitational pull it exerts on another body.

(B) Only elliptical orbits can account for the various phases of the moon as seen from Earth.

(C) Nonelliptical orbits violate the laws of celestial mechanics.

(D) The moons of the planet Uranus move in elliptical orbits.

(E) All celestial bodies move in elliptical orbits.

21. The Astonian government cited flagrant violations of human rights as the official reason for ceasing to provide military support to the embattled country of Cretia. But, at the same time, Astonia continues to provide military support to countries with far worse human-rights records than Cretia. Hence, despite the official explanation for this change in policy, this reversal cannot be accounted for solely by the Astonian government's commitment to human rights.

    Which of the following, if true, would most strengthen the conclusion in the preceding argument?

    (A) Cretia's neighboring countries recently entered into a nonaggression pact with one another.

    (B) Astonia recently entered into long-range trade agreements with Cretia's neighboring countries.

    (C) The newly elected head of the Cretian government is an avowed anti-Astonian.

    (D) Cretia has a longer record of human-rights abuse than other countries to which Astonia provides military support.

    (E) The Astonian government's decision to provide military support to a country is made mainly on the basis of the country's capability to defend itself from outside aggression.

22. Who the terrorists are and at whom their recent terrorist activities were aimed are currently under investigation by the bureau.

    (A) Who the terrorists are and at whom their

    (B) Whom the terrorists are and at whom their

    (C) Who are the terrorists and at whom their

    (D) Who they are and who the

    (E) Who the terrorists are and to whom their

23. Despite his admiration of the great jazz musicians that preceded him, Blakey opposed them trivializing the popular genre.

    (A) them trivializing the popular genre.

    (B) their trivializing of the popular genre.

    (C) their trivializing the popular genre.

    (D) the popular genre being trivialized by them.

    (E) them when trivializing the popular genre.

24. Even high school freshmen and sophomores, theories concerning the psychology of death and dying among the elderly can hold considerable significance and interest for many students.

    (A) Even high school freshmen and sophomores, theories concerning the psychology of death and dying among the elderly can hold considerable significance and interest for many students.

    (B) Even as high school freshmen and sophomore students with considerable interest in theories concerning the psychology of death and dying among the elderly, these theories can hold considerable significance.

    (C) Theories concerning the psychology of death and dying among the elderly, for many students, even high school freshmen and sophomores, can hold considerable significance and interest.

    (D) Theories concerning the psychology of death and dying among the elderly can hold considerable significance and interest for high school freshmen and sophomore students.

    (E) Considerable significance and interest for even high school freshmen and sophomores is held in theories concerning the psychology of death and dying among the elderly.

25. Unequal pay for men and women is a completely indefensible practice and one that must be stopped immediately. After all, can anyone seriously doubt that women have as much right to self-esteem as men? Surely this fact alone is reason enough to justify their right to earn as much money as men.

    Which of the following is an assumption on which the preceding argument depends?

    (A) High self-esteem is as important to women as it is to men.

    (B) People who do not have jobs lack self-esteem.

    (C) Women and men who perform similar jobs should earn similar salaries.

(D) Equal pay for equal work is a constitutionally guaranteed right of all workers.

(E) A person who has less money than another has less self-esteem.

26. The medical licensing board of this state maintains that only medical schools that are accredited by the board should be permitted to train doctors. The board's primary reason for this policy is that doctors who are trained at nonaccredited institutions may lack the training necessary to become competent practitioners. But since the licensing board is composed entirely of doctors and they obviously have a financial interest in limiting the supply of new doctors, the board's reasoning cannot be taken seriously.

Which one of the following argumentative techniques does this passage use?

(A) The passage undermines the licensing board's argument by pointing out that one of the statements used to support the conclusion is false.

(B) The passage discredits the licensing board's argument by questioning the motives of the board in advancing it.

(C) The passage discredits the licensing board's argument by showing that the board is not a reliable authority on the argument's topic.

(D) The passage discredits the licensing board's argument by pointing out that other institutions besides those accredited by the board can train competent doctors.

(E) The passage challenges the licensing board's argument on the grounds that the major premise on which the board bases its conclusion is highly questionable.

27. The pesticide Azocide, introduced to central valley farms three summers ago, has proven ineffective because other pesticides' chemical compositions already in wide use neutralizing its desired effect.

(A) because other pesticides' chemical compositions already in wide use

(B) because of the chemical compositions of the pesticides already in wide use

(C) due to other pesticides already in wide use, whose chemical compositions have been

(D) since, due to the chemical compositions of other pesticides already in use, those pesticides have been

(E) because of other pesticides and their chemical compositions already in use, which have been

**Questions 28–30 refer to the following passage:**

The 35-millimeter (mm) format for movie production became a *de facto* standard around 1913. The mid-1920s through the mid-1930s, however, saw a resurgence of wide-film formats. During (5) this time period, formats used by studios ranged in gauge from 55mm to 70mm. Research and development then slackened until the 1950s, when wide-screen film-making came back in direct response to the erosion of box-office receipts (10) because of the rising popularity of television. *This is Cinerama* (1952) is generally considered to mark the beginning of the modern era of wide-screen film-making, which saw another flurry of specialized formats, such as Cinemascope. In 1956, (15) Panavision developed Camera 65 for MGM Studios; it was first used during the filming of *Raintree Country*. Panavision soon contributed another key technical advance by developing spherical 65mm lenses, which eliminated the "fat (20) faces" syndrome that had plagued earlier CinemaScope films.

Some 40 "roadshow" films were filmed in wide-screen formats during this period. But wide-screen formats floundered due to expense, (25) unwieldy cameras, and slow film stocks and lenses. After the invention of a set of 35mm anamorphic lenses which could be used in conjunction with much more mobile cameras to squeeze a wide-screen image onto theatrical (30) screens, film technology improved to the point where quality 70mm prints could be blown up from 35mm negatives.

28. You can infer from the passage's information that wide-film formats were

    (A) in use before 1913.

    (B) not used during the 1940s.

    (C) more widely used during the 1920s than during the 1930s.

    (D) not used after 1956.

    (E) more widely used for some types of movies than for others.

29. The passage mentions all the following as factors contributing to the increased use of wide-film formats for moviemaking *except*:

    (A) spherical camera lenses

    (B) Panavision's Camera 65

    (C) television

    (D) anamorphic camera lenses

    (E) movie theater revenues

30. Which of the following statements is most strongly supported by the passage's information?

    (A) If a movie does not suffer from the "fat faces" syndrome, then it was not produced in a wide-film format.

    (B) Prior to the invention of the 35mm anamorphic lens, quality larger prints could not be made from smaller negatives.

    (C) The same factors that contributed to the resurgence of wide-film formats in the 1950s also led to the subsequent decline in their use.

    (D) The most significant developments in 35mm technology occurred after the release of *Raintree Country*.

    (E) Movie-theater revenues are not significantly affected by whether the movies shown are in wide-screen format.

31. The overall demand for used computers has risen dramatically in the past few years. Most of this increase is due to the explosion of entertainment software products aimed at young first-time computer users. As is to be expected, this demand has exerted an upward pressure on prices of used computers. As a result, we can expect that an increasing number of computer owners will be selling their old computers in order to buy the latest models.

Which of the following, if true, would most help to support the preceding argument's conclusion?

    (A) Computer technology is progressing so rapidly that computers purchased a year ago are now virtually obsolete.

    (B) Exciting new software is being developed that can run only on the latest computer models.

    (C) Most computer users do not know how to upgrade their old computers to accommodate the latest software products.

    (D) It is less expensive to buy a new computer than to buy the components and build one yourself.

    (E) The primary reason computer owners have not bought new computers or used computers that are newer models is that their old computers have little or no resale value.

32. When students receive individual tutoring, they invariably get good grades, and, as a general rule, when students get good grades their self-esteem is greatly enhanced. Thus . . . .

Which of the following provides the most logical completion of the preceding sentence?

    (A) individual tutoring enhances a student's self-esteem.

    (B) students who get good grades receive individual tutoring.

    (C) to enhance a student's self-esteem, it is necessary to give fair examinations.

    (D) only students who get good grades have high self-esteem.

    (E) students who get low grades have low self-esteem.

33. The nutrient value of animal products is indisputable. Complete protein—the kind with sufficient quantities of the eight amino acids—is found only in animal products. The human body cannot manufacture these eight amino acids, so they must be supplied through proper diet.

Which of the following is the preceding argument's main point?

(A) Animal products are the main source of the eight amino acids that make up complete protein.

(B) A proper diet must contain the eight amino acids.

(C) A proper diet must include animal products.

(D) The human body cannot manufacture amino acids.

(E) Animal products are nutritious sources of food.

34. New theoretical models about electromagnetic waves have actually enhanced astronomers' understanding of the evolution of stars to a greater extent than <u>observational data.</u>

(A) observational data.

(B) that of observational data.

(C) observational data has.

(D) have observational datum.

(E) have observational data.

35. Inventors have <u>yet to learn</u> that something that does two things does one of them better.

(A) Inventors have yet to learn

(B) Having not yet learned, inventors need to learn

(C) Inventors have not as of yet learned

(D) Inventors as yet have to learn

(E) Not having yet learned, inventors have to learn

36. The FatGo diet plan is simple and easy: Just drink a can of delicious fruit-flavored FatGo in place of your meals each day. Everyone who has tried it has lost weight, and losses of 10 pounds in the first week are not uncommon. Start drinking FatGo today, and next week you'll be the thin person that you've always wanted to be.

The faulty reasoning in which one of the following is most parallel to that in the preceding argument?

(A) My car was working perfectly until I let you drive it on Saturday. Now it won't even start. You must have done something to it that caused this problem.

(B) Studies reveal that people who do not smoke cigars or cigarettes are involved in far fewer serious automobile accidents than those who do. Thus, if you're involved in a serious accident, it's probably because you smoke.

(C) My former husband was a drunk and a wife beater. From that experience, I've learned that all men are no good.

(D) Unregulated commercial interactions will confer on this nation the advantages that result when there is an unrestricted flow of products among countries. That's why free trade will be good for this country.

(E) The main cause of illegal drug use in America is unemployment. Thus, to get rid of the drug problem, we have to develop public works programs so that we can provide jobs for everyone.

**Questions 37–39 refer to the following passage:**

(5) When Ralph Waldo Emerson pronounced America's declaration of cultural independence from Europe in his "American Scholar" address, he was actually articulating the transcendental assumptions of Jefferson's political indepen-
(10) dence. In the ideal new world envisioned by Emerson, America's becoming a perfect democracy of free and self-reliant individuals was within reach. Bringing Emerson's metaphysics down to earth, Henry David Thoreau's *Walden*
(15) (1854) asserted that one can live without encumbrances. Emerson wanted to visualize Thoreau as the ideal scholar in action that he had called for

in the "American Scholar," but in the end, Emerson regretted Thoreau's too-private indi-
(20) vidualism, which failed to signal the vibrant revolution in national consciousness that Emerson had prophesied.

For Emerson, what Thoreau lacked, Walt Whitman embodied in full. On reading *Leaves of*
(25) *Grass* (1855), Emerson saw in Whitman the "prophet of democracy" whom he had sought. Other American Renaissance writers were less sanguine than Emerson and Whitman about the fulfillment of the democratic ideal. In *The Scarlet*
(30) *Letter* (1850), Nathaniel Hawthorne concluded that antinomianism such as the "heroics" displayed by Hester Prynne leads to moral anarchy; and Herman Melville, who saw in his story of *Pierre* (1852) a metaphor for the misguided as-
(35) sumptions of democratic idealism, declared the transcendentalist dream unrealizable. Ironically, the literary vigor with which both Hawthorne and Melville explored the ideal showed their deep sympathy with it even as they dramatized
(40) its delusions.

37. The author of the passage seeks primarily to

(A) explore the impact of the American Renaissance writers on the literature of the late 18th Century.

(B) illustrate how American literature of the mid-18th Century differed in form from European literature of the same time period.

(C) identify two schools of thought among American Renaissance writers regarding the democratic ideal.

(D) point out how Emerson's democratic idealism was mirrored by the works of the American Renaissance writers.

(E) explain why the writers of the American Renaissance believed that an ideal world was forming in America.

38. Based on the passage's information, Emerson might be characterized as any of the following *except*

(A) a transcendentalist

(B) an American Renaissance writer

(C) a public speaker

(D) a political prophet

(E) a literary critic

39. With which of the following statements about Melville and Hawthorne would the author most likely agree?

(A) Both men were disillusioned transcendentalists.

(B) Hawthorne sympathized with the transcendental dream more so than Melville.

(C) They agreed as to what the transcendentalist dream would ultimately lead to.

(D) Both men believed the idealists to be misguided.

(E) Hawthorne politicized the transcendental ideal, whereas Melville personalized it.

40. New genetic testing procedures have been developed that can detect the presence or absence of dirolin in foods. Dirolin is the toxin that causes food poisoning in humans. While rarely fatal if identified and treated in its early stages, food poisoning causes severe intestinal illness and vomiting. It is for this reason that the Department of Public Health and Safety should require that all processed foods be subjected to the new testing procedures.

Which one of the following, if true, would require the author to reconsider the conclusion?

(A) A recent Disease Control Agency report states that reported cases of food poisoning have declined steadily over the past decade.

(B) Death as a result of food poisoning is extremely rare in modern first-world countries.

(C) Current processing procedures employed in preparing foodstuffs are extremely effective in preventing and detecting dirolin contamination.

(D) The bacillus that produces dirolin can be easily treated with modern antibiotics.

(E) Improper preserving and processing procedures are responsible for the presence of dirolin in prepared foods.

41. While few truly great artists consider themselves visionary, many lesser talents boast about their own destiny to lead the way to higher artistic ground.

(A) While few truly great artists consider themselves visionary, many lesser talents boast about their own destiny to lead the way to higher artistic ground.

(B) While many lesser talents boast about their own destinies to lead the way to higher ground, few truly great artists consider themselves as visionary.

(C) Many lesser talents boast about their own destiny to lead the way to higher artistic ground while few truly great artists consider themselves as being visionary.

(D) Few truly great artists consider himself or herself a visionary while many lesser talents boast about their own destinies to lead the way to higher artistic ground.

(E) While many lesser talents boast about their own destiny, few truly great artists consider themselves visionary, to lead the way to higher artistic ground.

# Quick Answer Guide

**Practice Test: Verbal Ability**

| | | | | | | | |
|---|---|---|---|---|---|---|---|
| 1. | C | 12. | D | 23. | C | 34. | E |
| 2. | B | 13. | B | 24. | D | 35. | A |
| 3. | D | 14. | C | 25. | E | 36. | A |
| 4. | A | 15. | B | 26. | B | 37. | C |
| 5. | B | 16. | D | 27. | C | 38. | E |
| 6. | E | 17. | C | 28. | A | 39. | D |
| 7. | A | 18. | B | 29. | D | 40. | C |
| 8. | E | 19. | B | 30. | B | 41. | A |
| 9. | E | 20. | D | 31. | E | | |
| 10. | B | 21. | E | 32. | A | | |
| 11. | B | 22. | A | 33. | C | | |

# Practice Test: Review of Section 4 (Verbal Ability)

## Today's Topics:

Today you will review yesterday's Verbal Ability practice test. Preceding each explanation, the question type and difficulty level are indicated.

### 1. Sentence correction (easier). Answer: C.

The original sentence A includes a misplaced modifying phrase (following the comma). The sentence's construction suggests that it is the *electorate* that cannot reasonably be disputed, although this makes little sense in the context of the sentence as a whole.

B suffers from a confusing syntax. It appears from the sentence's construction that the elected officials—rather than the fact that they ignored their electorate's wishes—cannot be disputed. B also misplaces the prepositional phrases "on this issue" between the gerund "ignoring" and the object of that gerund, "the wishes of the electorate."

C remedies the underlined phrase's faulty construction by rephrasing it as a noun clause.

D improperly uses a comma between two clauses that do not constitute independent sentences on their own. D also sets up a parallel between "were ignored . . . " and "cannot reasonably." Both phrases seem to refer to "the wishes of the electorate," although this is probably not the intended meaning.

E is faulty in its use of the passive voice rather than the preferred active voice.

### 2. Sentence correction (challenging). Answer: B.

The original sentence A is a long sentence fragment with no predicate.

B completes the sentence by reconstructing it.

C, like A, is a long sentence fragment.

D uses the idiomatically incorrect "which book is"; that phrase should exclude the word "book."
E is unclear as to whether Francis Craig wrote all the books in the series or just the first three books.

### 3. Sentence correction (moderate). Answer: D.

The original sentence A is faulty in two respects. First, the sentence treats the compound subject ("interest rates" and "the supply of money") as singular by using "either . . . or"; the predicate should agree by also referring to the subject in the singular form, using "a factor" rather than "factors." Second, the verb phrase "can . . . be" is improperly split. Third, the phrase "can . . . be factors contributing to" is redundant and wordy.

B is faulty in two respects. B improperly separates the components of the progressive verb "can be." Also, the phrase "one or the other" duplicates the earlier phrase "either . . . or," resulting in redundancy and unnecessary wordiness.

C improperly splits the progressive verb "can contribute," and also separates that verb from its modifying prepositional phrase "to the amount . . ."

D remedies all the original sentence problems by uniting the verb parts, rewording the predicate to agree in form with the subject, and removing the redundant language.

E improperly separates the preposition "to" and its object "the amount of . . . ," thereby confusing the meaning of the sentence (the improper construction suggests that interest rates and the supply of money contribute to the level of government spending).

## 4. Assumption (moderate). Answer: A.

Answer A is the best response. The passage's argument is essentially that the law should not require motorists to wear seat belts because wearing them might endanger motorists' lives. You can express the argument as follows:

> **Premise:** Wearing seat belts can endanger motorists' lives.
>
> **Conclusion:** Law should not require motorists to wear seat belts.

You must fill this argument's logical gap, which is the link between acts that the law requires and activities that might endanger people. Response A expresses the necessary link.

The passage implies B. The first sentence states that "contrary to popular belief, there are cases in which a seat belt can actually endanger one's life rather than protect it." This implies that most people believe that wearing a seat belt will save their lives.

The passage also implies C. The first sentence states that "contrary to popular belief, there are cases in which a seat belt can actually endanger one's life rather than protect it." This implies that wearing a seat belt does not necessarily protect the wearer in automobile accidents.

D is off focus. The argument's issue is not whether people should obey the seat belt law, but rather whether the law should exist in the first place.

E is a colloquial paraphrase of the passage's first sentence.

## 5. Reasoning error (easier). Answer: B.

B is the best response. In the passage's argument, the Republicans' failure to articulate good reasons in support of their opposition to cuts in social security is taken as evidence that they are in favor of cuts in social security. Of the answer choices, response B best describes this reasoning error.

Response A describes the passage's argument incorrectly. The passage does not mention any alternatives.

C is an incorrect response. The passage's argument does not conclude that *all* Republicans favor cuts in social security on the grounds that *some* do; instead, the passage makes this conclusion on the grounds that Republicans have failed to present evidence of their opposition to cuts in social security.

D and E describe the passage's argument incorrectly. The passage presents no cases or data.

## 6. Interpretation (moderate). Answer: E.

E is the best response. Statement E restates the author's point in the first paragraph that rates of species movement driven by human transformation of the natural environment and by human mobility dwarf natural rates by comparison.

The passage does not support response A. Although the author compares natural species movement to human-driven movement, the passage makes no such comparison between human modification of habitats and human mobility.

The passage also fails to support B. The author makes no attempt to compare rate (interpreted either as frequency or speed) of species movement to total amounts of movement (distance).

The passage does not support C. The author makes no attempt to compare natural expansions to natural contractions.

D is nonsensical. Human mobility (commerce, tourism, and travel) do not create "natural" environments. It is human mobility itself, not the "natural environment" created by it, that contributes significantly to species movement.

## 7. Interpretation (moderate). Answer: A.

Answer A is the best response. In the second paragraph's first sentence, the author claims that "[a] number of factors confound quantitative evaluation of the relative importance of various entry pathways." In the remainder of the paragraph, the author identifies three such problems: the difficulty of early detection, the inadequacy of port inspection, and the inherent subjectivity in determining the "importance" of a pathway.

B is off focus and too narrow. Although the author does mention that a species is usually not detected until it spreads to at least 10,000 acres, the author mentions this single "event" leading to detection as part of the broader point that the unlikelihood of early detection contributes to the problem of quantifying the relative importance of entry pathways.

C is off focus. Although the author mentions these factors, the passage does not discuss them in any detail, as response C suggests. Also, the second paragraph's primary concern is not with identifying the factors affecting species detection but instead with identifying the problems in quantifying the relative importance of various entry pathways.

D is too narrow. The author is concerned with identifying other problems as well as in determining the relative importance of various entry pathways.

E is off focus. Although the author asserts that it is difficult to trace an entry pathway once a species is well established, the author does not explain why this is so.

## 8. Explicit detail (easier). Answer: E.

E is the best response. Nowhere in the passage does the author either state or imply that the physical size of a species' members affects whether the entry pathway for the species can be determined.

Answer A is the second-best response. Unlike responses B, C, and D, response A is not supported explicitly by the passage. However, the author mentions in the final paragraph that federal port inspection is "a major source of information on nonindigenous species pathways, especially for agricultural pests." Accordingly, whether a species is an agricultural pest might have some bearing on whether port inspectors detect its entry.

The second paragraph explicitly mention B, C, and D as factors affecting how precisely the entry pathways of a species can be determined.

## 9. Sentence correction (easier). Answer: E.

The original sentence A confuses the subjunctive verb form (which deals with possibilities rather than facts) and past-perfect tense. Response A also includes a disagreement in pronoun reference; "scientific community" is singular in form, calling for the singular pronoun "it" rather than "they."

B includes a disagreement in verb tense. The progressive verb "would not be" is in the present-perfect tense, whereas the verb "had . . . become" is in the past-perfect tense. Moreover, in the context of the sentence as a whole, neither tense is appropriate; the subjunctive verb form should be used instead.

C properly uses the subjunctive form ("were") but fails to remedy the incorrect pronoun reference ("they") in the original sentence.

D improperly expresses the idea to be conveyed in the past tense ("when the scientific community became") rather than in the appropriate subjunctive verb form.

E remedies both problems in the original sentence. It uses the subjunctive form consistently—at both the beginning and end of the phrase. It also replaces the incorrect plural pronoun "they" with "scientists."

## 10. Assessing the effect of additional information (moderate). Answer: B.

B is the best response. The major assumption of the passage's argument is that there are no relevant differences between the conditions present during the previous drought and the current drought that would necessitate the water use restrictions imposed in response to the current drought. Response B undermines this assumption and, as a result, undermines the author's contention. The fact that there is a significant increase in the number of water users points to a relevant difference between the two situations that accounts for the difference in the restrictions.

A, C, D, and E are incorrect responses. The task in this problem is to find an answer choice that weakens the argument—that is, one that undermines the argument's major assumption, attacks a stated premise, or suggests an alternative conclusion that you can infer from the premises. These four responses accomplish none of these.

## 11. Reasoning error (moderate). Answer: B.

B is the best response. By arguing that "if it is true that everything in the universe is composed of invisible atoms, surely it follows that everything in the universe is invisible," the author relies on the mistaken assumption that the whole must have the same properties as its parts, or more generally, that what is true of the parts is necessarily true of the whole.

Answer A is an incorrect response. The passage cites no antecedent event as the cause of some other event.

C is also incorrect. Admittedly, the word "invisible" appears several times in the passage; however, its meaning remains the same in all occurrences—that is, that which the eye cannot see.

D is an incorrect response. Although the passage cites modern science as the origin of the view that everything in the universe consists of atoms, this fact is not taken as a reason for rejecting the view.

E is also an incorrect response. The argument does not rely on this belief. The passage makes no attempt to show that the claim that everything in the universe consists of atoms cannot be proven to be true.

## 12. Sentence correction (moderate). Answer: D.

The original sentence (A) suffers from faulty parallelism. The second occurrence of "from" should be deleted to restore the proper parallelism between the phrases "the host" and "the diplomat's." At the same time, the word "both" in A is redundant in light of the words "the other" at the end of the sentence, thereby confusing the meaning of the sentence.

B remedies the original sentence's problems but presents a usage problem. The phrase "each other" properly refers to only two persons or things. Because the potential number of "citizens" (guests) might exceed two, "one another" should be used instead.

C suggests a nonsensical meaning—that the *country* itself (rather than a person) seats its citizens. The construction also creates ambiguity as to what the rules require.

D remedies the original sentence's faulty parallelism by reconstructing the phrase, using the subjunctive form ("that . . . be").

E is faulty in two respects. It includes the word "to" twice; the second occurrence is redundant and should be excluded. Also, the use of double possessive adjectives—"diplomat's" and "country's"—is improper.

## 13. Sentence correction (easier). Answer: B.

Response A is faulty because the plural subject "benefits" is followed by the singular verb "is."

B remedies the original sentence's problem by using the plural "are," which agrees with "benefits."

C improperly uses the word "furthering," suggesting that exercise is a benefit or goal that is being furthered.

D improperly uses the subjunctive verb form ("would be") instead of the more appropriate present tense ("are").

E improperly uses the subjunctive verb form ("would be") instead of the more appropriate present tense ("are").

## 14. Sentence correction (moderate). Answer: C.

The original statement A includes an ambiguous pronoun reference. It is unclear whether "they" refers to the bounty hunters, their captives, or the authorities.

B is illogically constructed. It appears from B that the authorities turn over captives to themselves. Also, the antecedent of "them" is unclear.

C remedies the original sentence's ambiguous pronoun reference by reconstructing the sentence.

D is ambiguous and confusing. It is unclear whether the modifying phrase following the comma refers to bounty hunters, their captives, or the authorities.

E is faulty in two respects. First, it is awkwardly constructed; the modifying phrase (set off by commas) belongs at the beginning of the sentence so that the other two (related) parts of the sentence are closer to each other. Second, the plural "bounty hunters" disagrees with the singular "captive," thereby confusing the sentence's meaning.

## 15. Interpretation (easier). Answer: B.

B is the best response. According to the passage, the ambiguous position of Soviet scientists was that the Soviet government encouraged and generally supported scientific research, while at the same time it imposed significant restrictions on its scientists. Statement B restates this idea.

The passage does not support A. The author neither states nor suggests that the Soviets lacked sufficient funding; moreover, although statement A, if true, would indicate an ambiguous position for scientists, it is not the nature of the ambiguity to which the passage refers.

C is wholly unsupported. The author neither states nor suggests either assertion made in statement C.

The passage supports D (albeit, not explicitly) and, if D is true, it presents an ambiguous position for Soviet scientists. However, the ambiguity to which D refers fails to reflect the nature of the ambiguity to which the passage refers.

The passage does not support E. Although the government indeed punished some Soviet scientists, the author neither states nor implies that the government failed to identify those areas of research that it deemed most worthwhile. Moreover, although statement E, if true, would indicate an ambiguous position for scientists, it is not the nature of the ambiguity to which the passage refers.

## 16. Purpose of detail (moderate). Answer: D.

D is the best response. This part of the passage is concerned exclusively with pointing out evidence of the Soviet emphasis on a national science; given the content of the excerpt from *Literatunaya Gazeta*, you can reasonably infer that the author is quoting this article as one such piece of evidence.

B is the second-best response. The quoted article does indeed reflect the Marxist-Leninist ideal (at least as interpreted and promulgated by the government) and might in fact have been published only because the Soviet government sanctioned it. However, statement B is not likely to be the author's purpose in quoting the article, because this conclusion would require speculation and because the quoted excerpt does not mention government approval or disapproval of certain scientific notions.

Response A distorts the nature of the quoted article and runs contrary to the passage. The article illustrates the official Soviet position and possibly the sentiment among some members of the Soviet intellectual or scientific community. However, the article does not necessarily reflect the views of scientists from other countries.

C is not likely to be the author's purpose in quoting the article, because the author does not discuss disagreement and debate among Soviet intellectuals.

E is not likely to be the author's purpose in quoting the article. Although the assertion mentioned in response E might in fact be true and indeed be supported by the passage's information, the author gives no indication as to when the article was written or published; thus, the article itself lends no support to the assertion mentioned in statement E.

## 17. Primary purpose (moderate). Answer: C.

C is the best response. The passage as a whole is indeed concerned with describing Soviet attempts to suppress scientific freedom.

D is the second-best response. Although the last paragraph briefly discusses other attempts at suppression of scientific freedom in the 20th Century, the passage does not examine these attempts; thus, D is too broad.

Response A is off focus and far too narrow; moreover, the author does not actually discuss any specific events that might have caused the suppression of the refusenik movement; rather, the passage mentions this historical phenomenon simply as another example of the Soviet regime's long-term pattern of suppression.

B is off focus and misses the author's attitude. Although the author does define the concept of national science, the passage makes no attempt to dispel or disprove the concept.

E is too narrow and is off focus. Although the author does imply that scientific freedom and scientific internationalism are related, the passage makes no attempt to examine their differences; moreover, the author's broader concern is quite different than to examine the relationship between these two types of scientific freedoms.

## 18. Parallel reasoning (challenging). Answer: B.

You can restate the passage's argument as follows:

**Premise:** Lies are morally justified *only if* they are told to save a person's life.

**Premise:** *Most* lies are *not* told to save a person's life.

**Conclusion:** *Most* lies are morally *un*justified.

B is the best response. You can restate response B's argument as follows:

**Premise:** Capital punishment is justified *only if* the convicted offender is guilty.

**Premise:** *Many* convicted offenders are *not* guilty.

**Conclusion:** *Many* instances of capital punishment are *un*justified.

A comparison of this argument with the passage argument outlined previously reveals a close similarity between the premises and conclusions of these arguments. In each, you construct the first premise by connecting two independent clauses with the phrase "only if"; the second premise states the denial of the clause following "only if"; and the conclusion states the denial of the clause preceding "only if."

Answer A is an incorrect response. You can restate the argument in response A as follows:

**Premise:** Capital punishment is justified *if* it deters people from taking another's life.

**Premise:** Capital punishment does *not* effectively deter people from taking another's life.

**Conclusion:** Capital punishment is *un*justified.

Contrary to initial appearances, this argument's first premise is not comparable to the first premise of the passage argument outlined previously. A simple example demonstrates the difference. Compare the following two statements:

Combustion will occur *only if* oxygen is present.

Combustion will occur *if* oxygen is present.

These two statements have different meanings. The first states that the presence of oxygen is a necessary condition for combustion, the second states that it is a sufficient condition. The first is true, and the second is false.

C is an incorrect response. The first premise of the argument in response C is comparable to the first premise of the passage argument, but the second premise and the conclusion of these arguments are not comparable.

D is an incorrect response. You can restate the argument in response D as follows:

**Premise:** *If* the defendant in a murder trial is determined to be guilty beyond a reasonable doubt, *then* the maximum penalty allowed under the law can be imposed.

**Premise:** *Most* defendants in murder trials are *not* determined to be guilty beyond a reasonable doubt.

**Conclusion:** The maximum penalty is seldom imposed.

This argument does not have the same structure as the passage's argument.

E is an incorrect response. You can restate the argument in response E as follows:

**Premise:** Corporal punishment for persons who commit violent crimes is justified *only if* the punishment will alter the persons' behavior in the future.

**Premise:** *Most* persons who commit violent crimes are corporally punished *not* to alter their future behavior *but* only to exact revenge.

**Conclusion:** *Most* instances of corporal punishment are *un*justified.

This argument does not have the same structure as the passage's argument. The argument's first and second premises are not comparable to the first and second premises of the passage's argument.

## 19. Inference (moderate). Answer: B.

B is the best response. From the information stated in the passage, you can infer that one-half-inch cubes would require proportionately less cooking time than the 20 minutes required for one-inch cubes. Cooking them for 20 minutes would consequently result in severe overcooking, and this in turn would result in a significant lessening of their food value.

The passage does not support response A, which contradicts information stated in the passage ("undercooked potatoes cannot be properly digested").

The passage does not support C. The passage clearly states that only potatoes that are diced into one-inch cubes are properly prepared by being cooked in boiling water for 20 minutes; potatoes that are smaller than this would require proportionately less time to be properly digestible.

The passage also does not support D. The passage does not discuss other cooking methods.

Finally, the passage fails to support E, which is too broad. This applies only to potatoes that are diced into one-inch or larger cubes. Smaller cubes would require less than 20 minutes to be properly prepared.

## 20. Inference (moderate). Answer: D.

D is the best response. From the passage's information, you can reasonably assume that Uranus and its moons constitute a planetary system. From this assumption and the claim that in all the planetary systems mentioned the satellite moves in an elliptical orbit, you can infer that the moons of the planet Uranus move in elliptical orbits. This is exactly what response D asserts.

The passage does not support response A. That response states something that is true according to modern physics, but the premises in the passage do not provide any logical support for this claim.

B brings in information that the passage does not mention. The passage does not mention the phases of the moon as seen from Earth.

C makes too broad a claim. The author restricts information in the passage to laws governing planetary systems.

E is too broad. The passage concerns only planetary systems, not all celestial bodies.

## 21. Assessing the effect of additional information (challenging). Answer: E.

E is the best response. The task in this problem is to find an answer that strengthens the argument—that is, one that offers support for the argument's major assumption or that provides additional evidence for the conclusion. Of the answer choices, response E is the best choice because it does the latter—that is, it

provides a convincing rationale for the seemingly inconsistent action on the part of the Astonian government.

Response A is consistent with the claim that Cretia is an "embattled country." Although response A might provide a reason for Cretia's need for military support, it does not provide a rationale for the Astonian government's seemingly inconsistent action.

B is the second best response. Response B provides a plausible reason for the Astonian government's shift in policy, but to accept it as the best response you would have to make superfluous assumptions about how these trade agreements impact Astonia's foreign policy decisions.

C is the third-best response. Although response C provides a rationale for Astonia's shift in policy, to accept it as the best response would require making several superfluous assumptions about the Astonian government's foreign policy making principles.

D conflicts with information provided in the passage regarding Cretia's human-rights record as compared to other countries. Moreover, the fact that Cretia has a worse record than other countries to which Astonia provides military support does not provide a convincing rationale for Astonia's change in policy toward Cretia.

## 22. Sentence correction (challenging). Answer: A.

The original sentence A includes a compound subject, expressed as a noun clause (the first part of the sentence through "aimed"). Response A properly uses "who" as one of the sentence's subjects and properly uses "whom" as an indirect object.

B incorrectly uses "whom" as one of the sentence's subjects.

C is awkwardly constructed. "Who are the terrorists" poses a question and does not parallel the other subject ("at whom . . . aimed").

D omits the preposition "at," resulting in a nonsensical phrase. Also, D is vague as to whom the pronoun "they" refers.

E improperly uses the preposition "to" instead of "at," suggesting that the terrorists' activities were aimed *to* a particular target.

## 23. Sentence correction (moderate). Answer: C.

The original sentence A is faulty in its use of the pronoun *them* instead of the possessive *their* where the object of a verb ("opposed") is a verbal noun ("idealizing") that is not the musicians themselves but instead their actions or traits.

B improperly adds the word "of," resulting in a diction error. A person is said to trivialize something (direct object), not trivialize *of* something.

C corrects the improper use of "them," replacing it with the possessive "their," which properly precedes the gerund noun "trivializing."

D employs the awkward passive voice instead of the preferred active voice.

E is awkward and confusing. It is unclear whether the modifying phrase beginning with "when" refers to Blakey or earlier jazz musicians.

## 24. Sentence correction (moderate). Answer: D.

The original statement A misplaces the prepositional phrase "Even as high school freshmen and sophomores," suggesting that "theories" are high school students.

B is constructed in a way that confuses the meaning as well as nonsensically equating "high school students" with "theories."

C inserts the modifying phrase "for many high school freshmen and sophomores" between two closely related ideas. The author should connect those ideas syntactically by moving the modifying phrase to either the beginning or the end of the sentence.

D moves the initial prepositional phrase to the end of the sentence, clarifying the sentence's meaning.

E employs improper diction. It is awkward to speak of a person's interest as "held in" a particular subject.

## 25. Assumption (moderate). Answer: E.

E is the best response. The passage's argument is essentially that women have the right to earn as much money as men because they have as much right to self-esteem as men. You can represent the argument as follows:

> **Premise:** Women have as much right to self-esteem as men.
>
> **Conclusion:** Women have the right to earn as much money as men.

The logical gap in this argument that you must fill is the link between a person's self-esteem and the amount of money that person earns. The suggestion is the amount of money that a person has determines that person's self-esteem—the more money, the more self-esteem; the less money, the less self-esteem. Of the answer choices, response E best expresses this assumption.

Response A is off focus. The argument does not address relative importance of self-esteem to men and women. Response A does not express an assumption of the argument, but rather another plausible reason that women and men should receive equal pay.

B is off focus. The argument concerns only unequal pay for men and women. This implies that they have jobs.

C is a paraphrase of the passage's first sentence. This sentence states that "unequal pay for men and women is a completely indefensible practice." C is just another way of saying this.

D brings in information that the passage does not mention. The passage does not discuss the constitutionality of unequal pay for women and men.

## 26. Method (easier). Answer: B.

B is the best response. The medical licensing board's argument is criticized on the grounds that the board's membership consists of doctors who have a vested interest in limiting the supply of new doctors, and that it is this self-serving motive that is the real reason for their position.

Answer A is an incorrect response. The primary reason offered in support of the medical licensing board's conclusion is "that doctors who are trained at nonaccredited institutions may lack the training necessary to become competent practitioners." The passage does not challenge the truth of this claim.

C is off focus. The passage does not question the medical licensing board's expertise on the topic.

D is off focus. The passage contains no reference to the capability of other institutions to train competent doctors.

E is incorrect. The major premise on which the board bases its conclusion is "that doctors who are trained at nonaccredited institutions may lack the training necessary to become competent practitioners." The passage does not attack or criticize this premise.

## 27. Sentence correction (moderate). Answer: C.

The original sentence A is faulty in two respects. First, it improperly uses "because" instead of "because of." Second, the construction leaves it unclear as to whether the modifying phrase "already in wide use" refers to "other pesticides" or to "chemical compositions."

B misuses the phrase "because of." The author should follow this prepositional phrase with a modifying clause by inserting a comma followed by "which" after "in wide use" ("in wide use, which . . . ").

C corrects the misuse of "because" by replacing it with "due to."

D is redundant in its use of both "since" and "due to." This redundancy results, in turn, in an awkward construction.

E misplaces the adverbial clause "already in use," which is intended to refer not to "chemical compositions" but rather to "other pesticides."

## 28. Inference (moderate). Answer: A.

Answer A is the best response. The passage refers to the establishment of a *de facto* 35mm standard around 1913, followed by a "resurgence" of wide-film formats (in the mid-1920s to the mid-1930s). This resurgence suggests that wide-film formats were not new because they had been used before the 35mm standard was established—that is, before 1913.

B distorts the passage's information. The passage does indicate that research and development slackened between the mid-1930s and the beginning of the modern era of wide-screen moviemaking (the early 1950s). However, the author neither states nor implies that wide-film formats fell into complete disuse during this interim period.

C distorts the passage's information. The author makes no comparison between the 1920s and the 1930s in terms of the extent to which wide-film formats were used. The passage indicates only that "(t)he mid-1920s through the mid-1930s saw a resurgence of wide-film formats."

The passage does not strongly support D, but suggests only that the 25mm format began again to dominate film-making after 1956.

E alludes to information that the passage does not discuss. Nowhere in the passage does the author either state or imply that wide-film formats were used more commonly for some types of movies than for others.

## 29. Explicit detail (easier). Answer: D.

D is the best response. According to the passage's last sentence, anamorphic lenses, used with more mobile cameras, made it possible to create quality 70mm prints from 35mm negatives. In this respect, the invention of the anamorphic camera lens contributed to the demise (not the increased use) of wide-film moviemaking.

The passage discusses A as a key technical advance in wide-film format technology. The spherical 65mm lens eliminated the "fat faces" syndrome (presumably, wide-film images were thereby made to appear more realistic). Accordingly, this new type of lens contributed to the increased use of the wide-film format.

The author indirectly refers to B as a key technical advance in wide-film format technology. In mentioning that "Panavision soon contributed another key technical advance," the author implies that Camera 65 was also a key technical advance.

The second paragraph's first sentence mentions C as one of two factors that prompted the resurgence in the 1950s of the wide-film format.

The same sentence mentions E as one of two factors that prompted the resurgence in the 1950s of the wide-film format.

## 30. Interpretation (moderate). Answer: B.

B is the best response. The passage's final sentence states that after the invention of the 35mm anamorphic lens, quality 70mm (larger) prints could be made from 35mm (smaller) negatives. It is reasonable to assume that larger prints could not be made from smaller negatives prior to that invention.

Response A calls for an illogical inference that contradicts the passage's information. The author states that the invention of the spherical 65mm lens "eliminated the 'fat faces' syndrome that had plagued earlier CinemaScope films." CinemaScope was one of the specialized wide-film formats. Thus, if a particular movie does not suffer from the "fat faces" syndrome, it could very well have been produced in wide-film format with a spherical 65mm lens.

C runs contrary to the passage's information. According to the passage, the advent of television and the resulting decline in box-office revenues prompted the resurgence of wide-film formats in the 1950s. The author identifies several factors as contributing to the subsequent demise of wide-film formats: expenses, unwieldy cameras, slow film stocks and lenses, the invention of the anamorphic lenses, and mobile cameras. However, the passage does not mention the popularity of television or box-office receipts among those factors.

D distorts the passage's information. The only post-*Raintree Country* technological developments that the passage mentions are the invention of anamorphic lenses and more mobile cameras. Although such developments were probably significant in the development of 35mm technology, to suggest that these innovations were the most significant developments in 35mm technology (as response D suggests) exaggerates the author's point.

E runs contrary to the passage's information. The information in the second paragraph suggests that it was in response to eroding box-office revenues that the movie industry stepped up its efforts to improve wide-screen technology. Moreover, based on the author's discussion of the modern era of wide-screen filmmaking, these attempts apparently were successful, at least until other problems (such as expense, unwieldy cameras, and slow film stocks

and lenses) made continued use of wide-film format unfeasible.

## 31. Assessing the effect of additional information (moderate). Answer: E.

E is the best response. The task in this problem is to find an answer that strengthens the argument—that is, one that offers support for the argument's major assumption or that provides additional evidence for the conclusion. The primary reason that the argument gives for expecting an increasing number of computer owners to sell their old computers is that increased demand for used computers has exerted an upward pressure on prices of used computers. This suggests that the reason computer owners had not sold their old computers previously is that those computers did not have sufficient resale value to enable the owners to purchase newer models. Response E explicitly states this reason and thus provides additional evidence for the conclusion.

A, B, and C bring in information that the passage does not mention. Admittedly, each of these responses provides a reason that computer owners might sell their old computers and buy newer models. However, none of these responses provides a reason for the expected increase in the number of computer owners who will do so. Consequently, none of these responses provides additional evidence for the conclusion.

D does not provide additional evidence for the conclusion nor does it provide support for the argument's major assumption.

## 32. Unstated conclusion (easier). Answer: A.

You can rewrite the passage's argument as follows:

> **Premise:** If students receive individual tutoring, then they invariably get good grades.

> **Premise:** If students get good grades, then their self-esteem is greatly enhanced.

The main ideas in the passage are (1) receiving individual tutoring, (2) getting good grades, and (3) enhancing self-esteem. The first premise links 1 and 2; the second premise links 2 and 3. The unstated conclusion must link 1 and 3.

Answer A is the best response. Response A links 1 and 3.

B is an incorrect response. Response B links 1 and 2.

C brings in information that the passage does not mention.

D is an incorrect response. Response D links 2 and 3.

E brings in information that the passage does not mention.

## 33. Conclusion (moderate). Answer: C.

C is the best response. The argument's main point or final conclusion is not overtly stated. The last sentence states the intermediate conclusion: "so they must be supplied through proper diet." The pronoun "they" in this phrase refers back to the eight amino acids, which, the passage mentions earlier, are found in sufficient quantities only in animal products. Because these eight amino acids can be found only in animal products and they are necessary for a proper diet, you can conclude that a proper diet must include animal products. This is the argument's main point and is exactly what response C asserts.

Response A simply restates the argument's second sentence. This sentence functions as a premise—not a conclusion—in the argument.

B is the second-best response. This question asks you to find the main point or final conclusion. Response B states an intermediate conclusion, not the final conclusion.

D generalizes one of the passage's premises. The passage says that the "human body cannot manufacture these eight amino acids." Response D asserts this claim more broadly.

E restates the passage's first sentence, which is superfluous to the argument. Response E states neither a premise nor a conclusion of the argument; it functions merely to introduce the topic.

## 34. Sentence correction (moderate). Answer: E.

The original sentence A makes an illogical comparison between "the evolution of stars" and "observational data."

B makes an illogical comparison between "that of observational data" and "electromagnetic waves." The word "that" does not logically refer to anything and should be excluded.

C is idiomatically improper in its placement of "has" after (rather than before) "observational data."

D improperly uses the distinctively singular noun "datum" along with the plural verb "have."

E establishes the logical comparison between "new theoretical models" and "observational data" by including the verb "have." The noun "data" is plural, so the verb "have" is proper here.

## 35. Sentence correction (easier). Answer: A.

The original sentence A is correct in its use of the idiomatic phrase "have yet to."

B is redundant and awkward; "having not yet learned" and "need to learn" convey essentially the same idea. Also, it is unclear what inventors have not yet learned.

C uses the improper "as of yet."

D shifts perspective (tense) in midsentence from the present ("as yet") to the future ("have to learn").

E is redundant and awkward in a manner similar to B.

## 36. Parallel reasoning (moderate). Answer: A.

The passage's argument is an example of "after this, therefore because of this" reasoning—that is, regarding an event that preceded another as being the cause of the subsequent event. Basically, the passage's argument is that because the weight loss followed the ingestion of FatGo in place of meals, FatGo is the cause of the weight loss. The reasoning in this argument is faulty because it completely overlooks other possible causes for the weight loss.

Answer A is the best response. The reasoning in response A is that because the problem with the car followed the person's use of the car, the person's use of the car is the cause of the problem. The reasoning in A is similar to the reasoning in the passage.

B is an incorrect response. The reasoning in response B confuses a correlation between two events with a causal relation between those events. Although the occurrence of a correlation between events indicates the possibility that they are causally related, it is also possible that the correlation is just a coincidence. In any case, the reasoning in B is not similar to the reasoning in the passage.

C is an incorrect response. Response C is an example of reasoning to a general conclusion on the basis of insufficient evidence. The fact that one man behaves in a certain way is not sufficient grounds for the conclusion that all men behave in that way. In any case, the reasoning in C is not similar to the reasoning in the passage.

D is an incorrect response. Response D is an example of circular reasoning. The premise and the conclusion of the argument in D express the same thing. The reasoning in D is not similar to the reasoning in the passage.

E is an incorrect response. The premise of the argument in E states an oversimplified account of the cause of the problem. The conclusion states a solution to the problem that addresses the cause identified in the premise. The reasoning in E is not similar to the reasoning in the passage.

### 37. Primary purpose (moderate). Answer: C.

C is the best response. The passage describes an imaginary debate over the American democratic ideal among the writers of the American Renaissance, in which Emerson, Thoreau, and Whitman are grouped together in one school of thought while Hawthorne and Melville are paired in another.

The passage does not support response A. The author does not "explore" the impact of the American Renaissance writers to any extent.

The passage also fails to support B. The author makes no further attempt to distinguish American forms from European forms.

D is the second-best response. Admittedly, Emerson's idealism was reflected in the works of Thoreau and Whitman insofar as they too shared the transcendentalists' dream. However, response D distorts the passage's information. The author actually points out that Thoreau's "too-private individualism" was not in accord with what Emerson hoped for. In this sense, the author is pointing out how Thoreau's *Walden* failed to accurately mirror Emerson's idealism. In addition, although the passage does strongly suggest that, through his works, Whitman fully reflected Emerson's ideal American scholar, the passage does not discuss how Whitman's works serve this end. Thus, the passage does not support response D as well as response C.

E distorts the passage's information. The only event that the passage mentions that might have contributed to the idealist mind set of the times was Jefferson's declaration of political independence. However, the author does not actually claim that it was because of Jefferson (in whole or in part) that the writers of the American Renaissance believed that an ideal world was forming in America. Moreover, the passage does not discuss any other reasons that the American Renaissance writers might have believed as they did.

### 38. Interpretation (moderate). Answer: E.

E is the best response. Although in criticizing Thoreau's *Walden* (a literary work), Emerson could be viewed as playing the role of literary critic, this suggestion is a bit attenuated. Moreover, the passage supports all other answer choices more strongly.

The assertion that Emerson "was actually articulating the transcendental assumptions political independence" implies response A.

The statement that "the other writers of the American Renaissance were less sanguine than Emerson and Whitman about the fulfillment of the democratic ideal" implies B.

The passage's first sentence implies C, referring to Emerson's "American Scholar" address. The word "address" suggests a public speech, and it was Emerson himself who was the speaker (he "pronounced").

The passage supports D. The author asserts that Thoreau "failed to signal the vibrant revolution in national consciousness that Emerson had prophesied." Also, the passage supports the idea that Emerson anticipated and predicted that America would become "a perfect democracy of free and self-reliant individuals."

### 39. Interpretation (challenging). Answer: D.

D is the best response. According to the passage, Melville, through his story of *Pierre*, conveyed the notion that democratic idealism was based on "misguided assumptions." Although the author is not so explicit that Hawthorne also believed idealists to be misguided, Hawthorne's conclusion that transcendental freedom leads to moral anarchy can reasonably be interpreted as such.

Answer A is the second-best response. According to the passage, both men sympathized with the democratic ideal, which was part of the transcendental dream. In this respect, it can be argued that both men were transcendentalists at heart. Also, Hawthorne concluded that transcendental freedom would lead to moral anarchy, whereas Melville declared the dream unrealizable. In this sense, then, both men were disillusioned with the transcendental dream. However, the author states that for Emerson—a transcendentalist—the democratic ideal seemed "within reach," whereas for Hawthorne and Melville, the ideal was clearly not within reach. Accordingly, to categorize them as transcendentalists would contradict the author's description of the transcendental viewpoint.

The passage does not support B. The passage states that both men sympathized with the transcendental dream. However, the author neither states nor implies that one of these two men sympathized with the transcendental dream more than the other.

The passage also fails to support C. According to the passage, Hawthorne believed that personal "heroics" lead to moral anarchy, whereas Melville believed that the transcendental dream was unrealizable. This information suggests neither agreement nor disagreement between the two men as to what the transcendental dream would ultimately lead to.

E confuses the passage's information. The passage suggests just the opposite. It can be argued that Melville politicized transcendentalism in that, through his metaphorical story of *Pierre*, he revealed the problems of democratic idealism. At the same time, Hawthorne personalized transcendentalism through the actions of an individual character (Hester Prynne) in *The Scarlet Letter*.

## 40. Assessing the effect of additional information (moderate). Answer: C.

C is the best response. The task in this problem is to find an answer that weakens the argument—that is, one that undermines the argument's major assumption, attacks a stated premise, or suggests an alternative conclusion that you can infer from the premises. The argument's major assumption is that

current dirolin contamination detection methods are inadequate, ineffective, or completely lacking. Response C effectively undermines this assumption.

A, B, D, and E bring in information that neither undermines the argument's major assumption, attacks a stated premise, nor suggests an alternative conclusion that you can infer from the premises.

## 41. Sentence correction (challenging). Answer: A.

Answer A is the best response. The original sentence contains no grammatical errors, ambiguous references, or idiomatically improper words or phrases. The word "visionary," used as an adjective here, is proper, although you could use the word "visionaries" (a noun) instead.

B incorrectly uses the plural "destinies" to describe a singular idea. The word "as" in B is idiomatically incorrect and should either be deleted or replaced with the infinitive "to be."

C incorrectly omits a comma (between "ground" and "while") to separate the modifying clause from the main clause. Also, the phrase "as being" is idiomatically improper here and should either be removed or replaced with the infinitive "to be."

D is faulty in two respects. In the first part of the sentence, the subject and verb disagree in number: "few" suggests plurality, whereas "himself or herself" suggests singularity (as does "a visionary"). D, like B, incorrectly uses the plural "destinies" to describe a singular idea.

E is faulty in that the phrase following the second comma is separated from the term to which it refers ("destiny"). This misplaced modifier results in a confusing overall syntax that obscures the sentence's meaning.

# Evaluating Your Practice Test Scores

## Today's Topics:

1. Determining your Analytical Writing Assessment (AWA) score
2. Determining your Verbal, Quantitative, and total scaled scores
3. Interpreting your scaled scores

Today you score the practice test that you took during Days 25 through 29 and evaluate your performance. Before doing so, you might want to review the section "Scoring, Evaluation, and Reporting" from Day 1.

## DETERMINING YOUR ANALYTICAL WRITING ASSESSMENT (AWA) SCORE

To evaluate your performance on the AWA practice test that you took on Day 25, refer to the AWA scoring guide from Day 12. Score each of your two essays on a scale of 0 to 6, based on the scoring guide. Your final AWA score (0 to 6) is simply the average of these two individual scores, rounded off to the nearest one-half point.

## DETERMINING YOUR VERBAL, QUANTITATIVE, AND TOTAL SCALED SCORES

To determine your scaled score for either the Quantitative or Verbal section of the practice test, follow these steps:

1. Determine your total number of *correct* responses for the section, based on the answer keys. This is your *raw score*.

2. Subtract one-quarter point from that total for each *incorrect* response; round off this number to the nearest integer. The result is your *corrected raw score*. (This is how the pencil-and-paper GMAT penalizes test-takers for incorrect responses. Recall from day 2, however, that the computer-adaptive GMAT penalizes you for an incorrect response by posing easier subsequent questions, for which correct responses add fewer points to your score than do correct responses for more difficult questions.)

3. Refer to the appropriate column in the conversion table shown on the next page to convert your corrected raw score to the appropriate *scaled score* (0–60).

CONVERSION TABLE A:
VERBAL AND
QUANTITATIVE SCORES
(0-60)

| CORRECTED RAW SCORE | VERBAL | QUANTITATIVE | CORRECTED RAW SCORE | VERBAL | QUANTITATIVE |
|---|---|---|---|---|---|
| 41 | 52 | — | 19 | 27 | 31 |
| 40 | 51 | — | 18 | 25 | 30 |
| 39 | 50 | — | 17 | 24 | 28 |
| 38 | 48 | — | 16 | 23 | 27 |
| 37 | 47 | 53 | 15 | 22 | 25 |
| 36 | 46 | 52 | 14 | 21 | 24 |
| 35 | 45 | 51 | 13 | 20 | 23 |
| 34 | 44 | 50 | 12 | 19 | 22 |
| 33 | 43 | 49 | 11 | 18 | 21 |
| 32 | 42 | 48 | 10 | 17 | 20 |
| 31 | 41 | 47 | 9 | 16 | 18 |
| 30 | 39 | 45 | 8 | 15 | 17 |
| 29 | 38 | 44 | 7 | 14 | 16 |
| 28 | 37 | 43 | 6 | 13 | 14 |
| 27 | 36 | 41 | 5 | 12 | 13 |
| 26 | 35 | 40 | 4 | 11 | 12 |
| 25 | 33 | 38 | 3 | 10 | 11 |
| 24 | 32 | 37 | 2 | 9 | 10 |
| 23 | 31 | 36 | 1 | 8 | 9 |
| 22 | 30 | 34 | 0 | 7 | 8 |
| 21 | 29 | 33 | | | |
| 20 | 28 | 32 | | | |

4. To determine your total scaled score, add your two corrected raw scores together and convert the total corrected raw score to a scaled score (200–800) using the conversion table shown in this next figure.

CONVERSION TABLE B: TOTAL SCORE (200-800)

| CORRECTED RAW SCORE | TOTAL SCALED SCORE | CORRECTED RAW SCORE | TOTAL SCALED SCORE | CORRECTED RAW SCORE | TOTAL SCALED SCORE |
|---|---|---|---|---|---|
| 63 and up | 800 | 41 | 580 | 19 | 370 |
| 62 | 790 | 40 | 570 | 18 | 360 |
| 61 | 780 | 39 | 560 | 17 | 350 |
| 60 | 770 | 38 | 550 | 16 | 340 |
| 59 | 760 | 37 | 540 | 15 | 330 |
| 58 | 750 | 36 | 530 | 14 | 330 |
| 57 | 740 | 35 | 530 | 13 | 320 |
| 56 | 730 | 34 | 520 | 12 | 310 |
| 55 | 720 | 33 | 510 | 11 | 300 |
| 54 | 710 | 32 | 500 | 10 | 290 |
| 53 | 700 | 31 | 490 | 9 | 280 |
| 52 | 690 | 30 | 480 | 8 | 270 |
| 51 | 680 | 29 | 470 | 7 | 260 |
| 50 | 670 | 28 | 460 | 6 | 250 |
| 49 | 660 | 27 | 450 | 5 | 240 |
| 48 | 650 | 26 | 440 | 4 | 230 |
| 47 | 640 | 25 | 430 | 3 | 220 |
| 46 | 630 | 24 | 420 | 2 | 310 |
| 45 | 620 | 23 | 410 | 0-1 | 200 |
| 44 | 610 | 22 | 400 | | |
| 43 | 600 | 21 | 390 | | |

# INTERPRETING YOUR SCALED SCORES

## Understanding Scaled Scores

The purpose of converting raw scores to scaled scores is to account for slight variations in overall difficulty level and in the total number of questions among the different exams administered over the years. (This conversion process is referred to in the field of testing and measurement as *equating*.) Scores reported to the schools are scaled scores, *not* raw or corrected raw scores. The figures in conversion tables A and B are average conversion figures based on several previously administered pencil-and-paper exams. Keep in mind that scaled scores and percentile rankings vary slightly from exam to exam. Also keep in mind that these tables pertain to the pencil-and-paper version the GMAT, not the computer-adaptive version. Nevertheless, your scaled score on the practice test as determined by the two conversion tables should approximate the scores that you would attain on the GMAT CAT. As these tables illustrate, extremely high scaled scores (approaching 60 and 800) and extremely low scaled scores (approaching 0 and 200) are rare.

## Understanding Percentile Rankings

Your GMAT score report indicates not only your scaled scores but also your *percentile ranking* (0 to 99%) based on your Verbal, Quantitative, and total scaled scores. These three percentile rankings indicate how you performed relative to all others taking the GMAT over a recent multiyear period. A percentile ranking of 60%, for example, indicates that you scored higher than 60% of all test-takers (and lower than 39% of all test-takers). (Note: The testing service reports only the scaled scores, not percentile rankings, to the business schools.) Refer to this next figure's percentile ranking conversion chart to determine your rankings for the practice test.

Note the following observations about scaled-score/percentile-ranking conversions:

- You don't have to attain the highest possible Quantitative or Verbal score or a "perfect" total score of 800 to rank in the 99th percentile. Conversely, your scaled scores don't have to be as low as possible to rank among the lowest percentile.

## Percentile Rankings

| Total Scaled Score | Percentage Below |
|:---:|:---:|
| 740 | 99 |
| 720 | 99 |
| 700 | 98 |
| 680 | 97 |
| 660 | 95 |
| 640 | 93 |
| 620 | 89 |
| 600 | 85 |
| 580 | 80 |
| 560 | 74 |
| 540 | 68 |
| 520 | 61 |
| 500 | 53 |
| 480 | 46 |
| 460 | 39 |
| 440 | 32 |
| 420 | 26 |
| 400 | 20 |
| 380 | 15 |
| 360 | 11 |
| 340 | 8 |
| 320 | 6 |
| 300 | 4 |
| 280 | 2 |
| 260 | 1 |
| 240 | 1 |
| 220 | 0 |

| Verbal and Quantitative Scores | | |
|:---:|:---:|:---:|
| | **Percentages Below** | |
| **Scaled Scores** | **Verbal** | **Quantitative** |
| 50 | 99 | 99 |
| 48 | 99 | 99 |
| 46 | 99 | 97 |
| 44 | 98 | 95 |
| 42 | 95 | 91 |
| 40 | 92 | 87 |
| 38 | 87 | 82 |
| 36 | 82 | 75 |
| 34 | 75 | 68 |
| 32 | 67 | 60 |
| 30 | 59 | 52 |
| 28 | 50 | 43 |
| 26 | 42 | 34 |
| 24 | 34 | 27 |
| 22 | 26 | 20 |
| 20 | 20 | 14 |
| 18 | 15 | 9 |
| 16 | 10 | 5 |
| 14 | 7 | 3 |
| 12 | 4 | 1 |
| 10 | 2 | 0 |
| 8 | 1 | 0 |
| 6 | 0 | 0 |

- Assuming that you responded to all 78 multiple-choice questions, if you responded correctly to 40 of those questions (plus or minus one), you've performed better than about one out of every two test-takers!

## ADDITIONAL PREPARATION

Go back to the practice test answer keys to determine your particular strengths and weaknesses. If you performed particularly poorly in one area (geometry questions, for example), review the lessons pertaining to those questions.

# Notes

# Notes

# Notes

# Notes

# Notes

# Notes

# Notes